THE HUNDRED YEARS WAR REVISITED

PROBLEMS IN FOCUS SERIES

Each volume in the 'Problems in Focus' series is designed to make available to students important new work on key historical problems and periods that they encounter in their courses. Each volume is devoted to a central topic or theme, and the most important aspects of this are dealt with by specially commissioned essays from scholars in the relevant field. The editorial Introduction reviews the problem or period as a whole, and each essay provides an assessment of the particular aspect, pointing out the areas of development and controversy, and indicating where conclusions can be drawn or where further work is necessary. An annotated bibliography serves as a guide for further reading.

TITLES IN PRINT

European Warfare 1450–1815 *edited by Jeremy Black*
The Wars of the Roses *edited by A. J. Pollard*
The Reign of Henry VIII *edited by Diarmaid MacCulloch*
The British Problem, c.1534–1707 *edited by Brendan Bradshaw and John Morrill*
Culture and Politics in Early Stuart England *edited by Kevin Sharpe and Peter Lake*
The Origins of the English Civil War *edited by Conrad Russell*
Reactions to the English Civil War 1642–1649 *edited by John Morrill*
The Reigns of Charles II and James VII & II *edited by Lionel K. J. Glassey*
The Origins of the French Revolution *edited by Peter R. Campbell*
Enlightened Absolutism *edited by H. M. Scott*
European Warfare 1815–2000 *edited by Jeremy Black*
Popular Movements, c.1830–1850 *edited by J. T. Ward*
The Hundred Years War Revisited *edited by Anne Curry*

THE HUNDRED YEARS WAR REVISITED

Edited by
Anne Curry

BLOOMSBURY ACADEMIC
LONDON • NEW YORK • OXFORD • NEW DELHI • SYDNEY

BLOOMSBURY ACADEMIC
Bloomsbury Publishing Plc
50 Bedford Square, London, WC1B 3DP, UK
1385 Broadway, New York, NY 10018, USA
29 Earlsfort Terrace, Dublin 2, Ireland

BLOOMSBURY, BLOOMSBURY ACADEMIC and the Diana logo
are trademarks of Bloomsbury Publishing Plc

First published 2019 by RED GLOBE PRESS
Reprinted by Bloomsbury Academic, 2023

Copyright © Anne Curry and The Authors, 2019

The authors have asserted their rights under the Copyright,
Designs and Patents Act, 1988, to be identified as the Authors of this work.

All rights reserved. No part of this publication may be reproduced or transmitted in any form or by any means, electronic or mechanical, including photocopying, recording, or any information storage or retrieval system, without prior permission in writing from the publishers.

Bloomsbury Publishing Plc does not have any control over, or responsibility for, any third-party websites referred to or in this book. All internet addresses given in this book were correct at the time of going to press. The author and publisher regret any inconvenience caused if addresses have changed or sites have ceased to exist, but can accept no responsibility for any such changes.

A catalogue record for this book is available from the British Library.

A catalog record for this book is available from the Library of Congress.

ISBN: HB: 978-1-137-38986-2
PB: 978-1-137-38985-5
ePDF: 978-1-137-38987-9
ePub: 978-1-350-30764-3

Series: Problems in Focus

To find out more about our authors and books visit
www.bloomsbury.com and sign up for our newsletters.

Contents

Abbreviations	vi
Contributors	viii
Introduction by Anne Curry	xi

1. **English Politics and the Hundred Years War** — 1
   Gwilym Dodd

2. **French Politics during the Hundred Years War** — 33
   Graeme Small

3. **Financing the Hundred Years War** — 57
   Tony K. Moore and Adrian R. Bell

4. **The Hundred Years War and the Church** — 85
   Rory Cox

5. **The Hundred Years War 'At Home'** — 111
   Laura Crombie

6. **Chivalry and the Hundred Years War** — 133
   Andy King

7. **First-Hand Accounts and Reports of Warfare** — 153
   Craig Taylor

8. **Navies and Maritime Warfare** — 169
   Andrew Ayton and Craig Lambert

9. **Armies** — 203
   Gary Paul Baker

Index — 231

Abbreviations

Age of Edward III   *The Age of Edward III*, ed. J. Bothwell (Woodbridge, 2001)
Allmand   C. T. Allmand, *The Hundred Years War* (Cambridge, 1988)
Allmand, *Henry V*   C. T. Allmand, *Henry V* (London, 1992)
BEC   *Bibliothèque de l'École des Chartes*
BIHR   *Bulletin of the Institute of Historical Research*
BL   British Library
CCR   *Calendar of Close Rolls*
Contamine, *GES*   P. Contamine, *Guerre, état et société à la fin du moyen âge* (Paris and The Hague, 1972)
CPR   *Calendar of Patent Rolls*
Curry, *Sources*   A. Curry, *The Battle of Agincourt: Sources and Interpretations* (Woodbridge, 2000)
Cursed Kings   J. Sumption, *The Hundred Years War, Volume 4: Cursed Kings* (London, 2015)
Divided Houses   J. Sumption, *The Hundred Years War, Volume 3: Divided Houses* (London, 2009)
EcHR   *Economic History Review*
EHR   *English Historical Review*
Foedera   T. Rymer, *Foedera, conventiones, litterae et cuiuscunque generis acta publica* (London, 1704–35)
Friel   I. Friel, *Henry V's Navy: The Searoad to Agincourt and Conquest 1413–1422* (Barnsley, 2015)
Froissart (Brereton)   Froissart, *Chronicles*, ed. G. Brereton (Harmondsworth, 1978)
Froissart (Lettenhove)   *Oeuvres de Froissart*, ed. K. De Lettenhove, 25 vols (Brussels, 1867–77)
Froissart (Luce)   Jean Froissart, *Chroniques*, ed. S. Luce et al., 15 vols (Paris, 1869–1975)
Guerre et société en France   *Guerre et société en France, en Angleterre et en Bourgogne XIV–XVe siècle*, ed. P. Contamine, C. Giry-Deloison and M. H. Keen (Lille, 1991)

Hewitt	H. J. Hewitt, *The Organization of War under Edward III* (Manchester, 1966)
HYW	*The Hundred Years War: Problems in Focus*, ed. K. Fowler (Macmillan, 1971)
HYW. Wider Focus	*The Hundred Years War: A Wider Focus,* ed. L. J. A. Villalon and D. J. Kagay (Leiden, 2005)
JBS	*Journal of British Studies*
JMH	*Journal of Medieval History*
JMMH	*Journal of Medieval Military History*
Knights and Warhorses	A. Ayton, *Knights and Warhorses: Military Service and the English Aristocracy under Edward III* (Woodbridge, 1994)
La Roncière	C. de la Roncière, *Histoire de la marine française*, 6 vols (Paris, 1899–1932)
ODNB	*Oxford Dictionary of National Biography*
Ordonnances	*Ordonnances des roys de France de la troisième race, recueillies par ordre chronologique*, 22 vols (Paris, 1723–1849)
PROME	*The Parliament Rolls of Medieval England 1275–1504*, ed. G. Given Wilson, P. Brand, S. Phillips, M. Ormrod, G. Martin, A. Curry and R. Horrox (Stroud 2005)
Rose	S. Rose, *Medieval Naval Warfare, 1000–1500* (Abingdon and New York, 2002)
Society at War	C. T. Allmand, *Society at War* (2nd edn, Woodbridge, 1998)
Soldier Experience	*The Soldier Experience in the Fourteenth Century*, ed. A. R. Bell, A. Curry, A. King, D. Simpkin and A. Chapman (Woodbridge, 2011)
SLME	A. R. Bell, A. Curry, A. King and D. Simpkin, *The Soldier in Later Medieval England* (Oxford, 2013)
TNA	The National Archives
Trial by Battle	J. Sumption, *The Hundred Years War, Volume 1: Trial by Battle* (London, 1990)
Trial by Fire	J. Sumption, *The Hundred Years War, Volume 2: Trial by Fire* (London, 1999)
TRHS	*Transactions of the Royal Historical Society*
War, Government	*War, Government and Power in Late Medieval France*, ed. C. T. Allmand (Liverpool, 2000)
War, Politics	J. Sherborne, *War, Politics and Culture in Fourteenth-Century England*, ed. A. Tuck (London and Rio Grande, 1994)

Contributors

Andrew Ayton has published extensively on the military and maritime communities of late medieval England, and on the organisation and conduct of the king's wars in Scotland, France and at sea. His books include *Knights and Warhorses: Military Service and the English Aristocracy under Edward III* (1994) and (with Sir Philip Preston) *The Battle of Crécy, 1346* (2005). He is Honorary Senior Research Fellow in History at the University of Hull (where he lectured for thirty years prior to retirement in 2015) and Honorary Senior Research Fellow at Keele University.

Gary Baker is a Researcher in History at the University of Groningen, and has previously worked as a Research Assistant at the University of East Anglia and the University of Southampton. He completed his PhD at the University of Hull in 2012 looking at the English military community in the second half of the fourteenth century, and has published articles on war and the military community in the Hundred Years War. His research interests include military history more broadly, particularly of the medieval and early modern periods, and maritime history from the fourteenth to sixteenth centuries.

Adrian R. Bell is Professor in the History of Finance at the ICMA Centre, Henley Business School, University of Reading. He has published widely on soldier careers in the Hundred Years War and (jointly with Professor Anne Curry) is responsible for The Soldier in Later Medieval England online database (www.medievalsoldier.org). Professor Bell has also co-led a number of research projects on medieval finance, including wool forwards, credit finance and sovereign default, FX and Real Estate bubbles.

Rory Cox is Lecturer in Late Medieval History at the University of St Andrews. Dr Cox's interdisciplinary research engages with the ethics of war, violence and political theory over the longue durée. He has published widely on the just war tradition and applications of violence, and he is co-editor of the journal *Global Intellectual History*.

Laura Crombie was awarded her PhD from the University of Glasgow in 2011. The book based on her thesis was published as *Archery and Crossbow*

Guilds in Medieval Flanders, 1300–1500 in 2016, and she has published on both the military and the social aspects of the shooting guilds, as well as on other urban groups in the Flanders and on diplomatic relations between Britain and the Low Countries. She has taught at the Universities of Aberystwyth, York and Leicester, and she now lives and works in Glasgow.

Anne Curry is Professor of Medieval History at the University of Southampton where she was also Dean of the Faculty of Humanities from 2010 to 2018. She has worked extensively on the Hundred Years War, especially its fifteenth-century phase, and is particularly well known for her publications on the battle of Agincourt and Lancastrian Normandy, and the Parliament Rolls of Medieval England for the reign of Henry VI. She was editor of the *Journal of Medieval History* from 2001 to 2008, and is co-editor of the forthcoming *Cambridge History of War, Vol. 2: 400–1500*. With Adrian Bell she devised and directed The Soldier in Later Medieval England project (www.medievalsoldier.org), and is currently directing a project to make the Gascon Rolls from 1307 to 1468 available online (www.gasconrolls.org).

Gwilym Dodd gained his PhD from the University of York in 1998 before becoming a British Academy Post-Doctoral Fellow. In 2002, he joined the history department at the University of Nottingham where he has remained since. His research focusses on the politics, political culture and governance of late medieval England. He is the author of numerous articles and chapters in these areas and has edited multiple essay collections on the reigns of different late medieval English kings. He is also one of the commissioning editors of *Fourteenth Century England* published by the Boydell Press. Two central strands of his work are petitions and parliament. In 2007, he published the monograph *Justice and Grace: Private Petitioning and the English Parliament in the Late Middle Ages* and, in 2010, he co-edited, with Alison K. McHardy, the edition of sources *Petitions to the Crown from English Religious Houses, c. 1272 – c. 1485*. He is currently working on a major study of the late medieval English parliament.

Andy King is Lecturer in History at the University of Southampton. After completing his PhD, on the political society of fourteenth-century Northumberland, at Durham University, he worked there as a research assistant, leading to his edition of *Sir Thomas Gray: Scalacronica (1272–1363)*. He was subsequently employed at Southampton on the medieval soldier project, and co-authored the monograph *The Soldier in Later Medieval England* (with Adrian Bell, Anne Curry and David Simpkin). He wrote the volume on *Edward I* for the Penguin Monarchs series, and has co-written *England and Scotland, 1286–1603* (with Claire Etty). He has published articles on the Anglo-Scottish Marches, chivalry, treason and the laws of war, English armies and castles.

Craig Lambert is a maritime historian who has published widely on naval operations and maritime communities. Recently, he launched a free-to-access website containing the details of more than 50,000 ship voyages from more than 500 English, Welsh and Channel Islands ports (www.medievalandtudorships.org). His books include *Shipping the Medieval Military: English Maritime Logistics in the Fourteenth Century* (2011); as well as *Military Communities in Late Medieval England: Essays in Honour of Andrew Ayton* (2018; edited with Gary P. Baker and David Simpkin) and *Agincourt in Context: War on Land and Sea* (2018; edited with Rémy Ambhül).

Tony Moore is Lecturer in Finance at the ICMA Centre, Henley Business School, University of Reading. His main research interests are medieval English political and constitutional history and the development of financial markets in the Middle Ages. He is one of the series editors of Palgrave Studies in the History of Finance.

Graeme Small works on the political, social and cultural history of France, the Low Countries and Scotland in the late medieval and early modern periods. His current research focusses on vernacular chronicles, town records and medievalism. Among his publications are *Late Medieval France* (2009) and a contribution to the *Short Oxford History of France* (2003). He is a professor at Durham University.

Craig Taylor is Reader in Medieval History at the University of York. He is an intellectual and cultural historian who specialises in the politics and aristocracies of fourteenth- and fifteenth-century France and England. He has published books and articles on the Hundred Years War, chivalry, Joan of Arc, the Salic Law, propaganda, biography and the history of emotions. He was recently a co-investigator on an AHRC-funded project entitled *England's Immigrants 1350–1550*, and is currently collaborating with Professor Jane Taylor, University of Durham, to translate a series of fifteenth-century French chivalric biographies.

Introduction

Anne Curry

Kenneth Fowler's edited collection *The Hundred Years War* was published in Macmillan's Problems in Focus series in 1971. I started my degree course in History in the following year and soon discovered not only the fascination of Anglo-French warfare but also how valuable Fowler's collection was as a guide and stimulus to thinking about the subject. Throughout my teaching career, I have recommended the book to students, devising this current book as a complementary collection rather than as a substitute. It is dedicated to Professor Fowler in recognition of his substantial contribution to the study of the later Middle Ages, to which I shall return at the end of this introduction.

The contents of the 1971 volume were influenced, as Fowler noted in his preface, by 'those aspects of the war which are currently interesting historians or which have hitherto been neglected'. The first two chapters, John Le Patourel's study of 'The Origins of the War' and John Palmer's 'The War Aims of the Protagonists', provided succinct insights into the key problems of the Hundred Years War, which is customarily dated 1337–1453. England and France had been at war on many occasions before this time over the extent and tenurial nature of the lands which English kings held by hereditary right in France. In the treaty of Paris of 1259, Henry III formally abandoned his claims to lands in northern France, including Normandy which his father King John had lost in 1204, but had confirmed by the French king, Louis IX, his right to the duchy of Aquitaine in south-west France. Henry accepted an obligation to pay homage for this duchy.

When the Hundred Years War began in 1337, the English still held the duchy of Aquitaine and had also acquired the county of Ponthieu around the mouth of the Somme, through the inheritance Eleanor of Castile, queen of Edward I. While historians prefer to eschew the notion of inevitability, there can be no doubt that the holding of lands in one country by the king of another was a recipe for conflict. From the late thirteenth century onwards, concepts of sovereignty and identity had developed strongly, making such a situation unacceptable to both parties. In the late thirteenth and early fourteenth centuries, the English made efforts to avoid the humiliation of paying liege homage to their French counterpart. As for the French, they were increasingly keen to remove the English from French soil.

Into this problematic feudal relationship came a new dynastic factor in 1328: the claim of Edward III of England to be the rightful heir to the crown of France itself. Twelve years earlier, at the death of Louis X with only a daughter surviving, the French had decided against allowing a woman to inherit the throne. But there remained the grey area of whether a royal daughter could transmit a claim to her son. Edward III's claim was through his mother Isabella, the daughter of King Philip IV (d. 1314), whose three brothers had ruled in turn – Louis X (d. 1316, followed by his posthumous son John I who was technically king for the five days he was alive), Philip V (d. 1322) and Charles IV. When Charles died in 1328, Edward was his *nearest* male heir as the grandson of Philip IV but through the female line. His cousin through the male line, Philip VI of Valois (d. 1350), was preferred as king. It was hardly likely, after all, that the French would choose a king of England, a country with which they had been waging war during the last years of Charles IV's reign, in alliance with England's northern neighbour, the Scots.

Whether Edward III ever seriously intended becoming king of France, or whether he hoped to use his claim to the throne as a bargaining counter in existing feudal and territorial disputes, will continue to be debated as much as it was in 1971. As Le Patourel's article outlined, the same debate was applicable to all of Edward III's successors as kings of England. All called themselves kings of France, maintaining the claim to the French throne and continuing to exploit it by diplomatic as much as military means. Only briefly, between 1360 and 1369, had Edward III dropped the title in return for French acceptance of an extended Aquitaine and Ponthieu to be held by the English crown in full sovereignty without the need for any homage. This advantageous settlement (the treaty of Brétigny-Calais) had resulted generally from English military successes of the previous twenty years but specifically from the capture of the French king, John II (d. 1364), at the battle of Poitiers in 1356. By seeking to collect a large ransom for John, the English had to accept his kingship of France, but the prize of substantial territorial gain was deemed enough of a compensation. Not surprisingly, however, John's successor, Charles V (d. 1380), was keen to recover the lost lands and feudal authority. By reneging on the terms of the Brétigny-Calais settlement in 1369 he forced Edward III to resume his French title and claim, but had already gained advantage by swift military action. Thereafter, the war went badly for the English. By 1389, they held no more land in France than they had done in 1337. Yet the French had not managed to expel them from French soil. In 1396, both sides accepted the stalemate by agreeing a twenty-eight-year truce.

A change of dynasty in England and divisions in France between the Armagnac/Orleanist and Burgundian parties in France competing for control of the mentally incapacitated king, Charles VI (d. 1422), encouraged the English to invade again. Within five years of action, 1415–20, Henry V (d. 1422) was even more successful than Edward III had been, defeating the French in battle at Agincourt and conquering Normandy. In the treaty of Troyes of 1420 Henry was accepted by Charles VI as his heir, thereby establishing the prospect of a double monarchy of England and France and formally disinheriting the dauphin Charles and, indeed, the whole of the Valois line. Eleven years later, Henry VI (d. 1471), the son of Henry V by Catherine, daughter of Charles VI, was crowned in Paris as king of France in accordance with the settlement of 1420. The origins of the treaty of Troyes, however, lay in French domestic politics rather than in English war aims per se. There is ample evidence that Henry V would have been satisfied with territorial concessions: as Palmer had concluded in 1971, 'he was no bigoted idealist, inexorable in his pursuit of "just rights" to which he was mystically committed. Like Edward III he was a realist and an opportunist of genius.' The English 'triumph' of 1420 might have appeared to give England the final victory in the Anglo-French wars, but after a near-century of conflict there remained many French committed to their removal from French soil. As the tide turned in their favour from 1429 onwards – thanks to Joan of Arc's inspiration and the coronation at Reims of the dauphin Charles as Charles VII (d. 1461) – the English refused to compromise. In 1449–50, Charles recovered Normandy and, in subsequent years (1451–3), what was left of English Aquitaine. The English were left with only Calais, Edward III's conquest of 1347, and the empty title 'king of France'.

The events of the Hundred Years War are well known. Indeed they are better known now than they were in 1971 thanks to the magisterial volumes of Jonathan Sumption which have reconstructed the wars from both an English and a French context, the first works to attempt this in detail, using a substantial range of primary sources supported by extensive secondary reading. His first volume of this Hundred Years War series, published in 1990, *Trial by Battle*, dealt with the opening of the war to the surrender of Calais; the second, *Trial by Fire* (1999), to the treaty of Brétigny-Calais; the third, *Divided Houses* (2009) from 1369 to 1399; and the fourth, *Cursed Kings* (2015), from 1399 to 1422.[1] The completion of the series to 1453 is eagerly awaited. In addition, the Anglo-French conflict has been well served by single-volume analyses. Christopher Allmand's *Hundred Years War: England and France at War c.1300–c.1450*, originally published in the Cambridge Medieval Textbooks series in 1988 and available in a French version published by Seuil in 2015.² In addition to a brief chronological survey, Allmand, who contributed a pioneering article on 'War and the Non-Combattant' to Fowler's 1971 volume, included thematic chapters on a range of themes from institutional to literary considerations. My own *Hundred Years War* in the Palgrave Macmillan British History in Focus series, originally published in 1993 with a second edition in 2003, focussed more on diplomacy and military aims and outcomes, differentiating the phases of the war and considering how they involved most of Europe and not just England and France.³

A key advance in scholarly knowledge came through the publication in 1972 of Philippe Contamine's *Guerre, état et société: Étude sur les armées des rois de France 1337–1494*,⁴ the first major study of French military organisation in the period and beyond, which made a major contribution to the explanation of final French victory. Contamine's subsequent extensive work on warfare, including his synoptic volume *La guerre au moyen âge* of 1980, translated into English in 1986,⁵ as well as his studies of French noble society,⁶ previsaged by his chapter in Fowler's 1971 volume on 'The French Nobility and the War', has had a major influence in both England and France. Another chapter in the 1971 volume – H. J. Hewitt's 'The Organisation of War', a tight summary of his book *The Organization of War under Edward III 1338–1362*, published in 1966 – formed a *point de départ* for subsequent research as well as no doubt many undergraduate essays.⁷

The Hundred Years War has proved a popular topic at all levels of study and enjoyment. That fact in its own right would justify a new compilation of essays reflecting at least some of the research which has been carried out since Kenneth Fowler published his collection in 1971. My vision in putting this volume together was to emphasise the work of scholars younger than myself. The way history is studied does change over time. Approaches are much affected by contemporary issues and concerns. Hence questions of state finance, considered in this volume by Tony Moore and Adrian Bell (based in the Henley Business School of Reading University), have come to the fore in recent years, much influenced by major European projects, and adopting a much broader analysis than, say, the work of Michael Postan on the costs of the Hundred Years War.⁸ Debates on the role of the state in the transition from the medieval to early modern period have influenced recent studies of military organisation, as is elucidated in Gary Baker's study of armies in this volume, as well as studies of national engagement in international conflicts and of the central relationship of war and politics, as analysed in the chapters of Gwilym Dodd and Graeme Small on, respectively, English and French political contexts. Religion was little emphasised in the 1971 volume, save in the context of war and the non-combatant examined by Allmand. Here, it receives a separate study which sets the Hundred Years War within the 'spirit of the age' as well as the institutions of the Church.

Historiographical trends, not least the interest in 'mentalité', have also played their part in changing emphases in the study of the Hundred Years War. Chivalry, for instance, was absent as a separate theme in Fowler's volume, but in the light of the inspirational work of Maurice Keen could hardly now be ignored.[9] In this volume, the warrior mindset is explored not only through conduct in war, as in Andy King's chapter, but also through the question of reportage – so key to the nature as well as historians' analysis of narrative sources – which forms the theme of Craig Taylor's discussion of 'First-Hand Accounts and Reports of Warfare'. Work on the impact of wars on non-combatants across the ages has boosted an interest in this area of Hundred Years Wars studies, as examined by Laura Crombie in her chapter on 'The Hundred Years War "at Home"', which also links to studies of urban and rural environments as well as gender dimensions of war. New methodologies have also enabled new ways of looking at old problems; for example, through an online database of 250,000 soldiers serving the English crown (The Soldier in Later Medieval England) as well as the *New Oxford Dictionary of National Biography* and History of Parliament project researching biographies of all members of the English parliament,[10] it is possible to probe more deeply as well as more broadly into the English aristocracy at war than Michael Powicke was able to do in 1971. Such projects have influenced several of the chapters in this collection.

The current volume, therefore, reflects at least some of the major trends in research on the Hundred Years War since 1971. Its format is deliberately thematic, in order that the Anglo-French conflict can be set within a wider context of politics, society and economy in the later Middle Ages. Where possible, English and French developments have been considered in tandem. This is particularly valuable in discussions of armies and navies, where much detailed research has been carried out on both sides of the Channel over the last fifty or so years. The importance of the naval dimension of the war was emphasised by Colin Richmond in his chapter on 'The War at Sea' in Fowler's 1971 collection, but only recently has it been fully explored by Andrew Ayton and Craig Lambert thanks to new methodologies for data analysis.[11]

In no way, however, can a volume of this kind be complete or definitive. Other themes, such as technology, would have been worthily included, but all editors and publishers are faced with problems of space and length. The Hundred Years War has a strong regional as well as pan-European dimension; yet this book concentrates very much on England and France. My intention is to produce a second edited volume which approaches the war through studies of each of the many parts of Europe which it touched; this will also enable further thought on the intensity and impact of war, and on the conduct of international relations which was discussed in part by Fowler himself in his essay on 'Truces' in the 1971 collection.

At the point *The Hundred Years War: Problems in Focus* was published by Macmillan in 1971, Kenneth Fowler was Reader in Medieval History at the University of Edinburgh, having joined the medieval history department there in 1958. A graduate at undergraduate and doctoral level of the University of Leeds, by 1971 he had already published *The Age of Plantagenet and Valois* (Elek, 1967), which remains even more than fifty years later the best illustrated academic study of the Anglo-French wars, and a model biography in *The King's Lieutenant: Henry of Grosmont, First Duke of Lancaster 1310–1361* (Elek, 1961). Promoted to a chair at Edinburgh in 1974, he served as Dean of the Faculty of Arts in the early 1980s, retiring in 1988. Three years later appeared his magisterial study, *Medieval Mercenaries: Volume 1. The Great Companies* (Blackwell, 2001). This book reflected the extremely wide geographical range of his research, covering not only England, France and the Low Countries but also Italy and the Iberian peninsula. His articles have been published in the same range of locations and even as far afield as Romania, with a significant spread of topics from humanism to military discipline, from diplomacy to the costs of urban defence, from newsletters to visual images. Ken has shown himself as adroit in comparative studies as in synthesis, and in bringing to light not only wars of late medieval kingdoms but also the complex and often shadowy world of the condottieri. The authors join with me in thanking him for the stimulus he has given to Hundred Years War studies over many years.

Just as the Hundred Years War has engaged many historians on both sides of the Channel both before and after 1971, it is to be hoped, and expected, that it will continue to do so into the future, so that forty or fifty years from now we might expect a revisiting of Problems Revisited in this current volume.

NOTES

1 All volumes have been published by Faber and Faber. *The Hundred Years War: Volume 1. Trial by Fire* (London, 1990); *The Hundred Years War, Volume 2: Trial by Fire* (London, 1999); *The Hundred Years War, Volume 3: Divided Houses* (London, 2009); *The Hundred Years War, Volume 4: Cursed Kings* (London, 2015).
2 C. T. Allmand, *The Hundred Years War: England and France at War c.1300–c.1450* (Cambridge, 1988); *La guerre de Cent Ans*, translated by C. Cler (Paris, 2015).

3   A. Curry, *The Hundred Years War* (Basingstoke, 1993, second edn 2003).
4   P. Contamine, *Guerre, état et société: Étude sur les armées des rois de France 1337–1494* (Paris and The Hague, 1972).
5   P. Contamine, *La guerre au moyen âge* (Paris, 1980), translated by Michael Jones as *War in the Middle Ages* (Oxford, 1986).
6   P. Contamine, *La noblesse au royaume de France de Philippe le Bel à Louis XII* (Paris, 1997).
7   H. J. Hewitt, *The Organization of War under Edward III 1338–1362* (Manchester, 1966).
8   This began during the Second World War with M. M. Postan, 'Some Social Consequences of the Hundred Years' War', *Economic History Review*, 12 (1942), pp. 7–12. See also K. B. McFarlane, 'War, the Economy and Social Change: England and the Hundred Years War', *Past and Present*, 22 (1962), pp. 3–13, and Postan's riposte 'The Costs of the Hundred Years War', *Past and Present*, 27 (1964), pp. 34–53.
9   Especially M. H. Keen, *Chivalry* (London, 1984).
10 www.medievalsoldier.org, along with A. R. Bell, A. Curry, A. King and D. Simpkin, *The Soldier in Later Medieval England* (Oxford, 2013) (AHRC Research Grant AID 120386)); for the regularly updated online version of the Dictionary see www.oxforddnb.com, in addition to the print version of 2004; www.historyofparliament.org; for the biographies of MPs see *History of Parliament. The Commons 1386–1421*, ed. J. S Roskell, L. Clarke and C. Rawcliffe (Stroud, 1993), with volumes covering the remainder of the fifteenth century expected in the near future.
11 Their chapter draws on data from ESRC project (RES-000-22-4127) at Hull (Ayton and Lambert) and AHRC (AH/L004062/1) at Southampton (Lambert).

1 English Politics and the Hundred Years War

Gwilym Dodd

Politics directly affected the course, and ultimately the outcome, of the Hundred Years War. In the pre-modern era, and particularly in late medieval England, the relationship between politics and warfare was sharpened by the fact that the political system was highly evolved and the government greatly centralised. Crucially, 'politicians' were often also the commanders and captains on the battlefield. This meant that the fortunes of war significantly influenced the domestic political environment. But it also meant that the ability of the English to prosecute a successful war against the French was hugely dependent on the political leadership of the king and his nobles, as well as (and increasingly so, as time passed) on the broader support of the general populace. This points to an important truism: that the military effectiveness of a medieval kingdom must be measured not just in terms of the fighting capability of its armies, but also how effectively its resources (especially money and manpower) were mobilised in support of the war effort. These were the considerations which formed the basis of much of the discussion and internal political negotiation between the rulers and ruled of England during the Hundred Years War.

This chapter explores the nature and extent of the inseparable relationship between warfare and politics in the period. It demonstrates the extent to which the prosecution of warfare rested not just on the ability of the king to rally the support of his closest nobles, but also to an equal extent on his ability to win over the broader political community, including those of lower social status who have traditionally been excluded from political analysis. Thus, one of the central strands will be a consideration of how and why the Hundred Years War transformed the nature of warfare from the concern of a relatively small military caste into a truly national enterprise involving all the king's subjects. Another important focus is the role of the king himself. During the war, five English kings sat on the throne. We can exclude from our consideration

Henry IV (1399–1413), because a period of prolonged truce existed during his reign, and because as a usurper he was concerned more about preserving his position as king of England. This leaves four kings who for convenience can be placed into two categories: those under whose rule the war went well – Edward III (1327–77) and Henry V (1413–22); and those under whose rule it went badly – Richard II (1377–99) and Henry VI (1422–61). We will consider how and why these kings were so critical in determining the fortunes of war, as well as how political consensus could be built – or lost – depending on their personal abilities and interests.

Late medieval English political history has flourished since Kenneth Fowler published his collection in 1971. Each king who ruled during the period of the Hundred Years War has been the subject of a detailed scholarly biography in the Yale English Monarchs series.[1] There has also been a huge growth in more specialised discussions on different aspects of the government and governance of England, from investigation into the impact of taxation and the use of propaganda to consideration of the position of the Church, the development of political institutions and the careers of key individuals. Quite simply, we know much more than we did forty-five years ago about the impact of war on English politics and government. We have also seen the emergence of new historical techniques and a greater appreciation of the importance of close textual analysis. In this respect, the emergence of a 'new constitutional history', founded on the premise that we cannot truly comprehend late medieval political life without understanding the values, ideas and principles which underpinned it, through the study of language use, has been one of the most important historiographical developments of the past four decades.[2] Political history is no longer conceived just in terms of what administrative records tell us; it encapsulates a broader range of evidence, including theoretical works, literature, art and architecture. There has also been significant enhancement of some of the more traditional types of record thanks to research projects putting technology to good use, such as a new edition of the Parliament Rolls; a database of all taxes levied before 1689; and an online catalogue of Ancient Petitions.[3] All this has allowed more rounded and nuanced appraisals of how kings ruled and how the English polity functioned in the period.

PRELIMINARY CONSIDERATIONS

Two key considerations provide useful context for discussion of the central strands. First is the central place which military leadership and martial prowess held in contemporary expectations of what a king should be like and what he should do. Attitudes to warfare were markedly different in the fourteenth century than they are today: war did not represent a regrettable breakdown in international relations, bringing out the worst in human behaviour. Instead, it was thought to be an ennobling experience, an opportunity for individuals to demonstrate their valour, prowess and honour.[4] The political elite of England, as elsewhere in Europe, defined themselves in large measure by the military function which they performed, and by the martial culture and chivalric ethos which imbued their lives.[5] As studies of the nobility have shown, the commanders of English armies overwhelmingly comprised the king's senior magnates: social status and military leadership were two sides of the same coin.[6] The king, as the head of this elite, was naturally expected to be first among all the knights of his kingdom, and to be the very embodiment of the chivalric ideal.[7] Such sentiments are articulated in the *Secreta Secretorum*, a pseudo-Aristotelian tract on the nature of kingship and governance which was among the most widely circulated texts of its kind in the Middle Ages. All the great writers of the past, it asserted, were at one in judging that,

> the prowess and worthynesses of emperors, kings, and al othyr governors of chivalry ... [depends on their ensuring that] chivalry is not only kepete, savyd and mayntened by dedis of armes, but by wisdom and helpe of lawes, of witte, and wisdom of understandynge.[8]

The king was characterised as the 'governor of chivalry', expected not only to lead by example but to ensure that his nobles and gentry kept to the code and proved themselves worthy of the knighthood he had bestowed on them. Expectations were high, therefore, that kings would provide the right opportunities for these qualities to shine. In 1328, a royal clerk named Walter de Milemete wrote what is now the earliest surviving 'mirror of princes' written specifically for the instruction of an incoming king (i.e. Edward III). The treatise offered guidance on what it was to be a 'perfect prince', imploring the young Edward to follow the example of Alexander:

> Wherefore, most noble lord, if you will observe the foregoing writing regarding war, conflict and other things about fighting, once taught to the noble King Alexander, conqueror of the earth, by the philosopher Aristotle ... thereby you will enjoy conquest, honour, and grace on earth, and in Heaven, reigning with God and all his celestial host, you will have eternal glory.[9]

It was King Arthur, however, rather than King Alexander, who featured in many chronicles and literary works of the period, providing a compelling exemplar of the kingly ideal to the social elites who commissioned such writings. And it was the romance of Arthur's *military* exploits which above all captured their imagination. A poem celebrating Edward's victory at Crécy compared him with 'good King Arthur' in 'bringing woe to the French'.[10] Arthur was the ubiquitous model king of Plantagenet England.[11] This is not to say that late medieval English kings were expected to be warmongers; far from it. As we shall see, the wars kings fought were considered legitimate only if they were demonstrably defensive in nature. But, in the event of war, a king was expected to provide the leadership, direction and inspiration necessary to ensure victory.

The second consideration is the underlying tension that existed in the way in which the Hundred Years War was conceived by contemporaries. On the one hand, in legal and diplomatic terms, and in all official discourse, the war was defined not as a struggle between the peoples of England and France but as a conflict between their kings. The war turned on a dispute over succession to the French throne, and so to this extent when war broke out in 1337 it was not the case that England sought to recover its rights in relation to France, but that the English king sought to defend his inheritance from the French king. The war was thus, in its opening stages, fundamentally a dynastic war which involved the peoples of England and France by virtue of the fact that they were the subjects of their respective kings and owed loyalty and obedience to him at times of national crisis. To this extent, the war might also be described as feudal in nature, in as much as the involvement of the population of the kingdom was a matter of obligation, similar to a vassal's allegiance to his lord.

A good illustration is shown in the way that Edward III assumed the title of 'king of France' at the very beginning of the conflict. This was a decision that had monumental implications on the strategy, scope and even, perhaps, the eventual outcome of the war from the point of view of England, and yet the evidence suggests that Edward took the decision in private, making no attempt to consult more widely than his immediate circle of advisors. It is remarkable that Edward began using the title of king of France formally and officially from his base in Ghent on 26 January 1340, but did not think it was necessary to inform his subjects in England of this decision for another month when, on 21 February, the writs issued for summoning parliament contained the new royal style.[12] Another indication of the personal, even familial, nature of the conflict was the central place given to inter-dynastic marriage in Anglo-French diplomacy. To the modern observer it may seem strange to note how willing English kings were to marry into the French royal family (and for French kings to allow their female relations to become the consorts of English kings) as a means of cementing terms of truces and treaties. Both Richard II and Henry V had French kings as their fathers-in-law under such circumstances; Henry VI married Charles VII's niece as an opening move towards peace negotiations. Edward III's mother, Isabella, was a daughter of a French king – it was this family connection which constituted the principal cause of the war. It is going too far to suggest that the Hundred Years War boiled down to a squabble between the ruling families of the two most powerful kingdoms of Europe, but there is undeniably a sense in which the course of the conflict hinged on the making or breaking of inter-familial relations between the two royal dynasties.

Yet, for all the focus given to the king as the prime mover, he still needed the cooperation of his people to ensure the success of his policies and ambitions. Counterbalancing the obligation of the people to support their king's great enterprise was an equally powerful obligation on the part of the king to rule with the consensus of those subject to his authority. What was defined in legal terms as the king's war thus became, by default and for strongly pragmatic reasons, the concern of all his subjects. It was axiomatic that the sovereign did not rule his people by diktat but with their acquiescence. For centuries, English kings adhered to this principle by seeking the counsel of nobles and senior clergymen, but by the time of the outbreak of the Hundred Years War parliament had come to the fore as the key institutional context in which the king obtained wider affirmation for his military ambitions. This is easily explained. War was expensive, especially once armies were raised by paid contractual service. The king could only pay by tapping into public wealth through taxation: under the Roman law doctrine *quod omnes tangit ab omnibus approbetur* ('what touches all must be approved by all') he was under a constitutional obligation to seek the consent of all his subjects – through their representatives – to obtains these funds.[13] When war broke out in 1337, Edward was very careful to consult parliament on the matter, though this did not extend to the question of his claim to the French throne which was discussed only in closed council.[14] This was partly in fulfilment of his obligation to seek counsel and advice but it was also the act of a canny politician: by obtaining parliamentary consent to the war, the king was in effect obtaining parliamentary *commitment* to funding it. This was exactly the point made in 1346 when the chancellor declared that when 'our lord the king undertook the war by the common assent of all those in parliament, they promised that they would aid him with all the men and money at their power.'[15]

Parliament had traditionally been attended by the secular and religious elites of the realm, but from the end of the thirteenth century it was increasingly attended at royal behest by representatives of the counties (the knights of the shire) and boroughs or towns (the burgesses), because it was they who were empowered to grant taxation on behalf of their constituents. By the start of Edward III's reign in 1327 the knights and burgesses had become a permanent presence.[16] Although labelled 'the Commons', they were drawn from gentry and urban oligarchies respectively: they did not constitute the 'common people' of the realm, upon whose shoulders the burden of direct taxation principally fell.[17] In granting taxation, the Commons needed to balance the needs of the crown with the sustainability of heavy financial demands on the poorer members of society. In theory, the Commons had little choice but to grant the king taxation whenever he could prove his 'necessity'[18] (i.e. that it was vital for the defence of the kingdom's interest, even if these interests lay overseas), but this was not a straightforward process. What constituted 'necessity' was open to interpretation; while the Commons may have had a duty to provide funds where necessity was proved, *how much* they provided and what conditions were attached to their grants remained matters open to debate. Representation in parliament thus pushed the gentry and townsmen into an unprecedented position of political prominence, as the king directly solicited their support for his military projects and as they themselves grew in political maturity, learning to secure political concessions in return for grants of taxation. Waging war successfully was thus not simply a matter of the king providing effective leadership on the battlefield; it also required his political acumen and an ability to persuade his subjects that the war he wished to wage was worth them granting him the money to pay for it.

THE WAR GOES WELL

It is probably true of all wars that victory on the battlefield generates support on the home front: a victorious army can go far in persuading even the sternest critic that war is just and noble. The impressive body of support which Edward III and Henry V built up for their campaigns was undoubtedly brought about by the enthusiasm generated by the victories which the campaigns achieved. There was a strong element of cyclical causality here: military success generated political acquiescence, which translated into generous grants of taxation, which in turn led to more military success and further political and financial support. Neither Edward nor Henry found it hard to extract large grants of taxation from parliament in the wake of victories. Between 1344 and 1357 – the high-water mark of Edward's military successes – the king extracted no fewer than eleven direct subsidies from parliament and eight clerical tenths from convocation (the Church's equivalent of parliament). Altogether, this was worth, theoretically, £550,000.[19] The clearest example of the link between military success and political acquiescence occurred in the parliament which met on 4 November 1415. Barely a week after news had reached England of Henry V's momentous victory at Agincourt not only did MPs agree to the accelerated payment of a previous parliamentary subsidy, but they also endorsed a further grant of direct taxation and, extraordinarily, they permitted the king to levy the wool subsidy and tunnage and poundage for the rest of his life without further recourse to parliament, thus in effect rewriting a key element of the unwritten medieval constitution.[20]

Military victory turned into political goodwill and financial generosity not only because of the confidence it instilled in the leadership of the king and the belief that taxes (not to mention service in the army) would be put to good use, but also because it underlined the legitimacy and justness of the war against France. This was an age in which great store was placed on the connection between good – or bad – fortune and the will of God. Victories indicated that England's cause met with Divine approval. When Edward III won his first major victory of the war, the naval battle of Sluys in June 1340, he made a point of writing to all the bishops requesting masses and prayers in thanksgiving for this victory.[21] Henry V's remarkable and in some ways unexpected victory at Agincourt convinced many Englishmen, not least the king himself, that God was unquestionably on their side.[22] This spurred the faith which Englishmen had in the military policies of their king, and induced them to support and assist in realising his ambitions. Victory did not just make people feel good about themselves and their rulers; it could bring tangible rewards in the form of profit and advancement – and it was not just the men in the armies who benefitted materially. In 1348 the chronicler Thomas Walsingham recorded that 'throughout England it seemed to the English as if a new sun had risen on account of the sufficiency of peace, the abundance of supplies, and the glory of victories'. He went on to explain one of the reasons why morale was so high:

> For a woman was of no account who did not possess something from the spoils of Caen and Calais [recently captured by English armies], and other cities overseas in the form of clothing, furs, quilts, and utensils. Scattered throughout England in every house were to be seen table-cloths and jewels, bowls of murra [semi-precious stone or porcelain] and silver, linen and linen cloths.[23]

However, it would be wrong to conclude that all a king needed to do was win a battle and everything else would fall into place. This oversimplifies and significantly underestimates the challenges which he faced in mobilising not just resources but also his subjects in support of the war. Both Edward III and Henry V understood the crucial importance of securing the 'home front' before overseas campaigning. Henry famously spent the opening years of his short reign before his first campaign putting the realm to rights after the chronic instability and governmental malaise of his father's rule.[24] This involved an overhaul of the financial system so that crown revenue from feudal prerogatives and customs charges was collected more rigorously and royal expenditure was reduced significantly, especially in relation to the costs of the household and the distribution of annuities. It also hinged on a reassertion of the rule of law: Henry pacified the kingdom by reasserting his authority in Wales, by reinvigorating legal processes across England, and by taking on and defeating the threat posed by the Lollard heresy. This eliminated the sorts of issues which might otherwise have distracted a disgruntled political community from the effective prosecution of the war.

Edward III also excelled in his dealings with the political community, though, unlike Henry who learnt from the bad example of his father, Edward's appreciation of the importance of managing his subject's expectations derived from his own bitter experience and the mistakes he made early in his reign.[25] Edward's initial strategy involved the encirclement of France with a string of alliances which, by October 1339, had generated a debt of some £300,000,[26] almost nine times a standard grant of direct taxation (i.e. a fifteenth and tenth) which was reckoned to raise in one year (£38,000). More worryingly, in his single-mindedness to raise the exorbitant campaign funds necessary, the king showed complete disregard for the impact which these military and diplomatic strategies were having on his people. It was at this time, 1339–40, that the anonymous *Song Against the King's Taxes* was written castigating him for his extravagant living, while pointing out that he 'makes ordinary folk sell their cows, utensils and clothes to pay for his wars'.[27] Edward 'hit the buffers' in the parliament of April 1341.[28] The principal cause was the rift that had opened up between Edward and his military commanders in France, on the one hand, and the regency council left in England and charged to raise funds for the king's campaigns, on the other hand. Refusing to believe that there was a good enough reason to explain the council's inability to raise sufficient money for his needs, Edward returned home in secret in December 1340 determined to exact retribution on his hapless councillors, and to make a particular example of John Stratford, archbishop of Canterbury, who he held to be principally responsible for his troubles. But the king's petulance backfired spectacularly, and when parliament met in the spring he was faced with a formidable coalition of opponents made up of senior nobles, clergymen, gentry and merchants, as well as the weight of adverse public opinion. Edward was forced into a humiliating climb-down. It was at this point that peers won the right to be tried only by their fellow peers, in parliament and not by arbitrary judgement of the king. The Commons also used their control of taxation to force Edward into agreeing to a public audit of royal finances.[29] His obstinacy and recklessness thus resulted in the unedifying spectacle of a late medieval king being dictated to by his own people. Edward had discovered the hard way that he could not single-mindedly drain the realm of its resources without facing serious political repercussions.

The crisis of 1340–1 exposed the limitations of royal authority: the king had to work with the political community and win its support rather than dictate to it what he needed. This was an important lesson which held Edward in good stead for the remainder of his reign. From this point, he involved all his noblemen in the enterprise of war; with the exception of the elderly or infirm, *every* great earl and lord served in one or other of the campaigns of 1346–7. This new approach avoided the dangerous split which had occurred in 1338–40 when the lay and spiritual peers running the regency council in England became seriously disaffected from the king and his entourage who were campaigning in France. In the 1340s and 1350s, the regency councils were controlled not by noblemen but by the king's loyal ministers.[30] Edward also abandoned the alliance strategy of 1337–40 and instead developed multiple theatres of war. This gave noblemen the outlet they desired for their military ambitions and enabled the king to establish a clearer framework with which to appraise, through service, their loyalty to him.

It also reduced the costs of war, or at least the burden of war, by spreading the costs across a lengthier period. This, together with improvements in the management of royal finances and genuine attempts to curb the excesses of royal purveyance, made the sacrifices which war imposed on the population a more palatable proposition. It is a measure of just how far Edward had come since the crisis of 1340–1 that, in 1359, he was able to propose a major campaign to conquer France without needing parliament to finance the expedition by a grant of taxation – the king's own finances were deemed to be sufficient to cover the costs.[31] It was not just the nobility who were won over to the king's military enterprise. Over time, as the war became an accepted and normal part of national life, military service among the gentry intensified and became more widespread. Ayton has argued that in consequence there was a 'militarisation of the wider gentry'.[32] It was a phenomenon noted by Froissart, who remarked 'on account of their great conquests and the riches won in them the whole community of [England] is always more inclined to war than peace'.³³ The closer alignment of the (martial) interests of the king, nobles and gentry led, almost inevitably, to greater political cooperation.³⁴

While the impressive unity of purpose which Edward and Henry built up for their war aims was largely created and sustained by military success, some of this achievement can be attributed to their effective engagement with what might anachronistically be described as 'public opinion'. A king could not rely on his subjects' blind obedience to harness the resources of his kingdom in support of the war. Instead, he needed to persuade his subjects of the need to part with their money and goods. The art of persuasion lay as much at the heart of politics in late medieval England as in modern political life. English kings may have had a God-given right to the throne of France (as they saw it), but the case still needed to be made to the people. This challenge – of reconfiguring what was essentially a dynastic squabble into a conflict which concerned the whole nation – was, in some respects, a daunting one. War was very much removed from the experience of most English people. With the exception of French raids on the south coast and incursions by their Scottish allies in the north, fighting and destruction were confined to France, as discussed in Laura Crombie's chapter in this volume (Chapter 5). While this was something for the English to be grateful for, it heightened a sense in which the war was of little direct concern to most people, and it certainly gave a hollow ring to the claim that England's cause was defensive in nature and therefore necessary and unavoidable.

There was, in addition, the challenge of persuading people that the war was winnable. It is not just historians working with the benefit of hindsight who have claimed that the aim of Edward III and his successors to take the French throne was unrealistic; from the outset, contemporaries similarly expressed their disbelief that England would prevail. The French chronicler Jean le Bel suggested – not inaccurately – that it was risking ridicule for Edward to claim to be the king of a country that he did not possess, while an anonymous chronicler from Rochester commented acidly that Edward might as well call himself sultan of Babylon or king of heaven for all the good that would come of his claim to be king of France.³⁵ Such scepticism was well founded: France was widely considered to be the premier nation in Western Europe, a fact that even Edward acknowledged when he gave precedence to the French *fleurs de lis* over the English leopards in the newly quartered coat of arms of the 'double' monarchy.³⁶ Moreover, France had proved its military superiority in the more limited conflicts over the duchy of Guienne in 1294–7 and 1324–5. Modern historians, perhaps to a greater degree than when Fowler's collection was published, are in agreement that Edward and his successors never seriously contemplated actually *conquering* France. As Taylor has put it, the claim to the throne 'remained a secondary goal for the English during the Hundred Years War, at core a bargaining tool in their negotiations for an expansion of their continental empire and an end to French sovereignty over those lands'.[37] If true, it suggests a surprising level of insincerity about the stated war aims of the English and perhaps also, and more importantly, an acknowledgement at the very highest political level of the improbability of actually making good the king's claim.

The challenge, then, was to make the interests of the political community appear to accord with royal dynastic ambitions, and to present the war (and the taxation it required) as an unavoidable but worthwhile necessity. A good illustration of how this was attempted occurred in September 1346 when the representatives of the king (who was still campaigning in France) approached parliament hoping to secure a new tax grant to sustain the expedition. Although this was the first parliament to meet since the victory at Crécy in August, it was not this battle but the discovery of plans, at the capture of Caen in July, for an invasion of England by Philip VI and various Norman communities that Edward and his advisors chose as moral leverage to induce the Commons to grant a subsidy. The plans, which dated to 1339, were introduced with the following preamble:

> And thereon an ordinance was exhibited, made by the said enemy and some of the great men of France and Normandy, to destroy and ruin the whole English nation and language, to execute which ordinance the said enemy had appointed the count of Eu and the chamberlain, Tankerville, to go there with a great multitude of men-at-arms, Genoese and foot soldiers.[38]

Within the ordinance was a clause which must have sent shivers down the spines of all gathered in parliament:

> And [after the conquest of England] the other rights which the [English] nobles and the barons and other secular men have there will belong and remain to the churches, barons, nobles and good towns of Normandy.[39]

In the aftermath of Agincourt, in November 1415, the chancellor made a speech to parliament pushing other sorts of arguments. Explaining to the Lords and Commons how the expedition had come about, he declared,

> that despite frequent requests being made by our sovereign lord the king to his adversary of France, in order to have peace, to avoid the shedding of Christian blood, and to have the aforesaid rights restored in the said parts of

France, being nevertheless unable to secure restitution, and perceiving that he could not recover anything except by force of war, and, forsaking therefore all kinds of personal pleasure, comfort and safety, he undertook the same expedition and venture for that reason, believing wholeheartedly in his lawful quarrel and in Almighty God, in accordance with the words of the wise man who says, 'Strive thou for justice, and the lord shall fight with you'.[40]

The king was thus presented as a reluctant warrior. His desire was for peace. But he also strove for justice. His repeated overtures to the French king for restoration of his rights in France had all been rejected. He therefore had no choice but to wage war. In doing so, he forewent the luxuries and comforts to which he was accustomed, thus matching the sacrifices his subjects had been called upon to make; but the cause was fundamentally a just one – it was a *lawful quarrel* – and for this reason, and because the king was a pious man, England had God on its side. These were precisely the sorts of arguments the French employed in their declarations against the English.

It would be wrong to conclude from these examples that the crown's persuasive strategies were aimed only at the political or parliamentary elites. Modern scholarship has emphasised the much wider reach of the king's message, and the broader basis of 'public opinion'.[41] We ought to talk not of an elitist political community, but rather of an inclusive political nation, since the advent of national taxation meant that it was important for the crown to engage everyone with the arguments justifying the war. As Rory Cox discusses in Chapter 4 of this volume, the Church was a principal agent for wider dissemination.[42] Instructions were regularly sent by the crown to bishops ordering them to mobilise their clergy in support of the war. The clergy were able to reconcile their spiritual mission with support for war by offering prayers asking for peace; that is to say, peace on English terms, brought about by English victory. How a bishop might act is demonstrated by a letter sent to his clergy by William Wykeham, bishop of Winchester and Edward III's chancellor, in February 1370 admonishing them for not doing enough, for he reminded them that,

> We ... learning how much the dangers of war and of the invasions of our external enemies who are preparing to attack, invade and crush the borders of the realm of England, as much by land as by sea, with no small multitude of ships and of armed men, have ordered and caused processions to be made and celebrated and other devout prayers to be said and continued in all monasteries, churches and other sacred places of our diocese of Winchester.[43]

Since the Church was heavily taxed in support of the war effort, one suspects that as a loyal servant of the crown Wykeham's concerns were directed as much at ensuring the continued backing of the clergy for the king's great enterprise in France as at making sure that royal propaganda was being properly disseminated by his clergy to the wider population.[44]

In an age of limited literacy, the propagation of the 'official line' on the war was achieved as much through visual representation as by the written or spoken word. The appropriation by the English crown of the symbol of French monarchy – the *fleurs de lis* – and its ubiquitous use in the royal coat of arms which appeared on manuscript illuminations, buildings, royal standards, royal clothing, royal seals on official correspondence and on gold coinage (used mainly by the international merchant community) were as powerful as any procession or speech in reminding the people of the reality of their king's claim to the French throne.[45] Much less in evidence today but possibly one of the most important media transmitting the heraldry of the double monarchy in the period was stained glass both in churches and in private residences.[46]

Above all it was the personal dynamism of the king that determined his success in mobilising public opinion. Edward III and Henry V both possessed a natural charisma which drew people into their worlds. From the mid-1340s, Edward famously transformed his court into a replica of that of King Arthur, complete with sittings of a Round Table and a new Camelot – Windsor castle – which was substantially rebuilt to serve as the centre of the new Arthurian cult.[47] In 1348, he established the Order of the Garter and installed as its patron St George, described in 1351 as 'the most triumphant athlete of Christ whose name and protection the English race invoke as that of its special patron, in war especially'.[48] In a petition presented by the abbot of Vaudey (Lincs.) in 1347, Edward was described as the 'prince of chivalry' (*il est prince de chivalerie*), which says much about the effectiveness and reach of the king's projection of his martial image.[49] The king fired people's imagination and made them believe in the nobility and glory of fighting his wars. It was a measure of how successfully he did this, and the extent to which English society had become used to a war-footing mentality, that when, in the parliament of 1358, the king set forth terms for a proposed peace settlement with France, he was met with a distinctly lukewarm reception: MPs were anxious lest the dignity of the crown was in any way compromised by the concessions the king appeared willing to make.[50] Thus it can be seen that Edward had truly succeeded in making his war his people's war.

Henry V addressed his soldiers on the eve of the battle of Agincourt and led by example during the battle itself,[51] but he also showed great skill in the 'PR management' of his domestic audience. One of the most interesting and surprising manifestations of his manipulation of public opinion was the many letters he sent to the citizens of London while on campaign. These were basically newsletters: their purpose was, literally, to keep subjects informed of his progress, thus (it was hoped) keeping them interested in, and engaged with, his enterprise. They were sent to London as the richest city in the kingdom and the principal source of supplies and loans necessary for the king to carry on the war. In 1418, Henry sent a letter addressed to the mayor, aldermen and commons of London, in which he reported that,

> we haue leyd þe seige afore the cite of Roan [Rouen], which is the most notable place in fraunce saue Parys, atte which siege vs nedeþ gretly refreshing for vs and for our hoost … And pray you effectually, that in al the haste that ye may ye wille do arme as manie smale vessels as ye may, goodly with vitaille [victuals], and namly with drinke, for to come to Harfleu.[52]

London was the hub of the nation's social, economic and political life, so news sent there was quickly and efficiently disseminated throughout the kingdom. The letters show that Henry was an able communicator and could 'speak the language' of his subjects, quite literally – and deliberately – by using English (rather than the customary Anglo-Norman French) to convey his news.[53]

THE WAR GOES BADLY

The single most important factor to explain why English military fortunes declined in the reigns of Richard II and Henry VI was that neither possessed the personal attributes or willpower to prosecute the war against France effectively. In Henry's case, this statement requires little qualification: he was entirely unsuited to the rigours of kingship; his weakness of character, leading to complete mental collapse in the 1450s, proved catastrophic not only for England's military fortunes but for its public life in general, as political fragmentation led to civil war and eventually, in 1461, to replacement of the Lancastrian dynasty. We shall consider later how political dialogue shaped, and was itself shaped by, the English defeat in France in the crucial decade of the 1440s. We will establish how the political community coped with a king who apparently lacked any desire to reinvigorate English military fortunes. To some extent this shift of political dynamic was also evident in the reign of Richard II, but the abilities, motivations and failings of this king are far less easy to discern, and have commanded far less historical consensus than appraisals of Henry VI. Let us begin by considering the complex circumstances of this earlier reign.

Richard famously pursued a 'peace policy' in the latter stages of his reign, resulting in 1396 in a truce of twenty-eight years and his marriage to Isabella, daughter of Charles VI.[54] Nevertheless, historians have warned against assuming that Richard's desire to come to terms with the French meant that he had always longed to have peace and that he was, in a manner of speaking, innately anti-militaristic.[55] Richard was no pacifist: in 1385, he led a large royal expedition to Scotland, and he also undertook campaigns to Ireland in 1394–5 and 1399 – though it must be said that on none of these occasions were notable feats of arms accomplished. Palmer has suggested that the visual symbolism of the Wilton Diptych, an altarpiece commissioned by Richard for his personal use, indicates his desire to lead a crusade with the king of France, on the grounds that, while he abhorred the shedding of blood in a conflict between Christian nations, he had no such qualms in shedding the blood of Turks to liberate the Holy Land.[56] It was under Richard in the 1390s, and evidently with the king's encouragement, that there was some revival of the crusading ideal among the knights of the royal court.[57]

Yet the conflict which really mattered, because it remained the primary focus of the English nation, was the war against France. Here, understanding Richard's position, especially in the 1380s before the advent of his peace policy, is not at all straightforward. Traditionally, scholars have characterised Richard's attitude to the war as at best lukewarm and at worst actively disengaged. This interpretation hinges on the fact that Richard did not personally lead a campaign against the French. Arguments that he suffered from an inferiority complex, lest his own martial performance be compared unfavourably with his father's (the Black Prince) and his grandfather's (Edward III), seem less convincing than a lack of conviction in the belief that the chances of gaining glory on the battlefield outweighed the enormous risks of defeat, or even capture, that such an undertaking entailed. That Richard was less than enthusiastic about recovering his rights in France is suggested by a heated confrontation he is reported to have had with his uncle, Thomas, duke of Gloucester, and Thomas Arundel, bishop of Ely, in October 1386 when, responding to the political demands being made of him, the king declared that 'it seems best to us to turn to our cousin of France [i.e. Charles VI], and seek his support and aid against our enemies, and better to submit ourselves to him than to our subjects'.[58] His critics felt minded to remind the king that the king of France was not his friend but his 'chiefest enemy'.

A different interpretation on Richard's position has been articulated by Fletcher, who suggests that far from shying away from the conflict Richard's desire was to prove himself in battle, but that he was prevented from doing so by the parsimony of parliament whose members refused to provide sufficient funds for a royal expedition (far more expensive than any other type of expedition).[59] On at least three occasions (May 1382, and twice in 1383), chancellors had approached MPs declaring that it was the king's 'firm purpose' to lead an expedition to France, only to be rebuffed by subsidies which barely covered the standing costs of defence. In 1385, another royal uncle, John of Gaunt, duke of Lancaster, begged the king to launch a royal expedition to France, using the funds which parliament had provided the previous autumn, but members of the royal council vacillated and eventually rejected the proposal on the grounds that Scotland posed too great a risk, such that,

> he [i.e. Richard II] ought to remain in the security of his own country defending it from the incursions of his enemies, rather than make an unconsidered excursion into foreign parts adding thereby no lustre to his reputation.[60]

It was as a result of obstacles which parliament placed in his way and the other defence needs of the kingdom – so the argument runs – that the king and his advisors were reluctantly forced to concede that negotiated peace was the only viable way forward.

Where one stands in relation to these interpretations depends on how genuine the chancellors' declarations to parliament are judged to have been. While Fletcher takes them at face value, others have seen them as political gambits, strategies aimed at inducing the Commons to be as generous as possible by emphasising (disingenuously) the king's willingness to serve his kingdom.[61] The complication is that Richard's own voice is difficult to discern. In 1382 Richard was still only fifteen years old and was just emerging from the unofficial minority of the early years of his reign. Even in 1385, as the quotation above shows, it was not the king but his councillors who put forward the 'royal' point of view. What Richard thought about the war and whether he really wished to fight in France we may never be fully sure about. Yet, in a sense, what is important about the political dialogue of the 1380s is what it reveals about the state of politics and relations between all those with a stake in the war. It highlights serious divergences of opinion between the political community and the government. It also underlines the absence of a firm political direction and the concomitant weakness of royal authority. Let us consider these points in more detail.

In the 1370s and 1380s, England was obliged to continue the war against France devoid for the most part of a fully functioning king. By the mid-1370s, Edward III, by now a man in his sixties, had effectively withdrawn from politics and played little part in the conflict; in 1377, he was succeeded by his ten-year-old grandson, Richard, who would not fully emerge as a ruler in his own right until after the collapse of his magnate opponents in 1389. It is important to note that MPs did not use this prolonged period of royal deficiency to cut the amount of taxation granted in support of the war; on the contrary, they were remarkably generous with their constituents' money. The gross yield of all types of extraordinary taxation (i.e. lay, clerical and indirect) between 1368 and 1375 was in the order of £690,000; between 1376 and 1381, it amounted to £500,000.[62] These were among the most intensively taxed years of the Hundred Years War, suggesting that the political community very much rallied to the cause in spite of – indeed, perhaps because of – the absence of an active monarch. The real problem was that the political community had lost confidence in the ability of the government to spend taxation in a cost-effective and efficient way. Moreover, it was becoming increasingly clear as the 1370s progressed that the forbearance of the wider population to repeated demands for taxes was wearing thin. In 1381, resentment boiled over into outright rebellion as large portions of the population of south-east England marched on London in the most extraordinary act of popular resistance in the Middle Ages. The catalyst for the 'Peasants' Revolt' was the third poll tax of November 1380. Subsequently, the Commons were far less willing to make generous grants of taxation for fear of provoking further unrest.[63] Inevitably, this impacted on the level of military activity English armies could subsequently mount.

What was the cause of the breakdown in political consensus? First, nothing of any note militarily was achieved in these years. Between 1369 and 1389, as Palmer pointed out, no fewer than fourteen major expeditions were sent across the Channel (compared to just nine between 1337 and 1360),[64] yet when the commanders returned they had little to show for the huge public funds invested in their campaigns. The sums were enormous: Gaunt's expedition of 1369, from Calais to Harfleur and back again, cost in the region of £75,000; the earl of Buckingham's army of 1380-1, which traversed northern France and attempted, but failed, to take the city of Nantes, more than £100,000.[65] Altogether, between 1368 and 1381, England spent an estimated £1,061,750 on the war with France.[66] English strategy had failed to adjust to the new French policy of disengagement which effectively allowed enemies free rein over French territory but avoided decisive clashes of arms. In military terms, this resulted not in defeat for the English, but stalemate, and a very costly stalemate at that, for in addition to the regular *chevauchées*, there were also garrisons to support at Calais, Brest and Cherbourg as well as the defence of the seas and the border with Scotland.

The absence of strong royal leadership meant that overall direction of military strategy was lacking, as we can see in debates which raged during the parliament of October 1382 over whether Gaunt's proposed expedition to Castile, or the bishop of Norwich's plans to cross to Flanders, better served England's interests.[67] There were too many strategies to choose from, and a sense also that foreign policy was being made 'on the hoof' in response to external events and for inconsistent purposes. Perhaps inevitably, then, in the absence of a supreme authority in the person of the king, there was much suspicion, squabbling and recrimination. These decades saw the introduction of special war treasurers at the behest of the Commons because they did not believe that public money was being spent properly.[68] They also witnessed the emergence of the parliamentary process known as impeachment, which provided MPs with a recognised means of bringing government ministers and other public servants to account for their actions. Impeachment was used most extensively against individuals accused of squandering or embezzling money raised by taxation for the war. It was first employed in the Good Parliament of 1376, when the combined attack of the Lords and Commons on Edward III's ministers led to the temporary collapse of his government.[69] It was used in subsequent years to bring to trial in parliament commanders who were accused of failing to discharge their military duties satisfactorily.[70] Curry has suggested that at times of military crisis the Commons often elected Speakers with military backgrounds to represent their views to the crown: Sir Peter de la Mare, Speaker in 1376, and possibly the very first Speaker in history, may well have been chosen at this critical time for this reason.[71]

The other reason why the political community had lost faith in the government was because of its catastrophic failure to provide adequate defence for the people. In 1372, with the help of Castilian allies, the French destroyed the English fleet off La Rochelle, leaving the south coast vulnerable to attack. As the 1370s progressed, French raiding increased in intensity: the war was now being brought to English soil with a vengeance. In 1377, Rye, Folkestone, Portsmouth, Dartmouth, Plymouth, Winchelsea, Hastings and the towns of the Isle of Wight were burned.[72] Such was the level of destruction that, a few years later, it was reported that 'by being burned by the king's enemies and much more by the withdrawal of its burgesses, [Rye] is now so desolate and almost destroyed that the proprietorship of vacant plots and tenements can scarcely be known'.[73] In the first parliament of Richard II's reign, which met in October 1377, the Speaker of the Commons, once again

Sir Peter de la Mare, provided a scathing appraisal of the failings not of the crown but of the warrior class in general:

> whereas the illustrious knighthood of the kingdom had long been well nurtured, cherished, honoured, and nobly rewarded for their many good deeds, so had their knighthood been most keen and ardently willing to undertake great enterprises and deeds of arms ... whereby the kingdom had been greatly enriched and filled with all that was good ... and what is more, the fame of their nobility spread throughout the whole world. Now, however, since their knighthood had been rebutted and scorned, and furthermore, their goods, nobly won from their enemies in war, taken from them without just cause, and also their knighthood and all other virtue scorned, and vice prized, promoted, and honoured, and not punished or chastised at all, so had their same knighthood and the hearts of good and virtuous persons been greatly cast down, wherefore no man has any inclination these days, from what his past experience taught him, to do good: and so the kingdom has lately suffered great injuries and outrages from the said enemies from many parts.[74]

Late fourteenth-century poets expressed similar anxieties and criticisms about the purpose of the conflict and the conduct of the warrior classes, reflecting perhaps the views of the wider public.[75] One of the foremost writers of his day, John Gower, wrote that 'the number of knights increases, but their activity decreases. Thus their honour is empty, since it is without responsibility.'[76]

If all this indicated deep dissatisfaction about the shortcomings of the military caste, such sentiments took on a more dangerous hue during the Revolt of 1381, when the rebels specifically targeted the properties of Gaunt and Richard, earl of Arundel in Sussex because they were considered to have left their own tenants helpless and exposed to raiding.[77] The Speaker of the parliament which met after the Revolt in November 1381, Sir Richard Waldegrave, expressed a surprising degree of sympathy for the rebels by including in his appraisal of the causes of the Revolt the pointed observation that,

> although great sums are continually granted and levied from the commons [i.e. common people] for the defence of the realm, they are still no better defended or secured against the enemies of the kingdom, as far as they know, but are burned, robbed, and pillaged every year by the said enemies, by land and by sea, with their barges, galleys, and other vessels, against which no defence has ever been, nor is yet, provided.[78]

Waldegrave's views were probably not far off the mark. The rebels of 1381 were acutely aware of the vulnerability of their own communities to French attack, to the extent that they had left behind contingents of their own men to guard the coasts when they marched on London.[79]

There was thus a significant loss of confidence in the martial abilities of the kingdom. The difficulty for Richard – whether or not he *really* wanted to fight – was that as he grew older the inability of his government to deal with the threat from France came increasingly to be regarded as a reflection of the failings of his own kingship as well as the moral bankruptcy of his court. It was not a coincidence that Richard lost his power to a coalition of magnate opponents in 1386 at a point when England faced the very real possibility of a full-blown invasion by the French. Around 1388, the chronicler Walsingham penned his famous diatribe against Richard's entourage, describing them as 'knights of Venus rather than of Mars, showing more prowess in the bedroom than on the field of battle'.[80] The king's decision to negotiate with the French for peace once he had regained his power in 1389 was no doubt informed in large part by the realisation that the war had significantly undermined his political authority and that it would continue to do so in the face of unrealistic expectations from parliament that great military victories could be won with minimal financial outlay. 'Peace-making' was as central to the duties of kingship as military prowess, so, if Richard's policies in the 1390s set him apart from other English kings, they did not at the same time indicate that his kingship was a failure. He did not seek the reputation for himself as a 'warrior king', like his grandfather, but wanted to be known as a 'prudent and refined' monarch.[81] No doubt he regarded his pursuit of peace in the 1390s as a prime example of his wisdom. This may have been justified: there is reason to suppose that large sections of the population, now very war-weary, welcomed their king's rapprochement with France.

Many of the problems and challenges which existed in the reign of Richard II reappeared in the reign of Henry VI, but much magnified and with far greater consequences. Henry succeeded to the throne in 1422 as a nine-month-old baby, thus imposing minority government on the kingdom for fifteen years. When he came of age in 1437, it was clear that Henry possessed no aptitude for ruling, let alone military leadership. English resolve began to weaken in the face of lack of direction and leadership at home, coupled with a resurgence of French military fortunes; the political community gradually accepted the desirability of a negotiated peace, but military events overtook diplomatic aspiration and, by 1453, the English had, in effect, been defeated. One of the great ironies of this last stage of the Hundred Years War was that the conflict generally went much better for the English in the first half of

Henry VI's reign, when the king was a child and politically ineffective, than it did in the second half when he was an adult. This was largely because the war aims of the English in the earlier years were clear cut – namely, to preserve the French inheritance that Henry V had left for his son. This created a unity of purpose and, in broad terms, political consensus. When Henry VI officially came of age in 1437, the constraints on foreign policy were lifted, but the direction which it should take became a matter of contention. Henry abhorred war and wanted peace. That much was clear. This affected a discernible shift in emphasis from 1437. From 1444, after the disastrous campaign of the duke of Somerset of the previous year, English policy turned inexorably towards the goal of coming to terms with France. But how was peace to be achieved? What concessions ought the English be prepared to make to secure French coalescence? These were the difficult questions which informed the politics of the later 1440s.

It used to be thought that William de la Pole, earl of Suffolk, and court favourite of Henry, was the principal proponent of a 'peace at any price' policy, and that he effectively sold England 'down the river' to fulfil his own personal ambitions. These, at least, were the terms by which the nobleman came to be impeached in 1449–50, when the Commons sought someone to blame for the loss of Normandy and the imminent collapse of English power in France. Modern revision by Watts, however, casts more sympathetic light on Suffolk's motivations, highlighting the invidious position he was in by the mid-1440s as he sought to negotiate desperately needed respite for England without conceding the overall English claim to the French throne.[82] It was a measure of the extent to which the broader political elite had invested in the war that the king's highly controversial decision in 1444 to cede the territory of Maine to Charles VII in return for nothing more than tenuous promises of French goodwill was made by Suffolk in secret and kept that way until 1447 – partly by neutralising the arch-critic of the peace policy, Humphrey, duke of Gloucester. Yet did Suffolk have any choice? The tragic dilemma he faced, as Myers put it, was having to decide between a ruinous war or a shameful peace.[83] Neither option was politically attractive, but at least by handing over *some* territory to the French there was a chance of keeping the rest. In spite of their attempts to cover up their involvement a sizeable group of the nobility had agreed to this course of action. And the people, by now, wanted peace: when Richard, duke of York returned to England with the king's new French bride, Margaret of Anjou, in April 1445, her arrival was met with great pageants and celebrations in the streets of London as the people regarded her union with Henry as a signal that the war would soon be at an end.[84]

There is a strong argument to be made that, while Suffolk worked hard to fulfil the wishes of his sovereign and make the best of a bad situation, the political community buried its collective head in the sand in the naïve hope that the French monarchy would passively accept the continued occupation by English soldiers of large tracts of French territory. As the great enterprise of Lancastrian France unravelled in the late 1440s, Suffolk became the sacrificial lamb, used to cover up where the real responsibility for the loss of France lay, not just with an ineffective king committed to peace but also with a political community that had increasingly – and fatally – disengaged from the war. In December 1420, the Commons declared that the Treaty of Troyes had effectively brought to an end the need for parliament to grant taxation for the war, since English kings (they argued) could now draw exclusively from their French subjects to help them gain the throne.[85] Accordingly, between 1422 and 1427, no direct taxation was requested. When it resumed, the grants were paltry. In the eight years between 1428 and 1436, income from all types of taxation generated £207,821; in the seventeen years from 1436 to 1453, only £239,500.[86] This steady contraction resulted from smaller grants spread over longer periods of time, and was compounded by a massive reduction of the rate at which the wool subsidy was granted compared with previous reigns (i.e. 23 per cent).[87] In the critical year when Normandy was being overrun, in 1449, no realistic grant was made which might have saved the duchy by funding a large expeditionary army.

Two reasons explain this situation. First, as the fifteenth century progressed, a growing gap developed between the domestic political community and the relatively small group of quasi-professional soldiers who either had lands in France to defend or were pursuing long-term military careers there.[88] England was, in effect, becoming *de*-militarised. This weakened political resolve and probably reduced the ability of MPs to discern the seriousness of England's strategic position, and their willingness to fund major military activity. Secondly, by the 1440s, crown finances were in a state of complete meltdown.[89] The crown was finding it hard enough to pay for itself, let alone a foreign war. It was clear to everyone that Henry VI's priorities lay elsewhere. In 1444–5, £4,000 of duchy of Lancaster revenue was spent on the king's foundations of Eton and King's College, Cambridge.[90] Moreover, with the arrival of Queen Margaret, household costs soared, rising from £8,000 to £27,000 from 1444.[91] In a situation where it was likely the Exchequer would use the proceeds of taxation to alleviate the crown's growing insolvency – brought about by the king's profligate spending and his new, and distinctly unmartial, interests – it is understandable that parliament baulked at the idea of heavy and burdensome taxation.

The growing distance of the political community from the reality of England's position did not make eventual defeat any easier to swallow. The loss of France dealt a devastating blow to national pride, and the sense of betrayal was felt widely. After Suffolk's fall from grace in parliament in 1450 he was put on a ship to take him into exile, but was captured by a group of English sailors who had him summarily executed (allegedly with a rusty sword which required six swipes before the beheading was done). When shown the royal safe conduct which should have protected the duke, the sailors dismissed it on the grounds that

> they did not know the king, but they well knew the crown of England, saying that the aforesaid crown was the community of the said realm, and that the community of the realm was the crown of that realm.[92]

Such an extraordinary statement, which effectively separated the king from the crown and identified the latter with the people, has attracted considerable interest from political and constitutional historians. It signified a rejection of the king's authority and, by extension, a disassociation of the people with royal policy. It is commonplace to suggest that the late Middle Ages was an age of deference; but this statement, and the context in which it was made, indicates the contrary. 'Public opinion' was being formed and expressed independently of the views of the king and his nobles.[93] This also applied to national sentiment. One of the striking developments of the Hundred Years War was the way in which a sense of nation and nationhood developed as the conflict progressed. But, whereas under Edward III these sentiments had tended to be encouraged by, and to a large extent focussed on, the king and the crown, in the fifteenth century, in the absence of strong leadership and direction from the king, the focus turned more broadly to the abstract idea of England as a nation.[94]

Whereas Edward III had worked hard to induce a sense of ownership on the part of the political community towards a conflict he had started, by the mid-fifteenth century that sense of ownership was so strong that the crown's failure to defend English interests overseas, and its apparent willingness to concede defeat, provoked outrage and despair. What had started as a war between kings had ended up as a war between peoples. The shift was clearly manifested in the spontaneous outburst of indignation in 1435 when news filtered through of the duke of Burgundy's defection to the French at the treaty of Arras, and the jingoistic, xenophobic and vitriolic songs and poems that were widely circulated following the duke's subsequent unsuccessful attack on Calais.[95] The political community thus inhabited a contradictory, some might even say hypocritical, position: reluctant to commit the nation's wealth to saving the English position in France,[96] its members were nevertheless deeply committed – emotionally, psychologically and culturally – to the idea of maintaining English dominance on the continent.

CONCLUSIONS

Ultimately, England lost the war because its rulers, and its people, lost the political will to continue the fight. Edward III's great gamble, of claiming the French throne in a bid to secure substantial lands in France with full sovereignty, did not pay off. By 1453, England had little to show for its colossal expenditure of effort and resources except for a precarious toehold on the northern French coast. If, however, we view the outcome of the war through the lens of the 'home front', and the development of systems and institutions put into place to help England wage war more effectively, the story is different. It used to be thought that the onset of near continuous warfare in the late medieval period acted as a curb on state development in England. In a well-known and oft-quoted thesis, Richard Kaeuper argued that the era of great advancement in government and royal authority seen under the Angevins gave way to a period of stagnation and retreat under the Plantagenets, as all their attention was focussed on waging war.[97] The price paid by the crown to secure the support and cooperation of the political community was a diminution of royal authority, as power was handed over to the gentry and nobility on whom the crown increasingly relied for administration and justice in the localities. The 'law state' thus gave way to the 'war state'. In recent years, this hypothesis has been challenged and scholars are now broadly agreed that far from arresting state development, the Hundred Years War – and the preceding conflict with Scotland – acted as vital stimuli for change and innovation.[98] England lost the Hundred Years War, but the war profoundly and permanently altered the shape and nature of the English polity. The institutions of central government, and notably parliament, were transformed, as was political society, which became more integrated and complex as new and innovative ways were found to secure consensus, public finance and law and order in the localities.

If, ultimately, England was unable to overcome its French adversary, this did not dampen the enthusiasm of subsequent generations in harking back to the glory years of English triumph.[99] It was easy to overlook the political tension and instability which the war had generated. In 1472, John Alcock, bishop of Rochester addressed the Commons hoping to persuade them to grant a subsidy in support of Edward IV's proposed invasion of France. He began by reminding the gathered MPs of the long period of civil unrest which England had experienced in recent years. This had left many unhealed wounds and lawlessness was rampant. The best remedy for these problems, he argued, was foreign war, since this offered honourable employment to the disaffected under the king's leadership. He reminded his audience that justice, peace and prosperity had only been long-lasting in the days of those kings who went to war against foreign enemies – namely, Henry I, Henry II, Richard I, Henry III (when he had fought foreign enemies), Edward I, Edward III and Henry V. Notwithstanding his simple-mindedness, even Henry VI had stood in glory and honour while the war lasted, Alcock argued, but afterwards everything fell into decay.[100] It is difficult to escape the logic of Alcock's arguments. At times when English military fortunes were ascendant this tended to produce 'justice, peace and prosperity' at home, conditions which usually translated into political consensus and support.

There are many modern examples which testify to the timelessness of this underlying principle. In the fourteenth and fifteenth centuries, the link between foreign warfare and domestic politics was sharpened by the fact that the king was expected to be both politician and commander-in-chief. The absolute key to successful medieval kingship was man-management. Edward III and Henry V were successful kings because they knew how to command the respect and loyalty of their subjects; this had as much application in parliament or the council or in the king's dealings with the leading citizens of his cities as it did on campaign or in the heat of battle. But the connection between war and politics ran deeper than this, for it was not just the king who fulfilled a dualistic political/military function; the political community did too. The nobles and gentry who served in the army also constituted the nucleus of the political elite, because they served either as the king's closest advisors and councillors (the nobles) or as members of parliament and/or local office holders (the gentry). This meant that politics was particularly closely attuned to the changing fortunes of war. It also meant that the king's greatest supporters militarily could fairly rapidly turn into the king's greatest critics politically if it was felt that the war was being badly mishandled, as Richard II and Henry VI found to their cost.

But perhaps we should not be too hard on these two kings. They did not enjoy the immeasurable advantage which Edward III and Henry V enjoyed, of being able to establish a strong basis of political and military support from early in their reigns. Both Edward and Henry attracted men of their own generation to their military enterprises, whereas Richard and Henry VI came to power as minors in a political environment dominated by old soldiers who longed to return to the glory days of the past. Nor should we necessarily criticise the peace-making sentiments of Richard and Henry VI, when Edward and Henry V could just as easily be condemned for committing their subjects to massive burdens of taxation, a conflict seemingly without end, and for pinning the fate of their kingdoms, as well as their own personal safety, on the notoriously unpredictable outcome of a battle. What would the historical reputations of Edward and Henry V be had the battle of Crécy or Agincourt been lost – as well they might have been – and they themselves captured and kept in foreign captivity for an extended period of time, as happened to David II of Scotland following the battle of Neville's Cross in 1346 and John II of France following the battle of Poitiers in 1356? Were Edward III and Henry V reckless gamblers *as well as* heroic warriors?

We need also to consider the extent to which all these kings were free to choose their political and military destinies. A key theme is the emergence, in the course of the Hundred Years War, of 'popular politics' and public opinion. More than any other dynamic, and to an extent never previously seen, the conflict brought the people into the political life of the kingdom. Overall strategy was no longer decided by the king and a few of his closest advisors; it was now determined by the political will of the people. The success or failure of the English war effort could thus ultimately be said to have been as much dependent on the commitment of the king's subjects to the conflict as it was on the personal qualities and wishes of the king.

NOTES

1. For the series (published in New Haven, CT and London), W. M. Ormrod, *Edward III* (2011); N. Saul, *Richard II* (1994); C. Given-Wilson, *Henry IV* (2016); C. T. Allmand, *Henry V* (1992); and B. Wolffe, *Henry VI* (1981). See also R. A. Griffiths, *The Reign of Henry VI* (London, 1981).
2. E. Powell, 'After "After McFarlane": The Poverty of Patronage and the Case for Constitutional History', *Trade, Devotion and Governance: Papers in Later Medieval History*, ed. D. Clayton, R. G. Davies and P. McNiven (Stroud, 1994), pp. 1–16; C. Carpenter, 'Political and Constitutional History: Before and After McFarlane', *The McFarlane Legacy*, ed. R. H. Britnell and A. J. Pollard (Stroud, 1995), pp. 175–206.
3. PROME; http://www.nationalarchives.gov.uk/e179/; 'Medieval Petitions: A Catalogue of the "Ancient Petitions" [SC 8] in the National Archives', led by Prof Ormrod and Dr Dodd.
4. J. Barnie, *War in Medieval English Society* (London, 1974), pp. 70–7; and M. H. Keen, 'Chivalry, Nobility, and the Man-at-Arms', *War, Literature and Politics in the Late Middle Ages*, ed. C. T. Allmand (Liverpool, 1976), pp. 32–45.
5. M. Keen, *Chivalry* (New Haven, CT, 1984); J. Watts, *Henry VI and the Politics of Kingship* (Cambridge, 1996), pp. 31–8.
6. J. Sherborne, 'John of Gaunt, Edward III's Retinue and the French Campaign of 1369', *Kings and Nobles in the Later Middle Ages*, ed. R. A. Griffiths and J. Sherborne (Gloucester, 1986), pp. 41–61; A. R. Bell, *War and the Soldier in the Fourteenth Century* (Woodbridge, 2004), pp. 83–96; *SLME*, pp. 23–53; N. A.

Gribit, *Henry of Lancaster's Expedition to Aquitaine, 1345–46* (Woodbridge, 2016). Although concerning an earlier period A. Spencer, *Nobility and Kingship in Medieval England: The Earls of Edward I, 1272–1307* (Cambridge, 2014), pp. 76–86, is valuable.

7   M. Keen, 'Chivalry and English Kingship in the Later Middle Ages', *War, Government and Aristocracy in the British Isles, c. 1150–1500*, ed. C. Given-Wilson, A. Kettle and L. Scales (Woodbridge, 2008), pp. 250–66. See also C. Taylor, 'Henry V, Flower of Chivalry', *Henry V: New Interpretations*, ed. G. Dodd (Woodbridge, 2013), pp. 217–47.

8   *Three Prose Versions of the Secreta Secreotrum*, ed. R. Steele, Early English Text Society, extra series, 74 (1898), p. 121.

9   W. de Milemete's *Treatise on the Nobility, Wisdom and Prudence of Kings*, translated in *Political Thought in Early Fourteenth Century England*, ed. C. J. Nederman (Tempe, Arizona, 2002), p. 61.

10 *Political Poems and Songs*, ed. T. Wright, 2 vols (London, 1859–61), I, p. 31.

11 R. Radulescu, '"Talkyng of Cronycles of Kynges and of other polycyez": Fifteenth-Century Miscellanies, the *Brut*, and the Readership of *Le Morte Darthur*', *Arthurian Literature*, 18 (2001), pp. 125–42. For the enthusiasm of Edward I and Edward III for Arthur, C. Shenton, 'Royal Interest in Glastonbury: Two Arthurian Itineraries, 1278 and 1331', *EHR*, 114 (1999), pp. 1249–55 and J. Vale, *Edward III and Chivalry* (Woodbridge, 1983), chaps. 1 and 4.

12 See two articles in the *Age of Edward III*: W. M. Ormrod, 'A Problem of Precedence: Edward III, the Double Monarchy, and the Royal Style', pp. 146–7; C. Taylor, 'Edward III and the Plantagenet Claim to the French Throne', pp. 165–6.

13 G. Post, *Studies in Medieval Legal Thought: Public Law and the State 1100–1322* (Princeton, 1964), pp. 163–238.

14 Ormrod, *Edward III*, pp. 190–6.

15 *PROME*, parliament of 1346, item 7.

16 J. R. Maddicott, *The Origins of the English Parliament, 924–1327* (Oxford, 2010), pp. 331–52.

17 J. R. Maddicott, 'The English Peasantry and the Demands of the Crown, 1294–1341', *Landlords, Peasants and Politics in Medieval England*, ed. T. H. Aston (Cambridge, 1987), pp. 285–359; C. Dyer, 'Taxation and Communities in Late Medieval England', *Progress and Problems in Medieval England: Essays in Honour of Edward Miller*, ed. R. H. Britnell and J. Hatcher (Cambridge, 1996), pp. 168–90; W. M. Ormrod, 'Poverty and Privilege: The Fiscal Burden in England (XIIIth–XVth Centuries)', *La fiscalità nell'economia europea secc. XIII–XVIII*, ed. S. Cavaciocchi, 2 vols (Florence, 2008), II, 637–56; M. Forrest, 'The Distribution of Medieval Taxation in Southern England: New Evidence from Surrey, Middlesex, and Dorset', *Southern History*, 31 (2010), pp. 27–47; W. M. Ormrod, 'Henry V and the English Taxpayer', *Henry V*, ed. Dodd, esp. pp. 200–15.

18 G. L. Harriss, *King, Parliament and Public Finance in Medieval England to 1369* (Oxford, 1975), pp. 3–48, 314–20, summarised in idem, 'War and the Emergence of the English Parliament, 1297–1360', *JMH*, 2 (1976), pp. 35–56.

19   W. M. Ormrod, 'Edward III and the Recovery of Royal Authority in England, 1340–60', *History*, 72 (1987), pp. 4–19 (p. 17).
20   *PROME*, parliament of 1415, items 4–5.
21   A. K. McHardy, 'Some Reflections on Edward III's Use of Propaganda', *Age of Edward III*, p. 190.
22   For contrasting views, see C. J. Rogers, 'Henry V's Military Strategy in 1415', *HYW. A Wider Focus*, pp. 399–428 – Henry was a military genius; and G. Dodd, 'Agincourt: Henry's Hollow Victory', *History Today*, 65 (2015), pp. 19–26 – Henry was a reckless adventurer.
23   Thomas Walsingham, *Chronicon Angliae*, ed. E. M. Thompson (London, 1874), p. 26.
24   E. Powell, 'The Restoration of Law and Order', and G. L. Harriss, 'Financial Policy', *Henry V: the Practice of Kingship*, ed. G. L. Harriss (Oxford, 1985), pp. 53–74, 159–79.
25   Ormrod, *Edward III*, chap. 8. Useful context is also given in E. B. Fryde, 'Parliament and the French War, 1336–40', reprinted in *Historical Studies of the English Parliament*, ed. E. B. Fryde and E. Miller, 2 vols (Cambridge, 1970), I, pp. 242–61.
26   *PROME*, parliament of October 1339, item 4.
27   *Anglo-Norman Political Songs*, ed. I. S. T. Aspin (Anglo-Norman Text Society, xi, 1953), p. 112.
28   Harriss, *King, Parliament*, pp. 294–302, offers the best discussion of this parliament. For a useful summary of these crisis years 1339–41, see Ormrod, *Edward III*, chap. 8.
29   The concessions won by the Commons were made into legislation: *Statutes of the Realm*, 11 vols (London, 1810–28), I, 295–8.
30   Ormrod, 'Edward III and the Recovery', pp. 6, 13–17.
31   Harriss, *King, Parliament*, pp. 346–7.
32   A. Ayton, 'Armies and Military Communities in Fourteenth-Century England', *Soldiers, Nobles and Gentlemen: Essays in Honour of Maurice Keen*, ed. P. Coss and C. Tyerman (Woodbridge, 2009), pp. 215–39 (p. 221).
33   Froissart (Lettenhove), XIV, p. 384.
34   See Ormrod, 'Edward III and Recovery', pp. 10–13.
35   *Chronique de Jean le Bel*, ed. J. Viard and E. Déprez, 2 vols (Paris, 1904–5), I, pp. 167–8, as noted by Le Patourel, *Feudal Empires, Norman and Plantagenet* (London, 1984), chap XII, p. 180; *Chronicon de Lanercost*, ed. J. Stevenson (Edinburgh, 1839), p. 344; Ormrod, *Edward III*, p. 293.
36   M. Michael, 'The Little Land of England is Preferred Before the Great Kingdom of France: The Quartering of the Royal Arms by Edward III', *Studies in Medieval Art and Architecture Presented to Peter Lasko*, ed. D. Buckton and T. A. Heslop (Stroud, 1994), pp. 114–26; A. Ailes, 'Heraldry in Medieval England: Symbols of Politics and Propaganda', *Heraldry, Pageantry and Social Display in Medieval England*, ed. P. Coss and M. Keen (Woodbridge, 2002), pp. 83–104.

37 Taylor, 'Edward III and the Plantagenet Claim', p. 155.
38 *PROME*, parliament of 1346, item 6.
39 Ibid, item 7.
40 *PROME*, parliament of 1415, item 1.
41 J. Watts, 'The Pressure of the Public on Later Medieval Politics', *The Fifteenth Century IV* (2004), pp. 159–80; J. Watts, 'Public or Plebs: The Changing Meaning of 'The Commons', 1381–1549', *Power and Identity in the Middle Ages: Essays in Memory of Rees Davies*, ed. H. Pryce and J. Watts (Oxford, 2007), pp. 242–60; D. Rollison, *A Commonwealth of the People: Popular Politics and England's Long Social Revolution, 1066–1649* (Cambridge, 2010), esp. chaps 4 and 5.
42 See also W. R. Jones, 'The English Church and Royal Propaganda During the Hundred Years War', *JBS*, 19 (1979), pp. 18–30; pp. 18-30; A. K. McHardy, 'Liturgy and Propaganda in the Diocese of Lincoln during the Hundred Years War', *Studies in Church History*, 18 (1982), 215–28; A. K. McHardy, 'Some Reflections on Edward III's Use of Propaganda', *Age of Edward III*, pp. 171–92.
43 *Wykeham's Register*, ed. T. F. Kirby, Hampshire Record Society (2 vols, 1899), II, p. 105; McHardy, 'Some Reflections', pp. 183–4.
44 A. K. McHardy, 'The English Clergy and the Hundred Years War', *Studies in Church History*, 20 (1983), pp. 171–78; eadem, 'Clerical Taxation in Fifteenth-Century England: The Clergy as Agents of the Crown', *The Church, Politics and Patronage in the Fifteenth Century*, ed. R. B. Dobson (Gloucester, 1984), pp. 168–92. Clerical contribution to war finance led, on occasion, to clerical criticism of, and even revolt against, royal fiscal policies; W. M. Ormrod, 'The Rebellion of Archbishop Scrope and the Tradition of Opposition to Royal Taxation', *The Reign of Henry IV: Rebellion and Survival, 1403–13*, ed. G. Dodd and D. Biggs (Woodbridge, 2008), pp. 162–79.
45 Ormrod, 'Problem of Precedence', pp. 133–5, 149–50. See also E. Danbury, 'English and French Artistic Propaganda during the Period of the Hundred Years Wars: Some Evidence from Royal Charters', *Power, Culture and Religion in France c. 1350–1550*, ed. C. T. Allmand (Woodbridge, 1989), pp. 75–98.
46 McHardy, 'Some Reflections', pp. 186–8.
47 W. M. Ormrod, 'For Arthur and St George: Edward III, Windsor Castle and the Order of the Garter', *St George's Chapel, Windsor, in the Fourteenth Century*, ed. N. Saul (Woodbridge, 2005), pp. 13–34; J. Munby, R. Barber and R. Brown, *Edward III's Round Table at Windsor* (Woodbridge, 2007).
48 *CPR, 1350–54*, p. 127. See Vale, *Edward III and Chivalry*, pp. 76–91; R. Barber, *Edward III and the Triumph of England* (London, 2013). On the appropriation of St George by the English crown, see D. A. L. Morgan, 'The Banner-bearer of Christ and Our Lady's Knight: How God became an Englishman Revisited', *St George's Chapel*, pp. 51–61.
49 TNA, SC 8/239/11914.
50 *Historia Anglicana*, ed. H. T. Riley, 2 vols (London, 1863–4), I, p. 285; Ormrod, *Edward III*, pp. 393–4.

51　A. Curry, *Agincourt: A New History* (Stroud, 2005), pp. 200 and 221–2; eadem, 'The Battle Speeches of Henry V', *Reading Medieval Studies*, 34 (2008), pp. 77–98.

52　*A Book of London English, 1384–1425*, ed. R. W. Chambers and M. Daunt (Oxford, 1931), pp. 73–4; J. L. Kirby, 'Henry V and the City of London', *History Today*, 26 (1976), pp. 223–31.

53　The pioneering work is J. H. Fisher, 'A Language Policy for Lancastrian England', *Publications of the Modern Language Association of America*, 107 (1992), pp. 1168–80. See also M. Vale, 'Language, Politics and Society: The Uses of the Vernacular in the Later Middle Ages', *EHR*, 120 (2005), pp. 15–34. Henry's use of English represented an important development, but we should not see it as part of a comprehensive 'language policy', still less an expression of linguistic patriotism: see G. Dodd, 'The Spread of English in the Records of Central Government, 1400–30', *Vernacularity in England and Wales, c. 1300–1550*, ed. E. Salter and H. Wicker (Turnout, 2011), pp. 225–66, and also M. Vale, *Henry V: The Conscience of a King* (New Haven, CT and London, 2016), pp. 114–25.

54　Saul, *Richard II*, chap. 10.

55　As argued by A. Curry, 'Richard II and the War with France', *The Reign of Richard II*, ed. G. Dodd (Stroud, 2000), pp. 33–50 (pp. 41–2).

56　J. J. N. Palmer, *England, France and Christendom, 1377–99* (London, 1972), pp. 242–4. See also N. Saul, 'A Farewell to Arms? Criticism of Warfare in Late Fourteenth-Century England', *Fourteenth Century England II* (Woodbridge, 2002), pp. 131–46 (143–5).

57　T. Guard, Chivalry, *Kingship and Crusade: the English Experience in the Fourteenth Century* (Woodbridge, 2013), pp. 169–71, 199–206. For Richard's chivalric/martial ethos, see articles in *The Age of Richard II*, ed. J. L. Gillespie (Stroud, 1997), by J. L. Gillespie, 'Richard II: Chivalry and Kingship' (pp. 115–38), and 'Richard II: King of Battles?' (pp. 139–64).

58　*Knighton's Chronicle, 1337–1396*, ed. G. H. Martin (Oxford, 1995), pp. 357–9.

59　C. Fletcher, *Richard II: Manhood, Youth, and Politics, 1377–99* (Oxford, 2008), pp. 97–126.

60　*The Westminster Chronicle, 1381–1394*, ed. L. C. Hector and B. F. Harvey (Oxford, 1982), p. 113.

61　M. Aston, 'The Impeachment of Bishop Despenser', *BIHR*, 38 (1965), pp. 127–48 (p. 138); Saul, *Richard II*, p. 157.

62　J. W. Sherborne, 'The Cost of English Warfare with France in the Later Fourteenth Century', reprinted in idem, *War, Politics and Culture in Fourteenth-Century England* (London, 1994), pp. 55–70 (p. 62).

63　J. A. Tuck, 'Nobles, Commons and the Great Revolt of 1381', *The English Rising of 1381*, ed. R. H. Hilton and T. H. Aston (Cambridge, 1984), pp. 194–212.

64　Palmer, *England, France and Christendom*, p. 1.

65　Sherborne, 'Cost of English Warfare', pp. 56 and 68.

66　Ibid, p. 69.

67　*PROME*, parliament of October 1382, items 11–12, and items 23 and 46 (XXIII).

68 *PROME*, parliament of October 1377, item 27; parliament of January 1380, item 14; parliament of 1381, item 1; parliament of November 1384, item 1; parliament of 1385, item 10.
69 G. Holmes, *The Good Parliament* (Oxford, 1975). A summary is provided by Ormrod, *Edward III*, pp. 550–62.
70 R. Ambühl and G. Dodd, 'The Politics of Surrender: Treason, Trials and Recrimination in the 1370s', *Ruling Fourteenth Century England: Essays in Honour of Christopher Given-Wilson*, ed. R. Ambühl, J. Bothwell and L. Tompkins (Woodbridge, 2019), pp. 227–61.
71 A. Curry, 'Speakers at War in the Late Fourteenth and Fifteenth Centuries', *Parliamentary History*, 29 (2010), pp. 8–21.
72 Sumption, *Divided Houses*, pp. 281–91.
73 *CPR, 1381–85*, p. 425.
74 *PROME*, parliament of October 1377, item 16.
75 See Barnie, *War in Medieval English Society*, pp. 127–38; R. F. Yeager, '*Pax poetica*: On the Pacifism of Chaucer and Gower', *Studies in the Age of Chaucer*, 9 (1987), pp. 97–121; and Saul, 'Farewell to Arms?'.
76 *Vox Clamantis*, book 5, chap. 8 (printed in *The Major Latin Works of John Gower*, ed. E. W. Stockton (Seattle, 1962), pp. 207–8).
77 E. Searle and R. Burghart, 'The Defense of England and the Peasants' Revolt', *Viator*, 3 (1972), pp. 381–2.
78 *PROME*, parliament of 1381, item 17.
79 As reported by the *Anonimalle Chronicle*; *The Peasants' Revolt of 1381*, ed. R. B. Dobson (London and Basingstoke, 1983), pp. 126–7.
80 *The St Albans Chronicle, Volume 1 1376–1394*, ed. J. Taylor, W. R. Childs and L. Watkiss (Oxford, 2003), p. 815; W. M. Ormrod, 'Knights of Venus', *Medium Ævum*, 73 (2004), pp. 290–305.
81 Saul, *Richard II*, pp. 356–7.
82 Watts, *Henry VI*, pp. 221–34; C. Carpenter, *The Wars of the Roses: Politics and the Constitution in England, c. 1437–1509* (Cambridge, 1997), pp. 95–105.
83 A. R. Myers, *England in the Later Middle Ages*, 8th edn (Harmondsworth, 1971), pp. 15–16 (Myers was describing the situation faced by the English monarchy in the fourteenth century, but his observation applies with equal force, and perhaps more so, to the circumstances of the fifteenth century).
84 H. E. Maurer, *Margaret of Anjou: Queenship and Power in Late Medieval England* (Woodbridge, 2003), pp. 17–24.
85 *PROME*, parliament of December 1420, item 25 (XIIII). For comment, see G. L. Harriss, 'The Management of Parliament', *Henry V*, ed. Harriss, pp. 137–58 (pp. 149–50).
86 G. Bernard, *War, Taxation and Rebellion: Henry VIII, Wolsey and the Amicable Grant of 1525* (New York, 1986), p. 127.
87 W. M. Ormrod, 'The Domestic Response to the Hundred Years War', *Arms, Armies and Fortifications in the Hundred Years War*, ed. A. Curry and M. Hughes (Woodbridge, 1994), pp. 83–101 (pp. 93–4).

88 M. Powicke, 'Lancastrian Captains', *Essays in Medieval History Presented to B. Wilkinson*, ed. T. A. Sandquist and M. R. Powicke (Toronto, 1969), pp. 371–82; M. Keen, 'The End of the Hundred Years War: Lancastrian France and Lancastrian England', *England and Her Neighbours 1066–1453: Essays in Honour of Pierre Chaplais*, ed. M. Jones and M. Vale (London, 1989), pp. 297–311. See also S. Payling, 'War and Peace: Military and Administrative Service amongst the English Gentry in the Reign of Henry VI', *Soldiers, Nobles and Gentlemen*, ed. Coss and Tyerman, pp. 240–58.
89 See G. L. Harriss, 'Marmaduke Lumley and the Exchequer Crisis of 1446–9', *Aspects of Late Medieval Government and Society: Essays Presented to J. R. Lander*, ed. J. G. Rowe (Toronto, 1986), pp. 143–78.
90 Carpenter, *Wars of the Roses*, p. 105.
91 Ibid.
92 Quoted in R. Virgoe, 'The Death of William de la Pole, Duke of Suffolk', *Bulletin of the John Rylands Library*, 47 (1964–5), pp. 489–502 (p. 499).
93 D. McCulloch and E. D. Jones, 'Lancastrian Politics, the French War, and the Rise of the Popular Element', *Speculum*, 58 (1983), pp. 95–138.
94 R. A. Griffiths, 'The Island of England in the Fifteenth Century: Perceptions of the Peoples of the British Isles', *JMH*, 23 (2003), pp. 177–200; A. Ruddick, 'National Sentiment and Religious Vocabulary in Fourteenth-Century England', *Journal of Ecclesiastical History*, 60 (2009), pp. 1–18; D. Green, 'National Identities and the Hundred Years War', *Fourteenth Century England VI* (Woodbridge, 2010), pp. 115–30; A. Ruddick, *English Identity and Political Culture in the Fourteenth Century* (Cambridge, 2013).
95 J. A. Doig, 'Propaganda, Public Opinion and the Siege of Calais in 1436', *Crown, Government and People in the Fifteenth Century*, ed. R. E. Archer (Stroud, 1995), pp. 79–106; J. Scattergood, 'The Libelle of Englyshe Polycye: The Nation and Its Place', *Nation, Court and Culture: New Essays on Fifteenth-Century English Poetry*, ed. H. Cooney (Dublin, 2001), pp. 28–49; D. Grummitt, *The Calais Garrison: War and Military Service in England, 1436–1558* (Woodbridge, 2008), pp. 31–43.
96 On blame for the English defeat linked to lack of sufficient funds for the army, see C. Nall, 'Perceptions of Financial Mismanagement and the English Diagnosis of Defeat', *The Fifteenth Century VII* (Woodbridge, 2007), pp. 119–35.
97 R. W. Kaeuper, *War, Justice and Public Order: England and France in the Later Middle Ages* (Oxford, 1988).
98 G. L. Harriss, 'Political Society and the Growth of Government in Late Medieval England', *Past and Present*, 138 (1993), pp. 28–57. See also A. Musson and W. M. Ormrod, *The Evolution of English Justice: Law, Politics and Society in the Fourteenth Century* (Basingstoke, 1999); C. Carpenter, 'War, Government and Governance in England in the Later Middle Ages', *The Fifteenth Century VII*, pp. 1–22.
99 D. A. L. Morgan, 'The Political After-Life of Edward III: The Apotheosis of a Warmonger', *EHR*, 112 (1997), pp. 856–81; Allmand, *Henry V*, pp. 426–43.
100 J. B. Sheppard (ed.), *Literae Cantuarienses*, Rolls Series, 3 vols (1887–9), iii, pp. 274–85, summarised in *PROME*, parliament of 1472 (third roll, June 1474–March 1475), Appendix, item 1.

2 French Politics during the Hundred Years War

Graeme Small

It has become something of a commonplace to explain the political development of late medieval Europe in terms of the impact of warfare, nowhere more so than in French historiography.[1] A hundred years of war followed 'le beau siècle de Saint Louis' (Louis IX, 1226–70), and confounded the upwards trajectory of Capetian achievement.[2] Warfare led to the weakening and recasting of royal power thereafter, a process interpreted variously by scholars as one of fragmentation, decentralisation or, most recently, 'deconcentration'.[3]

By the later fifteenth century, however, the Hundred Years War had created something new: it brought about nothing less than the 'genèse médiévale de la France moderne' ('the medieval genesis of modern France').[4] The Valois monarchy was able to expel the English from every part of French soil bar Calais thanks to success in establishing permanent taxation, and thereby being able to fund a national army garrisoned across the kingdom. A sacralised monarchy promoted and drew strength from ideological currents which, together, have been described as 'the birth of France the nation'.[5]

A small number of French scholars have written histories of the Hundred Years War primarily as a military conflict, much like their Anglophone counterparts.[6] For most, however, *La guerre de Cent Ans* is a 'découpage chronologique' ('chronological break') in its own right – quite as much a defining period in French political history as the Mervovingian era of the early Middle Ages, or the numbered Republics of modern times.[7] Clearly it would be impossible within the scope of the present chapter to do justice to the range of writings that have appeared since the late 1960s when Kenneth Fowler's original volume of essays was in preparation. In what follows, we seek to capture some of the salient trends that have emerged, but also to offer other ways of looking at French political society in the period.[8]

TRENDS IN THE POLITICAL HISTORY OF LATE MEDIEVAL FRANCE

In the late 1960s, it would not necessarily have been obvious that the study of the political history of late medieval France was set to make a major comeback.[9] With its emphasis on creating a narrative of events (called in French *l'histoire événementielle*) and describing how institutions of government had emerged and developed, political history as it was written in the late nineteenth century and the first decades of the twentieth came to seem irrelevant to a generation of French scholars influenced by the rise of the *Annales* school in the 1930s. Gradually, in the work of historians such as Raymond Cazelles (1917–85) and Bernard Guenée (1927–2010), the political history of late medieval France was to be re-established as an area of research, with particular emphasis on the development of the state. The revival of political history since the 1970s is most apparent in the study of men and ideas – areas in which some of the *Annalistes*' approaches, such as prosopography and the study of mentalities, were most readily adapted.

Although there were earlier attempts to identify the men who served the state in medieval France, the task of setting the careers of royal servants in context began in earnest with Cazelles's study of political society under Philip VI and, around the same time, Guenée's work on the men involved in the regional administration of royal justice.[10] Thereafter, prosopographical approaches began to appear, further deepening our understanding of the ruling elites of the kingdom across a variety of governmental organisms.[11] The royal state as it emerged from these studies was, as Françoise Autrand observed (1986), a small thing in terms of the number of people involved (which was of course what made a prosopographical approach feasible in the first place): perhaps just 200 office holders or so were enough during the reign of Charles VI to run the king's *Parlement* (for justice), the *Chancellerie* (for correspondence), the *Chambre des comptes* and *Trésor* (for the finances of the king's domain), and finally the mint. Clearly it would be a mistake to overestimate the administrative capacity of such thinly staffed organisms, or to make the development of the institutions of the state the main story of late medieval political history, as French historians were once inclined to do.

Knowing who served the king, and understanding the relations between these men, has nonetheless subsequently enabled the study of factions within the governing elite, and an examination of their role in political change (including how the war with the king of England developed in any given phase). The so-called 'Marmousets', an influential group of counsellors in the reign of Charles V (1364–80) and the early years of Charles VI, are an illustration of this point. The group was reputedly given its pejorative name ('little monkeys', referring to the humble origins of its members) early in the reign by supporters of the young king's uncles, whose involvement they managed to thwart until 1392. The 'Marmousets', foremost among them the Breton noble Olivier V de Clisson, the Burgundian Bureau de La Rivière and the king's treasurer, Jean Le Mercier, are attributed with a number of successful policies which helped stabilise the French position in the second phase of the Hundred Years War (1369–89) – notably the adoption of Fabian tactics to counter English arms during the reign of Charles V, and the conservation of royal resources during the early years of his son's reign.[12] Other factional groupings whose composition and actions have been studied include 'le parti navarrais' – the Navarrese party, the supporters of Charles 'the Bad', king of Navarre – which had caused so much trouble for John II in the 1350s.[13] Office-holding by influential adherents of the rival Burgundian and Armagnac camps in the internecine wars which paralysed the kingdom in the first and second decades of the fifteenth century has also been scrutinised.[14]

The study of men at the political centre, and the groupings they formed, has done much to show how far the Hundred Years War can be understood as a series of conflicts within the French polity rather than simply a war between the king of England and the king of France. Quite how conflicts at the centre of the kingdom shaped events across the realm can still be very difficult to follow, however. The insights of Peter Lewis (1931–2014) into the mechanisms of brokerage, the distribution of power and the construction of clienteles between the 'centre' and the 'periphery' of political society provide a framework that has yet to be taken up by French scholars in a systematic way. We will return to this point later in this section.[15]

Political ideas and mentalities is the other area of considerable research and comment since the late 1960s. The remarkable effort to 'penser le pouvoir' (to 'think about power') by a great many French writers of the later Middle Ages tends to be linked, in modern scholarship, to the repeated cycle of crisis and recovery which the Hundred Years War brought to political life.[16] In tracts and longer treatises, verse works of varying form and purpose, chronicles, sermons and a proliferation of other literary texts, predominantly composed in the vernacular rather than in Latin, writers reflected on who or what was responsible for the miserable state of the kingdom, or advocated solutions to the sins of the times, usually by calling for reform and a strengthening of the monarchy.[17] Many of these writers were linked in some way to royal government: Geoffroi de Charny, among the first to address the failings of the nobility in the 1350s, was the royal standard bearer at the battle of Poitiers, where he was killed; royal secretaries and notaries such as Jean de Montreuil and Alain Chartier were both involved in the political processes which inspired their polemical writings. Jean de Montreuil was murdered by the Burgundian party in Paris in 1418. It is not surprising that the troubles of the kingdom should have been felt particularly acutely in such circles, or that the glorification of the monarchy seemed to them essential in French political life.[18] At least one king, Charles V, took a hand in commissioning new writing about the monarchy (on matters such as succession arrangements or the coronation ritual, for example), and some of these texts found their way into the great royal library at the Louvre which the king developed. It is to Charles V's reign, and the group of intellectuals at the heart of power whom he cultivated, that the origins of the late medieval outpouring of reflection and polemic is most convincingly traced.[19]

It is far from certain that such writers were articulating opinions that were more widely held.[20] Nor can we be sure that these men – and one woman, Christine de Pizan – were able to influence public opinion to any great extent. Even figures whom we might describe as 'public intellectuals', such as the chancellor of the University of Paris, Jean Gerson, were still read and heard within fairly well-defined 'distribution circles'.[21] Ideas circulated in late medieval France in many ways. Political communication also developed through royal entry ceremonies, the study of which has advanced considerably since it began in earnest in the late 1960s. These infrequent but highly memorable events were occasioned by a visit of the king and his entourage to a town or city, less often by another member of the royal family, during which the progress of the royal party through the town to its place of residence was accompanied by symbolically charged street theatre and decorations which were arranged and paid for by the municipality and civic groups.[22] The study of gestures and rituals associated with the exercise of justice, or with the making of peace, are other ways in which we now understand the nature of political authority, and how its ambitions and purpose were communicated to the king's subjects.[23] By these means and others, the monarchy was becoming the natural focus of a regnal community which was imagined by contemporary writers as a beautiful garden, tended by the king; as a fine tree in blossom, to be preserved from drought; as a desolate mother, whose children (the nobility, the clergy, the people) had failed to protect her and her possessions.[24] Because it gave rise to these popular tropes, the Hundred Years War is rightly seen as an important phase in the development of French identity.

The emphasis we have placed thus far on the smallness of the apparatus of the state and the softness of its power stands in contrast to the view that the key development of the Hundred Years War was the dramatic and enduring growth in the coercive capacity of the monarchy, above all in its ability to raise money. We now understand far better than we did in the late 1960s the possibilities and limitations of the various experiments by which the monarchy attempted in the first half of the fourteenth century to raise funds to fight its wars: further discussion is also provided in a later chapter in this volume.[25] The main breakthrough, as John Bell Henneman (1935–98) demonstrated, came in the wake of the crisis of John II's capture at Poitiers in 1356, when one of the traditional grounds for seeking a subsidy, namely to pay the king's ransom, provided the springboard for the levying of more sustained taxation.[26] Apart from the risk that it might provoke wide-scale revolt, an obvious danger of increasing fiscal revenues was the potential it created for infighting among covetous parties around the king.[27] Maurice Rey explained the fiscal collapse of the second half of Charles VI's reign in this light, as political factions either sought to monopolise the king's riches or else called for the abolition of certain taxes in an effort to deny them to their rivals.[28] These policies contributed significantly to the straitened circumstances that afflicted the monarchy from the 1410s, through the Burgundian–Armagnac conflict, and well into Charles VII's reign (1422–61), both of which will be discussed further in the section 'Men of the East' and 'Men of the West'. Not entirely coincidentally, these were also years in which English successes in France were at their height. The eventual establishment of a 'fiscal system' in the second half of Charles VII's reign was in many respects simply a return to tax-raising practices which had proved successful under Charles V. The main differences between the two reigns are that, in the 1440s, Charles VII was surrounded by a less extensive and less powerful royal family than his grandfather had been; and he ruled over subjects who, after yet more decades of war and internal strife, were more accepting of tax burdens than their predecessors in the 1370s.[29] The period of greatest expansion and innovation in matters of taxation occurred during the reign of Louis XI (1461–83), after the English had been driven from most of France, but at a time when their return in arms under a warlike monarch, and an alliance of that enemy with some of the great princes of France, could not be ruled out.[30] Despite his great revenues, an isolated Louis XI nonetheless came perilously close to defeat during the War of the Public Weal in 1465.[31] Fiscal revenues did indeed increase greatly from 1300 to 1500, but in fits and starts, and on their own they did not guarantee Valois supremacy. For growing taxes to translate into military success, the political conditions had to be right.[32]

By comparison with their French counterparts, as Gwilym Dodd's chapter shows, English kings were generally more successful at winning consent for taxation because they could negotiate with leading figures in English political society through a single representative assembly, Parliament.[33] In France too there was a single representative assembly for the entire realm, the Estates-General, which had first met in the reign of Philip IV (1285–1314) during that king's dispute with Pope Boniface VIII. But it proved to be an unwieldy and ineffective means of raising money in the first decades of the fourteenth century. The radical role adopted by the Estates in the political turmoil following the battle of Poitiers (1356), the next most intense period of meetings, ensured that later kings, with one notable exception to which we shall return, were not always keen to summon and consult the main representative assembly of their realm. As long as it had to seek agreement for taxes, the royal administration generally resorted to many smaller negotiations through its officers in the localities, either with regional or local assemblies or directly with local municipal authorities (or indeed at both levels). Peter Lewis produced an important summation of these points in an article which, by implicit comparison with England, elected to emphasise the 'failure' of the Estates in late medieval French history.[34]

It would be fair to say that historians have since chosen to nuance Peter Lewis's emphasis. James Russell Major (1921–98) in particular drew attention to the importance of regional and local representative assemblies across the kingdom in our period: not just in the so-called 'pays d'états' (quasi-independent by partly autonomous principalities) which were absorbed into the kingdom at various points in the fifteenth century, like Burgundy (1477), Normandy (1450) or Provence (1481), but elsewhere in the kingdom too, where they were active in a variety of necessary and important roles for as long as they existed. Regional Estates occupied themselves in revising customary law, for example, or promoting local interests by calling for the creation of a regional *Parlement*, as happened in Languedoc.[35] The monarchy which emerges in Major's work is not the proto-absolutist political authority which some studies persist in holding up as the product of the Hundred Years War, but rather a relatively fragile entity that very much needed the cooperation of local elites to exercise power, some of which was won through the regional Estates.[36]

One possible reason for the relatively limited impact of the Estates on French political life lay in noble attitudes towards these bodies. Although the middling nobility did participate in the meetings of most regional Estates and the Estates-General, they were less concerned than many of their fellow delegates in the central business of negotiating taxes because they did not contribute to levies themselves. And the highest nobility, the princes of the blood and great lords, according to Lewis, 'had long outgrown' such gatherings.[37] At one time this might not have seemed much of a loss to representative assemblies because the French nobility were long perceived by historians to have been a spent force by the later Middle Ages. This was the view of Augustin Thierry (d. 1856) and Jules Michelet (d. 1874), who chose to contrast the triumphant march of the monarchy and its principal ally, the bourgeoisie (foremost among them the lawyers who put royal power on a sovereign footing), with the diminishing power of great lords and the church.[38] The renewal of interest in rural history by historians from the 1960s seemed to lend additional weight to the view that the late Middle Ages was a period of aristocratic decline, as scholars found evidence of an erosion of seigneurial revenues resulting from the man-made and natural disasters of the period. Guy Fourquin's work on the region around Paris presented a hard-up regional aristocracy dividing patrimonies among multiple heirs or else selling up to wealthier urban dwellers, while Guy Bois's study of rural Normandy talked of nothing less than a 'crisis of feudalism'.[39]

As we have since learned, however, news of the demise of aristocratic power in late medieval France has been greatly exaggerated. Pierre Charbonnier's work on the Auvergne, Michel le Mené's on Anjou and Jean Tricard's on the Limousin have reversed the view that the nobility was a class in decline.[40] These historians and others point to evidence of the relative economic buoyancy of the aristocracy, as well as the continuing social and political importance of lordship and noble families in the social and political life of rural localities across the kingdom. In this 'other France', the nobility retained a firm hold on the countryside: through their fortified dwellings and military training, their exercise of justice and ability to keep the peace, and their networks which could be mobilised in times of need. This power could be disrupted or indeed corrupted during periods of intense conflict, as Nicolas Wright has shown.[41] Noble networks were, in part, the product of the ties of kinship, lordship and regional association which had shaped crusade participation among the nobility in earlier times. The bonds of vassalage were still commonly used to produce war bands and armies when required, despite the supposed weakening of the feudal tie in the later Middle Ages. In addition, new forms of social relations were taking hold within the aristocracy, in which money replaced land as the principal means of retaining the loyalty and service of useful noblemen.[42] Finally, other means of creating loyalties were emerging, such as the granting of office in a great lord's service, the award of pensions, membership of chivalric orders, or 'brotherhood-in-arms' agreements.

Networks so constituted were of particular importance for the political history of late medieval France. Singly or in alliance, they created the power base of a great lord within any given locality or region, or indeed across a number of regions. In turn, these networks might connect upwards via brokerage and patronage, as Peter Lewis rightly pointed out, to form clienteles of national significance. To demonstrate the point we can take Emily Lebailly's 2006 study of the circle of Raoul I, count of Eu and Guînes, who was made constable of France by Philip VI in 1329. Unusually good evidence relating to the constable's circle reveals the importance of his power base in Normandy and Picardy, where the vast majority of the nobles who served in his household or military entourage came from. Even after the constable's death at a joust in 1345, his supporters remained an identifiable interest group. Many entered the service of the count's son, another Raoul, who inherited his father's office as constable (the leading military figure in the whole realm). In other words, noble networks were durable entities capable of transferring allegiance and service from one leader to another, albeit in this instance simply from father to son. Raoul II was captured at the battle of Crécy in the following year, and was Edward III's prisoner until 1350. Within months of the constable's release and return to France he attracted the suspicion of John II and was executed for treason. There was scant regard for due process, it seemed to Raoul II's supporters, and the king committed the additional mistake of failing to mollify the noble networks concerned. The upshot was that John II created a powerful and well-connected group of enemies for himself in Normandy and Picardy. Some of the original group of Normans who had served Raoul I and his son subsequently took up the cause of Charles 'the Bad', king of Navarre, and were among the murderers in 1352 of Raoul II's successor as constable, Charles of Spain (who – not coincidentally – happened to be a favourite of the king). Lebailly argues that men from the very same Eu–Navarre network emboldened John's son and successor, the future Charles V, to adopt an independent attitude towards his father during his time as duke of Normandy (1355–6), provoking another drastic intervention by the royal administration and yet more executions for treason, as well as the imprisonment of Charles of Navarre himself (1356–8).[43] Noble networks within a region could thus have a marked impact upon the political life of the kingdom, in this case for more than a decade during what was a key phase of Anglo-French relations.

THE KING AND THE PRINCES OF THE REALM

How might one write a history of French politics in this period that takes account of the changing composition, ambitions and influence of the myriad noble networks which surely existed across France?[44] Compared to England, the evidence is thin and the subject is vast. Equally, nor can the actions of the 'political class par excellence' be ignored.[45] Whatever wealth a ruler might have from taxation, much hung on his ability to mobilise the energy and to retain the loyalty of military elites.

One influential answer to our question was formulated by Édouard Perroy (1901–74) in a short article which emphasised not the power of the king but rather the power of the princes of the realm in fifteenth-century France.[46] According to Perroy, the fundamental problem was that noble networks were mobilised at the regional level by increasingly autonomous princely states, to the detriment of the unity of the kingdom. This period constituted, in his view, a new age of principalities in French history, echoing in some ways the fragmentation of public authority during the tenth and eleventh centuries (another subject he had published on). Whether principalities emerged as the result of a military victory, as was the case in Brittany (1364), or from a deliberate decision by a king to create an apanage for a member of the royal familial community, as happened in Berry (1360) and Burgundy (1363), these political units are perceived to have striven for ever greater autonomy in similar ways: through the development of 'state' institutions such as princely households and courts, counting houses, agents for raising taxation and, in a few cases, sovereign courts of law.[47] Perroy spent much of his early career teaching and researching in the United Kingdom, and his ideas had particular influence on that side of the Channel.[48] John Le Patourel (1909–81) traced the origins of the French princely state to the fourteenth century, and some of the most important and enduring work on the subject has since been written by British scholars, above all Michael C. E. Jones on Brittany and Richard Vaughan on Burgundy (1927–2014).[49] Some French historians have adopted a similar approach, such as André Leguai (1923–2000) or Jean Kerhervé.[50]

The notion of a 'princely state' is useful in some respects, not least because it draws attention to the regions of France and the ways in which authority at that level might overlap with local identities, most convincingly in the case of Brittany. But there are problems with the concept too, which all of these historians are fully aware of – not least the limited reach of the developing administrations which were answerable to local rulers, and the ability of their royal counterpart to intervene in a prince's affairs. Perhaps most importantly, the attitude of regional nobilities to the growing power of princes 'on their patch' was not always a welcoming one. As Olivier Mattéoni's work on the duchy of Bourbon has shown, some of the men (usually the most influential) who served a regional prince were the servants of two or more masters, the other master often being the king.[51] There are many examples of princely power being profoundly compromised by the dual or indeed multiple allegiances of leading noblemen and noble networks. Despite the victory of the Montfortist party in the Breton civil war (1341–64), for example, Jean IV, duke of Brittany managed to alienate a substantial sector of the nobility in the duchy, leading some Breton barons, such as Olivier V de Clisson, to enter the service of the French crown. The extent of internal opposition to Jean IV eventually forced him to take exile in England (1373–9), resulting in a period of royal dominance in the duchy which might well have reversed the outcome of the Breton civil war. Even in fifteenth-century Burgundy, so often taken to be the prime example of a 'princely state' in late medieval France, the willingness of leading nobles to accept royal blandishments and their desire to maintain a leading role in the political life of the realm could provoke a crisis – something Duke Philip the Good (1419–67) clearly understood, but which his son Charles the Bold (1467–77) signally failed to appreciate.[52] If one is to take account of the actions of the nobility as the single most important political group in late medieval France, then it is difficult to see the value of writing the history of the realm as a mosaic of semi-autonomous principalities. The 'princely state' is perhaps a more fragile construct than the historiography currently recognises it to have been.

'MEN OF THE EAST' AND 'MEN OF THE WEST'

A different way forward was offered as long ago as 1958 by Raymond Cazelles in his work on political society under Philip VI. His approach has yet to win the recognition and detailed development it deserves and it is only possible to offer a sketch of it here, along with some further thoughts on how his ideas can be followed up. Cazelles identified an important geopolitical distinction between, on the one hand, a 'continental' France in the east which had recently expanded to the borders of the Empire, and in some places even further where forms of French were spoken; and a 'coastal' France in the west and north, connected along its length by the sea, where horizons were less confined by political and linguistic borders. The temptation for western noble networks – *les hommes de l'Ouest* – to resist their Valois king, and even to ally with the king of England, was highly significant at key points in the Hundred Years War. After all, fourteenth-century English kings remained tied to France by profound dynastic and cultural bonds.[53] They were major territorial princes at various points along the length of coastal France, not just in Gascony where the English king was duke. Last but not least, they became claimants to the French throne itself. Equally, as Cazelles noted, eastern noble networks – *les hommes de l'Est* – sought to play a role in the kingdom too. This was a long-term characteristic of French political life stretching back to the late Capetian period when the dukes of Burgundy showed themselves to be reliable royal vassals, their line providing royal spouses, their households generating noble servants of the crown, and their administration supplying influential figures in organs of state, such as the chancellery and *Parlement*.

At the start of our period, Cazelles found a core of advisors around Philip VI who came from eastern France, their presence reflecting the influence at the royal court of Philip's father-in-law, Odo IV, duke of Burgundy. In the field, by contrast, the new Valois king tended to rely on 'men of the west' for military leadership. The western party was given its head in 1339 when the king agreed to a Norman plan to lead the first French invasion of England since 1216. The English naval victory at Sluys (1340) put paid to the scheme and led to the loss of a great many French, Normans, Gascons, Bretons and Genoese (the latter supplying some of the shipping). The defeat marked the start of a gradual deterioration in relations between the king and the 'men of the west', evinced most clearly in the rebellious attitude of the Norman baron Godefroy of Harcourt, who eventually took exile in England (where dissident westerners usually found a welcome). In Brittany, meanwhile, the succession crisis which erupted in the Duchy in 1341 gave Edward III further opportunity to undermine Valois influence in the west. The region descended into internecine warfare which would fester on for more than two decades. When Edward III next landed on the continent in person to make good his claims in France, in 1346, he came through Normandy in the company of Godefroy of Harcourt. This was the campaign which culminated in the first major land defeat of the French at Crécy.

The ensuing crises of John II's reign (1350–64) have often been attributed to the personal failings of the king. In an age of personal monarchy, a ruler's qualities could have a decisive impact in determining the course of events. But here too the role of western and eastern noble networks had a fundamentally important role to play. Before John came to the throne, there seemed to be an opportunity for the monarchy to reconnect with western noble networks when Philip VI gave him the title of Duke of Normandy (1347). Close analysis of John's time in the duchy reveals that the chance was not taken, however: we now know that the heir to the throne spent little time in the duchy, and that few Normans found a place in his circle as king.[54] The summary execution of Raoul II d'Eu, discussed earlier, alienated key sectors of the Norman nobility. Moreover, a new and potentially powerful rival emerged in the region in the form of Charles of Navarre (1332–87), who had come into possession of his family's extensive and strategically important territories grouped near the Seine. As the grandson of King Louis X (1314–16) through the female line, this young prince also had a potential claim to the throne of France. John was clearly aware of the threat and sought to win Navarre over, but his efforts were inconsistent and sometimes counterproductive, creating a new figure of national significance for disaffected elements of Norman political society to rally around. The king's decision to give his own son and heir, Charles, the administration and title of the duchy of Normandy in 1355 offered the possibility of reconnecting the monarchy once more with regional noble networks in the west. Perhaps under the influence of supporters of his murdered constable, Charles of Spain, it seems that John chose not to allow this process to develop. Instead, as we have seen, he had Navarre arrested and several of his Norman allies executed. All the while, the erratic unfolding of the war of dynastic succession in Brittany was further undermining the Valois position in western France.

John might have been able to compensate for these difficulties if, like his father before him, he had been able to rely on powerful noble networks elsewhere in the kingdom. Unfortunately the king's party was a relatively weak political grouping, with few territorial princes of note in its ranks, and little Burgundian support following the death of Odo IV in 1350 (leaving only a minor for an heir). John sought to compensate for his weak links among noble networks in both east and west by novel means, creating an order of chivalry, the Order of the Star, in 1352. Ambitiously, the Star was intended to bring together a membership of no fewer than 500 knights. The king hoped by these means that 'a tranquil peace [might] be reborn in our reign'.[55] Unfortunately a great many of the members of the order were killed on 14 August 1352 at the battle of Mauron, a victory for the English and their Monfortist allies in Brittany. When the Black Prince won his famous victory and captured John near Poitiers in 1356, the monarchy's relationship with key noble networks across the realm was therefore particularly weak. The terms of the treaty of Brétigny which permitted John's release four years later proposed to make matters far worse: the monarchy was to be left with no firm foothold along the Atlantic seaboard of the realm; only limited stretches of the Norman coastline under its control; and vast swathes of the interior in the south-west of France beyond its reach. The west looked set to slip from Valois control for good.

The story of how the crown recovered under Charles V (1364–80) is usually told in terms of the contribution of key members of the royal family, new military tactics and the greatly improved tax-raising powers mentioned above.[56] But it can also be seen as a function of the king's success in mobilising noble networks in both east and west. The defeat of Charles of Navarre at the battle of Auray in 1364 and the failure of the victor in the Breton civil war, the Montfortist duke Jean IV, to win the loyalty of key members of the Duchy's nobility, combined to bring a great many 'men of the west' into the royal orbit. As a result, the king's military establishment was enhanced in a decisive manner: Philippe Contamine has shown that the majority of the leadership and rank-and-file in the armies of Charles V's reconquest were either Breton or Norman, foremost among them Olivier V of Clisson, who had fought on the winning Montfortist side at Auray in 1364, but who became royal constable in 1380.[57] The granting of apanages to the king's brothers reconnected the monarchy to noble networks in other ways, in both the west (where Louis I, duke of Anjou was militarily active), and the east of the realm (where Philip the Bold established himself as duke of Burgundy). The right political conditions had been created for the monarchy's growing resources to be used to good effect, producing the first Caroline reconquest (the second Caroline reconquest being the recovery of Normandy and Guienne from the English by Charles VII).

After the stability of Charles VI's minority (1380–8) and rule by the 'Marmouset' group, the collapse of royal fortunes under Charles VI (1380–1422) is commonly attributed to the onset of the king's mental illness in 1392, and the devastating struggle for power which emerged within the extended royal familial community as a result.[58] Initially, in a period lasting roughly from 1392 to 1404, the main protagonists in this internal struggle were the unfortunate king's most powerful remaining uncle, Philip the Bold, and the only royal brother, Louis of Orléans. On Philip's death in 1404, leadership of the Burgundian party passed to Philip's son, John the Fearless. John's position within the royal familial community was relatively lowly, at least compared to his father's, and in a second phase of the struggle for power around Charles VI (1404–7), the Burgundian camp found itself increasingly on the back foot. John the Fearless's remedy to his predicament was bold and shocking: Louis of Orléans was murdered on his orders in 1407. Thereafter, the Burgundian camp wrestled against a series of factional coalitions which are commonly called 'Armagnac' on account of the fact that they were led for part of the time by Louis of Orléans's father-in-law, Bernard VIII Count of Armagnac.[59] In September 1419, elements of the 'Armagnac' party would take revenge for the killing of Orléans, and the long periods of Burgundian dominance which followed, by butchering John the Fearless at Montereau. Against this backdrop of intrigue and murder, some of the greatest military achievements of the English in France occurred, notably victory at Agincourt; the conquest and settlement of parts of northern France; and eventually the supposed 'final peace' of Troyes in May 1420, which envisaged a united France under Lancastrian rule.

Emphasis on the importance of the king's madness and factional infighting is very helpful in understanding the crises of the long reign of Charles VI. Building on the work of Cazelles, however, John Bell Henneman drew out the continuing importance behind these events of western noble networks.[60] To his point we might an additional dimension of our own, namely the fact that long-term divisions between 'men of the west' and clearly identifiable eastern rivals are also all too apparent behind the political turmoil. At the centre of eastern noble networks when Charles VI succeeded to the throne was the duke of Burgundy, just as had been the case earlier in the fourteenth century. Duke Philip the Bold was only distantly related to his Capetian predecessors in the duchy, but like them he sought to exercise influence at the royal centre. He had far more success in doing so than any Burgundian duke before (or indeed after). Additionally, Philip the Bold used royal resources to add to his patrimony much like the other uncles of Charles VI, save that here too he was a more successful dynast, acquiring by marriage and other means a number of territories and claims which carried Burgundian political influence into the Low Countries and the Empire, particularly the counties of Flanders and Artois, and the imperial county of Burgundy. In Philip the Bold, eastern noble networks therefore had a powerful leader to whom they could look for preferment with a great deal of confidence. From 1384 onwards, when the duke of Burgundy came fully into possession of the county of Flanders, Burgundians began to acquire titles and office in the duke's northern territories.[61]

By contrast, the westerners who had played a key role in the victories of Charles V's reign had far more restricted opportunities. Many had found service in the armies which Louis I of Anjou led in the first Caroline reconquest, but this oldest royal uncle died while pursuing recently acquired dynastic claims in Sicily in 1384 – the very same year which saw Burgundian expansion reach new heights. It was not until the 1390s that a credible leader of western noble networks emerged in the shape of the king's brother, Louis of Orléans. When Orléans was himself murdered in 1407, as we have seen, opposition to Burgundian power passed to the series of coalitions and groupings of noble networks which can loosely be described as 'Armagnac' but which were still essentially western in leadership: other than Bernard VIII of Armagnac, leading figures included Louis II, duke of Anjou; Jean I, duke of Alençon (whose county had been elevated into a duchy in 1414); and Charles, duke of Orléans, Louis's eldest son. The western party had some success, particularly in winning control of the king's person and of Paris from 1413 to 1418. But they also suffered some notable disasters, not least on the field at Agincourt where, although they were joined by some Burgundians in the royal army which was defeated by Henry V, it was primarily leading western leaders who were captured (Charles of Orléans) or killed (Jean I of Alençon).

Unlike Edward III in his wars in France, Henry V now embarked upon a campaign of conquest and settlement in Normandy which would continue elsewhere in northern France in the 1420s under his brother, John, duke of Bedford. Western nobles were faced with the prospect of accepting English rule or abandoning family lands. Leadership of these threatened networks fell to Charles VI's last surviving male heir, the dauphin Charles. The advisors around the dauphin during his negotiations with John the Fearless, duke of Burgundy in 1419 which were intended to achieve unity against the English were predominantly Angevins, Bretons and Normans, and it was in this essentially western political milieu that the idea of murdering John, leader of dominant eastern noble networks, was hatched and executed on 10 September that same year. The military establishment which subsequently formed around the dauphin Charles was predominantly Orleanist or Armagnac in terms of its traditions of service. When the new duke of Burgundy, Philip the Good, reacted to his father's murder by allying with Henry V, making possible the treaty of Troyes of May 1420 and the prospect of a double monarchy of France and England, western and eastern noble networks were thus once again in direct confrontation. Cazelles's model for understanding political change in late medieval France therefore remains relevant to the events of the first quarter of the fifteenth century.

Given the nature of his allies among the French nobility when he acceded to the throne in 1422, Charles VII was certainly not in a wholly disastrous position. Nevertheless, it must have seemed that nothing short of a miracle would be required for a second Caroline reconquest to occur. Against the unanointed nineteen-year-old-king, declared an outlaw and disinherited by his own father in 1420, stood, not just the Valois dynasty's traditional English enemy, now recognised by many as the rightful heir, but its traditional ally, the Burgundian leader of eastern noble networks. Compared to Charles V's position in 1369, the young king's finances were in ruins after years of fiscal decline, and his capacity to raise manpower was naturally far weaker than his grandfather's had been. Measures taken in the 1420s to meet the challenge of raising money and men were, by their nature, of limited long-term value: devaluing the coinage was a highly unpopular measure which the king's subjects soon found ways of circumventing, while the large-scale use of Scots mercenaries to form the king's army, although successful at Baugé in 1421, produced fewer positive benefits thereafter, with defeats at Cravant in 1423 and Verneuil in the following year.[62]

In the late 1420s, a miracle did occur – Joan of Arc erupted onto the political stage.[63] The Maid's intervention in the conflict led to the raising of the siege of the strategically important city of Orléans, the recovery of Champagne, and the crowning of Charles VII in Reims cathedral on 17 July 1429. Although these were important gains, there are good grounds for not overemphasising the importance of Joan's brief political career.

English attacks deep into Valois territory persisted. The Anglo-Burgundian alliance remained in force, and in control of Paris.[64] Burgundian action against the armies of Charles VII was more intense in this period than it had ever been in the 1420s, notably in 1433–4. Finally, it was politically hazardous for Charles to be associated with Joan's actions after her execution on the marketplace at Rouen in 1431 on charges of heresy.

In fact, there was no single turning point in the royal recovery under Charles VII, but rather a series of incremental gains which enabled the king to raise money and men. Despite the fact that the monarch and western noble networks had little option but to rely on one another, it proved very difficult for Charles VII, much like all his predecessors save his grandfather Charles V, to guarantee the loyalties of the 'men of the west'. A certain amount could be achieved by simply allowing the western military classes to take their living from the land while they resisted the English threat to their patrimonies and the southern half of the kingdom, as happened on the frontiers of the duchy of Anjou in the 1420s. But it was the king's subjects who suffered most from such policies. When Charles tried to distribute his limited resources among his military establishment to channel their energies, as he did by taking the drastic step of alienating portions of the royal domain in western France to military leaders, he simply risked alienating those who received less of his largesse. One result was the open warfare between the king's constable, Arthur de Richemont, and his favourite, Georges de la Trémoille, which severely impeded the Valois war effort between 1427 and 1433. Allowing lords to raise levies to hire troops themselves created further potential for disorder, boosting the careers of mercenary captains, such as the infamous Rodrigo de Villandrando.

The recovery had to be built from more stable financial and political bases. In terms of the former, the crucial development was the most intensive period of consultations and negotiations with representative assemblies since the 1350s, above all in the period 1428–36. It now became possible to restore the *aides*. The most significant military achievement of this period was the recovery of Paris in 1436. Substantial financial reforms in the early 1440s further strengthened the king's resources, which were supplemented by heavy borrowing, notably from the king's *argentier*, the international merchant Jacques Coeur.[65] The political foundations of the recovery, meanwhile, were gradually built on firmer alliances within the western military classes, in particular an Angevin party which became influential around Charles VII from the early 1430s onwards.[66] The king's brother-in-law Charles, count of Maine, was the initial lynchpin in this Angevin network, joined later by Maine's brother René, duke of Anjou, and the seneschal of Anjou, Pierre de Brézé, who became the leading figure at Charles VII's court in the 1440s. The Angevins had the advantage of being core members of both the royal familial community and western noble networks, but their ascendancy did not go unchallenged. In 1440, in an episode known as the Praguerie, a western coalition led by the dauphin Louis; Jean II, duke of Alençon; and others tried, and failed, to oust Maine. Thereafter, however, Angevin ascendancy was secure.

It was in this milieu in 1445 that the decision was made to use the king's improving finances to bring the leading mercenary captains directly into royal service, and to negotiate from a position of strength for the remainder to disband their forces. The result of these measures was the creation of the standing army which, under western leadership, drove the English from Normandy and Gascony, and which is discussed more fully in Gary Baker's chapter later in this volume. Politically, of course, the standing army settled another fundamental issue that had dogged the monarchy for decades. As Contamine observed, 'the budget of the state [had become] to some extent a budget of noble assistance'.[67] We might add that the principal beneficiaries of this budget were the 'men of the west'.

The second Caroline reconquest (Normandy 1449–50, Gascony 1451–3) was not just more extensive than the first; it differed in another key respect: it did not involve 'the men of the east' under their traditional leader, the duke of Burgundy. Charles VII made peace with Philip the Good in 1435 at Arras, weaning him away from his English alliance on terms that seemed far too advantageous in the eyes of some western commentators. Thereafter, however, the Burgundians were not readmitted to the king's favour, and relations remained cool. The royal council had been dominated by easterners under Philip VI, but, under Charles VII, they were almost entirely absent; it was the westerners who predominated.[68] It has seemed to posterity that Duke Philip found more than enough compensation in his growing empire in the Low Countries which now extended from Artois to Zeeland and was further expanded by the acquisition of the Somme towns by the terms of the treaty of Arras (1435) and the duchy of Luxembourg by inheritance (1443). One tradition of scholarship, ultimately traceable to the great Belgian historian Henri Pirenne (1862–1935), even insists that Philip the Good had turned his back on France, and was effectively creating an autonomous Burgundian state. But Philip and those around him continued to aspire to a role in the kingdom of France, as the duke's political actions in the 1430s and 1440s reveal.[69] The ideal opportunity for the 'men of the east' to re-establish their influence in the kingdom seemed to present itself when the dauphin Louis fled from his father and took exile in the Burgundian territory of Brabant between 1456 and 1461. But when he came to the throne in 1461, Louis XI turned out to be just as resistant to Burgundian domination as his father had been. At certain points in his reign it looked as though the king of France would once again have to face a powerful Anglo-Burgundian coalition. Charles the Bold replaced his father as duke of Burgundy in 1467, and took as his bride Edward IV's sister (1468). But when English invasion eventually came, in 1475, Edward was bought off by Louis XI, and returned home with the large army he had brought to march on Reims.

Little over sixteenth months later Charles the Bold died in battle at Nancy fighting a coalition led by Duke René II of Lorraine. His lands in eastern France were quickly absorbed by the French king, while many of the duke's northern territories were eventually secured by Maximilian I, the Habsburg husband of Charles's female heir Mary of Burgundy. Only at this point does the role of eastern and western noble networks in French political life, first identified by Raymond Cazelles, developed by John Bell Henneman and traced further here through the events of the fifteenth century, begin to lose its explanatory force.[70] At the same time, the possibility of a renewal of the Anglo-French conflict based on substantial internal French support finally abated. From the perspective of the development of French political life, 1475 seems a better date for the close of the 'Hundred Years War' than the traditional endpoint of 1453.

THE KING AND THE TOWNS

Highly schematic though the foregoing must be, it is possible to consider French politics during the Hundred Years War not simply from the monarchy's perspective or in connection with emerging princely states, but in terms of the ambitions and actions of noble networks. By contrast, it might be argued, towns and townsmen had limited agency in dictating the ebb and flow of political life in France. No city shaped events on the regnal stage, with the possible exception of Paris during the period 1356–8, when the provost of the merchants Étienne Marcel sought to use the estates to achieve his ends.[71] Certainly, the city walls which sprang up across the kingdom in the fourteenth century could halt an enemy's advance and thereby alter the course of the Hundred Years War: at Tournai in 1340, when Edward III failed to build on his victory at Sluys; or at Orléans in 1428–9, when the English were denied a firm grip on the Loire. Nevertheless, the reach of any town or city beyond its own region, and even beyond its immediate locality, was often limited. Urban networks encouraged the development of mutual defence pacts and information-gathering, but these were relatively passive forms of political action. Given these points, it is perhaps understandable that monographs on the history of individual towns in late medieval France long lived in the shadow of Henry Sée's *Louis XI et les villes* (1890), which emphasised the gradual domination of urban communities by the monarchy by the end of the Hundred Years War.

It would be fair to say that we have now arrived at a more balanced recognition of the importance of urban communities in the political life of the realm. Foremost among the scholars who has altered our perception in this regard is Bernard Chevalier, who demonstrated that the late Middle Ages, rather than the twelfth or thirteenth centuries, was the great period of urban emancipation and institutional development in France.[72] These processes were initiated and accelerated by the crown's need to rely on municipalities to defend themselves through wall-building, a massive undertaking paid for by taxes which, strictly speaking, had to be authorised by the crown, but which were raised and spent by civic administrations. The holding of municipal assemblies to consent to taxes and deliberate on other matters was becoming a fundamental means of influencing public opinion. The developing political importance of municipalities was no straightforward process, of course, marked as it was by an intensification of revolts by urban populations which were exposed more than most of the king's subjects to fiscal demands, and by the proclivity of some among the urban elites to support leaders of noble networks against the king, notably Charles of Navarre in the 1350s and (especially) the Burgundian party in the 1410s. But by the 1440s, Chevalier finds a 'perfect accord' to have existed between the monarchy and its 'bonnes villes': towns which were 'good' because they were loyal to the crown.[73] Other historians have since brought out further dimensions of the growing closeness of the king and municipal governors. Gisela Naegle has shown how both came to see themselves as common defenders of the public weal, for example.[74] More recently, David Rivaud has argued that the relationship between the king and civic administrations was based on the premise of a shared burden of responsibility to ensure 'le bon ordonnancement du royaume' ('the good governance of the realm').[75]

Are we in danger of simply returning to a revised version of Augustin Thierry's model of a triumphant monarchy allying with a rising bourgeoisie in the late Middle Ages? Perhaps, with the obvious proviso that the corollary of this view, the decline of the aristocracy, no longer holds sway. But at least we now understand how much of what we call 'the state' in late medieval France was in key respects no more – and no less – than the sum of many municipal parts. Each of these parts had its own characteristics shaped by local context. And all of them were forming at the same time as, and often in tandem with, the growth of royal administration. The story of French politics during the Hundred Years War therefore no longer ends with the emergence of a centralised state, but rather with a monarchy that had succeeded to a greater extent than ever before in absorbing and channelling the energies of noble and urban elites, and which was dependent on them for the effective exercise of its authority.

NOTES

1. J. Watts, *The Making of Polities: Europe, 1300–1500* (Cambridge, 2009), p. 19.
2. J. Bradbury, *The Capetians* (London, 2007); *France in the Central Middle Ages*, ed. M. Bull (Oxford, 2002); E. Hallam and J. Everard, *Capetian France, 987–1328* (originally published 1980, rev. 2nd edn, London, 2001).
3. L. Dauphant, *Le royaume des quatre rivières: L'espace politique français (c. 1380–1515)* (Seyssel, 2012).
4. M. Mollat, *La genèse médiévale de la France moderne* (Paris, 1981); A. Derville, *La société française au Moyen Age* (Paris, 2000), p. 120.
5. C. Beaune, *Naissance de la nation France* (Paris, 1986); trans. S. R. Huston, ed. F. Cheyette as *The Birth of an Ideology: Myths and Symbols of Nation in Late-Medieval France* (Berkeley, 1991).
6. Since 1971, the main studies are: A. Leguai, *La guerre de Cent Ans* (Paris, 1974); J. Favier, *La guerre de Cent Ans* (Paris, 1980).
7. In the *Bibliographie annuelle de l'histoire de France*, for example, the primary rubric for political history in the late medieval period is 'Guerre de Cent Ans'. This work is still the standard bibliographical tool for French historians. Another way of illustrating the point would be to cite the titles selected for the late medieval volumes for recent general histories of France: B. Bove, *Le temps de la guerre de Cent Ans: 1328–1453* (Paris, 2009); M. Pastoureau, *Histoire de France illustrée, 3: La guerre de Cent Ans: le redressement de la France, 1328–1492* (Paris, 1986); J. Glénisson and Y. Bruand, *La France de la guerre de Cent Ans* (Paris, 1976).
8. See also *France in the Later Middle Ages*, ed. D. Potter (Oxford, 2002); G. Small, *Late Medieval France* (Basingstoke, 2009).
9. B. Guenée and J.-F. Sirinelli, 'L'histoire politique', *L'histoire et le métier d'historien en France 1945–1995*, ed. F. Bédarida (Paris, 1995), pp. 301–12.
10. G. Dupont-Ferrier, *Gallia regia ou état des officiers des bailliages et sénéchaussées de 1328 à 1515*, 7 vols (Paris, 1942–66); R. Cazelles, *La société politique et la crise de la royauté sous Philippe de Valois* (Paris, 1958); idem, *Société politique, noblesse et couronne sous Jean II et Charles V* (Paris, 1982); B. Guenée, *Tribunaux et gens de justice dans le bailliage de Senlis à la fin du Moyen Age (vers 1380-vers 1550)* (Paris, 1963).
11. Prosopography is essentially an investigation of common characteristics using a collective rather than individual biographical approach. A. Demurger, 'Guerre civile et changements du personnel administratif dans le royaume de France de 1400 à 1418: l'exemple des baillis et sénéchaux', *Francia*, 6 (1978), pp. 151–298; A. Lapeyre and R. Scheurer, *Les notaires et secrétaires du roi sous le règne de Lous XI, Charles VIII et Louis XII*, 2 vols (Paris, 1978); F. Autrand, *Naissance d'un grand corps d'état: les gens du Parlement de Paris, 1345–1454* (Paris, 1981); *Prosopographie et genèse de l'État moderne*, ed. F. Autrand (Paris, 1986).

12 J. B. Henneman, 'Who were the Marmousets?', *Medieval Prosopography*, 5 (1984), pp. 19–63; idem, *Olivier de Clisson and Political Society in France under Charles V and Charles VI* (Philadelphia, 1996).
13 R. Cazelles, 'Le parti navarrais jusqu'à la mort d'Étienne Marcel', *Bulletin de philologie et d'histoire* (1960), pp. 839–69; P. Charon, 'Un hôtel royal et ses dignitaries au XVe siècle. L'exemple de l'hôtel de Charles II de Navarre', *Revue historique*, 667 (2013), pp. 597–48; X. Pindard, 'L'entourage criminel de Charles de Navarre d'après les dépositions de 1378', ibid, pp. 549–74.
14 A. Demurger, 'Le rôle politique des baillis et sénéchaux royaux pendant la guerre civile en France (1400–18)', *Histoire comparée de l'administration (IVe–XVIIIe siècle)*, ed. W. Paravicini and K. Werner (Munich, 1980), pp. 282–90.
15 Collected in P. S. Lewis, *Essays in Later Medieval French History* (London, 1985), especially pp. 41–68, 127–38, 151–68; plus 'Reflections on the role of royal clienteles in the construction of the French monarchy (mid-XIVth/end XVth centuries)', *L'État ou le roi. Les fondations de la modernité monarchique en France (XIVe-XVIIe s.)*, ed. N. Bulst and R. Descimon (Paris, 1996), pp. 51–67. Also key is G. Prosser, '"Decayed Feudalism" and "Royal Clienteles": Royal Office and Magnate Service in the Fifteenth Century', *War, Government*, pp. 175–89.
16 *Penser le pouvoir au Moyen Age. Études d'histoire et de littérature offertes à Françoise Autrand*, ed. D. Boutet and J. Verger (Paris, 2000).
17 The key author is Jacques Krynen, especially his *Idéal du prince et pouvoir royal en France à la fin du Moyen Age (1380–1440): Étude de la littérature politique du temps* (Paris, 1981); and *L'empire du roi: Idées et croyances politiques en France, XIIIe–XVe siècles* (Paris, 1993).
18 C. Taylor, 'War, Propaganda and Diplomacy in Fifteenth-Century France and England', *War, Government*, pp. 70–91; idem, *Chivalry and the Ideals of Knighthood During the Hundred Years War* (Cambridge, 2013).
19 F. Autrand, *Charles V Le Sage* (Paris, 1994), especially, pp. 728–31.
20 B. Guenée, *L'opinion publique à la fin du Moyen Age d'après la 'Chronique de Charles VI' du Religieux de Saint Denis* (Paris, 2002).
21 D. Hobbins, *Authorship and Publishing before Print: Jean Gerson and the Transformation of Late Medieval Learning* (Philadelphia, 2009).
22 B. Guenée and F. Lehoux, *Les entrées royales françaises de 1328 à 1515* (Paris, 1968); L. Bryant, *The King and the City in the Parisian Royal Entry Ceremony: Politics, Ritual and Art in the Renaissance* (Geneva, 1986); J. Blanchard, 'Le spectacle du rite: les entrées royales', *Revue historique*, 305 (2003), pp. 475–519; N. Murphy, *Ceremonial Entries, Municipal Liberties and the Negotiation of Power in Valois France, 1328–1589* (Leiden-Boston, 2016).
23 C. Gauvard, *'De Grace especiale': Crime, état et société en France à la fin du moyen âge*, 2 vols (Paris, 1991); J. Chiffoleau, 'Les processions parisiennes de 1412. Analyse d'un rituel flamboyant', *Revue historique*, 284 (1991), pp, 38–76; N. Offenstadt, *Faire la paix au moyen âge: Discours et gestes de paix pendant la guerre de Cent Ans* (Paris, 2007).
24 Beaune, *Naissance de le nation France*, passim.

25 A. Rigaudiere, 'L'essor de la fiscalité royale du règne de Philippe le Bel (1285–1314) à celui de Philippe VI (1328–1350)', *Europa en los umbrales de la crisis, 1250–1350: XXI Semana de Estudios Medievales de Estella, 18 a 22 julio de 1994* (Pamplona, 1995), pp. 323–91. See also essays in E. Brown, *Politics and Institutions in Capetian France* (London, 1991). For a general overview of what follows, see J. B. Henneman, 'France in the Middle Ages', *The Rise of the Fiscal State in Europe, c. 1200–c.1815*, ed. R. Bonney (Oxford, 1999), pp. 101–22.

26 J. B. Henneman, *Royal Taxation in Fourteenth-Century France: The Development of War Financing, 1322–56* (Princeton, 1971); idem, *Royal Taxation in Fourteenth-Century France: The Captivity and Ransom of John II, 1356–70* (Philadelphia, 1978); N. Murphy, *The Captivity of John II, 1356–60: The Royal Image in Later Medieval England and France* (New York, 2016).

27 Among much work see S. K. Cohn, *Lust for Liberty: The Politics of Social Revolt in Medieval Europe, 1200–1425* (Cambridge, MA, 2006).

28 M. Rey, *Les finances royales sous Charles VI: Les causes du défécit* (Paris, 1965).

29 M. Wolfe, *The Fiscal System of Renaissance France* (New Haven, CT, 1972).

30 J.-F. Lassalmonie, *La boîte à l'enchanteur: Politique financière de Louis XI* (Paris, 2002).

31 J. Krynen, 'La rebellion du Bien Public', *Ordnung und Aufruhr im Mittelalter: Historische und juristische Studien zur Rebellion*, ed. M. T. Fögen (Frankfurt, 1995), pp. 81–97.

32 For a comparison see D. Grummitt and J.-F. Lassalmonie, 'Royal Public Finances (c. 1290–1523)', *Government and Political Life in England and France, c.1300–c.1500*, ed. C. Fletcher, J.-P. Genet and J. Watts (Cambridge, 2015), pp. 116–49.

33 For a broad comparative survey, see M. Hébert, *Parlementer: Assemblées représentatives et échanges politiques en Europe occidentale à la fin du Moyene Age* (Paris, 2014).

34 P. S. Lewis, 'The Failure of the French Medieval Estates', *Past and Present*, 23 (1962), pp. 3–24.

35 J. R. Major, *Representative Government in Early Modern France* (New Haven, CT, 1980); idem, *From Renaissance Monarchy to Absolute Monarchy: French Kings, Nobles and Estates* (Baltimore, MD, 1994).

36 For a more 'absolutist' monarchy see E. Le Roy Ladurie, *The French Royal State, 1460–1610*, trans. J. Vale (Oxford, 1994), and the review by S. Carroll in *French History*, 8 (1994), pp. 474–5.

37 Lewis, 'The Failure of the French Estates'.

38 B. Guenée, 'The History of the State in France at the End of the Middle Ages as seen by French Historians of the Last One Hundred Years', *The Recovery of France in the Fifteenth Century*, ed. P. S. Lewis (London, 1971), pp. 324–53.

39 G. Bois, *The Crisis of Feudalism: Economy and Society in Eastern Normandy, c.1300–1550*, trans. J. Birrell (Cambridge, 1984); G. Fourquin, *Les campagnes de la région parisienne à la fin du moyen âge* (Paris, 1964).

40 P. Charbonnier, *Une autre France: La seigneurie rurale en Basse Auvergne du XIVe au XVIe siècle*, 2 vols (Clermont-Ferrand, 1980); M. Le Mené, *Les campagnes angevines*

à la fin du moyen âge (Nantes, 1982); J. Tricard, *Les campagnes limousines du XIVe au XVIe siècles: Originalité et limites d'une reconstruction rurale* (Paris, 1996).

41 N. Wright, *Knights and Peasants. The Hundred Years' War in the French Countryside* (Woodbridge, 1998). On the disruptive power of noble networks in southern France (among many other things) see J. Firnhaber-Baker, *Violence and the State in Languedoc, 1250–1400* (Cambridge, 2014).

42 The pioneering work of Peter Lewis is summarised and brought up to date in Prosser, '"Decayed Feudalism" and "Royal Clienteles"'.

43 É. Lebailly, 'Le connétable d'Eu et son cercle nobiliaire. Le réseau d'un grand seigneur au XIVe siècle', *Cahiers de recherches médiévales et humanistes* 13 (2006), pp. 41–52. On Charles as duke of Normandy, see Autrand, *Charles V*, p. 173.

44 The only attempt to take fuller account of the role of the nobility in events of the period is M.-T. Caron, *Noblesse et pouvoir royal en France (XIIIe–XVIe siècle)* (Paris, 1994).

45 Quotation from G. Prosser, 'The Late Medieval French *noblesse*', *France in the Later Middle Ages*, ed. Potter, pp. 189–209, 229–31, at p. 231.

46 E. Perroy, 'Feudalism or Principalities in Fifteenth-Century France', *BIHR*, 20 (1943–5), pp. 181–5.

47 F. Autrand, *Jean de Berry: l'art et le pouvoir* (Paris, 2000).

48 Perroy taught at the University of Glasgow from 1924 to 1934, where he prepared his thesis on England during the Great Schism: É. Fournial, 'Édouard Perroy (1901–1974)', *Cahiers de civilisation médiévale*, 17 (1974), pp. 399–400.

49 J. Le Patourel, 'The King and the Princes in Fourteenth-Century France', *Europe in the Late Middle Ages*, ed. J. Hale, R. Highfield and B. Smalley (London, 1965), pp. 155–83; M. C.E. Jones, *The Creation of Brittany: a Late Medieval State* (London, 1988); R. Vaughan, *Philip the Bold* (2nd edn, Woodbridge, 2002); idem, *John the Fearless* (2nd edn, Woodbridge, 2002); idem, *Philip the Good* (2nd edn, Woodbridge, 2002) (2nd edn, Woodbridge, 2002); idem, *Charles the Bold* (2nd edn, Woodbridge, 2002).

50 His main synopsis since 1971 (with references to earlier work) is 'Royauté et principautés en France aux XIVe et XVe siècles: L'évolution de leurs rapports au cours de la guerre de Cent Ans', *Le Moyen Age*, 101 (1995), pp. 121–36. See also J. Kerhervé, *L'État Breton aux XIVe et XVe siècles: Les ducs, l'argent et les hommes*, 2 vols (Maloine, 1987).

51 O. Mattéoni, *Servir le prince: les officiers des ducs de Bourbon à la fin du Moyen Age* (Paris, 1998), pp. 275, 282, 394–5, 444.

52 G. Small, *George Chastelain and the Shaping of Valois Burgundy* (Woodbridge, 1997), pp. 42–9, 52–127, 162–96. This argument has now been taken up and developed in E. Lecuppre-Desjardin, *Le royaume inachevé des ducs de Bourgogne (XIVe–XVe siècles)* (Paris, 2016).

53 M. Vale, *The Angevin Legacy and the Hundred Years War (1250–1340)* (Oxford, 1990), republished as *The Origins of the Hundred Years War*; A. Butterfield, *The Familiar Enemy: Chaucer, Language and Nation in the Hundred Years' War* (Oxford, 2009).

54 J. Tricard, 'Jean duc de Normandie et héritier de France: Un double échec?', *Annales de Normandie*, 29 (1980), pp. 23–44.

55 D'A. J. D. Boulton, *The Knights of the Crown: The Monarchical Orders of Knighthood in Later Medieval Europe (1325–1520)* (2nd edn, Woodbridge 2000), p. 185.
56 Autrand, *Charles V*, passim.
57 Contamine, *GES*, pp. 152–3.
58 F. Autrand, *Charles VI: La folie du roi* (Paris, 1986). There is interesting comment on his illness in R. Famiglietti, *Royal Intrigue: Crisis at the Court of Charles VI, 1392–1420* (New York, 1986).
59 B. Schnerb, *Les armagnacs et les bourguignons: La maudite guerre* (Paris, 1988); B. Guenée, *Un meurtre, une société: L'assassinat du duc d'Orléans, 23 novembre 1407* (Paris, 1992); B. Schnerb, *Jean sans Peur: Le prince meurtrier* (Paris, 2005).
60 J. B. Henneman, *Olivier de Clisson and Political Society in France under Charles V and Charles VI* (Philadelpha, 1996).
61 See M.-T. Caron, *La noblesse dans le duché de Bourgogne, 1315–1477* (Lille, 1987).
62 H. Miskimin, *Money and Power in Fifteenth-Century France* (London, 1984); N. Sussmann, 'Debasement, Royal Revenues and Inflation in France during the Hundred Years' War, 1415-22', *Journal of Economic History*, 53 (1993), pp. 44–70; B. Ditcham, '"Mutton Guzzlers and Wine Bags": Foreign Soldiers and Native Reactions in Fifteenth-Century France', *Power, Culture and Religion in France, c.1350–1550*, ed. C. T. Allmand (Woodbridge, 1989), pp. 1–13.
63 C. Taylor, *Joan of Arc: La Pucelle* (Manchester, 2006).
64 G. L. Thompson, *Paris and Its People under English Rule* (Oxford, 1991).
65 M. Mollat, *Jacques Coeur ou l'esprit d'entreprise au XVe siècle* (Paris, 1988).
66 M. Vale, *Charles VII* (London, 1974), pp. 70–114.
67 P. Contamine, 'The French Nobility and the War', *HYW*, p. 151.
68 P.-R. Gaussin 'Les conseillers de Charles VII (1418–61): Essai de politologie historique', *Francia*, 10 (1982), pp. 67–130.
69 See the collected essays of P. Bonenfant, *Philippe le Bon: Sa politique, son action* (Brussels, 1996).
70 Cf. J. Watts, 'Conclusion', *Government and Political Life in England and France*, ed. Fletcher and Grant to Fletcher, Genet and Watts, pp. 368–9.
71 R. Cazelles, *Étienne Marcel, champion de l'unité française* (Paris, 1984).
72 B. Chevalier, *Tours ville royale, 1356–c.1520: Origine et développement d'une capitale à la fin du Moyen Age* (Paris-Leuven, 1976); idem, *Les bonnes villes de France du XIVe au XVIe siècle* (Paris, 1982).
73 A. Rigaudière, 'Qu'est-ce que c'est qu'une bonne ville dans la France du Moyen Age?' in his *Gouverner la ville*, pp. 53–112; B. Chevalier, 'L'État et les bonnes villes au temps de leur accord parfait (1450–1550)', *La ville, la bourgeoise et le genèse de l'État moderne, XIIe–XVIIIe siècles*, ed. N. Bulst and J.-P. Genet (Paris, 1988), pp. 71–85.
74 G. Naegle, *Stadt, Recht und Krone. Französische Städte, Königtum und Parlement im Spätenmittelalter*, 2 vols (Husum, 2002).
75 D. Rivaud, *Les villes et le roi: Les municipalités de Bourges, Poitiers et Tours et l'émergence de l'État moderne* (Rennes, 2007).

3 Financing the Hundred Years War

Tony K. Moore and Adrian R. Bell

Cicero's dictum that 'money is the sinews of war' was well understood in the Middle Ages and only became more relevant as state capacity increased from the thirteenth century onwards in both England and France, driven by the pressures of interstate competition.[1] In particular, the English kings needed to mobilise the resources of their kingdom effectively in order to compete with the larger and wealthier French kingdom.[2] This chapter will consider three key aspects of the financing of military activity. First, it will gauge the scale of royal financial resources in the two countries and how these changed during the period. Second, it will consider how kings raised this money. Third, it will investigate how this money was transferred to where (and, vitally, when) it was needed, introducing the key role played by financial intermediaries, with special reference to England.

It is difficult to reconstruct reliable estimates for royal revenues over time and between countries. As a result, some previous studies have preferred to consider the subjective experience of taxation.[3] This chapter argues, however, that it is still useful to develop rough quantitative figures to facilitate comparison of the relative scale of resources available to English and French kings. The options chosen here are either to consider revenues in relation to contemporary Gross Domestic Product (GDP; the monetary value of all goods and services produced in a given country per year), where modern reconstructions are available, or to convert currencies into their silver equivalents based on the precious metal content of the coin.[4] The latter does not account for differences in purchasing power and can be difficult to calculate for France given changes in the silver content of the coinage. These problems are less significant for England because of the relative stability of the coinage but it should be stressed that these figures are speculative and aim only to give an indication of the relative orders of magnitude.

DEMAND FOR MONEY

The financial costs of raising armies were heavy. For England, Fryde estimated that Edward III spent around £400,000 (equivalent to 128 tonnes of silver) over the first three years of the war, with at least half being promised to his continental allies.[5] The cost of the largest campaigns, comprising 10,000–12,000 men and led by the king himself, ran into hundreds of thousands of pounds: the Crécy-Calais campaigns of 1346–7 cost around £200,000 (58 tonnes), the Poitiers campaign of 1355–6 £100,000 (26 tonnes). During the Reims campaign of 1359–60, some £134,000 (35 tonnes) was spent on wages alone.[6] Even a force of 3,000 men-at-arms and 3,000 archers to serve for six months in 1382 was projected to cost £60,000 (16 tonnes).[7] English kings also had to defend territory they held in France. Garrisons were especially expensive because they were manned year-round. The Calais garrison cost £10,000–20,000 per annum, a constant drain on English resources as there were few local revenues to deploy.[8] Sherborne has reconstructed total expenditure on garrisons, naval and expeditionary forces of approximately £1,139,000 (nearly 300 tonnes of silver) in the twelve years between 1369 and 1381.[9]

There is less data about French military expenditure given the loss of records and the fact that much was disbursed locally. As noted, it is difficult to draw comparisons over time given frequent changes in silver content and hence value of the *livre tournois*. French military spending seems to have been broadly comparable to that of the English. In March 1339, a memorandum estimated the costs of war at 253,000 *livres tournois* from March to May, and 1 million *livres tournois* during the key campaigning months of June to September (equivalent to 49 tonnes of silver). The French *états généraux* estimated the costs of war at 3 million *livres tournois* (61 tonnes) in 1343 and 5 million *livres tournois* (81 tonnes) in 1355.[10] In 1372, the royal army was expected to cost 50,000 *livre tournois* per month (24 tonnes of silver annually).[11] The maintenance of Charles VII's *Compagnies d'ordonnance* of 1445, often described as the first standing army, required a sizeable and, importantly, continuous funding stream of around 744,000 *livres tournois* per annum (21.8 tonnes).[12]

Fighting a war was an expensive business over and above ordinary royal expenditure on household, administration and so on. For such extraordinary expenditure, both kings needed to mobilise their subjects' resources. This was a particular challenge for the English kings as they drew on a significantly smaller tax base than their opponents. England's geographical area was c.130,000 km^2 compared to 460,000 km^2 for areas under the control of the French king. English kings also controlled Wales, Ireland and Gascony but these did not produce a significant surplus. However, at certain times during the Hundred Years War, the effective influence of the French king was more limited. In the 1420s, provinces loyal to Charles VII totalled 173,835 km^2 compared to 136,930 km^2 controlled by the Burgundians and 224,420 km^2 by the English.[13] This reversed the traditional balance of power between the English and French kings. Estimates vary, but, at its pre-plague peak, the population of Valois France was probably around three to four times greater than that of England (15–20 million compared to 5–6 million). After the Black Death, European populations fell by around a half and did not recover until the sixteenth century but the ratio between France and England probably did not change dramatically (8 million against 2 million).[14] For a largely agrarian economy, size (in terms of area and population) is a reasonable proxy for economic capacity. For England, we have more precise reconstructions of national economic productivity. Broadberry and his team suggested an average GDP for England of £4.2 million per annum between 1337 and 1453, with a minimum of £2.7 million in 1441 and a maximum of £6.6 million in 1370.[15] Ridolfi has conducted a detailed investigation into economic output in medieval France: his figures suggest that in 1300 French GDP per capita may have been slightly higher than that of the English ($843 and $757 respectively in 1990 Geary–Khamis dollars). After the Black Death, however, English GDP per capita increased significantly to $1,103 in 1400 whereas French GDP per capita was relatively stagnant at $985.[16] However, since the population of France was so much greater than that of England, total French GDP would still have been significantly larger by a factor of 3.5. The simple geographical disparity between the two countries gave an advantage to the French kings.

For England, surviving sources allow the approximate reconstruction of revenues on an annual basis. Over the whole war, the English government raised nearly £9.3 million pounds from direct taxes on surplus income and indirect taxation on exports and imports.[17] On average, therefore, the extraordinary tax burden was over £79,400 per annum. This can be compared to a gross income of around £20,000–£30,000 from the crown's ordinary (or domain) revenues – although it should be noted that most of the latter was spent on the king's domestic administration and was not available to fund military campaigns. It may be more illuminating to consider war expenses in relation to the kingdom's economic output. Figure 3.1 shows both the nominal value of extraordinary revenues and their share of reconstructed GDP: this suggests that £100,000 for a substantial expeditionary force for France would require the king to mobilise 2–3 per cent of England's GDP in excess of his traditional income (which represented about 0.5 per cent of GDP). Royal tax revenues, at their greatest level, reached 3.4 per cent of GDP in 1416,

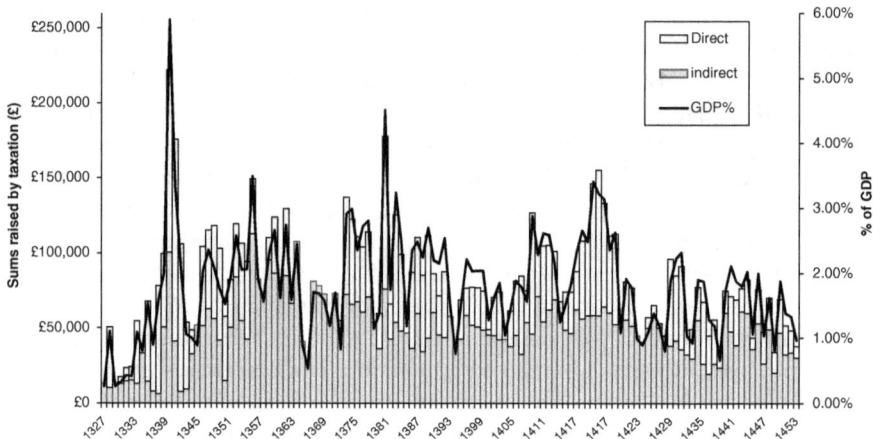

Figure 3.1 English extraordinary revenues in nominal figures and as a share of GDP

Source: Data from the European State Finance Database (http://www.esfdb.org/table.aspx?resourceid=11334; http://esfdb.org/table.aspx?resourceid=11593).

Figures for direct and indirect taxation from http://www.esfdb.org/table.aspx?resourceid=11334 adjusted to include the farms paid when the customs were held by the merchant companies 1344–50; Estimates for nominal GDP from Broadberry et al., *English Economic Growth*.

3.5 per cent in 1354, 4.5 per cent in 1378 and 5.9 per cent in 1339. This may not seem high by modern standards (in 2015 tax revenues were 32.5 per cent of GDP in England and 45.2 per cent in France) but it was an impressive achievement for a medieval administration.

For France, we have to make do with indicative estimates for certain years, summarised in Table 3.1. Because of changes in the value of the coinage we have converted nominal revenues for the selected years into their silver equivalents to show changes in effective royal income more clearly. To aid comparisons, the table also shows English royal revenues in silver for the same years. There are no estimates of annual GDP for France although, for Normandy in 1461, Philippe Contamine has estimated that royal taxes accounted for around 2.6 per cent of estimated GDP (as extrapolated from daily agricultural wages).[18] This is comparable to England in most years although it should be noted that Normandy was probably the most heavily taxed region of France and consistently contributed the most to royal coffers. Table 3.1 also shows the proportion of French royal income that was derived from the crown's ordinary revenues (domain lands and regalian rights) and extraordinary revenues (from taxation including seigniorage).

Table 3.1 French revenues

Year	Nominal total (*livres tournois*)	Ordinary revenues	Extraordinary revenues	France (tonnes of silver)	England (tonnes of silver)
1328-1332 (average)	574,446	50.7%	49.3%	49.7	18.0
1337	546,689	57.2%	42.8%	44.2	31.9
1338	521,560	65.9%	34.1%	38.2	40.8
1339	899,504	49.0%	51.0%	51.4	80.4
1340	1,261,327	46.0%	54.0%	54.8	64.9
1341	933,726	63.3%	36.7%	28.5	42.8
1342	1,129,283	60.6%	39.4%	26.5	26.1
1344	543,860	59.7%	40.3%	25.9	23.3
1349	781,746	6.7%	93.3%	20.4	24.5
1372	2,180,625	8.3%	91.7%	85.2	39.1
1390	1,770,000	10.2%	89.8%	61.5	21.0
1408	584,166	31.5%	68.5%	20.2	36.8
1418-20 Charles VI (average)	608,840	14.2%	85.8%	5.9	33.7
1461	1,800,000	2.8%	97.2%	46.5	14.0

Sources: Henneman, Development of War Finance, pp. 348-50; Lot and Fawtier, Institutions françaises, pp. 236, 269; Rey, Domain du roi, as qualified by Charles Radding, 'Royal Tax Revenues in Later Fourteenth Century France', Traditio, 32 (1976), pp. 361-8; Lassalmonie, La boîte à l'enchanteur, p. 60. English silver totals have been converted from Figure 3.1 with an addition for ordinary revenues.

Comparing the data in Figure 3.1 and Table 3.1, we can divide the fiscal chronology of the war into four periods.[19] Shortly before the war, between 1328 and 1332, Edward III's ordinary income averaged around one-third of that of Philip VI, in rough proportion to the relative sizes of their realms. Between the outbreak of war in 1337 and the treaty of Esplechin in 1340, however, the English king's total income was around 20 per cent greater than that of his French rival. In 1339, Edward raised 60 per cent more than Philip. Edward's advantage in military spending power was even greater if we include his use of credit, since much of this was only repaid much later, if it was repaid at all. This English financial advantage, or at least parity, continued into the 1350s. Edward III's ability to extract large sums of extraordinary income through direct and indirect taxation, combined with his access to credit, enabled him to compete on a level playing field with the much larger French monarchy, which was still reliant on traditional sources of royal revenue supplemented by ad hoc taxes.[20]

However, the English initial advantage was not maintained as the pressure of military competition and the need to pay John II's ransom of 3 million *écus* forced the French to revamp their own finances. In 1360, regular indirect taxes (the *aides* and *gabelle*) were introduced, followed by direct taxes (the *fouage* and later *taille*) in 1363. Importantly, these were collected even during peacetime.[21] As a result, total French revenues rose to be two or three times greater than those of the English, again reflecting the relative sizes of the two realms. It is clear from Table 3.1 that, from this point onwards, taxation formed the basis for French royal finances rather than traditional (domain) sources of revenue. This fiscal advantage coincided with a period of French military resurgence and English losses.

In the later fourteenth and early fifteenth centuries, the incapacity of Charles VI made it difficult to maintain political unity and the efficacy of the fiscal system. Royal income was diverted as nobles, royal officials and towns sought to capture royal revenues in their areas of influence.[22] Looking to attract popular support, the *tailles* were discontinued in 1413 and the *aides* in 1418. By contrast, although Henry IV faced numerous internal challenges to his rule after the deposition of Richard II, his son Henry V was able to stabilise English royal finances and secure repeated grants of direct taxes to fund his campaigns into France. After the treaty of Troyes, the dauphin (the future Charles VII) continued to resist but his control was limited to south-east France and, lacking a territorial base or tax revenues, he was forced to rely on seigniorage revenue from debasing the coinage.

There was a fourth and final reversal of fortunes in the 1430s and 1440s when Charles VII was able to restore his grandfather's fiscal system and to secure the right to impose effectively permanent direct taxation. By contrast, Henry VI was unable to rebalance the English tax system away from its reliance on declining wool exports. This allowed the French to reassert their fiscal superiority and, combined with English political and military failures, to eject the English from Normandy in 1450 and Gascony in 1453. As the pressure to raise taxes in order to compete with France diminished, English finances in the later fifteenth century underwent a partial return to a domain state. In their survey of English state finance from 1485 to 1815, O'Brien and Hunt make the startling observation that 'for roughly three centuries down to the Civil War English monarchs and their financial advisers struggled (and more often than not failed) to appropriate in real terms the levels of taxation collected by their predecessors in the 1340s'.[23]

Although this brief survey has suggested that the country with superior finances tended also to enjoy military ascendancy, we should be cautious about proposing any direct causal relationship. First, although it was essential that a king had sufficient funds to put a credible force into the field, the outcome of any battle was famously uncertain. Secondly, the state of the kingdom's finances and its military success were both reflections of the abilities of its ruler; a strong king could mobilise the military and economic resources of his subjects while a less competent ruler found it difficult to do either. The fiscal chronology proposed above bears more than a passing resemblance to Guy Bois's reconstruction of broader economic and social trends for Normandy, which he divided into four similar periods.[24] Thirdly, the transition from a domain state to a tax state was not a teleological inevitability and could be reversed; Henneman identified a successive 'rise, fall and revival' of the French tax state while Ormrod has argued that later fifteenth-century England saw a 'simple reversion' from the nascent Edwardian tax state to 'the older household organisation of royal financial that had existed in the twelfth and thirteenth centuries'.[25] Fiscal systems did not run themselves but required constant political attention and frequent rebalancing in order to remain effective.

RAISING MONEY

The increasing costs of military competition put unprecedented pressure on finances and required a fundamental change in the nature of state finance. This has been conceptualised as the transition from a domain state to a tax state.[26] The following discussion will explore the chief sources of royal revenues in England and France, starting with the king's ordinary or domain revenues, and then considering extraordinary revenues from direct and indirect taxes and debasement of the coinage. The next stage in the evolution of state finance was the fiscal state which integrated a system of public credit into the tax state. Whether the use of credit by medieval England and France can be considered as reaching the level of a fiscal state will be considered in the third section of this chapter.

Despite the contemporary belief that the king should 'live of his own', the demands of war quickly outstripped traditional sources of revenue from the royal domain estates, feudal prerogatives and fines for royal favour, and the profits of justice. In England, at least at first glance, the revenue from these sources held up well. Henry I's income in 1130 was around £22,000 and, 200 years later in 1330, it was still around £17,000. However, when these sums are adjusted for inflation, it can be calculated that Edward III enjoyed roughly one-fifth as much purchasing power as Henry I.[27] Moreover, these figures record gross income not net: much was devoted to the king's ordinary expenses and not available for military spending. There was some change in emphasis in the fifteenth century. After Henry Bolingbroke seized the throne in 1399, the vast duchy of Lancaster estates were joined to the royal domain, increasing gross ordinary income to more than £30,000, although most of this additional income was already committed to paying annuities to duchy officials and supporters.[28] Under the Yorkist kings (1461–85) royal estates and other forms of Crown property produced around half of total revenue, which partly reflects a renewed focus on exploiting the royal domain but also the reduced demands for extraordinary taxation following the end of the Hundred Years War.

In France, the succession of Philip VI, while providing Edward III with his claim to the French throne, also brought the Valois estates into the royal demesne, augmenting the landed resources available to the French kings. While Charles IV had received an average of 17 tonnes of silver from his ordinary revenues, under Philip this increased to 25 tonnes.[29] By comparison, Edward III's gross ordinary revenues averaged about 6.6 tonnes of silver. This built-in advantage meant that the French kings had less need to raise taxes. Instead, their fiscal policy during the initial stage of the Hundred Years War was 'to run the domain state at maximum capacity'.[30] However, ordinary revenues were inelastic and difficult to expand rapidly in wartime. The one exception was seigniorage, the income received at the royal mints which will be considered later as a form of extraordinary income. In the later fourteenth century, French ordinary revenues collapsed, falling to *c.* 50,000 *livres tournois* in 1374 (2.0 tonnes of silver). This partly reflected what Bois termed a 'seigneurial crisis' as a result of plague, the disruption caused by fighting in the countryside and the erosion of nominal rents by inflation. It may have had the effect of encouraging the French aristocracy to enter royal service in search of pensions or exemptions from tax.[31] Although French ordinary income recovered to around 180,000 *livres tournois* (*c.* 6 tonnes) between 1388 and 1409, this still only represented around 7 per cent of total revenues. By 1461, ordinary revenues had fallen back to 50,000 *livres tournois*, contributing less than 3 per cent of total French royal revenues. The French experience is thus a mirror image of the English.

Clearly the king's personal and feudal revenues were not sufficient to meet the demands of later medieval warfare. Fortunately, later medieval political theory held that subjects had a duty to assist the ruler in the case of necessity, such as during a war.[32] In England, from the 1290s onwards, such grants of extraordinary taxation needed the consent of the Commons in parliament. Lay subsidies were usually only granted for specific purposes in wartime – the absence of direct taxes during the truce of 1360–9 can clearly be seen in Figure 3.1. One exception was during the truce of the 1390s when Richard II received several grants of subsidies even though there was no military necessity. This 'tyranny' was one of the justifications for his deposition.[33] Moreover, although subjects were bound to assist their ruler in cases of genuine necessity, there was room for negotiation. In 1380, for example, the minority council requested £160,000 from parliament to fund a new campaign to France. After much debate, the Commons ultimately agreed to a grant of 100,000 marks (£66,666 13s 4d) to be raised by the third poll tax in four years, the harsh collection of which helped to spark the Peasants' Revolt. Conditions might be attached by the Commons to a grant, most frequently that it would not set a precedent or that it should only be spent on a designated war purpose. Such negotiations also allowed the Commons to push for redress of grievances in return for tax grants: this leverage contributed to its political role and the result was a centralised and national system of taxation and political representation.

The lack of visible military activity at the start of the Hundred Years War meant that Philip VI found it difficult to persuade his subjects of the necessity of taxes. When he was able to raise taxes, although he utilised many of the same techniques as later rulers (hearth and sales taxes), these were mostly ad hoc and negotiated with individual provinces and towns.[34] After Poitiers, the need to fund John's ransom and the depredations of the *routiers* created a state of 'evident necessity' that justified the imposition of royal taxation on a new scale and, importantly, during peacetime too. However, the French kings tended to negotiate with particular regions, towns and interest groups rather than a single national assembly, which reflects deep-seated provincialism in France. When Charles VII sought to rebuild the tax system from the 1430s, it was still the provincial Estates that played a more important role. The result was to stifle the growth of a national political assembly along English lines and to confirm the diversity of the French fiscal system.[35] In 1439, it was recognised that the imposition of *tailles*, the chief form of direct taxation, was a royal prerogative. Thereafter, Charles VII was able to levy direct taxes annually, even during the truce with England between 1444 and 1449. This established a firm fiscal foundation for the early modern French monarchy and enabled a more absolutist form of royal government.[36]

There were significant practical differences between English and French tax systems. The bulk of English taxation (59.9 per cent) was raised from indirect taxes with the remainder coming from direct taxes on the laity (28.5 per cent) and on the clergy (11.5 per cent). This partly reflects the fact that indirect taxation became a permanent imposition during this period, although income varied depending on the level of exports and the rates charged, while direct taxation was generally only granted during time of war. The situation was reversed in France, where direct taxation became more important than indirect (representing 58.7 per cent and 38.5 per cent respectively of total royal revenues in 1461) and, as we have seen, ultimately permanent.

For England, the total revenue generated by indirect taxation is shown in Figure 3.2, along with the volume of wool and cloth exports (expressed in sacks of wool or the equivalent). Wool was England's main export and, as a high-value commodity in great demand in foreign markets, it could support a high rate of tax. That it was shipped from a small number of ports made exports easier to monitor. The customs duty on wool exports was introduced at the rate of 6s 8d per sack in 1275 to which was added the 'new custom' charged to foreign merchants of 3s 4d from 1303. From 1337, the English kings were able to levy additional subsidies of between 40s and 60s per sack, for which they needed consent by assemblies of merchants or, later, parliament.[37] Right from its inception, the wool custom was integrated into the royal credit system as security for the repayment of loans, as we shall explore later in this chapter. Indirect taxes were also levied on other imports and exports, including tunnage of 2s per tun of wine imported; poundage, an ad valorem duty of 6d in the pound; and a relatively modest duty on cloth exports.[38] However, these only brought in a fraction of the revenue generated by the wool custom, which posed a fundamental threat to royal finances in the fifteenth century when cloth exports began to rise at the expense of wool. Since wool exports were more heavily taxed than cloth, the result was a significant drop in royal tax revenues.[39] Henry VI was unable to increase export taxes on cloth or find an alternative revenue stream to compensate for this, undermining the basic foundation of Edwardian state finance.

France lacked a staple export commodity such as wool. As a result, indirect taxation took the form of sales taxes on internal transactions rather than customs duty on imports and exports. In 1360, the *aides* were introduced as part of the arrangements to raise John's ransom. This was set at 1 sou per livre (5 per cent) of the value of goods sold, excluding small transactions

Financing the Hundred Years War 67

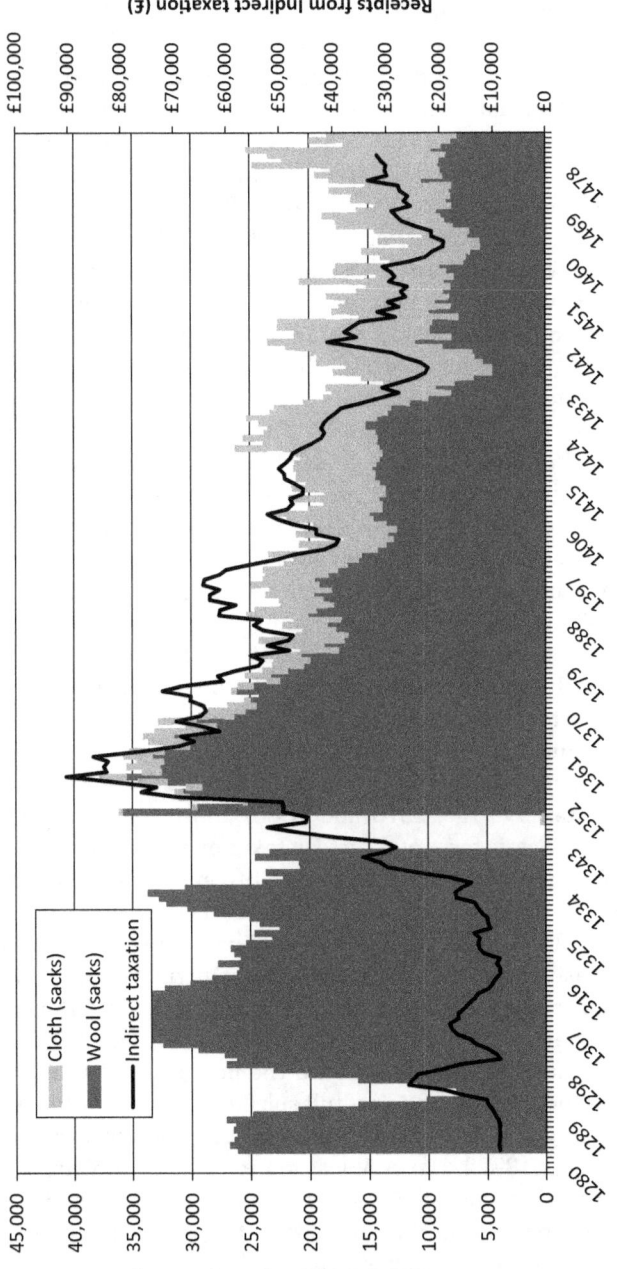

Figure 3.2 English wool and cloth exports and income from indirect taxation (five-year moving averages)

Source: Data from the European State Finance Database (http://www.esfdb.org/table.aspx?resourceid=11334; http://esfdb.org/table.aspx?resourceid=11593). Cloth exports were recorded in pieces but have been converted into their equivalent in sacks of wool at the rate of 4.3 pieces of cloth per sack (Harriss, *Shaping the Nation*, p. 257).

of less than 5 sous. Wine was taxed at a higher rate, initially 1d per sou but later increased to 5 sous (25 per cent or the *quatrième*).[40] It was more administratively complex to monitor and tax all internal transactions than imports and exports at a small number of ports. By the fifteenth century, the French employed several thousand tax collectors compared to a handful in England.[41] There were also internal differences within France. The estates of Languedoc preferred direct taxes to indirect and offered the king a set sum in exchange for the *aides*. This give rise to the odd situation whereby transactions in Languedoil were taxed and those in Languedoc were not. To avoid the possibility for tax avoidance, an internal customs border was erected with a duty of 5 per cent on goods moved from Languedoil to Languedoc known as the *imposition foraine*.[42] On his death in 1380, Charles V released the new taxes, including the *aides*, but the revenue they raised was too important to give up and they were reintroduced in 1382. Their effectiveness was undermined under Charles VI, however, as he granted leading nobles the right to a share, usually one-third but sometimes one-half, of the *aides* collected in their areas. The aides were released in 1418 by the Burgundians in an attempt to secure public support against their Armagnac rivals.[43] As Charles VII sought to rebuild the fiscal foundations established under his grandfather, the *aides* were restored in 1427 and, by 1461, they comprised 29.7 per cent of total royal income, and the *gabelle* (salt tax) contributed a further 8.9 per cent. Here, again, the French approach differed from the English as indirect taxation became less important than direct taxation.

The English government was successful in imposing direct taxes on clergy and laity. Although there was some experimentation with taxes in kind (the ninth of 1340), poll taxes (1377, 1379 and 1380) and income taxes (1404, 1411, 1435, 1450), the classic form of direct lay taxation was the fifteenth and tenth.[44] This was supposed to be assessed at one-fifteenth of surplus production in rural areas and one-tenth in urban.[45] However, from 1334 the gross value of a fifteenth and tenth was fixed at £37,000 based on the contribution of each community as assessed in 1332. How this contribution was divided within each community was left to the local elites, which reduced the burden on the royal administration and may have allowed the wealthiest members of local society to shift much of the burden onto the poorest. Parliament could grant fractional subsidies – half-subsidies, full subsidies, 1½ subsidies or even double subsidies – or grant multiple subsidies to be collected over several years. In the ten years 1413–22, Henry V was granted the equivalent of 10 ⅓ subsidies: in only one year of his reign, 1420, was no subsidy collected.[46] After 1422, the government found it increasingly difficult to raise money: the total sum expected from a subsidy was reduced by £4,000 in 1433 and a further

£2,000 in 1446. This coincided with the fall in revenues from indirect taxation discussed earlier, leading to a significant reduction in royal income from extraordinary taxes after 1422, as can clearly be seen from Figure 3.1.

In 1363, the French king was granted direct taxation to supplement the *aides* in the form of a *fouage*, a graduated hearth tax set at 3 francs per household. At first sight, this seems closer to the English poll tax than the fifteenths and tenths. In practice, however, the numbers of hearths became fixed and the sums demanded were apportioned locally, in a similar way to the fifteenths and tenths in England. The monies collected from the *fouage*, however, were spent locally rather than distributed centrally.[47] Like the *aides*, the *fouage* was released by Charles VI on his deathbed in 1380. Also like the *aides*, it was quickly replaced by the *taille*. This was a direct tax similar in form to the *fouage*, except that it was not a permanent imposition but had to be granted by regional assemblies for specific purposes. During 1384–8, Charles VI was granted nearly 5 million *livres tournois* (185 tonnes of silver), and, in 1402–6, 2.6 million (89 tonnes) for the war effort. In 1411–12, the Burgundians, then in power, raised 900,000 *livres tournois* (34 tonnes) to fight against the Armagnacs.[48] Between 1421 and 1432, the dauphin Charles raised 7 million *livres tournois* (149 tonnes) from those parts of France under his control and a further 2.7 million *livres tournois* between 1439 and 1444 (79 tonnes).[49] At his death in 1461, the *taille* was worth 1,055,000 *livres tournois* (27 tonnes or 58.6 per cent of total royal income).[50]

The question of clerical taxation had been a contentious issue at the end of the thirteenth century but had been settled in the king's favour and both kings took full advantage. In England, direct taxes on the clergy raised £1,067,700, equivalent to roughly 40 per cent of the sums raised from direct taxes on the laity. Consent was given by convocations of the archdioceses of Canterbury and York, which were usually summoned at the same time as parliament – a standard grant from the former being worth £15,200 compared to £2,000 from the latter. This can be partly explained by the larger size of the archdiocese of Canterbury but also reflects the economic damage caused by Scottish raids in the North. The burden of clerical taxation was heavy; over the course of the fifteenth century, Canterbury was taxed every other year and York every third year.[51]

The French kings benefitted from a particularly close relationship with the papacy especially in the fourteenth century. They were frequently granted the clerical tenths (*decime*) imposed by the popes on the French clergy. Henneman estimated that the *decime* was worth around 44,500 silver marks (10.4 tonnes of silver) per year, comprising around one-fifth of royal revenues. In 1344, Clement VI acquitted Philip VI of the money that he had collected from the crusading tenth (valued at 2.8 million florins), while also lending him substantial sums.[52] From 1360, direct clerical taxation became less significant and stopped being collected every year. Instead the clergy paid occasional *decimes* as a counterpart to the *tailles* imposed on the laity. The church's landed revenues had been depleted as part of the general seigniorial crisis and, by the later fourteenth century, revenue from the *decimes* had halved to around 150,000 livres (5 tonnes).[53]

Another major difference between English and French fiscal policy was their attitude towards debasement of the coinage.[54] The medieval economy became increasingly monetised, as the commercial revolution led to a demand for a reliable money supply to conduct trade and, not least, pay taxes. Rulers asserted the right to issue coins within their territories, which contained a (greater or lesser) proportion of precious metal. Royal mints charged a fee (seigniorage) for minting new coins, which could be increased by altering the precious metal content. Figure 3.3 shows the prescribed silver content of the main unit of account.[55] Since the standard of the French coinage was sometimes changed several times in the same year, this figure shows the minimum silver content of the nominal denier in each year. To make the figure more understandable, the silver contents of the two currencies have been plotted on different axes with different scales. We can see a marked trend in the relative silver contents of the two coins. At the start of the period, the to penny sterling contained around four times as much silver as the denier *tournois*, a ratio that dated back to the thirteenth century. By the end of the war, sterling contained ten times as much silver as *tournois*. The silver content of the

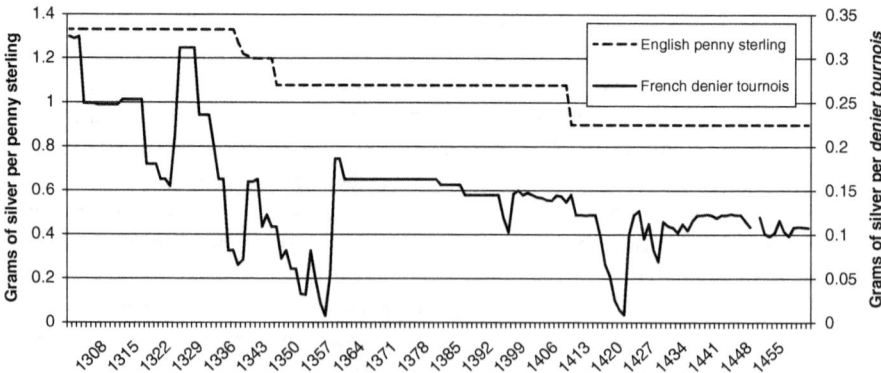

Figure 3.3 Silver content of the English and French currencies

Sources: Allen–Unger Global Commodity Price Database; Miskimin, *Money, Prices and Foreign Exchange*; idem, *Money and Power*.

French currency was also far more volatile than the English, resulting from the frequent recourse by the French kings to monetary alterations to generate revenue through seigniorage.

There were two major periods of serial debasement in France. The first was between 1337 and 1360 and the second between 1417 and 1429. Just before the start of the war, each *denier tournois* contained 0.24 grams of silver. At its nadir in 1360, it was a mere 0.0078 grams. In the later fourteenth century, the silver content was relatively stable at 0.14–0.16 grams, only to be progressively reduced from 1417 to 0.009 grams in 1422. This had a dramatic impact on royal revenues; in 1349, profits from seigniorage accounted for 70.6 per cent of royal revenues rising to 85.6 per cent in 1418–20, compared to only 0.7 per cent of treasury receipts in 1384, a period of (relatively) strong money.[56] It is apparent that periods of debasement coincide with periods of fiscal instability. When the tax system was established and functioning reasonably well between 1363 and 1415 and again in the 1430s and 1440s, the value of the coinage was maintained. French kings resorted to debasing the coinage to raise income from seigniorage because it did not require consent. Debasement raised money more quickly than taxes could be assessed and collected, but it had economic consequences. It usually led, after a lag, to inflation as prices rose to reflect the decreased value of the coinage. This had political repercussions since this inflation 'tax' hit those classes with fixed incomes. Trade was also damaged by the uncertainty caused by fluctuations in the value of the coinage.

Although the English kings did reduce the metallic content of the coinage on occasion, these were 'defensive' adjustments to maintain parity with other coinages rather than 'aggressive' debasements for fiscal purposes. Average gross revenue from seigniorage in England was £1,336 between 1337 and 1377, around 1 per cent of total royal income. The ability of English kings to raise taxes from parliament meant that they did not have to resort to such tactics which would have been unpopular with the very people (the landed classes and merchants) who sat in parliament. English monetary consistency stands in stark contrast to the instability in France. Edward III sought to appeal to French dissatisfaction by promising, on claiming the French throne in 1340, that he would not engage in such monetary manipulations.[57] This does not mean that the English kings did not have a monetary policy. Rather, they followed a 'bullionist' policy that, instead of raising revenue, aimed to maintain a strong currency by encouraging imports of gold and silver. This would both boost the domestic money supply and ensure a source of funds for the garrison at Calais.[58]

In general, there seems to have been a reasonable match between the extraordinary expenditure and extraordinary revenues of the English and French crowns at war, at least over the medium term. Sherborne estimated that English military expenditure between 1368 and 1375 was around £672,000 compared to tax receipts of £690,000, and that between 1376 and 1381, military expenditure was *c.* £467,000 against receipts of *c.* £500,000.[59] The Exchequer has been criticised for being a purely auditing body and not engaging in any form of forward-looking planning but, in fact, the close correspondence between the sums raised and spent suggests some form of budgeting.[60] This was a substantial achievement and should not be overshadowed by the undoubtedly dramatic but rare occasions on which the system broke down and large arrears were accumulated. In the early 1340s, Edward III owed around £300,000. A century later, Henry VI managed to top this figure. The treasurer, Lord Cromwell, presented royal debts of £168,000 before parliament in 1433. By 1449, this had probably doubled to more than £300,000.[61] To examine how medieval kings could amass this level of debt, it is necessary to consider the workings of the contemporary financial system.

MOVING MONEY

Our overview has suggested that the English and French kings were, for the most part, able to raise enough money from extraordinary revenues to meet their military expenses but it was necessary to bridge the gap between the two. First, taxes were often voted in *response* to a military emergency and took time to collect in full. Second, any monies raised had to be transported from the point of collection to the war theatre where they were needed. This required a financial system to move money in space and time. During the fourteenth and fifteenth centuries, the main financial intermediaries were merchants as, in Murray's words, 'money and credit flow along with trade'.[62] While the sensible use of credit could help the king to anticipate and transfer his revenues, it was possible for royal borrowing to get out of control. This section will focus on the better-documented case study of England, but will highlight where similar mechanisms appear to have been used in France.

It might be thought that the safest policy was for the king to build up a cash reserve sufficient to meet any unexpected military expense. Counterintuitively, however, the possession of a large war chest did not necessarily strengthen the king's position. The two wealthiest English kings of the later Middle Ages were Edward II and Richard II, both of whom had substantial sums in their treasury when deposed.[63] By contrast, Edward I and Edward III, two of the most successful and respected medieval kings, were frequently in debt. A popular king could be confident that he could secure grants of taxation from parliament and so did not need to stockpile treasure, which could rather signal political insecurity.

Of course, where military expenditure was anticipated and taxes could be gathered in advance (or, as we shall see, money borrowed on the security of those taxes) before the departure of the army, it was possible to make payments in cash. Yet it could be expensive and risky to transport large sums in cash: Fryde has estimated that it cost Edward I 2–3 per cent to transport cash to the continent in 1297 while an English fleet sailing to Gascony in 1372 with £12,000 in cash was defeated off La Rochelle and the money lost. The alternative was to engage in cashless transfer, which was often linked to a credit transaction. In 1338–40, Edward III only shipped £6,000 in cash from England to the Low Countries, a tiny portion of the £400,000 that he spent overseas.[64] The remainder was raised on the continent by borrowing from merchants abroad and then repaying them in England, often by allowing them credit against the customs duty owed for wool exports.

When considering the use of credit by English kings, it is important to draw a distinction between long-term and short-term borrowing. Unlike the Italian city-states, there was no long-term funded public debt in England or France. Why not? One explanation focusses on the supply-side; English kings were not sufficiently credit-worthy borrowers for anyone to be willing to lend on a long-term basis at acceptable terms.[65] Another focusses on the demand side; English and French kings did not need to issue long-term debt to fund their wars since, as we have seen earlier, they were usually able to raise sufficient income from extraordinary taxes. Instead, they faced a short-term liquidity issue of bridging the gap between the start of conflict and the eventual receipt of taxes. To use a modern analogy, the English and French kings drew on their credit card while the Italians used a mortgage.

At the start of the war, Edward III could draw upon the services of the great Italian merchant societies of the Bardi and the Peruzzi – a continuation of a long-standing tradition; since 1275, English kings had engaged a series of Italian merchant societies as 'bankers to the Crown'. In effect, the Italians advanced money to the king or made payments on his behalf and were repaid from customs revenues.[66] Philip IV had made similar use of the Franzesi brothers 'Mouche' and 'Biche' in the 1290s and 1300s but Philip VI preferred to extort money from foreign moneylenders on the pretext of their usury. Although this raised useful sums in the short term, such policies impaired the French kings' access to international credit in the longer term.[67] Royal finance was not solely an Italian perquisite – domestic merchants such as William de la Pole in England in the 1330s and Jacques Coeur in France in the 1440s played a similar role.[68] After the collapse of the Peruzzi and the Bardi in 1343 and 1345 respectively, Edward III sought to continue the basic system by farming the customs – crucial for credit systems as it provided a regular revenue stream – to a series of English merchant companies between 1343 and 1350.[69] These great merchants did not necessarily fund their advances to the king from their own resources but seem to have raised money from consortia of smaller lenders. It was more convenient for the king to deal with one intermediary than directly with hundreds of individual creditors. In return, the merchant companies received grants of interest and trading privileges, which increased their profitability and thus their ability to continue lending to the crown.

Ultimately, the increasing scale of royal demands outstripped the resources of all of these groups and kings had to adopt a more decentralised credit system, literally cutting out the middleman. From the second half of the fourteenth century, the English government relied on a larger number of smaller loans from individuals and corporations. Some particularly wealthy figures made major contributions – Henry Beaufort, bishop of Winchester, alone loaned a total of £216,000 (47 tonnes in silver) to Henry V and Henry VI, although his exposure at any one time was only a fraction of this sum.[70] Likewise, Pope Clement VI (a former councillor to Philip VI) and his brother Guillaume, vicomte de Beaufort lent 622,000 florins (roughly 20 tonnes of silver) to Philip between 1345 and 1348, which they later wrote off.[71] On a smaller scale, both the English and the French crowns sought to raise smaller loans from individual landowners or towns, usually in anticipation of the collection of local taxes. In England, commissions *de mutuo faciendo* were dispatched to try and secure loans from landowners in the counties. On 13 May 1421, for example, Henry V raised £9,000 from no fewer than 501 small loans.[72] Equally important were loans from the mercantile class, either as individuals or collectively through corporations such as towns, especially London. During the reign of Richard II, the city advanced £66,000 compared to a total of only £12,000 from all the other provincial towns of England.[73] Merchants of the Staple based at Calais also had a strong incentive to support the garrison of the town.[74] The situation was similar in France where it was common for town councils and, especially, royal officials to advance loans against their future tax obligations.[75]

The king also employed credit in another way. In England, soldiers' wages were supposed to be paid in advance at least for the first stage of the campaign. This initial cash payment was often borrowed by the king as discussed.

Captains might also receive security for later periods in the form of a pledge or an assignment on future tax revenues. However, some royal captains had to wait longer to be paid in full – sometimes as long as ten years.[76] The king could also buy goods on credit or use his right of purveyance (at least until the 1360s) to make compulsory purchases. Delaying payment on obligations was a traditional method by which the king could manage his short-term cashflow. As a result, there was often a queue of such involuntary royal creditors awaiting payment on wardrobe or Exchequer bills for services or goods rendered. There was no set priority and well-connected creditors could often muscle their way to the front of the line.[77] As well as formal loans, therefore, the English kings could effectively borrow by running up arrears on their accounts payable.

Kings sought, but were not always able, to prioritise military payments. In the case of arrears for military service, it is not entirely clear on whom this burden would have fallen. If captains paid their own soldiers upfront even if they only received payment in arrears, then they would have been extending credit to the king – which might have been expensive if they had to borrow this money themselves. Alternatively, the captains may have been able to pass this burden down onto their soldiers by delaying payment of their wages until money had been received from the crown. If soldiers' wages were left unpaid for long enough, it could lead to refusals to fight, insurrection or even attacks on allies and locals. During the long siege of Calais in 1347, William de Bohun, earl of Northampton, warned the king that, unless he received the sums owed to him, he would have to withdraw his troops as he could not pay them.[78] In winter 1406–7, after years of late or underpayment, the garrison at Calais mutinied and seized the wool held by the merchants of the Staple.[79] Yet such situations did not seem to dent enthusiasm for military service.

The problem of royal credibility could be partly mitigated by the use of security or collateral. In extreme cases, the royal jewels could be used as pledges. Edward III had to pawn his crown, which then passed through several hands before he could redeem it, and Henry V pledged his jewels to his captains before the Agincourt campaign.[80] Alternatively, repayment could be assigned against a future source of royal revenue – usually on the collectors of the customs but sometimes on future instalments of direct taxes. As evidence, the creditor would receive a tally, a stick of wood cut with notches representing sums of money and split into two so that both parties had a record of the transaction.[81] Originally, tallies were issued to a collector of royal revenues as proof that he had paid money into the treasury. By the fourteenth century, however, the tally had become a credit instrument. It was a particularly useful instrument since the recipient may have been able to pledge it as security for a loan or to trade it again on the secondary market. This system continued in use until the nineteenth century.

Unlike the Italian city-states, there was no organised and official secondary market for English royal debt but there is scattered evidence for the trading of royal obligations. In 1415, some of the royal jewels pledged to retinue captains as security for payment of future instalments of their wages ended up in the hands of London merchants, suggesting that the captains had used the jewels as pledges for their own loans in order to have ready cash to pay their soldiers.[82] The same happened with tallies. The trading of government debt was explicitly sanctioned by Edward III, at least for a select group, including the king's major financiers, who received royal licences to buy up and redeem royal debts. The recipients could profit by buying these obligations at a discount from desperate royal creditors and then presenting them to the king at face value. Contemporaries complained that merchants were buying up these debts at the rate of 1s or 2s in the pound, a discount of 90–95 per cent of their face value: this was confirmed by an Exchequer investigation. As much as £84,000 of distressed royal debt was redeemed between 1343 and 1355 in this way.[83] There are indications of similar practices in France, with desperate royal creditors offering to sell 10,000 francs of royal debt for only 100 francs, a 99 per cent discount.[84] This allowed the king to kill two birds with one stone: clearing up some of his old debts and rewarding his financiers without the appearance of usury but at the expense of the smaller royal creditors.

That English kings could fund themselves by issuing tallies on future revenues or running up arrears for services rendered may seem like a 'free lunch' at the expense of royal creditors. As Sir John Fortescue, the late fifteenth-century theorist, observed: 'the poor man would rather have 100 marks (£66 13s 4d) in hand than a hundred pounds by assignment, which perhaps shall cost him very much before he can get his payment, and perhaps never be paid thereof.' However, it is unclear who would have borne this cost. Fortescue went on to suggest that '[the king's] creditors will win upon him the fourth or fifth penny of all that he spends'.[85] In other words, the king would have to promise to repay the creditor more than he had actually received to compensate them for the risk of late or even non-repayment. Steel found several examples from the Receipt Rolls between 1379 and 1386 where royal creditors were recorded as lending a certain sum with part noted as paid and the rest as *pro eisdem* (for the loan). Such entries cease after 1386, possibly because they left 'much too clear an indication of an openly usurious transaction in the rolls'.[86] It is possible, however, that such payments continued to be made but were concealed by inflating the value of the debt recognised. There is at least one similar case from France in 1416–17 where Guillaume Cenatui was accused of taking a quarter of the sum supposedly lent for his private profit.[87] If this was a standard practice, then the headline figures for royal revenues given in the accounts may overstate the king's effective buying power.

In modern finance, of course, a key indicator of creditworthiness is the interest rates charged by lenders. As we have already seen, any consideration of this is complicated because of the usury prohibition.[88] Some lenders may have been motivated by political duty; there is no explicit evidence that Cardinal Beaufort sought any interest on his loans to Henry V and VI.[89] Towns or royal officials who advanced money to the king against future tax revenues probably did so freely out of a sense of obligation or to secure their political position. Yet some clearly expected to receive a financial return on their investment, either by disguised interest payments or through monetising trading privileges. When the accounts of the Bardi and the Peruzzi were being heard in the 1340s, a royal clerk calculated that the Bardi had been promised £84,087 and the Peruzzi £38,366 as 'gifts in the name of usury' since they had started lending money to the king.[90] It is not possible to calculate precise interest rates for many of these transactions, but it seems that kings could borrow at between 15 per cent and 25 per cent per annum during peacetime but had to pay rates of 40–60 per cent, or even higher, during wartime.[91] It seems that kings could borrow at between 15 per cent and 25 per cent per annum during peacetime but had to pay rates of 40–60 per cent, or even higher, during wartime. In France, the university and city of Paris complained in 1413 that the king had been borrowing from Italian merchants at interest rates of 50 per cent or 60 per cent, costing the crown some 300,000 *livres tournois* (8.8 tonnes of silver) each year.[92]

Both English and French kings therefore seem to have enjoyed reasonable access to credit. Generally this was a boon but there was always the risk that the king would overextend himself. Using tallies to anticipate future income effectively assumed receipt of those monies before they had actually been collected. We see this in the so-called 'fictitious loans' on the Receipt Rolls. In the event that the creditor was not able to collect on a tally, the Receipt Roll entry would be cancelled and replaced by a new 'fictitious loan' from that creditor, effectively rolling over the debt. It has been suggested that this can be used as a barometer of royal fiscal management and that the much lower proportion of 'fictitious loans' under Henry V compared to his father and son reveals his tight control over his finances and his discipline in not borrowing or promising more than his revenues could reasonably cover.[93] The most famous example of financial mismanagement is Edward III's 'default' in the 1340s which has been blamed for the failures of the Bardi and the Peruzzi. While it is true that he owed them huge sums of money, the true picture is more nuanced. First, the majority of this debt represented promises of interest rather than principal advanced. Moreover, when Edward issued a 'stop' on assigned payments from the Exchequer in May 1339, he specifically excluded the Bardi and the Peruzzi. Edward also never formally repudiated his debts, and both he and his grandson continued to make occasional repayments to the Bardi until the remaining debt was forgiven in 1391. Finally, both the Bardi and the Peruzzi owed money to their own creditors in England but both Edward and Richard II protected them from legal proceedings.[94] In general, then, both English and French kings seem to have tried to deal with their creditors in good faith, although these good intentions were often overtaken by events.

Overall, in both France and England short-term borrowings were often linked to future tax revenues through tallies of assignment or advances from tax farmers. This system was usually effective in bridging the gap between the king's need for money and the usually much slower collection of his revenues. On occasion, however, royal expenditure could outstrip medium-term revenues, leading to infrequent but spectacular debt crises. The fact that neither country introduced a long-term public debt, however, means that they cannot be considered as having developed into true fiscal states during the Middle Ages.

CONCLUSION

Both kingdoms were able to raise sufficient amounts of finance to put armies into the field. The new demands of later medieval warfare forced kings to turn to new forms of revenue, ultimately introducing tax systems with the consent of public assemblies. This was combined with the use of short-term credit, both to anticipate future revenues and to transfer money to the war theatre. The relative financial capacities of the English and French states varied over time, leading to a 'see-saw' of fiscal and, arguably, military advantage. At least initially, the English kings could draw on a more developed tax system, compensating for the smaller size of their realm. However, the French reforms of the 1360s and 1430s allowed them to reassert their greater resource base. Although periods of military dominance usually coincided with fiscal stability, it is too simplistic to argue that the latter caused the former. We can rather conclude that an efficient fiscal and financial system may have been a *necessary* condition for success in war but it was far from *sufficient*. Moreover, the fiscal transition from a domain state to a tax state was driven by the pressure of military competition. After the end of the Hundred Years War, England retreated from large-scale European entanglements and, freed of this external pressure, underwent a partial reversion to a domain state. Ultimately, it was the outbreak of the 'second Hundred Years War' (1689–1815), and the renewed need to compete with France, that drove England to create a long-term funded national debt, thereby transitioning into a fiscal state.

NOTES

1   For this view of state formation as driven by a competition or 'tournament', see C. Tilly, *Coercion, Capital and European States, 990–1992* (Cambridge, MA, 1992); S. Epstein, *Freedom and Growth: Markets and States 1300–1750* (London, 2000); P. Hoffman, *Why Did Europe Conquer the World?* (Princeton, NJ, and Oxford, 2015).
2   For comparative overviews, see E. Fryde, 'The Financial Policies of the Royal Governments and Popular Resistance to Them in England and France, c.1270–1420', *Revue Belge de philologie et de d'histoire*, 57 (1979), pp. 824–60; W. M. Ormrod, 'The West European Monarchies in the Later Middle Ages', *Economic Systems and State Finance*, ed. R. Bonney (Oxford, 1995), pp. 123–60; D. Grummit and J.-F. Lassalmonie, 'Royal Public Finance (c.1290–1523)', *Government and Political Life in England and France, c.1300–1500*, ed. C. Fletcher, J.-P. Genet and J. Watts (Cambridge, 2015), pp. 116–49. For England, see W. M. Ormrod, 'England in the Middle Ages', *The Rise of the Fiscal State in Europe c.1200–1815*, ed. R. Bonney (Oxford, 1999), pp. 19–47. For France, see J. B. Henneman, 'France in the Middle Ages', *Rise of the Fiscal State*, ed. Bonney, pp. 101–22.
3   Grummitt and Lassalmonie, 'Royal Public Finance', pp. 119–23 for important caveats about using statistical evidence.
4   GDP figures for England are from S. Broadberry, B. Campbell, A. Klein, M. Overton and B. van Leeuwen, *British Economic Growth, 1270–1870* (Cambridge, 2015). For France, we used estimates for GDP per capita from Leonardo Ridolfi, 'The French Economy in the *longue durée*: A Study on Real Wages, Working Days and Economic Performance from Louis IX to the Revolution (1250–1789)', unpublished PhD thesis (IMT School for Advanced Studies, Lucca, 2016). The silver content of the English penny sterling is from the Allen–Unger Global Commodity Prices Dataset, available from http://www.gcpdb.info [accessed 23 December 2017]. The silver content of a nominal denier *tournois* was calculated from appendices in H. Miskimin, *Money, Prices and Foreign Exchange in Fourteenth-Century France* (New Haven, CT, and London, 1963) and idem, *Money and Power in Fifteenth-Century France* (New Haven, CT, and London, 1984).

5   E. Fryde, 'Financial Resources of Edward III in the Netherlands, 1337–40', *Revue Belge de philologie et d'histoire*, 57 (1979), pp. 1142, 1180.
6   W. M. Ormrod, *Edward III* (New Haven, CT, and London, 2011), pp. 297, 342, 398.
7   The parliament of 1382 considered this necessary to fund a campaign of that size and length (*PROME*, VI, p. 271) but earlier that year John of Gaunt requested the same sum for only 2,000 men-at-arms and 2,000 archers for an Iberian expedition (pp. 247–48).
8   D. Grummitt, 'The Financial Administration of Calais during the Reign of Henry IV, 1399-1413', *EHR*, 113 (1998), p. 277.
9   J. Sherborne, 'The Cost of English Warfare with France in the Later Fourteenth Century', *BIHR*, 50 (1977), p. 149.
10 Fryde, 'Financial Policies', p. 839; B. Bove, *Le temps de la guerre de Cent Ans: 1328–1453* (Paris, 2009), p. 90.
11 M. Rey, *Le domaine du roi et les finances extraordinaires sous Charles VI 1388–1413* (Paris, 1965), pp. 36–8.
12 P. Solon, 'Valois Military Administration on the Norman Frontier, 1445–1461: A Study in Medieval Reform', *Speculum*, 51 (1976), pp. 92–4.
13 These have been calculated from modern French regions as given in Institut National de la Statistique et des Études Économiques, *La France et ses Territoires* (Paris, 2015), p. 99, online at https://www.insee.fr/fr/statistiques/fichier/1373022/FST15.pdf [accessed 23 December 2017].
14 Broadberry et al., *British Economic Growth*, pp. 3–33; *Histoire de la population française I. Des origines à la Renaissance*, ed. J. Dupâquier (Paris, 1988), pp. 259–64, 322–46.
15 Broadberry et al., *British Economic Growth*.
16 Ridolfi, 'French Economy', pp. 195–7.
17 The best overview of royal revenues is Ormrod, 'England in the Middle Ages', with data on European State Finance Database (www.esfdb.org). See notes to Figure 3.1 for more details.
18 P. Contamine, 'Guerre, fiscalité royale et économie en France (deuxième moitié du XVe siècle)', *Des pouvoirs en France, 1300–1500*, ed. P. Contamine (Paris, 1992), pp. 123–30 at 129.
19 This chronology is based on our reconstruction of royal revenues in Figure 3.1 and Table 3.1, but largely mirrors that in Ormrod, 'England in the Middle Ages' and Henneman, 'France in the Middle Ages'.
20 For details, see J. Henneman, *Royal Taxation in Fourteenth Century France: The Development of War Financing, 1322–1356* (Princeton, NJ, 1971).
21 See J. Henneman, *Royal Taxation in Fourteenth Century France: The Captivity and Ransom of John II, 1356–1370* (Philadelphia, PA, 1976). For their subsequent operation under Charles V and VI, see Rey, *Domaine du roi*.
22 M. Rey, *Les finances royales sous Charles VI: Les causes du déficit 1388–1413* (Paris, 1965).

23 Ormrod, 'West European Monarchies', pp. 149–54; P. O'Brien and P. Hunt, 'England 1485–1815', *Rise of the Fiscal State*, ed. Bonney, p. 58.
24 G. Bois, *The Crisis of Feudalism: Economy and Society in Eastern Normandy c.1300–1550* (Cambridge, 1984), pp. 277–368.
25 Henneman, 'France', p. 118; Ormrod, 'West European Monarchies', p. 150.
26 For an elaboration of this typology, see W. M. Ormrod and R. Bonney, 'Introduction: Crises, Revolutions and Self-sustained Growth: Towards a Conceptual Model of change in Fiscal History', *Crises, Revolutions and Self-Sustained Growth: Essays in European Fiscal History, 1130–1830*, ed. W. M. Ormrod, M. Bonney and R. Bonney (Stamford, 1999), pp. 1–21.
27 N. Barrett, 'English Royal Revenue in the Early Thirteenth Century and Its Wider Context', *Crises, Revolutions and Self-Sustained Growth*, p. 96.
28 C. Given-Wilson, *Henry IV* (New Haven, CT, and London, 2016), p. 175.
29 Calculated from Henneman, *Development of War Financing*, p. 349.
30 Ormrod, 'West European Monarchies', p. 142.
31 Henneman, *Captivity and Ransom of John II*, pp. 6–7.
32 E. Isenmann, 'Medieval and Renaissance Theories of State Finance', *Economic Systems and State Finance*, ed. R. Bonney (Oxford, 1995), pp. 28–44. See also G. Harriss, *King, Parliament and Public Finance in Medieval England to 1369* (Oxford, 1975) and L. Scordia, *'Le Roi doit vivre du sien': La théorie de l'impôt en France, XIIIe–XVe siècles* (Paris, 2005).
33 N. Saul, *Richard II* (New Haven, CT, and London, 1997), pp. 256–61.
34 Henneman, *Development of War Financing*, pp. 116–41.
35 Henneman, *Captivity and Ransom of John II*, pp. 307–9.
36 J.-F. Lassalmonie, *La boîte à l'enchanteur: Politique financière de Louis XI* (Paris, 2002), pp. 27–30. We have followed Henneman in stressing continuity between Charles V and Charles VII, but Martin Wolfe has argued that fifteenth-century changes were more fundamental (*The Fiscal System of Renaissance France* (New Haven, CT, and London, 1972), pp. 25–52).
37 Harriss, *King, Parliament and Public Finance*, pp. 447–9.
38 W. M. Ormrod, 'The Origins of Tunnage and Poundage: Parliament and the Estate of Merchants in the 14th Century', *Parliamentary History*, 28 (2009), 209–27.
39 G. Harriss, *Shaping the Nation: England 1360–1461* (Oxford, 2005), pp. 256–8.
40 Henneman, *Captivity and Ransom of John II*, p. 118.
41 Grummitt and Lassalmonie, 'Royal Public Finance', pp. 124–8.
42 Henneman, *Captivity and Ransom of John II*, pp. 161–70.
43 Rey, *Domaine du roi*, pp. 269–75, 370.
44 Lloyd, *English Wool Trade*, p. 160. M. Jurkowski, C. Smith and D. Crook, *Lay Taxes in England and Wales 1188–1688* (Chippenham, 1988), pp. xxxiv–xxxix.
45 All tax grants are detailed in Jurkowski et al., *Lay Taxes in England and Wales*.
46 W. M. Ormrod, 'Henry V and the English Taxpayer', *Henry V: New Interpretations*, ed. G. Dodd (Woodbridge, 2013), pp. 187–216.
47 Henneman, *Captivity and Ransom of John II*.

48 Rey, *Domaine du roi*, pp. 390–404.
49 F. Lot and R. Fawtier, *Histoire des institutions françaises au moyen âge: tome II* (Paris, 1958), p. 271.
50 Lassalmonie, *La boîte à l'enchanteur*, p. 60.
51 A. McHardy, 'Clerical Taxation in Fifteenth-Century England: The Clergy as Agents of the Crown', *The Church, Politics and Patronage in the Fifteenth Century*, ed. R. B. Dobson (Gloucester, 1984), pp. 168–70.
52 M. Faucon, 'Prêts faits aux rois de France par Clément VI, Innocent VI et le comte de Beaufort (1345–1360)', *BEC*, 40 (1879), p. 571.
53 Rey, *Domaine du roi*, pp. 340–7.
54 See M. Allen, 'Currency Depreciation and Debasement in Medieval Europe', *Money in the Western Legal Tradition: Middle Ages to Bretton Woods*, ed. D. Fox and W. Ernst (Oxford, 2016), pp. 41–52.
55 Note that in England the unit of account was identical with a physical coin, the penny sterling, but, in France, the denier tournois (as 1/240 of a *livre tournois*) had become an imaginary coin. Instead, the mints struck different coins with a face value of a set number of pence tournois (e.g. the gros, the blanc, or plaque).
56 Miskimin, *Money, Prices and Foreign Exchange*, p. 43; Lot and Fawtier, *Institutions françaises*, p. 269.
57 M. Allen, *Mints and Money in Medieval England* (Cambridge, 2012), pp. 164, 209–10.
58 J. Munro, 'Bullionism and the Bill of Exchange in England, 1272–1663: A Study in Monetary Management and Popular Prejudice', *The Dawn of Banking* (New Haven, CT, and London, 1979), pp. 174–87.
59 Sherborne, 'Cost', pp. 140–2, 149.
60 G. Harriss, 'Budgeting at the Medieval Exchequer', in *War, Government and Aristocracy in the British Isles, c.1150:1500: Essays in honour of Michael Prestwich*, ed. C. Given-Wilson, A. Kettle and L. Scales (Woodbridge, 2008), pp. 179–96.
61 R. Griffiths, *The Reign of Henry VI* (London, 1981), pp. 110, 377.
62 J. Murray, *Bruges, Cradle of Capitalism, 1280–1390* (Cambridge, 2005), p. 230.
63 C. Carpenter, 'Resisting and Deposing Kings in the Fourteenth and Fifteenth Centuries', *Murder and Regicide in European History, 1300–1800*, ed. R. van Friedeberg (Basingstoke, 2004). This partly reflected the two kings' pacific policy towards France, so their financial exactions were seen as enriching themselves personally.
64 Fryde, 'Financial Resources of Edward III', p. 1143.
65 D. Stasavage, *States of Credit: Size, Power and the Development of European Polities* (Princeton, NJ, 2011), pp. 34–35.
66 A. Bell, C. Brooks and T. Moore, 'Le crédit au moyen âge: Les prêts à la couronne d'Angleterre entre 1272 et 1345', *Ressources publiques et construction étatique en Europe XIIIe–XVIIIe siècle*, ed. K. Béguin (Mayenne, 2015).

67 J. Henneman, 'Taxation of Italians by the French Crown, 1311–1363', *Mediaeval Studies*, 31 (1969), pp. 15–43.
68 E. Fryde, *William de la Pole: Merchant and King's Banker (†1366)* (London, 1988); Michel Mollat, *Jacques Coeur ou l'espirit d'entreprise au XVe siècle* (Paris, 1988).
69 E. Fryde, 'The English Farmers of the Customs, 1343–51', *TRHS*, 5th series, 9 (1959), 1–17.
70 G. Harriss, *Cardinal Beaufort: A Study of Lancastrian Ascendancy and Decline* (Oxford, 1988), pp. 401–6.
71 Henneman, *Development of War Finance*, pp. 197, 233.
72 H. Kleineke, 'The Commission de *Mutuo Faciendo* in the Reign of Henry VI', *EHR*, 106 (2001), pp. 1–30; Steel, *Receipt*, pp. 162–3. On the same day, however, Beaufort lent £17,666 13s 4d.
73 C. Liddy, *War, Politics and Finance in Late Medieval English Towns: Bristol, York and the Crown, 1350–1400* (Woodbridge, 2005), pp. 21–43 (figures quoted at 41–42).
74 Grummitt, 'Financial Administration', pp. 291–2.
75 B. Chevalier, 'Fiscalité muncipale et fiscalité d'état en France du XIVe a la fin du XVIe siècle: Deux systems liés et concurrents', *Genése de l'état moderne: prélèvement et redistribution*, ed. J.-P. Genet and M. Le Mené (Paris, 1987); Fryde, 'Financial policies', pp. 827–9.
76 Sherborne, 'Costs', pp. 145–6.
77 G. Harriss, 'Preference at the Medieval Exchequer', *BIHR*, 30 (1957), pp. 18–23.
78 R. Partington, 'The Nature of Noble Service to Edward III', *Political Society in Later Medieval England: A Festschrift for Christine Carpenter*, ed. B. Thompson and J. Watts (Woodbridge, 2015), pp. 83–4.
79 Grummitt, 'Financial Administration of Calais', pp. 288–92.
80 J. Stratford, '"Par le special commandement du Roy": Jewels and Plate Pledged for the Agincourt Expedition', *Henry V: New Interpretations*, ed. Dodd, pp. 157–70.
81 T. Moore, 'Score it Upon My Taille: The Use (and Abuse) of Tallies by the Medieval Exchequer', *Reading Medieval Studies*, 39 (2013), pp. 1–24.
82 Stratford, 'Par le special commandement', pp. 164, 167–8.
83 A. Bell, C. Brooks and T. Moore, 'The Non-use of Money: Credit Finance in the Middle Ages', *Money and Its Use in Medieval Europe – Three Decades On: Essays in Honour of Professor Peter Spufford*, ed. M. Allen and N. Mayhew (London, 2017), pp. 145–50.
84 A. Bossuat, 'Étude sur les emprunts royaux au début du XVe siècle: La politique financière du connétable Bernard d'Armagnac (1416–1418)', *Revue historique du droit français et étranger*, 4th series, 28 (1950), pp. 352–3.
85 Sir John Fortescue, *On the Laws and Governance of England*, ed. S. Lockwood (Cambridge, 1997), pp. 92–3.
86 A. Steel, *The Receipt of the Exchequer, 1377–1485* (Cambridge, 1954), pp. 18–20.
87 Bossuat, 'Les emprunts royaux', p. 353 n. 2.

88 A. Bell, C. Brooks and T. Moore, 'Interest in Medieval Accounts: Evidence from England, 1272–1340', *History*, 94 (2009), pp. 411–33.
89 But see Steel, *Receipt*, pp. 156–7 for a bookkeeping anomaly that may result from the failure to include a disguised interest payment in one of Beaufort's loans.
90 TNA, C 47/13/6.
91 A. Bell, C. Brooks, and T. Moore, 'Le crédit au moyen âge: les prets à la couronne d'Angleterre entre 1272 et 1345', Resources publiques et construction étatique en Europe XIII-XVIIIème siècle, Colloque organise par l'IGPDE avec l'Université Paris 1 Pantheon Sorbonne et ses laboratoires (IDHE, LAMOP, EA 127, SAMM) et le laboratoire d'excellence ReFi (heSam) (2015), pp. 117-130. English version of French published text available at "https://eur03.safelinks.protection.outlook.com/?url=http%3A%2F%2Fcentaur.reading.ac.uk%2F40292%2F&data=01%7C01%7CA.E.Curry%40soton.ac.uk%7C4bfc025a5e664c22af7a08d6eb1eceb9%7C4a5378f929f44d3ebe89669d03ada9d8%7C0&sdata=FWaDYDTadEONveakEI9waOjYm1iIOtsah8Tr5z9X8tU%3D&reserved=0"http://centaur.reading.ac.uk/40292/
92 Fryde, 'Financial Policies', pp. 858–9.
93 G. Harriss, 'Financial Policy', in *Henry V: The Practice of Kingship*, ed. G. Harriss (Oxford, 1985), pp. 160–64.
94 Bell et al., 'Crédit au moyen âge', pp. 123–5; A. Beardwood, *Alien Merchants in England 1350–1377* (Cambridge, MA, 1931), pp. 4–9, 122–3.

4 The Hundred Years War and the Church

Rory Cox

The European Middle Ages have often been described as an 'age of faith', but in truth historians know very little about the personal beliefs of the vast majority of medieval men and women. This is not to say that faith or, perhaps more accurately, religion was unimportant: far from it. The Middle Ages was a period in which institutionalised religion, in the shape of the Latin Church, played a central role in European society. The Church and its constituent elements – clergy, doctrine, law, property, administration, finances – touched upon all aspects of medieval daily life and was a fundamental force in shaping the attitudes and actions of peasants and nobles, civilians and soldiers.

Since the late 1970s, historians have shown an increasing interest in, and sensitivity to, what might be termed the social structures of war; that is to say, the wider political, economic and cultural conditions in which wars are fought. These social structures both affect and in turn are affected by the prosecution of war. During the course of the Hundred Years War, religion – primarily in the form of the institutional Church in England and France – was drawn into the war in a variety of ways, both directly and indirectly.

As a major landowner in both England and France, access to the material resources of the Church was vital to the war efforts of Plantagenet and Valois kings. To this extent, the clergy could hardly avoid becoming politicised; indeed, many were more than happy to involve themselves in the conflict and some even took up arms. While this involvement was often voluntary and could be to the advantage of individual clergy or religious houses, just as often such involvement was against the wishes of the clergy or papacy, and very much to the Church's detriment. For example, the destruction of ecclesiastical property was particularly acute in the areas of France most affected by the war, and English religious houses along the south coast and northern marches (along with Scottish religious houses) also suffered extensive damage.[1]

In terms of indirect involvement, Plantagenet and Valois kings appealed to divine authority in order to legitimate their political claims; thus English and French clergy were at the front line of the propaganda war. Theologians and canon lawyers were called upon to sanction violent actions according to well-established traditions of justifiable Christian warfare, and bishops and preachers were instructed to buoy public support from the pulpit by offering prayers or organising processions. At the level of high politics, the Avignon papacy was intermittently involved in negotiations for peace between the warring parties, yet Englishmen accused this Francophile institution of being partisan to the Valois cause. Whether the war brought about the effective 'nationalisation' of the English and French churches remains open to debate, but it is certain that in both countries the Church was politicised and became increasingly so over the course of the fourteenth and fifteenth centuries.[2] In the evolving rhetoric of the French and English crowns, one can see how a secular conflict began to be described in the language of holy war: it quickly became a war *in defensio fidei et defensio regni* ('in defence of the faith and in defence of the realm').[3] A further layer was added to this veneer of religious rhetoric by the Great Schism (1378–1418), during which international support for the popes in Rome or Avignon was largely determined by political agendas and divisions, with England and her allies favouring the Roman pontiff against France and her allies who supported the pope in Avignon.

It is clear, then, that in order to approach a fuller understanding of the Hundred Years War, one must give due attention to the influence and role of the Church and religion. This chapter will begin by examining the direct and practical involvement of the Church with the war, looking at the financial, administrative, military and diplomatic contributions of English and French ecclesiastics. The indirect involvement of the Church will then be assessed, principally the role played by the Church in shaping public opinion through disseminating royally mandated propaganda. Finally, the potential benefits and losses experienced by the clergy and institutional Church will be considered, as well as the theological underpinnings that justified the Anglo-French violence of the fourteenth and fifteenth centuries.

Military activity on the scale and duration of the Hundred Years War required the development of sophisticated governmental machinery. Nowhere was this more evident than in the fiscal systems that were required to fund the vast expenses of sustained warfare, and from which ecclesiastical institutions and persons were by no means exempt. In France, Capetian monarchs had long fostered their title as *rex Christianissimus* ('most Christian king'), and technically all churches in France were under the king's protection. Inheriting this Capetian legacy, Valois kings wielded significant influence and control over French churches, as expressed by the bishop of Arras in the *Parlement* of 1380:

> the king our lord has not only temporality but also divinity. For he is anointed [*iniunctus*] and gives benefices by royal right [*en régale*] as well as having the administration of the temporalities of bishoprics during vacancies, up until there are new bishops. He also has the care of all the churches in his kingdom.[4]

It was customary for French clergy to be largely immune from the direct taxes levied on the laity; they were also exempted from some indirect taxes, notably the *aides* (excise duty on wine, etc.) and extraordinary taxes, such as the later *taille*. This did not mean, however, that the financial resources of the French Church escaped royal taxation. As a result of Philip IV's humbling of Pope Boniface VIII at the turn of the fourteenth century, French kings were able to levy taxes of 10 per cent of ecclesiastical property (an ecclesiastical 'tenth') between 1302 and 1378 without having to seek papal permission, and the majority of this revenue was diverted to military expenditure. While post-Schism popes after Clement VII began to claw back some control over royal taxation of the Church, clerical immunity from direct lay taxes was all but suspended between 1386 and 1416. The financial relationship of French religious houses to the Anglo-French war was also considerably complicated after the treaty of Troyes (1420), which effectively split the French Church between those dioceses controlled by the Anglo-Burgundians and those controlled by the nascent 'court of Bourges' under the dauphin, later King Charles VII.[5] Nevertheless, both parties continued to request ecclesiastical tenths. In 1432, Charles VII complained that French benefices were being given to aliens, with the result that French money was funding his political enemies.[6] Exactly the same complaints had been made by Edward III regarding English benefices from the 1340s onwards, and had led to the royal seizure of a considerable number of 'alien' ecclesiastical benefices and priories throughout England and Wales.

The relationship between French kings and their domestic clergy, while generally amicable, was not without moments of animosity, primarily caused by the crown's financial demands. Even in the early years of the Hundred Years War, French churchmen complained about the financial pressures imposed by royal policies. The debasement of the coinage was especially unpopular, so much so that Edward III highlighted it as a criticism of Philip VI in his 1340 proclamation to the French public.⁷ One French prelate, Gilles li Muisis (d. 1352), the abbot of St-Martin de Tournai, wittily observed:

> Money and the currency are most obscure things,
> They keep on going up and down and no-one knows why,
> If you want to win you lose however hard you try.⁸

The relationship between the French crown and the French prelates was particularly tested in 1356 following the defeat at Poitiers and the capture of John II. The Parisian Estates-General of October 1356, summoned by the dauphin's council, elected a joint committee of eighty members, including the outspoken bishop of Laon, Robert le Coq, and headed by the archbishop of Reims, Jean de Craon. Rather than simply granting the dauphin large sums of money to address the political and military crisis, the committee of the Estates presented a list of complaints that focussed on the mismanagement of royal taxes, the debasement of the coinage and the abuses of certain ministers of the royal court, including the Chancellor, Chamberlain and chief financial officers. Moreover, the dauphin was to be advised by a permanent commission of twenty-seven clerics and laymen appointed by the Estates. If these demands were granted, the clergy and nobility agreed to grant 15 per cent of their revenues for a year while the towns would provide one soldier per one hundred hearths. In spite of the political instability, these demands were simply unacceptable to the dauphin; he rejected them and suspended the Estates, being fortunate that the hostility of the capital was not matched in the provinces.⁹ Nevertheless, this was not a unique example of criticism of royal policy by leading French ecclesiastics over the demands placed upon the resources of the Church. Even in the 1450s, Jean Juvénal des Ursins, archbishop of Reims, complained to Charles VII that 'By all the kings whom God has helped in time past, neither ecclesiastical persons nor ecclesiastical jurisdiction was so trampled on, and is so trampled on, as in your time.'¹⁰

In England, the Church arguably played an even more important role in financing Plantagenet military ambition. It is beyond doubt that the sums committed to the war were staggering: by the end of 1337, before any major hostilities had even taken place, Edward III had already committed to paying £124,000 to his leading continental allies; by the end of 1340, Edward had spent nearly £400,000, with little to show for his huge outlay.¹¹ It has also been calculated that between 1369 and 1381 the English crown spent more than a million pounds on the war, with few tangible gains.¹² Direct and indirect taxation of the laity – particularly customs on wool – provided the majority of this money, but the Church also contributed a substantial share. As in France, the most effective royal tax on the Church was the ecclesiastical tenth, requested of the Convocations of the two archdioceses, Canterbury and York. Over the course of Edward III's reign, both provinces granted 23 tenths, totalling over £421,000. In addition, Edward was granted a further special subsidy of £50,000 in 1371, after significant pressure applied by the Black Prince.[13] Indeed, Edward III was able to secure unprecedented levels of taxation from parliament and Convocation, beginning with the 1337 triennial grant of a tenth from the Church and a fifteenth from the laity. It was probably assumed that this generous grant 'represented a final effort which would be rewarded with victory and peace', but this proved to be overly optimistic.[14] As the Rolls of Parliament repeatedly attest, the reasons given for the ongoing financial assistance of the clergy and laity was the 'compelling necessity' of the kingdom's defence and upholding the honour of the king.

As mentioned, the principal means of extracting money from the Church was the ecclesiastical tenth. The value of an ecclesiastical tenth in England during fourteenth century was about £20,000, with Canterbury province having to raise £16,000 of that sum. As a rough estimate, the crown could have raised £432,000 from Canterbury from 1337 up to the end of the fourteenth century, with a further £466,000 during the fifteenth-century phase of the war.[15] Of course, it was rare for medieval governments to realise the full value of their potential tax revenue: corruption, administrative failings and the inability to collect or to enforce payment in peripheral territories were just some of the obstacles. But it would be fair to say that kings could expect ecclesiastical taxes to arrive with fewer difficulties than taxes on the laity, and it should not be forgotten that many clergymen acted as tax collectors.

Aside from direct taxation, there were a number of other ways that the English Church could be compelled to contribute. Kings could 'request' loans (a demand in all but name), although ecclesiastical individuals and institutions were not as extensively mined for credit as leading lay subjects – the de la Poles, for example – and the Italian banks. Kings also exploited their traditional feudal rights, directing the income of ecclesiastical offices during periods of vacancies (at the same time ensuring that certain offices remained vacant as long as possible), and seizing the temporalities of prelates who opposed royal policies.

From very early in the war, a marked distrust and resentment of foreign clergy and the pro-French Avignon papacy led to the prohibition of payments to popes or cardinals in Avignon. French clergy in particular were suspected of espionage. In 1338, French monks were removed from

St Michael's Mount and Lewes, and during English campaigns clerical envoys were rarely allowed within sight of the main army, out of fear that they would divulge valuable strategic information to the enemy.[16] The crown turned xenophobia into financial profit with the seizure of income from benefices held by foreigners and from so-called 'alien priories', that is, religious houses that were the dependencies of foreign (usually French) mother-houses. The Statutes of Provisors (1351 and 1390) and of Praemunire (1353 and 1393) were part of a process in which the government tested how far it could resist the distant authority of the papacy and secure tighter control of ecclesiastical incomes, especially those belonging to alien clergy. Indeed, Richard II's minority government went so far as to expel foreign clergy from England in 1378, while, in 1414, under Henry V, alien priories theoretically ceased to exist, being entirely taken over by the crown and their property distributed among royal courtiers and existing or new religious foundations.[17]

Taken as a whole, clergy in both France and England were remarkably acquiescent to the financial demands of various kings between 1337 and 1453. This can be partly explained by the fact that, as a divinely instituted ruler, the demands of the king were not easily refused by ecclesiastics, especially in cases pertaining to national defence or royal honour. To withhold aid from the king in such matters was tantamount to questioning the very legitimacy of the king's authority and cause. Not only were most churchmen unwilling to take this step, many bishops, especially in England, proved themselves to be enthusiastic supporters of royal military policy. This support went far beyond financial contributions and involved the clergy directly in military administration and even military service. Indeed, perhaps the most important function of clergymen during wartime was their capacity to act as administrators, ensuring that the numerous logistical challenges of military expeditions ran as smoothly as possible. Clergymen could also find themselves – willingly or unwillingly – participating more directly in military service. Such involvement was not new. The First Lateran Council (1123) had issued a prohibition against the fortification of churches but this precept of canon law met with little recognition in practice. Laymen and ecclesiastics across Europe were responsible for encouraging the militarisation of Church architecture, particularly in marcher zones where the threat of raiding was most acute and chronic.[18] As great landowners with various legal functions, bishops and abbots were often the natural foci for the organisation of local defences. In the north of England, for example, bishops of Durham and Carlisle and archbishops of York were frequently engaged in resisting Scottish incursions. It was Archbishop Zouche of York and Bishop Kirkby of Carlisle who defeated and captured David II of Scotland at the battle of Neville's Cross in 1346. Likewise, bishops and abbots along the Channel coast were increasingly called upon to organise and lead local defences against Franco-Castilian naval raids from 1337 onwards.

This active military service contravened the strictures of canon law, which allowed clerics to exhort others to fight in a just war but generally prohibited clerics from bearing arms. Admittedly, the prohibitions against shedding blood were subject to various interpretations, with some canonists permitting self-defence if absolutely unavoidable (i.e. to save one's own life) and others recognising that bishops with temporal functions were obliged to respond to their sovereign's call to arms.[19] Moreover, when it came to clerical arms-bearing, the application of canon law had always been subject to occasional lapses or loose interpretation in practice. The story of Bishop Odo of Bayeux fighting at the battle of Hastings with a velvet-padded mace (so as not to shed blood) is a favourite example of historians and undoubtedly verges on the comic. But there were many examples throughout the Middle Ages of aristocratic churchmen choosing to share in the violent activities of their social peers, and the emergence of monastically inspired military orders such as the Templars, Hospitallers and Teutonic Knights arguably helped to erode further the hazy divide between lay and clerical violence.[20] Needless to say, the Hundred Years War provided ample opportunities for individual clerics to indulge their martial tastes, as well as forcing others into service which they would otherwise have wished to avoid. The military participation of clergy on both sides of the conflict did not escape the notice or criticism of the papacy. Pope Innocent VI addressed the kings of England and France in 1356, denouncing the involvement of clergy – whether as victims or participants – in the Anglo-French war. It is not without some irony, therefore, that during John II's captivity in Bordeaux following his defeat at the battle of Poitiers that same year, the king's leading advisor was Guillaume de Melun, archbishop of Sens, who had fought at Poitiers with his own retinue of two dozen men-at-arms.[21]

While such examples occurred relatively frequently, military service by individual (usually aristocratic) clerics did not reflect universal practice. In England, however, this was subject to a dramatic change in 1368, when Edward III took the seemingly unprecedented step of directly commanding arrays of the clergy across the country.[22] To achieve this, Edward required the express permission of the bishops in Parliament, which he was granted. The first royal writ of array was issued on 6 July 1368, timed to coincide with the imminent expiration in the following year of the Brétigny peace settlement, and at least ten further writs of array were issued at irregular intervals until 1418. All the writs stressed the threat of invasion posed by England's enemies and, with only a few exceptions, ordered bishops to:

> Cause all abbots, priors and men of religion and other ecclesiastical persons of your diocese whatsoever to be armed and arrayed, furnished with arms every man between the ages aforesaid [16 and 60] according to his estate and means, and put in thousands, hundreds and twenties, so that they shall be ready with other of the king's lieges to march against the said enemies within the realm, with God's help to overcome and destroy them, defeating and crushing their insolence and malice.[23]

These writs were intended to help form a militia, in addition to arrays of the laity, that could provide a first response against raiding or a last line of defence against invasion. Indeed, the arrays of the clergy were identical to the arrays of the laity as stipulated under the 1285 Statutes of Winchester, and included every rank of clergyman.[24] Nor were these arrays insignificant in terms of manpower. Bruce McNab has calculated from the surviving records that the clerical arrays of 1415 and 1418 would have recruited a minimum of 11,769 and 15,487 men respectively.[25]

Why the practice of arraying the clergy ceased in 1418 is unclear. It may have been that the threat of French raiding was perceived to be greatly diminished after Henry V's successes in Normandy, or that clerical resistance to the practice, which had always existed, had gradually increased. The Convocation of York had tried (unsuccessfully) to secure immunity from array as a condition of the triennial subsidy granted to Edward III in 1370.[26] Likewise, the array returns from the bishop of Lincoln in 1418 record that the Lincoln convent of Friars Minor obstinately refused to be arrayed, and it is likely that many other religious houses were less than enthusiastic about the demands for array. Nonetheless, taken as a whole, bishops and the wider clergy seem to have acquiesced quite readily to their own militarisation; bishops even went so far as to impose canonical penalties on clergy who refused to take up arms.[27]

If one asks why English clergy agreed to arm themselves during this period, then simple necessity must have been an important motivation. Royal proclamations predicting invasion and ordering preparations were repeatedly issued from 1345 onwards, encouraging public fear and support for Edward III's military ventures by fostering a state of emergency. This fear may have been exaggerated, but it was not entirely baseless. Even after the English military successes of the 1340s and 1350s, the burning of Winchelsea and several other south coasts towns in 1359 was a potent reminder of the vulnerability of many Channel ports. Franco-Castilian raiding during the 1370s was particularly severe; in response, the abbot of St Augustine Abbey Canterbury and the abbot of Battle Abbey were both vigorous in local defence. In short, if clergy – whether in the south or the north – agreed to take up arms in defence of their property and persons, it was often because no one else was going to do it for them. Furthermore, the government played on ecclesiastical fears of an existential threat to the English Church itself, with each writ stressing that the defence of the realm was inextricably bound to the protection of the Church of England against a pro-French and ever cash-hungry papacy.[28]

The religious and political problems generated by a partisan papacy were significantly exacerbated by the Great Schism of 1378. The schism added a religious dimension to Anglo-French animosity which led to further opportunities for clergy to directly involve themselves in warfare, against what had become a schismatic adversary. One notable opportunity for English clergy to take the field was the Flanders Crusade of 1383, led by the bellicose bishop of Norwich, Henry Despenser. Although ostensibly a holy war sanctioned by the Roman pope, Urban VI, the expedition became embroiled in the political exigencies of the English government. After an initially successful but ultimately confused and aimless expedition in the Low Countries, which culminated in ignominious retreat, Bishop Despenser was eventually impeached in the autumn of 1383 for his various failures on the Continent.[29] In England, the crusade was bitterly opposed by, among others, the pacifist theologian John Wyclif.[30] Nevertheless, the Flanders Crusade is a manifest example of how religious divisions emanating from the papacy must be considered within the political framework of the Anglo-French conflict and vice versa.

With these divisions in mind, it is hardly surprising that the role of the papacy as a peacemaker in the Hundred Years War was consistently undermined by perceptions of impartiality. Following the election of Clement V in 1305 and the beginning of the Avignon residency from 1309, the papacy was widely – and it must be said, quite fairly – regarded to be in thrall to the French crown. A good example of this partisanship in practice can be seen in the case of the papal envoy, Cardinal Talleyrand of Périgord, who was active in negotiations prior to the battle of Poitiers (1356) and during John II's subsequent captivity in Bordeaux. In England, not only was Talleyrand 'distrusted as an adherent of the French crown', he was also singled out by Parliament 'as one of the most notorious papal beneficiaries in England'.[31] As if this was not bad enough, Talleyrand's position as a disinterested mediator was further tarnished by the fact that his own retainers had fought for the French at Poitiers. Although Froissart insists that this was done without the cardinal's knowledge, the Black Prince took an exceedingly dim view of it.[32]

With two popes contesting legitimacy in Rome and Avignon in a papal schism from 1378 to 1418, which was finally resolved at the Council of Constance (1414–18), and the continuing weaknesses of the papacy during the subsequent conciliar process that dragged on until the late 1440s, individual popes lacked the universal support or authority necessary to impose any kind of peace settlement on either France or England. This, coupled with the tenacity and obstinacy of personalities such as Edward III, Philip VI, Charles V, Henry V and Charles VII, produced a toxic mix strong enough to poison any serious negotiations that could have brought about a final peace. Indeed, one should not underestimate the degree to which, on many occasions, one or both sides *desired* conflict.

In light of this inherent weakness, the efforts of Benedict XII to prevent the outbreak of hostilities in the 1330s, or the role of Clement VI in brokering the Truce of Malestroit (1343) and sponsoring the Avignon Peace Conference (1344), or the Guînes peace talks (1352–4) encouraged by Innocent VI and the Bruges Conference (1375–7) organised by Gregory XI, were all ultimately doomed to failure. An additional stumbling block was the papal interpretation of the English king-duke's relationship to the French crown, which popes such as Benedict XII and Clement VI understood as a problem of a recalcitrant vassal owing service and loyalty to his overlord, the king of France. English demands to hold an enlarged Aquitaine in full sovereignty were not looked upon favourably, while the Plantagenet claim to the French throne was never recognised by the papacy. Pope Martin V (1417–31) refused to endorse the treaty of Troyes, which disinherited the dauphin Charles and named Henry V as Charles VI's legitimate successor; this policy was continued by Eugenius IV (1431–47), who officially recognised Charles VII as the king of France in 1434, therefore scuppering his authority, in the eyes of the English, as a mediator at the Congress of Arras (1435).[33]

While the papacy met with little success in tempering or halting the Anglo-French war, members of the clergy nonetheless played a vital role in the diplomatic corps of the major players. University-trained clergy provided a ready supply of personnel who possessed the literacy and administrative skills necessary – individuals trained in civil and canon law were particularly sought after. Throughout the duration of the conflict, ecclesiastics fulfilled a variety of diplomatic functions, from ambassador to messenger, advisor to clerk. Moreover, the customary ecclesiastical privilege of immunity from violence was a useful asset for what was potentially dangerous employment, although it was by no means a guarantee of safety.

These, then, were some of the ways in which religion and the Church were directly involved in the Anglo-French conflicts. Of equal importance, however, were the various ways in which religion and the Church could be utilised to influence the prosecution of the conflict through indirect means. The theoretical underpinnings of justified violence largely stemmed from the Church itself. A doctrine of justifiable violence had been developed over several centuries by Christian theologians and canon lawyers, who built upon the foundations laid by classical authors such as Aristotle and Cicero. A distinctly Christian legitimation of violence is identifiable as early as the fourth century and was constructed around three key principles: the existence of a just cause, the presence of a proper authority to declare and wage war, and the maintenance of correct intention prior to and during war – that is, war had to be waged out of a love for justice and a wish to protect the innocent, *not* out of a desire to conquer or a vindictive lust for revenge.[34] The rhetoric produced by Plantagenet and Valois kings appealed to these commonly accepted principles in order to justify and legitimate their political claims and their extensive use of violence as a means by which to achieve them.[35] On the one hand, we may be inclined to be sceptical about the extent to which either side took such rhetoric seriously, and believe that they simply paid lip service to such legal niceties. On the other hand, late medieval France and England were remarkably litigious societies, and one should not underestimate the importance that people through all levels of society attached to legal rights, precedent and procedure. War was considered part of a legal process, and waging a lawful war was therefore integral to any claim of legitimate ownership of territory or spoils; most importantly of all, it was integral to any legitimate claim of lordship (*dominium*), which was at the very heart of the Anglo-French dispute.

Appeals to God and justice are recurrent in Edward III's 1340 proclamation of his rights to the French throne, and were part of a strategy to present his war as essentially defensive:

> Sir Philip Valois ... seized the kingdom [of France] by force, against God and justice ... We have now, after good and mature deliberation, and placing our faith in God and the good people, taken up the title to the government of the said kingdom, as is our duty ... And be informed that although we have, on several occasions, offered reasonable ways of peace to the said Sir Philip, he has been unwilling to make any such proposals to us, and has made war against us in our other lands, and is trying to defeat us utterly with his power; thus we are compelled by necessity to defend ourselves and to seek our rights.[36]

Naturally, French kings and ecclesiastics responded with similar claims to legal right and divine justice. In a sermon preached in 1414, the abbot of

Saint-Denis relied upon biblical references to portray Henry V of England as 'a subject who is unfaithful to his lord ... who rebels against his prince ... who seizes his lord's lands'; in response, Charles VI must punish him 'by force of arms', for the king is 'God's lieutenant, [and] must avenge himself of the sin'.[37] When the fifteenth-century English commander Sir John Fastolf observed that 'God, the sovereign Judge, in the pursuing of their right has ever greatly favoured [King Henry and his predecessors] ... and given them many worthy victories; or else it should be said and deemed that the king had no power or puissance with which to sustain his right', he was expressing a commonly held view that the Anglo-French war, like any other question of justice, was ultimately dependent upon the will of God.[38]

Possessing a body of law and precedent that legitimated violent action was all very well, but a far greater challenge faced by English and French monarchs was how to disseminate this message to their subjects, for it was they who would be required to provide the material resources for the defence of their monarch's 'rights'. It is difficult to exaggerate, therefore, the importance of the capacity of domestic clergy to shape public opinion, that thing which 'does not immediately control policy, but it sets limits within which the men who make policy must operate'.[39] The historian's attempt to establish medieval public opinion has been likened to 'astronomers trying to prove the existence of a new heavenly body which they have not yet seen'.[40] It is true that the shifting opinions of the late medieval English and French publics remain largely veiled from us, but we can be confident of attempts made to try to shape those opinions. The Church was uniquely placed in this regard: clergy had a pastoral duty to preach, churches were frequently the focus of community life (particularly public displays of piety or communal support for the king), and the administrative structures of the diocesan system, as well as the ability of many clerics to read and write, made them vital conduits for disseminating news into the parishes. Alongside this, there was in the later Middle Ages what John Watts has referred to as an 'expanding discursive community', ready and willing to receive and partake in news, debate and politics.[41]

As both kingdoms made ever-increasing demands on their public to provide the resources necessary for war, it became ever more important for royal governments to influence public attitudes about the war in order to ensure a continuing level of compliance.[42] It was Herbert Hewitt who first drew attention to the extensive use made of the Church in the arena of war propaganda during Edward III's reign, and this has been followed by further work on the subject by several scholars, above all Alison McHardy.[43] As she notes, Edward III 'was heir to a well-established tradition when he sought divine help for his military and political enterprises'; prayers for the king had been part of daily worship since the eleventh century.[44] The same was true for French kings who had long fostered the title *rex Christianissimus* and had benefitted from sophisticated religious propaganda, particularly in association with the royal abbey of Saint-Denis. From the thirteenth century down to 1461, French kings commissioned the production there of the *Grandes Chroniques de France* as well as the *Chronique du Religieux de Saint-Denys* (1380–1422).

Valois commission and dissemination of complex and varied media (chronicles, manifestos, pamphlets) are evidence of the refined and subtle qualities of French royal propaganda during the Hundred Years War. The English crown, in contrast, favoured the more direct medium of the royal writ as the principal method for disseminating its message through the Church: writs were issued to demand specific actions, to justify royal military and fiscal policy, and to rally the support of the public.[45] The most common requests were prayers for the well-being of the king (*ora pro rege*) and the success of specific military expeditions. Requests for votive masses, preaching tours to drum up public support, public processions for intercession or thanksgiving, vigils, almsgiving and bell ringing were also frequently issued. Bishops were even co-opted into disseminating the campaign letters that were regularly sent back to England as news bulletins and pieces of pro-government propaganda.[46]

Religious processions provided an opportunity for a very public display of piety and support for the crown, with the added incentive that indulgences could be earned through attendance. Processions could be either penitential in nature, designed to seek divine favour for a forthcoming expedition, or celebratory, organised in the wake of a recent victory. Importantly, processions brought together clergy and laity in a communal action of support, such as those ordered in Winchester by Bishop William Edington prior to the English campaign of 1346. The bishop decreed that there should be processions 'on market-days, going around the church or through the market-place, *as weather permits*'.[47] This stereotypically English concern for the weather could be interpreted as evidence of a less than enthusiastic response to royal demands for processions; however, it more likely reveals a pragmatic realisation that conducting processions in bad weather would simply serve to dampen (quite literally!) the spirits of the inhabitants of Winchester rather than bolster their support for the war and the inevitable demands upon their resources that accompanied it. In France, too, religious processions were a feature of royal propaganda. Following the French conquest of Normandy and Gascony towards the end of the war, Charles VII ordered processions 'such as it is usual to perform in such cases, when Our Lord has bestowed such very great favours upon us and upon our kingdom'.[48]

The relative lack of sophistication and volume of English royal propaganda compared to that of their Valois competitors might partly be explained by the fact that, for much of the war, the English appeared to have the upper hand. Victory was in the hands of God: divine approval was thus self-evident in victory, rendering further efforts to convince the public of legitimacy or success superfluous. In comparison, the Valois were on the back foot for significant stretches of time (1340–69 and 1392–1429), and arguably had much more work to do to convince their subjects that justice and God were truly on their side.[49] It is telling that serious and sustained criticism of the war only emerged in England from the late fourteenth century – when defeat indicated a withdrawal of divine favour – and originated from a diverse range of clerical sources. These included orthodox clergy such as Bishop Thomas Brinton, but also more radical clergy such as the Oxford theologian John Wyclif and his Lollard successors, men such as William Swinderby and Walter Brut. Condemnations of war can be found throughout Wyclif's theological and political treatises as well as his numerous Latin sermons. From the early 1370s until his death in 1384, Wyclif developed what can only be described as the earliest doctrine of absolute pacifism to emerge from the medieval West. Not only did he criticise the war in France, but he went as far as to deny the right of self-defence, claiming that it was always better to die as a martyr for Christ than to condemn one's own soul by committing homicide. However, while his pacifist teachings had some immediate influence on the Lollard and Hussite movements, and perhaps a modicum of influence on writers like William Langland, Wyclif's pacifism had no major impact on late medieval clerical attitudes to war.[50]

In terms of communicating royal propaganda, the greatest value of the Church for English and French kings was its ability to influence public opinion from the pulpit. This could be exercised through preaching, conducting special services and offering prayers for success or thanksgiving. Indeed, this role may have had a fundamental impact on English Church liturgy, as the dissemination of war propaganda via religious services was a major catalyst in bringing about the regular use of English language in churches.[51] We have a good knowledge of Plantagenet requests for these practices since many are preserved in the English chancery records and in various bishops' registers. In Lincoln diocese alone, special prayers were requested on fifty-one occasions between 1337 and 1453, and, of these, thirty-four were principally concerned with the war.[52] From the king to the bishops, from the bishops to the archdeacons, and from the archdeacons to rectors, vicars and parish priests, the machinery of the Church could reach all corners of the kingdom and, more importantly, all levels of society.[53]

That medieval governments fully recognised the potential of the clergy to sway public opinion is evinced through the English treatment of the Church in Normandy during their occupation. As Henry V steadily conquered the duchy between 1415 and 1419, winning the good graces of the Norman clergy – or at least avoiding their outright opposition – was a strategic priority and crucial to consolidating English rule. The Norman Rolls show that it was frequently individual clerics who led their parishioners to swear fealty to the new king.[54] The English essentially adopted a carrot and stick policy: rewarding those clergy who swore fealty to the new regime, while confiscating the benefices of those clergy who fled the duchy and refused to accept English rule. The advantage of the confiscations was that these offices could then be redistributed to clergy who *were* willing to accept English rule, consequently creating a patronage network of individuals indebted to the English government. Broadly speaking, this policy seems to have been successful. While secret anti-English sentiments may have existed below the surface, there is very little evidence of overt hostility from the Norman clergy. Indeed, in 1430 John, duke of Bedford, was bestowed with the honour of being elected as a canon of Rouen cathedral. But it should come as little surprise that there was limited opposition to English rule from the Norman Church. Ultimately the clergy benefitted from governmental stability and the economic prosperity that it engendered. Up until the late 1430s the English provided these conditions, and thus their tenure was met with either support or acquiescence.

In the kingdoms of England and France, religious buildings had traditionally provided an important focal point for news distribution and collection. Edward III's 1340 proclamation explaining his rights to the French throne was to be disseminated in France by being 'proclaimed publicly and ... displayed on the doors of churches and in other public places, so that it may come to the notice of all'.[55] When English soldiers fortuitously 'discovered' a French invasion plan (dated 23 March 1339) during the sack of Caen in 1346, it was promptly shipped back to London and read aloud at St Paul's Cross by Archbishop Stratford of Canterbury, *ut per hoc excitaret populum regni* – 'so that this might rouse the people of the kingdom'.[56] Indeed, the physical structure of a religious building could itself become a medium for propaganda, with stained glass and sculpture reaching exceptional levels of sophistication during the late Middle Ages.[57] The Great East Window of the Benedictine Abbey of St Peter, now Gloucester cathedral, was probably the largest window in England at the time of its construction (*c.* 1350–60). The Gloucester window, nicknamed the 'Crécy window', depicts a number of lords who fought at the battle of Crécy or who later joined the siege of Calais. It has been argued that the window was commissioned to celebrate these English victories and directly associate them with divine providence.[58] The Collegiate Chapel of St George at Windsor, founded by Edward III in 1348 as the spiritual home for his Order of the Garter, is adorned with a blend of sacred and chivalric imagery intended to inspire the English military elite and to project an image of a martial dynasty in harmony with the sacred. Similarly, the tombs of Edward III and Henry V in Westminster Abbey were religious and political sculptures, just as the Abbey of Saint-Denis and the Sainte-Chapelle in Paris provided the setting for Capetian and Valois religious-political art of a similar vein. The French royal arms were themselves subject to politico-religious considerations, with Charles V ordering a reduction in the number of *fleurs de lis* to three in February 1376, in order to honour the Trinity and to differentiate the French arms from Plantagenet uses of the *fleur de lis*, which Edward III had quartered into the English royal arms in 1340.[59]

The patronage of religious institutions and art served a variety of functions, from seeking divine favour for future political projects to displaying a very worldly image of power. Perhaps the most important function it served was as an act of penance, fulfilling the desire of the patron to mitigate divine punishment for sin and ease the transition into heaven by completing 'good works' on earth. In this regard, the Anglo-French war – in providing countless opportunities for sin – was highly conducive to religious patronage, as soldiers engaged in a form of spiritual money-laundering, converting their fortunes derived from violence into a form of wealth that could benefit their souls. Prominent English commanders of the Hundred Years War certainly founded chapels and churches, including the collegiate churches endowed by Henry of Grosmont, duke of Lancaster at Leicester (1356), Sir Robert Knolles at Pontefract (1385), Sir Hugh Calveley at Bunbury (1386) and Edward, duke of York at Fotheringhay (1411). While not all such projects were funded directly from war booty, they were expressions of an aristocratic culture that blended penance with largesse and display. This is particularly notable in the exquisite architecture of Saint-Mary's Warwick, which was patronised by the Beauchamp earls of Warwick over the course of the fourteenth and fifteenth centuries.[60] Some of the most notorious English captains in France, such as Knolles and Grosmont, were conversely some of the most generous patrons of religious institutions in England; Grosmont even went on to compose the devotional work *Le livre de seyntz medicines* (1353).[61] Following the example of Edward III, English monarchs particularly favoured English saints such as Thomas Becket, Edmund of Bury and Edward the Confessor, which Ormrod has described as 'an attempt to promote national pride and to drum up support for the king's wars'.[62] From the reign of Edward I, St George was increasingly appropriated as an 'English' saint, and this was accelerated by Edward III's devotion to St George and the saint's association with the Order of the Garter.[63] In this sense, patronage of religious institutions could provide a potent combination of penance, displays of personal wealth and power, and proto-nationalist sentiment.

The complex relationship between the violent actions of individual soldiers fighting in the Hundred Years War and their private penance can also be seen in the persistence of the crusade ideal within both the English and the French military class. Even by 1389, the French courtier Philippe de Mézières still blamed the English for causing Philip VI to abort his planned crusade of 1337.[64] But during the relatively peaceful decade of 1390s, during which the Truce of Leulinghem was extended and Richard II agreed to marry Charles VI's daughter, Isabella, English troops were willing to join French and other crusaders in an expedition against the Ottoman Turks. While the crusade culminated in a disastrous defeat of the Christian army at Nicopolis on 25 September 1396, it demonstrates that the appeal of crusade was still very much alive for soldiers who also participated in the Anglo-French conflict in the fourteenth century. Indeed, a famous example of international knightly camaraderie based upon the shared experience of crusade can be seen during the English sack of Caen in July 1346, during which, according to Froissart, the Count of Eu and the Count of Tancarville (the Constable and Chamberlain of France, respectively) sought the protection of the English knight Sir Thomas Holland, with whom 'they had campaigned together in Granada and Prussia and on other expeditions'.[65]

While certain religious houses might have benefitted from the patronage of returning soldiers, this generosity was a double-edged sword for the Church as a whole, for while one hand gave to the Church the other hand took away. The type of sin that could prick the conscience of a soldier might well include the devastation or looting of religious property, which occurred on a vast scale during the course of the Hundred Years War. Quite aside from the various seizures of domestic Church property and income undertaken by English and French kings, the Church suffered extensive destruction of its property as a direct effect of military operations. Like any civilian property, churches, chapels, abbeys and monasteries offered soft targets for armies on campaign, and very often housed significant wealth. For soldiers who fully expected to supplement their wages by taking booty, these targets were too inviting to be ignored. Given the fact that the majority of fighting took place on the Continent, it was French ecclesiastical houses that bore the greatest material losses as a result of the war. Nonetheless, substantial levels of destruction and looting also inflicted upon religious property in Scotland, the northern English Marches and the Low Countries. There is evidence that commanders issued disciplinary edicts instructing their troops to spare ecclesiastical property and persons: Edward III did so in 1346, Richard II in 1385 and Henry V did so on several occasions. However, these edicts did not guarantee universal ecclesiastical immunity, and commanders were clearly prepared to plunder certain religious houses when it suited their strategic objectives or financial requirements.[66]

Henri Denifle's study and compilation of documents relating to losses suffered by French religious houses remains the seminal work on this subject. Documents produced by religious houses, detailing or summarising their losses, were preserved in the cartularies of the houses themselves, in the French royal chancery and in the papal archives. In one such document – a letter sent to Pope Martin V in 1429 from the Augustinian monastery of St Marie de Cella in Poitou – the abbot pleaded poverty 'on account of the whirlwinds of war (*propter guerrarum turbines*), deaths from pestilences and other vexatious events'.[67] Documents such as this were produced not simply to record damages and loss of income, but to request aid or, more usually, to request exemption from royal or papal taxation. With this in mind, these documents are far from uncomplicated, as each institution had a financial incentive to emphasise or even exaggerate the level of damage suffered. Moreover, as the records collected by Denifle show, while many ecclesiastical losses were the direct result of warfare, this was not always the case: disease, famine and weather all played their part as well.

While not disregarding other factors, the conflict remained a major cause of destruction and depopulation in the areas that it touched – predominantly the south-western, north-western and northern counties of France. The fifteenth-century French bishops Jean Juvénal des Ursins and Thomas Basin both wrote movingly about the suffering of the clergy and other non-combatants in northern France. This suffering was exacerbated by the fact that the targeting of non-combatants was not restricted to periods of open hostilities or campaigns, nor was it committed solely by English soldiers. The activities of *routiers* and *écorcheurs* were a plague on the French kingdom from the 1350s onwards and showed scant regard for the Church or anybody else. Famously, the company of Arnaud (Regnault) de Cervoles, nicknamed 'the Archpriest', held Pope Innocent VI to ransom at Avignon in 1358, only departing after being paid 1,000 gold florins.[68] The actions of the Archpriest's company showed a remarkable disregard for papal or spiritual authority. Even troops taking royal pay indulged in predatory behaviour, as attested by Jean Juvénal des Ursins in a letter dated 1433:

> I certainly do not mean to say that these crimes are committed only by the enemy; for they have also been carried out by those who call themselves

the king's men, who have, with the pretext of *appatis* and otherwise, taken prisoner men, women, and small children, without distinction of age or sex; raped women and girls, captured husbands and fathers and killed them in the presence of their wives and daughters ... kidnapped priests, monks, clergy, and labourers; put them in shackles and other instruments of torment called "monkeys", and then beaten them, by which some were mutilated, others driven mad.[69]

The accounts of Ursins and Basin are unquestionably histrionic in their descriptions of suffering and were intended to be moralistic in tone, meaning that one must take a cautious approach to their descriptions of wanton destruction; but nor should they be entirely dismissed. As early as 1373, Charles V recognised that his troops had been responsible for pillaging and robbing his subjects, and issued ordinances that sought to 'prevent these aforementioned harms and several others concerning the war'. This was repeated almost verbatim sixty-five years later by Charles VII in the preamble to his military ordinances (1439), explaining that military reform was necessary 'in order to take precautions against and to provide a remedy to bring an end to the great excesses and pillages made and committed by the soldiery, who for a long time have lived on the people without the order of justice'.[70] Much of the problem derived from unreliable wage payment, with soldiers and commanders expecting to replace or supplement irregular wages through plundering or extorting the civilian population, including the clergy.

The suffering inflicted upon the civilian population – lay and clerical – did not go unnoticed by the papacy. In the aftermath of Edward III's campaign in the north-east of France in 1339, Pope Benedict XII granted 6,000 gold florins for the relief of the inhabitants of Cambrai, concerning which a full report survives of how this money was paid out in two instalments (totalling 9,020 *livres tournois*) through Bertrand Carit, the archdeacon of Eu. Although this type of generous financial relief was not frequently forthcoming from the papacy, Benedict XII's successors did repeatedly write to French and English monarchs complaining of the pillaging and destruction of churches and the violence done to clergy and other non-combatants, particularly women, as a result of the Anglo-French conflict.[71]

In spite of the many damages that the Hundred Years War inflicted upon the Church, it should be remembered that warfare could also offer significant opportunities for advancement and profit for certain individuals and institutions. The endowment or embellishment of churches and chapels in England, either paid for by war booty or partly motivated by violent actions committed on the Continent, has already been noted. For ambitious clerics, the war could provide unique opportunities for career progression. Climbing the ranks of the ecclesiastical hierarchy had always required the support of influential patrons, and those clerks who were attached to magnates involved with the war could find themselves particularly valued as administrators within a campaigning army or a newly conquered territory, or as trusted envoys. John Harewell, a cleric in the retinue of the Black Prince, rose to become bishop of Bath and Wells and was made the first English Chancellor of Aquitaine (1364–70).[72] Many knights took their own priests with them on campaign, and sought the necessary papal licences for private confessors and portable altars. Many of the clergy who applied for licences to leave their parish (*licencia absentandi ab ecclesia*) in order to go on campaign appear to have been junior-level parish priests, willing to risk the dangers of war and foreign travel in return for the potential rewards that such service could bring.[73] In providing for the religious needs of the army – especially hearing confessions and performing Masses prior to battle – clerics helped to maintain morale among the troops.

The link between religion and morale was nowhere better illustrated than in the person, actions and influence of one the most famous and divisive figures to emerge from the Hundred Years War – Joan of Arc.[74] The meteoric rise of *la Pucelle* ('the Maid'), her brief prominence and her tragic end are evidence of how religious conviction could have startling effects on military success. Indeed, her actions and legacy continue to stimulate fascination and disagreement in scholarship and popular history to this day.[75]

Joan grew up in the village of Domrémy in Lorraine, and, according to her testimony given at her later trial, 'at the age of thirteen she had a voice from God to help her and guide her'. This voice was followed by the voices of angels and saints, which told her 'that she should raise the siege of the city of Orleans'.[76] Remarkably, her persistence and sincerity managed to secure her an audience with the dauphin Charles at Chinon in March 1429. Joan claimed that she had been instructed by God to have Charles anointed as king of France at Rheims; the dauphin and his court, after showing considerable caution, eventually allowed her to accompany a relief force sent to Orleans, which had been besieged by an Anglo-Burgundian force since October 1428. Joan's role in inspiring the beleaguered garrison and populace of Orleans to throw off the siege in May 1429 was both unexpected and impressive. However, given the inadequate number of Anglo-Burgundian troops – patently insufficient to blockade a city the size of Orleans – it was hardly miraculous. Nevertheless, the victory at Orleans had a general rallying effect, and was later mythologised by learned commentators. Christine de Pizan (1429), among others, wrote in praise of Joan's actions; indeed, the most elaborate literary homage was a 20,000-line poem named *Le Mistère du Siege d'Orléans*.[77]

Yet, following Charles's coronation at Rheims on 17 July 1429, Joan was quickly distanced from the royal circle, and her capture by Burgundian troops at the siege of Compiègne a year later (23 May 1430) probably came as something of a relief for Charles VII and the Church. As the anointed king of France, Charles was God's sacred representative, and the continuing presence and popularity of *la Pucelle* must have created uncomfortable competition for Charles and senior clergymen alike. Joan's claim that she received direct commands from God, as well as her military actions and her defiance of traditional gender roles, must have stimulated a profound unease among many men of the day – clerical or otherwise. Even the pro-dauphinist archbishop of Reims, Regnault de Chartres, criticised Joan after her capture for being 'haughty and proud'.[78] When the duke of Burgundy eventually ransomed Joan to his ally, Henry VI, the English king almost immediately handed her over to the Church to face trial in Rouen as a heretic. The matter was settled when Joan was burned as a relapsed heretic on 31 May 1431.[79]

The relationship between religion and the Hundred Years War was thus constituted of a series of complex interactions that were integral to the many changes that were brought about in England and France by sustained warfare. Religion could be utilised by kings to legitimate or glorify their political claims and military ambitions, it could be used to motivate soldiers or to offer them consolation, and the administrative infrastructure of the Church could be co-opted to disseminate propaganda and persuade public opinion regarding the necessity of war and the taxes and manpower which it consumed. At the same time, war also shaped the evolution of the Church as well as the fate of individual churches and clerics. Religious houses in territories touched by fighting could be devastated and their clergy abused, the wealth of the Church was subject to constant attrition through taxation and other demands, and clerics themselves were even embroiled in the armed violence which canon law prohibited. More positively, some ambitious and talented clergy could make their fortune through the opportunities offered by military activity, some religious houses benefitted from generous endowments directly or indirectly connected to the war, and the liturgical and devotional practices of the English Church may have been fundamentally changed through the increasing use of the English tongue, brought about by the need to constantly discuss and justify the war in France. Above all, then, this was a reciprocal relationship, and to treat either the Church or the Anglo-French conflict of the fourteenth and fifteenth centuries in isolation would be to misunderstand the nature of both.

NOTES

1. The authoritative survey remains H. Denifle, *La désolation des églises, monastères et hopitaux en France pendant la guerre de Cent Ans*, 2 vols (Paris, 1897-9); see also R. Cox, 'A Law of War? English Protection and Destruction of Ecclesiastical Property during the Fourteenth Century', *EHR*, 128 (2013), pp. 1381–417.
2. See C. Burgess, 'An Institution for All Seasons: The Late Medieval English College', *The Late Medieval English College and Its Context*, ed. C. Burgess and M. Heale (York, 2008), pp. 3–27; G. E. St John, 'War, the Church, and English Men-at-Arms', *Fourteenth-Century England VI* (2010), pp. 73–93.
3. St John, 'War, Church', p. 75.
4. Pierre Masuyer, bishop of Arras, to *Parlement* (1380), cited in F. L. Cheyette, 'La justice et le pouvoir royal à la fin du Moyen âge français', *Revue historique de droit français et étranger*, ser. 4, 40 (1962), p. 391; P. S. Lewis, *Later Medieval France: The Polity* (London, 1968), pp. 207, 306–7.
5. The French Church had eleven archdioceses: Reims, Rouen and Sens in the north; Tours, Bordeaux and Auch to the west; Toulouse and Narbonne in the south; Lyon and Vienne in the east; and finally Bourges in the heart of the kingdom. Three Provençal archdioceses – Arles, Aix and Embrun – were added after 1481: Lewis, *Later Medieval France*, pp. 289–90.
6. Lewis, *Later Medieval France*, pp. 312, 325.
7. *Society at War*, pp. 147–9.
8. Lewis, *Later Medieval France*, p. 58, from A. D'Haenens, 'Les mutations monétaires du xive siècle et leur incidence sur les finances des abbayes bénédictines: le budget de St.-Martin de Tournai de 1331 à 1348', *Revue belge de philologie et d'histoire*, 37 (1959), p. 332.
9. *Trial by Fire*, pp. 255–8.
10. Cited in Lewis, *Later Medieval France*, pp. 308–9; also *Ecrits politiques de Jean Juvénal des Ursins*, ed. P. S. Lewis, 3 vols (Paris, 1978–92).
11. E. B. Fryde, 'Financial Resources of Edward III in the Netherlands, 1337–40 (2nd part)', *Revue belge de philologie et d'histoire*, 45 (1967), pp. 1142–216; G. L. Harriss, *King, Parliament, and Public Finance in Medieval England to 1369* (Oxford, 1975), p. 233.
12. J. W. Sherborne, 'Costs of English Warfare with France in the Later Fourteenth Century', *BIHR*, 50 (1977), pp. 135–50; A. Tuck, 'Richard II and the Hundred Years War', *Politics and Crisis in Fourteenth-Century England*, ed. J. Taylor and W. Childs (Gloucester, 1990), p. 122. For further discussion see the chapter by Moore and Bell in this present volume.
13. W. M. Ormrod, *Edward III* (Stroud, 2005), pp. 150–1; W. M. Ormrod, *Edward III* (New Haven and London, 2011), pp. 526–7; A. K. McHardy, 'The English Clergy and the Hundred Years War', *The Church and War*, Studies in Church History 20 (Oxford, 1983), p. 171 n. 2.
14. Harriss, *King, Parliament, Public Finance*, pp. 234–5.

15 M. McKisack, *The Fourteenth Century* (Oxford, 1959), p. 287; McHardy, 'English Clergy', pp. 171–2.
16 H. J. Hewitt, *The Organization of War under Edward III, 1338–1362* (1966), pp. 150–1, 166.
17 Alison McHardy, who has done so much to advance our knowledge of the English Church during the period, has explored the fate of the alien priories in detail: A. K. McHardy, 'The Alien Priories and the Expulsion of Aliens from England in 1378', *Church, Society and Politics*, Studies in Church History, 12 (Oxford, 1975), pp. 133–141; 'The Effects of War on the Church: The Case of the Alien Priories in the Fourteenth Century', *England and Her Neighbours, 1066–1453: Essays in Honour of Pierre Chaplais*, ed. M. Jones and M. Vale (London, 1989), pp. 277–95; A. McHardy and Nicholas Orme, 'The Defence of an Alien Priory: Modbury (Devon) in the 1450s', *Journal of Ecclesiastical History*, 50 (1999), pp. 303–12.
18 K. Haines, 'Attitudes and Impediments to Pacifism in Medieval Europe', *Journal of Medieval History*, 7 (1981), p. 378.
19 On the evolution of attitudes to clerical arms-bearing, see C. L. Reid Jr., 'The Rights of Self-Defence and Justified Warfare in the Writings of the Twelfth- and Thirteenth-Century Canonists', *Law as Profession and Practice in Medieval Europe*, ed. K. Pennington and M. Harris Eichbauer (Farnham and Burlington, VT, 2011), pp. 73–91; L. C. Duggan, *Armsbearing and the Clergy in the History and Canon Law of Western Christianity* (Woodbridge, 2013).
20 Most members of the military orders were lay brothers (e.g. sergeants and knights) and thus not ordained clerics.
21 B. McNab, 'Obligations of the Church in English Society: Military Arrays of the Clergy 1369–1418', *Order and Innovations in the Middle Ages*, ed. W. C. Jordan, B. McNab and T. E. Ruiz (Princeton, 1976), p. 294; *Trial by Fire*, p. 261.
22 McHardy, 'English Clergy', p. 174, suggests the practice may have existed as early as 1340.
23 Cited McNab, 'Obligations of the Church', p. 295. Similar writs were issued for 1372, 1373, 1377, 1385, 1386, 1391, 1400, 1402, 1415 and 1418.
24 McNab, 'Obligations of the Church', p. 297; McHardy, 'English Clergy', p. 174.
25 Figures are based on surviving records of eleven dioceses for 1415 and twelve dioceses for 1418, thus total numbers, inclusive of dioceses without surviving records, would have (presumably) been significantly larger. See McNab, 'Obligations of the Church', p. 312.
26 Ormrod, *Edward III* (2005), p. 156.
27 McNab, 'Obligations of the Church', pp. 304, 312–13.
28 Harriss, *King, Parliament, Public Finance*, pp. 315–17; McNab, 'Obligations of the Church', pp. 298–9, 312.
29 M. Aston, 'The Impeachment of Bishop Despenser', *BIHR*, 38 (1965), pp. 127–48; M. Wilks, 'Roman Candle or Damned Squib: The English Crusade of 1383', *Wyclif: Political Ideas and Practice. Papers by Michael Wilks*, ed. A. Hudson (Oxford, 2000), pp. 253–72; C. K. Paine, 'The Bishop of Norwich's Crusade, its Origins and Participants', unpublished. MLitt. dissertation, University of Oxford (1995).

30 R. Cox, *John Wyclif on War and Peace* (Woodbridge, 2014), pp. 104–8.
31 N. P. Zacour, *Talleyrand: the Cardinal of Périgord (1301–1364)* (Philadelphia, 1960), p. 45.
32 Froissart (Lettenhove), v, pp. 441–442; Froissart (Brereton), p. 133; Zacour, *Talleyrand*, pp. 52–3.
33 J. A. Wagner, *Encyclopedia of the Hundred Years War* (Westport, CT, 2006), pp. 142–3, 238–9; J. J. N. Palmer, 'The War Aims of the Protagonists and the Negotiations for Peace', *HYW*, pp. 51–74.
34 See R. Cox, 'The Ethics of War up to Thomas Aquinas', *The Oxford Handbook of Ethics of War*, ed. S. Lazar and H. Frowe (New York, 2018), pp. 99–121.
35 See P. S. Lewis, 'War Propaganda and Historiography in Fifteenth-Century France and England', *TRHS*, 15 (1965), pp. 1–21.
36 *Society at War*, pp. 147–149.
37 *Society at War*, p. 21.
38 Lambeth Palace Library, MS. 506, folio 31v, *Letters and Papers Illustrative of the Wars of the English in France during the Reign of Henry the Sixth, King of England*, ed. J. Stevenson, 2 vols (London, 1864), II.2, pp. 575–6; Lewis, 'War Propaganda', pp. 8–9 (English modernised).
39 J. R. Strayer, 'The Historian's Concept of Public Opinion', *Common Frontiers of the Social Sciences*, ed. M. Komarovsky (Glencoe, IL, 1957), pp. 263–8 at 266.
40 Strayer, 'Public Opinion', p. 263.
41 John Watts, 'The Pressure of the Public on Later Medieval Politics', *The Fifteenth Century IV* (2004), p. 162.
42 W. R. Jones, 'The English Church and Royal Propaganda during the Hundred Years War', *JBS*, 19 (1979), p. 18; see also J. B. Henneman, *Royal Taxation in Fourteenth Century France* (Princeton, 1971); Harris, *King, Parliament and Public Finance*.
43 Hewitt, *Organization*, esp. pp. 160–8; Jones, 'English Church and Royal Propaganda'; A. K. McHardy, 'Some reflections on Edward III's Use of Propaganda', *The Age of Edward III*, ed. J. S. Bothwell (Woodbridge, 2001), pp. 171–89; eadem, 'Liturgy and Propaganda in the Diocese of Lincoln During the Hundred Years War', *Religion and Identity*, Studies in Church History, 18 (Oxford, 1982), pp. 215–27; eadem, 'English Clergy and Hundred Years War', pp. 171–8. See also A. Rigg, 'Propaganda of the Hundred Years War: Poems on the Battle of Crécy and Durham (1346): A Critical Edition', *Traditio*, 54 (1999), pp. 169–211; E. Danbury, 'English and French Artistic Propaganda during the Period of the Hundred Years War: Some Evidence from Royal Charters', *Power, Culture, and Religion in France c. 1350– c. 1550*, ed. C. T. Allmand (Woodbridge, 1989), pp. 75–97.
44 McHardy, 'Edward III's Propaganda', p. 173.
45 Jones, 'English Church and Royal Propaganda', p. 19; McHardy, 'Edward III's Propaganda', p. 172.
46 Jones, 'English Church and Royal Propaganda', pp. 19–20; McHardy, 'Edward III's Propaganda', p. 175; G. E. St John, 'War, the Church, and English Men-at-Arms',

Fourteenth-Century England VI (2010), p. 74; G. R. Owst, *Preaching in Medieval England: An Introduction to Sermon Manuscripts of the period c. 1350–1450* (New York, 1965), pp. 202–3.

47 *The Register of William Edington Bishop of Winchester 1346–1366, Part I*, ed. S. F. Hockey, Hampshire Record Society 7 (Winchester, 1986), p. 8, cited in McHardy, 'Edward III's Propaganda', p. 177 (author's emphasis).
48 G. du Fresne de Beaucourt, *Histoire de Charles VII*, 6 vols (Paris, 1881–91), V, pp. 38, 52–3, cited in Lewis, *Later Medieval France*, p. 61.
49 Lewis, *Later Medieval France*, p. 66.
50 Cox, *Wyclif on War and Peace*, esp. pp. 135–64. Also N. Saul, 'A Farewell to Arms? Criticism of Warfare in Late Fourteenth-Century England', *Fourteenth Century England II* (2002), pp. 131–145; B. Lowe, *Imagining Peace: A History of Early English Pacifist Ideas, 1340–1560* (Pennsylvania, 1997); R. F. Yeager, 'Pax Poetica: On the Pacifism of Chaucer and Gower', *Studies in the Age of Chaucer*, 9 (1987), pp. 197–221.
51 McHardy, 'Edward III's Propaganda', p. 189.
52 McHardy, 'Liturgy and Propaganda in Lincoln', p. 216.
53 Hewitt, *Organization*, pp. 134–64; Jones, 'English Church and Royal Propaganda', p. 20; McHardy, 'Edward III's Propaganda', pp. 174–6.
54 For what follows see C. Allmand, 'The English and the Church in Lancastrian Normandy', *England and Normandy in the Middle Ages*, ed. D. Bates and A. Curry (London, 1994), pp. 287–98.
55 *Society at War*, pp. 147–9.
56 Adam Murimuth, *Continuatio Chronicarum Robertus de Avesbury, De Gestis Mirabilibus Regis Edwardi Tertii*, ed. E. M. Thompson (London, 1880), p. 211.
57 R. Marks, *Stained Glass in England during the Middle Ages* (Toronto, 1993).
58 McHardy, 'Edward III's Propaganda', pp. 187–8.
59 Danbury, 'English and French Artistic Propaganda', p. 87.
60 K. Fowler, *The Age of Plantagenet and Valois: The Struggle for Supremacy 1328–1498* (London, 1967), pp. 199–200.
61 St John, 'War, Church, and Men-at-Arms', pp. 89–93; *Le livre de seyntz medicines: The Unpublished Devotional Treatise of Henry of Lancaster*, ed. E. J. Arnould (Oxford, 1940).
62 W. M. Ormrod, 'The Personal Religion of Edward III', *Speculum*, 44 (1989), p. 859.
63 See J. Good, *The Cult of Saint George in Medieval England* (Woodbridge, 2009), pp. 52–8, 63–73.
64 Philippe de Mézières, *Songe du vieil pèlerin*, ed. G. W. Coopland, 2 vols (Cambridge, 1969), II, pp. 398–9, cited in C. J. Tyerman, 'Philip VI and the Recovery of the Holy Land', *EHR*, 100 (1985), p. 48.
65 Froissart (Brereton), p. 75; cf. Letter of Bartholomew Burghersh to John Stratford, archbishop of Canterbury (29 July 1346), *The Life and Campaigns of the Black Prince*, ed. R. Barber (London, 1979), pp. 17–18.
66 Cox, 'Law of War?', esp. pp. 1389–98, 1403–10.

67 Denifle, *Désolation*, I, pp. 171, §421.
68 Denifle, *Désolation*, II, pp. 188–211, esp. 209. *Froissart* (Brereton), p. 148, puts the ransom at 40,000 crowns.
69 *Écrits Politiques de Jean Juvénal des Ursins*, 1, pp. 56–7, in C. J. Rogers, 'By Fire and Sword: *Bellum Hostile* and "Civilians" in the Hundred Years' War', *Civilians in the Path of War*, ed. M. Grimsley and C. J. Rogers (Lincoln, NA and London, 2002), p. 47. See also Thomas Basin, *Histoire de Charles VII*, ed. C. Samaran, 2 vols (repr. Paris, 1964–5), I, pp. 31–3, 56–9, 104–15, 196–203; II, pp. 52–7.
70 Translated from *Ordonnances*, V, p. 658; XIII, p. 306.
71 Hewitt, *Organization*, pp. 124, 132–5.
72 Ormrod, *Edward III* (2005), p. 145. For John de Harewell in the Gascon Rolls, www.gasconrolls.org/en/indexes/entity-018764.html.
73 St John, 'War, Church, and Men-at-Arms', pp. 73–83; also D. S. Bachrach, 'The Organisation of Military Religion in the Armies of King Edward I of England (1272–1307)', *JMH*, 29 (2003), pp. 265–86.
74 *Joan of Arc: La Pucelle*, ed. C. Taylor (Manchester, 2006).
75 Useful are C. W. Lightbody, *The Judgements of Joan* (Cambridge, MA, 1961); A. L. Barstow, *Joan of Arc: Heretic, Mystic, Shaman* (New York, 1986); *Joan of Arc: Reality and Myth*, ed. J. van Herwaarden (Hilversum, 1994); *Fresh Verdicts on Joan of Arc*, ed. B. Wheeler and C. T. Wood (New York and London, 1996); K. DeVries, *Joan of Arc: A Military Leader* (Stroud, 1999); D. A. Fraioli, *Joan of Arc: The Early Debate* (Woodbridge, 2000).
76 *The Trial of Jeanne d'Arc*, trans. W. P. Barrett (New York, 1932), pp. 42–4.
77 *Le mistère du siege d'Orléans*, ed. F. Guessard and E. de Certain (Paris, 1862); Basin, *Histoire de Charles VII*, I, pp. 126–67. For an analysis of Christine's *Ditié de Jehanne d'Arc*, see Fraioli, *Joan of Arc*, pp. 103–25.
78 *Joan of Arc*, ed. Taylor, p. 21.
79 *Joan of Arc*, ed. Taylor, pp. 22–39, 207–24; J. Favier, *La Guerre de Cent Ans* (Paris, 1980), pp. 428–528.

5 The Hundred Years War 'At Home'

Laura Crombie

Traditional approaches to the Hundred Years War favoured battles, sieges and heroic deeds. Over the last four decades, an increased understanding of the impact of the war for non-combatants has emerged, as will be shown in an examination of the experiences of both urban and rural populations. French towns and villages suffered devastating *chevauchées* which destroyed lives and livelihoods. England did not escape unscathed, with raids, the needs of defence and military readiness, as well as financial demands, helping towns to develop a sense of their own communities. Beyond immediate destruction, war had implications for law and order for both countries, even playing a role in popular protests. Women were, of course, part of these civic and rural responses, but their role as both victims and agents merits analysis to avoid older interpretations that medieval warfare had little impact on and relevance to the female experience. Finally, and perhaps hardest to quantify, the lasting influence of the conflict in both England and France was a new sense of national awareness, even an emotional engagement, with royal actions. In looking at royal communications with the population, which could be called – to use a modern term – propaganda, scholars have debated the extent to which war became a truly *national* endeavour, no longer linked simply to the dynastic ambitions of kings.

TOWNS

Around 1300, few French towns had walls or defences of any significant value, while, by 1500, walls were synonymous with being urban. On the eve of the Hundred Years War, French towns were centres of culture, trade and intellectual life, but they were not well defended nor had they a need to be. When Caen was attacked by Edward III in 1346, it fell in less than a day. Froissart was quick to blame citizens and their incompetence, but Decaëns has emphasised the walls were in a poor state and could not have withstood a prolonged siege.[1] The contrast with fifteenth-century urban fortifications is well evidenced in *The Siege of Rouen*, a poem on the siege of the Norman capital in 1418–19.[2]

It was in the second half of the fourteenth century that walls became a feature of French urban life. Graeme Small has demonstrated that walls, and the expense and organisation required to build them, became the driving force in transforming urban society.[3] The inhabitants of Toulouse, whose walls had been pulled down in 1229, rebuilt them from 1345, introducing new taxes and investing all they could in keeping their town safe. The south reacted to the campaigns of the Black Prince, while in the north the campaigns of Edward III prompted swift civic responses. When the French town of Lille heard that Edward III had taken Calais in 1347, walls were rapidly rebuilt and repaired and emergency measures passed, with most residents working on, and watching, the walls for fear that an English army, or freebooting English soldiers, were about to arrive.[4]

The war, then, had a major physical impact on towns, changing what had been sprawling and rather open settlements into closed, walled towns. The cost drove urban moves towards better organisation and better taxation, but walls had other significances. Several studies have analysed the walls as part of civic identity. Reyerson, for instance, has shown that walls defined and united towns as their costs demanded civic responsibility and civic investment. Walls became part of what made a town a town, they demarcated the limits of civic space, creating a physical differentiation with the countryside, and helped townsmen to develop a stronger sense of their identity and community, representing their growing autonomy and their improved administration through an enclosed, even idealised, space.[5]

As well as being built, walls had to be manned and maintained: the development of military responsibilities drove towns to become more militaristic and organised. Town contingents had served in war before the 1340s; civic militias had supported Philip Augustus in his campaign to take Normandy from King John and were present at the battle of Bouvines in 1214. With the heightened tensions of the fourteenth century, civic militias took on a new significance. Ensuring defence became a priority – watching the wall was the most important way of protecting the town – and an important part of civic organisation and self-conception. In theory, all townsmen were responsible for the watch to protect against external threats and internal dangers: 'the watch mobilised the population like no other civic organisation.'[6]

As representatives of urban communities, and as embodiments of a newly militarised urban society, confraternities or guilds of archers and crossbowmen began to appear across France. In 1358, the dauphin Charles, acting as regent during his father's captivity, issued an ordinance to Caen. He praised the town, described as 'on the frontier' of his kingdom, for 'the loyalty and good love' that the inhabitants had always had for France. So that the town would remain 'most diligently guarded in obedience to' the crown the inhabitants were permitted to 'elect' 50 crossbowmen 'who are good and sufficient' for defending the town; the crossbowmen were granted tax exemptions and the freedom to bear arms in Caen and elsewhere. A few weeks later, in August 1358, Paris was permitted to elect an 'assembly called confraternity' dedicated to Saint Denis of 200 crossbowmen. The crossbowmen were, as in Caen, given rights and privileges. The charter made clear that the rights given to the Parisian confraternity were not new, but were the same as those granted to the 'confraternities' in Rouen, Amiens, Arras and Saint Omer. The crossbowmen, and any of their families or servants, were to be exempt from the jurisdiction of the provost of Paris and not to be brought to civic trial, except for rape, murder, treason or arson, being also exempt from a range of taxes and charges. They were also exempt from the watch, unless Paris was under direct threat, and were allowed to bring goods into the city free of toll.[7] Similar groups of archers and crossbowmen received rights from Charles V and Charles VII in Laon, La Rochelle, Rouen, Mantes, Tournai and other towns.[8] These confraternities in France still need detailed study but their prestige and the value kings placed upon them is clear from the numerous ordinances granted. As in Flanders, the shooting guilds or confraternities rose to civic prominence with princely support as a militarised part of civic society.[9]

Fourteenth-century warfare changed French towns physically and psychologically as they defended themselves against the English and against *routiers*. The picture becomes more complex in the fifteenth-century, with some coming under English rule and others becoming isolated. Henry V enjoyed a formal entry to Paris on 1 December 1420 as regent and heir to Charles VI; the city remained loyal to the Plantagenet king until recovered by the Valois in 1436. Paris was not ruled by force nor was an effort made to anglicise it; rather it was ruled as a French city. The English set out to respect the customs and privileges of French towns and to be accepted by the local population. Paris had already experienced the effects of civil war in Burgundian–Armagnac conflicts before 1420, most famously the murder of Louis of Orleans, brother of the king, in 1407. Fascinating insights into civic life between 1405 and 1449 can be gained from the anonymous *Journal d'un bourgeois de Paris*, written by a cleric in the city.[10] Those living in Paris did not, on the whole, see the period as a new period of foreign occupation but rather as continuation of civil war. As Thompson has shown, Parisian society accepted Lancastrian rule as long as that meant peace, but that often those in power showed more loyalty to the Burgundian cause than to the English or 'French'.[11]

Many Norman towns had significant numbers of English inhabitants, with Henry V and then his brother the duke of Bedford, as regent for Henry VI, encouraging immigration and giving out urban properties as well as fostering urban identity through the confirmation of privileges. Such policies helped to build a strong community: the towns of Normandy generally supported their English rulers and contributed much taxation for the defence of the duchy. Intermarriage between English men and Norman women, the first example dating back to the siege of Caen in 1417, encouraged integration but caused tensions when the duchy was reconquered, with some men renouncing their English status and swearing loyalty to the French crown for the sake of keeping their wife's lands.[12]

Some towns did remain committed to the Valois, even in the chaos of the 1420s. Tournai, an episcopal city surrounded by Burgundian lands, continually emphasised its loyalty to the French kings. The council minutes, published before the archives were destroyed in another war in May 1940, demonstrate this attachment.[13] The loyalty of the town was recognised by others, with letters from both Joan of Arc and Charles VII praising civic trustworthiness.[14] Tournai was relatively untouched by the war. It had been besieged by an Anglo-Flemish force briefly in 1340 and subsequently sent men (as in 1415) and money to the French kings, but was not devastated as were other parts of France. Tournai's relative isolation fostered a special kind of civic identity, at once proudly independent and unwilling, even in 1477 when at the centre of a new war, to accept a garrison, yet fiercely loyal to the French crown. The magistrates of Tournai even worked to obtain guarantees that the town would not be, as Amiens had been, mortgaged to the dukes of Burgundy. The response of French towns to the violence of the fourteenth century and to the conquests and occupations of the fifteenth varied, but towns developed a new sense of their own importance, as demonstrated by their walls and their administrations, and a more nuanced relationship with their king, whichever king they supported as ruler of France.

Towns in England were not subjected to the long-term violence experienced by those on the continent, but that is not to say they were unaffected. In 1338, French fleets raided Portsmouth, Southampton and the Channel Islands, with Guernsey being captured and held until 1340. The English ports were caught unprepared, and as they lacked walls they were violently attacked. As a maritime centre of war and trade, Southampton should have been better prepared. Civic regulations from the early fourteenth century set out how defences should have functioned, with aldermen responsible for wards and holding the right to muster men for defence, who should have been armed and paying watch. Yet, when the French attacked Southampton on 5 October 1338, the town was burnt and badly damaged. The sources note that local men required to watch the walls and defend the town had 'basely fled' on sight of the enemy, while others had paid bribes to avoid performing their watch at all.[15] Like Caen in 1346, the south coast of England was unprepared for the first onslaught of war: towns were caught unprepared and did not have walls.

As in France the war forced the building of urban fortifications. Moffett's work on Southampton has demonstrated the rapid development of walls and arms after 1338. At first this was at the initiative of the king, as Edward III revoked civic authority and installed royal keepers in light of the town's failure to defend itself. As Southampton recovered its autonomy, the mayor and aldermen engaged fully in organising their own defence and acquiring weapons. As in France, too, the militarisation of Southampton allowed for a greater sense of authority and better civic organisation.

England was never invaded by France but the psychological effects of war and the fear of invasion can still be traced. In 1385 and 1386, the French gathered a substantial invasion fleet at Sluis with the purpose of joining up with the Scots, to whom troops had also been sent, to launch a two-pronged attack on the north and south. The project came close to fruition and caused a wave of fear within England.[16] Thomas Walsingham, monastic chronicler of St Albans, describes in typically extreme language 'a countless host who like locusts would cover the whole land of the kingdom'.[17] Knighton similarly describes the impact of the planned invasion, believing the French had vowed not to leave England until it was 'either depopulated or conquered, so putting an end to the war between the kingdoms'.[18] Walsingham went on to criticise English responses to the crisis, especially the chancellor Michael de la Pole, and English ships who saw the French but 'did not take action, being prevented from doing so by quarrels among themselves or prevented from doing so by stupidity'.[19] English towns were rarely physically affected by war, save where they remained undefended as in the case of Winchelsea which never recovered from attack, but insecurity was a major concern, linked also to concerns of merchants for the security of shipping in the Channel.

England did not experience a 'total war' but the militaristic society still had an impact on those at home, indeed Ormrod has estimated that 10% of the adult male population was engaged in warfare.[20] England, like France, had to be prepared for war, even if war did not come. English kings expected their population to be ready and able to defend and to serve if called upon for local defence and also overseas until the use of shire levies abroad ended in the mid fourteenth century. In 1363, Edward passed the first of several decrees requiring all men to 'learn and practise the art of shooting' the longbow. All able-bodied men were required to practise at local butts on feast days, and were forbidden to play 'vain games of no value' including football and cockfighting. Royal demands were repeated: all artisans and labourers, for instance, were required to practise archery by the statutes of Cambridge in 1388.[21] Port towns like York and Bristol were required to provide ships for the royal navy, showing the collaboration between town and crown as a result of the war.[22] England was becoming a more militaristic and more militarily aware society, with walls and defences as well as military training, even if warfare on English soil was comparatively rare.

Mention must also be made of the wider role of non-combatants in equipping and feeding the army. Small ports, like Winchelsea, suffered but the hegemony of London increased over the period of the Hundred Years War and Bristol, well connected to the wine trade, similarly prospered.[23] Studies have shown that townsmen served in the armies of Edward III and Henry V, and that many ships were requested or requisitioned, a contrast with the situation before the Hundred Years War where towns had played a very limited role in warfare. The wealth of towns meant that English kings had to work with them in the war effort. Towns were a source of loans especially after Edward III's debts had helped to bankrupt the Italian Peruzzi and Bardi banks.[24] In 1357, the mayor of London was able to write to requesting to have civic privileges confirmed, and reminded the king of the loans and soldiers provided by the town.

THE COUNTRYSIDE AND THE HUNDRED YEARS WAR

English and French towns were threatened, occasionally sacked, during the Hundred Years War but the full brunt of devastation caused by war was borne by the French countryside. This devastation has long been appreciated; studies written in France in the 1940s likened the destruction of the Hundred Years War to that which they saw in their own day. Such dramatic descriptions are not limited to twentieth-century observers. Petrarch, writing in 1360, wrote that France was in such chaos that 'I had to force myself to believe it was the same country I had seen before'. In the next century, Jean Juvénal des Ursins described France as 'deserted, dissipated, laid waste and broken down'.[25] Other records, such as the distribution of papal alms, back up this image of destruction and devastation caused by English *chevauchées* in particular.[26]

Despite the miserable picture that emerges, it is important to avoid generalisations. Important contrasts can be seen because of the change in English strategy. While the fourteenth-century *chevauchées* were intended to cause disruption, the fifteenth-century policy was to try to win over the local population to the English cause through order and justice. The Treaty of Troyes confirmed the need to preserve existing French laws and customs. Complaints of violence and insecurity continued, but not all of the soldiers, who were in any case decreasing in number in years of peace, were living off the land and there were repeated efforts to curb those who were. Equally, not all areas were as damaged even in the fourteenth century. Taylor has emphasised how careful Edward III and his sons were not to allow pillaging on the lands of their allies in France.[27] Yet, for much of the French rural population in much of the first half of the Hundred Years War, the situation was bleak indeed. Numerous studies have highlighted the value of letters of remission (essentially pardons) for an understanding into the chaos of France in this period, and we have ample other evidence to go on.[28]

Villages were destroyed; peasants had to pay ransoms to protect themselves. Tales of horrors are all too common, especially under the 'freebooters', mercenary soldiers from across Europe who flocked to France to fight on both sides and who, when the kings made peace in 1360, turned into private armies, often called 'the Great Companies'. How far Froissart's account of the activities of the captain of one such company, Bascot de Mauléon, can be relied upon is debatable, but the general picture, of thousands of extremely well-trained military men suddenly unemployed setting out to exploit the land for their own gain has been accepted.[29] Studies have highlighted the number of young boys taken prisoner, to serve as pages, even as military slaves, in combat as their families could not ransom them, as well as men forced to act as 'pillagers' against their own people. For many in the French countryside, there was immense suffering and the images of depopulation, given by Petrarch and Basin, may not be gross exaggerations. As Firnhaber-Baker has shown, in wake of Poitiers 'the signature experience for many, perhaps even most, French men and women was violence'.[30]

It is not fair, however, to paint rural dwellers simply as passive victims of war. As Wright has shown, peasants could often take the initiative in defending themselves: villagers were aware of the dangers they were in and kept watch. If an approaching army was seen the entire population could flee, sometimes to a fortified parish church, a cave, or to forests where the people would be relatively safe. Fortified churches could not hold out for long against an invading army but could be enough to deter a small fast-moving host, with at least some, though clearly not all, discouraged from attacking a holy building. Rural dwellers in regions such as the rich wine-growing area around Auxerre, put a good deal of effort into fortifying their churches.[31]

Rural dwellers in France were not able to build walls, as those in towns were, but this does not mean they were unable to take action to protect themselves. They could, and did, take up arms. As Pégeot has shown, men were not necessarily capable of securing prestigious weapons, but efforts were made in many communities to prepare a force capable of some form of self-defence.[32] Efforts at fortification and a well-devised system of watching out for danger strengthened rural society just as it did urban society. There is less evidence of patriotism in the countryside, and peasants could not gain the sorts of rights that town dwellers did, yet rural people were not passive victims; they were able to organise and defend themselves and their communities against aggression.

DISORDER

With such violence going on, domestic responses that included disorder should come as no surprise. Perhaps the most famous example of resistance, of rural action and popular protest, were the events of May–June 1358 in France known as the Jacquerie. On 28 May, at Saint-Leu, near Chantilly, rural men attacked a group of men-at-arms, killing four knights and five squires led by Raoul de Clermont, who were seen to be abusing local customs. Two weeks later, on 10 June, Charles 'the Bad', king of Navarre, slaughtered numerous 'rustics' in Clermont, effectively ending the rebellion. It is easy to draw a simple connection between the violence of war and the actions of the Jacquerie, to state that the so-called peasants took action, angry at their military leaders for failing to protect them. Recent studies have shown that far from being the poorest labourers, many of the rebels indicted and those mentioned in letters of remission were from the better of levels of rural society, and that numerous urban groups joined with the rebel cause, at least temporarily. It would be simplistic to say that the war was the only cause for the Jacquerie: the famines of 1315 had destabilised grain prices; the Black Death, beginning in 1348, had destabilised the labour market. Yet it is clear that the war, and particularly John II's capture at Poitiers in 1356 and the ensuing political disruption caused by the absence of the king, created the circumstances in which the rebellions could happen.[33]

Traditional narratives of the Jacquerie focus on the chronicler Froissart's account of the rebels as 'wicked people' who were 'rampaging' all over France, and, by his statement, that 'when you asked them why they had done what they did, they responded that they did not know'.[34] A more nuanced understanding of the event can be drawn from the numerous other sources, including letters of remission, studied by Cohn; these show the movement to have been, at least initially, well organised and its leaders able to reach out to urban forces.[35] Far more sympathetic to the rebels was the Carmelite Friar Jean de Venette. His chronicle notes the horrors inflicted on the 'peasants' and their suffering from war and natural disaster. Before recounting the actions of the Jacquerie, Venette notes that 'everyone robbed them of their goods and there was no one to defend them' and that 'the wrong and oppression inflicted on them on every side and seeing that the nobles gave them no protection but rather oppressed them as heavily as the enemy'. Venette was not entirely on the side of the rural uprisings, describing 'monstrous business', and claiming that the men 'subjugated noble ladies to their vile lust, slew their innocent little children', but he does show an understanding of the circumstances of the violence.[36]

There is no doubt that the French countryside suffered a good deal of violence in the 1340s and 1350s, or that the Jacquerie was itself violent. The former is not the only explanation for the latter but they are connected. Popular anger and resentment about paying exceptionally high taxes, and enduring *chevauchées* and raids from the English and the Great Companies, and on occasion even from their own countrymen, found an outlet in the actions of May to June 1358. The Jacquerie was not the only time France saw disorder in the Hundred Years War, with tax riots and more complicated rebellions in the 1380s, disorder in Paris in the 1410s, not to mention the rebellions of Flanders in the 1340s and again in the 1380s, but it is a powerful demonstration of the role war had in destabilising law and orders.

In England, war may have played a role, thought a less direct one, in several popular rebellions of the period. The famous events of 1381, known as the Peasants' Revolt, were linked to war and the poll taxes required to pay for it, though the debates on the causes of, and extent of, the rebellion continue.[37] As Cohn has shown, the breakdown of law and order in England was usually linked to weak or absent kingship, so the circumstances created by an overextended king, in 1347, or an ineffective king losing the war, as in 1450, provided the circumstances for rebellion. The Hundred Years War was, then, a factor in creating the situation in which protests occurred, in both France and England, even if it was only an indirect factor in the large-scale popular protests.

Disorder did not simply mean rebellion or popular protest: the impact of the war on the functioning of law and order, especially in England, has attracted much attention. Many writers have commented on the number of criminals who served in the fourteenth-century armies of the English kings in return for a full pardon, as well as those who were pardoned for later crimes in light of their former service to the king.[38] Goldberg has brought to light numerous sources that shed light on women's experiences in this context in late medieval England. These include legal records that allow for an understanding of how war affected those who were not in the conflict zones and had little direct appreciation of war. In 1350, Nicholas de Bolton was accused of having raped Eleanor de Merton, but he was pardoned 'in consideration of good service in a late conflict at Calais' and so was not to be indicted or charged for the alleged crime.[39] This is just one example of a man who did not claim innocence, but who used his military service to escape any trial or accusation of crime.

Pardoning men accused, or convicted, of a crime was not new in the Hundred Years War. Edward I had recruited many of those who served in his armies from among accused criminals. The change in the Hundred Years War was one of scale. Hanawalt has shown that contemporaries blamed war for increased crimes both because of the increase in violence and because many homes would be left undefended. Men who had been outlaws before they joined the army, and who had spent a few months, or even years, fighting in France were unlikely to return peacefully to English society. Hanawalt's quantitative approach to this problem has shown that incidences of crime were much higher during French campaigns, for example during 1342–7, than they were in the ten preceding years, with particular increases in Norfolk, Essex and Somerset, such increases being linked to returning troops. By 1347, the Commons complained to the king that 'murders, wounding, robbers, homicides, rapes, and other felonies and misdeeds without number are done and maintained in the kingdom because the evil doers are granted charters of pardon … to the great destruction of the people'.[40] Individual pardons had been issued for military service from the thirteenth century, but the campaigning of the 1340s onwards created a pattern, showing that the course of justice was influenced by war. Again, war is not the only explanation for the growth of disorder, with famine, plague and economic changes, but it was an important factor among many for the changes in the legal system and for some of the disorders of the 1340s and 1350s.[41]

WOMEN

Separating women out as a category is in some ways artificial; women participated in some of the disorder discovered in the previous section, and were often victims of the alleged criminals pardoned in light of service. Yet medieval writers clearly saw women as a separate category,[42] so it is worth considering them separately within the context of the Hundred Years War at home. It should also be noted at the outset that the most famous woman of the War, Joan of Arc, will not be discussed here as her role was on the battlefield and in the royal courts, not at home. Numerous excellent studies have covered her career in depth and detail, with Taylor's extensive translation of sources allowing for an analysis of Joan, her life, trial and memory.[43]

Just as French rural dwellers were often seen as victims in war, women could often be seen as bearing the brunt of suffering. In his study of letters of remission, Wright has commented that soldiers or unpaid mercenaries capturing women for sexual purposes were 'mentioned so often in the remission records that it has been reduced to a bland formula'. He details numerous cases of *routiers*, like Guiot de Pin, and notes that rapes and adductions of women were 'customary' with numerous soldiers' confession to 'violation of women' and 'raping women and deflowering virgins'.[44] Chronicle accounts of warfare often include the rape or murder of women to emphasise the brutality of a particular event; Castilians were criticised for their violence in the 'ravishing of our wives and daughters' in Brittany in 1385.[45] The wars of the fourteenth century, with their brutality and the motivations for booty, a category in which women were all too often included, created the situation for a huge increase of violence, particularly sexual violence, against women. As Ramsay has noted, late medieval society was ambivalent about rape in times of war: it was not on the scale described by Carol Cohn for modern wars, with rape becoming a tool of ethnic cleansing to undermine bloodline and ethnicity, but it was certainly tolerated as a consequence of warfare. Curry has shown that many theorists, most famously Bovet, as well as military ordinances tried to limit violence against women and non-combatants with ordinances becoming more specific and 'secular' under Henry V, but that the levels of sexual violence in medieval war cannot be known.[46]

The violence of the fourteenth century was, at least partially, a result of the armies that set out to pillage and to carry off booty. The campaigns of the fifteenth century saw some changes. As Curry has shown, Henry V's army and the forces that occupied Normandy until the very end of the war had a rather more pragmatic approach to relations with the local female population. Ordinances were passed against anyone in the English army keeping a concubine. The English ordinances were unlikely to have been motivated by care for the local population, rather they wanted soldiers focussed, and not in conflict with each other over women, and feared the possibility of women acting as spies, though as Curry notes there was 'something of the prude' about Henry V.[47]

For many women, war brought misery and suffering; yet to view women simply as victims does them a disservice. Drawing on Cohn's comments for modern war, and the need both to understand the horrors of war and to see women's part as active agents and as part of collective responses, consideration must be given to women taking action. Direct evidence of women on the battlefield is very limited, and records of them highly problematic.[48] For instance, in his *Scotichronicon* Walter Bower describes a female lancer who had killed her opponent, at the battle of Boroughmuir in 1335, at the same moment that he had killed her. Her gender was only discovered when the bodies were being stripped of their armour at the end of the engagement.[49] The unnamed woman had been fighting for the Count of Namur against the Scots, and Bower uses her presence to vilify the continental ineffective fighters. The more famous figure of Jeanne Laisné (Hachette), who helped to save Beauvais from Burgundian assault in 1472, is even harder to interpret. Several accounts mention women defending the town walls as Burgundians attacked, and in 1473 Louis XI granted privileges to the 'femmes et filles' of Beauvais for their aid in defence of the town 'in imitation of men' and he particularly praises Jeanne Laisné, daughter of Mathieu, for throwing the Burgundian banner down from the walls.[50] Accounts of Jeanne's actions made the civic victory against a large Burgundian army seem all the more miraculous. Jeanne quickly became famous – indeed, Louis may be evoking the heroism of Joan of Arc in his father's armies to emphasise the divine nature of his rule and his war against Burgundy. As well as privileges, Louis allowed women to precede the men in the town's annual procession in memory of Jeanne's bravery.[51] Her fame endured; known as 'hachette' (axe) for the weapon she carried, she was immortalised in an 1851 statue by Vital Gabriel Dubray and Beauvais still celebrates Les Fêtes Jeanne Hachette at the end of June.

In any important war, the trope of women attacking or defending the walls is common, as shown in studies of women attacking the walls of Jerusalem in the First Crusade, and in trying to defend those walls against Saladin's attacks a century later.[52] Jeanne Laisné and her compatriots may be seen in the same way, as an effective way of adding drama to an important event rather than as a literal recording of siege warfare. Certainly some women led armies, as Isabella of Lorraine did after her husband Rene of Anjou was captured in the battle of Bulgnéville, and Margaret of Anjou did in England in the Wars of the Roses, but they are unlikely to have participated personally.[53] Landowning women would owe military service just as men did, and, as Christine de Pizan made clear, women had a responsibility to defend their husband's property if he was absent. They also had the responsibility to take action on behalf of their underage sons, as Jeanne of Flanders did in Brittany. After the death of her husband, Jean de Montfort, in 1341, Jeanne rallied support for their infant son, also Jean, to protect his inheritance.[54] Similarly in Scotland, Agnes of Dunbar defended Dunbar castle against English attack in 1338, and Julienne du Guesclin, nun and sister of Bertrand, apparently heroically defending Pontorson in her brother's absence in 1363.[55] In each case, women acted on behalf of their families as no male leader was available.

Women could, on occasion, take direct action. In the chaos of the Languedoc in the 1360s, a minor noble women, Mura Causit, and her husband, Guillaume, together occupied a castle near Béziers that Mura believed to be part of her inheritance.[56] She hired mercenary captains to claim her castles, their names, including 'le Negre' and 'le Bastard d'arse' probably, as Firnhaber-Baker notes, men of 'less exalted status' than the more famous captains, but Mura was the active participant here. Her father had been a castellan, her husband was a burgess, and they occupied the castle of Savignac against Johannes Columberii and his sons, though sadly the outcome is not clear.[57] Gilbert has found other examples of women involved in sieges, including pouring water over attackers and repairing and rebuilding besieged walls and houses.[58] Women were not, on the whole, recognised parts of a medieval fighting force, but they were able to act in defence of their rights, their families and their lands in times of necessity. Such temporary roles could include spying. As noted, governors of Lancastrian Normandy had some concern about intermarriage in case women were spying or gathering information. There is some evidence of both sides using women as spies in the war, and beyond, as the Journal of Jehan Nicolay, describing the events of the Franco-Burgundian war of 1477, makes regular mention of women carrying messages.[59] After the loss of Normandy, there were fears about Englishmen with foreign wives still living in the enemy's obedience: such men, it was urged, should not be privy to any secrets and should only cross and return from France with permission.[60]

It is clear that war meant suffering for a huge number of women, but some women found themselves in new situations. In looking at war widows, Rosenthal has noted that analysis of women in property records and wills can provide only 'tantalising glimpses' and not 'satisfying answer' to the power and position of widows in the fifteenth century. Rosenthal's short but insightful study is based on widows of the Wars of the Roses, and shows that noble women who were widowed, whether old or young, were unlikely to suffer profound economy distress, but that some could become influential figures, often as matriarchs through their children in both England and France.[61] No large-scale studies have been undertaken on widows during the Hundred Years War, but a study by Bertrand Schnerb of the minor aristocracy around Tournai in the aftermath of Agincourt shows the possibilities for women to act as widows or as heiresses.[62] As is well known, Agincourt was a particularly bloody battle for the French, not least as the prisoners were killed part of the way through the battle. In looking at a small area, the landholding of the nobility around Tournai, Schnerb has shown that in the years following the battle several aristocratic titles appear in feminised versions for the first time. As Rosenthal noted in England, frustratingly little can be uncovered about the real power and authority wielded by such women, but in the brutal wars of the early fifteenth century a new situation presented itself in which, for certain families, there simply were no men left to take over the titles.

More broadly, the dual impact of plague and war did offer some women new opportunities. This is not to dispute the horrors of war, nor the terrible psychological impact of the death and absence of men, but war forced or allowed some women to enter the workplace, and even to run businesses while men were away. For some women, husbands, fathers, even sons, did not return and so they took over the running of businesses. For these women, as for the noblewomen of Tournai, gains would not be permanent – an heir would come of age and balance would be restored; yet their actions should not be ignored. Women's slightly improved economic position, combined with debates over female inheritance influenced by Edward III's claim to France through his mother and the influence of some of the queens of the period as leaders and as intercessors, Green argues, had an impact on changing perceptions about women.[63] There may be an element of over-reaching here, as numerous examples of powerful women before 1337 could be offered.[64] But the more general points advanced by Rosenthal, Schnerb and Green, that war and loss of male populations gave some women some autonomy, are hard to refute.

MEMORY AND VALUES

The war brought change to towns, with walls as well as a sense of self and a growing appreciation of their own power; war also brought suffering and disruption, as well as some opportunities, to wider parts of society. For English and French societies as a whole, the lasting influence of the war was one of national identity, and a shared sense of memory and investment within the business of nationhood.[65] The debates around national identity are huge, and signs of attachment to France or England can be detected in sources that predate the war; but, in briefly looking at the efforts undertaken by kings to engage with their subjects, and what can even be termed propaganda, it can be shown that attitudes had changed between 1337 and 1453.

We have already seen how the relationship between Edward III and London developed as a result of war, but more can be said about the collective experience felt by England as a result of the war. Financial demands had been part of this. Of course, tax demands were never popular, but, as Ormrod has noted, even in their darkest hours of the war, there were few indeed in England who advocated a policy of cutting their losses and admitting defeat. What he has termed an 'information system' was set up in England, with sheriffs making proclamations to their local areas and the clergy encouraged to perform masses and organise processions in support of their king (this last activity being discussed in more detail in the chapter by Rory Cox in this volume). This 'propaganda' can be seen in illustrations within capitals on royal letters, in buildings, in rituals, in tournaments and in heraldry. All forms of public representations of kingship were utilised by the kings of England to encourage support for the wars. Edward III used ritual to his advantage, staging entrances into London, as did Henry V after his victory at Agincourt, and so too did his son Henry VI, with his English coronation in 1429 and an entrance into London after his French coronation in 1432 both inspiring loyalty.[66]

A great deal more could be said about the efforts of the kings to inspire loyalty in their citizens; but, in considering the war at home, it is the citizens' response to these efforts that demands attention. The so-called Agincourt Carol, which seems to have been circulating within a decade of the battle if not sooner, is evidence of the pride and attachment those at home felt for their glorious king:[67]

> Owre kynge went forth to Normandy
> With grace and might for chyvalry
> ther God for hym wrought mervelusly
> wherefore Englonde maye calle and cry
> Deo Gracias Anglia
> Redde pro Victoria
> [To God give thanks, O England, for the victory]

The first word here is significant – *our* king. In looking at a letter from James Gresham to John Paston, in 1450, Keen argued that the words 'we have now not a foot of land left in Normandy' was similarly revealing, the wording shows how 'Englishmen had come to identify their king's claims ... (as) embodying the community and its interests'.[68] The carol shows the same attachment to Henry and to Normandy; it repeats 'our' king on two further occasions, making clear the attachment felt to the heroic king. As well as showing that Henry and his 'chyvalry' (i.e. his army) were highly thought of and respected, it also emphasises that the victory was seen to have been won through God and was to be celebrated by England, not simply by the army or the nobility, but by the English nation. We do not necessarily have to believe Adam of Usk's statement that 'happiness filled the people' to understand that Agincourt quickly became part of English consciousness. Henry's victory was remembered in 1475 when Edward IV visited the field, and the author of the First English Life of Henry V urged Henry VIII to emulate his illustrious name sake when launching his expedition to France in 1513.[69]

We have seen that, for French towns, their relationship with their king, and their idea of 'Frenchness', was rather more complicated. Some of their reaction was simply xenophobic, with some desires to rid the country not just of the English but of foreign mercenaries, with the Scots and Spanish in particular coming in for criticism.[70] As in England, priests and their sermons became an important way in which the war was brought into the home, with Charles VI's reign seeing a huge increase in the number and elaborate nature of processions in Paris. As Guenée has shown, procession for the king had a role to play well before 1380, but the liturgy and the ceremonial nature of the processions organised in Paris had, by 1422, become part of daily life, even an instrument of propaganda, linking the town to the king.[71]

Again, a far longer discussion of the efforts the French kings went to in winning over their subjects could be put forward, with Charles VII's innovation in striking medals to celebrate his victories in 1450 showing a conscious effort to win over his people.[72] Taylor has produced an excellent study of the propaganda employed by notaries, chroniclers and historians in the fifteenth century. This short study can do little to add to his findings that, despite imperfections in the evidence, most polemics written for the Valois kings 'were primarily intended to serve as manuals for administrators and diplomats', with claims for a wider audience being 'far from convincing'.[73]

However, what can be added, as a final detail in appreciating the impact the war had upon French society, is an example of emotional attachment to the crown, bringing in the changing nature of towns, their greater sense of self and their more militarised societies.

In 1455, two years after the reconquest of Normandy, the crossbow confraternity of Tournai staged an elaborate competition. The event was one of the largest shooting competitions of the fifteenth century. In advance of their event, the crossbowmen sent out an elaborate letter of invitation, making clear that they wished to hold a competition to please and honour the French king and to rebuild peace and community between the town and their neighbours. As well as giving numerous prizes, all bowls, cups or jugs engraved with the arms of Tournai, of Saint George (patron saint of the Guild) and of the king, the Tournai guild encouraged guilds to stage plays on the theme 'of the great, miraculous and victorious deeds of the King of France', in particular the reconquest of Normandy.[74] This great urban event, within a town that had always been loyal to the French king, behind walls that had withstood a siege of Edward III in 1340, celebrated French identity as well as local identity. Prizes all bore the mark of the king, reminding all winners of the power of the newly victorious French king. The prize for best *chant roial* received a silver royal *écu*; the second best was to receive a silver dolphin – the text does not elaborate on the choice of this animal, but it would be obvious to all that the prize was a celebration of the dauphin as well as of the king and of France.

The Hundred Years War brought much misery to both French and English societies, with towns sacked, fields destroyed and innocents killed and raped. Yet the impact of the war upon society was one of inspiring a greater degree of administrative organisation, inspiring a sense of urban identity, and a belief among some rural dwellers in their ability to stand up for themselves. How far the war created a sense of national identity is a far larger question than can be addressed here; but, in carols and in public celebrations, the war inspired a devotion to the kings of France and England despite, or perhaps because of, all of the suffering that it brought with it.

NOTES

1   *Froissart* (Brereton), pp. 76–7; J. Decaëns, 'Le château et la ville de Caen pendant la guerre de Cent Ans', *La Normandie dans la guerre de Cent Ans, 1346–1450*, ed. J.-Y. Marin (Caen, 1999).
2   *John Page's The Siege of Rouen*, ed. J. Bellis (Heidelberg, 2015).
3   G. Small, *Late Medieval France* (London and New York, 2009), pp. 186–7.
4   P. Solon, '*Tholosanna Fides*: Toulouse as a Military Actor in Late Medieval France', *HYW. Wider Focus*, pp. 262–98; G. Bliek and L. Vanderstraeten, 'Recherches sur les fortifications de Lille au moyen âge', *Revue du Nord*, 70 (1988), pp. 107–22. Lille was, for much of the later Middle Ages, part of Flanders, but between 1305 and 1369 it was ruled directly by the French crown. See L. Crombie, 'The Low Countries', *The Hundred Years War: A Geographical Approach*, ed. A. Curry (Palgrave, forthcoming).

5   P. Contamine, 'Les chaines dans les bonnes villes de France (specialement Paris) XIV–XVI siècle', *Guerre et société en France*, pp. 293–314; P. Contamine, 'Les fortifications urbaines en France à la fin du moyen âge: Aspects financiers et économiques', *Revue Historique*, 260 (1978), pp. 23–47; D. Le Bilevec, *Défendre la ville dans les pays de la Méditerranée occidentale au moyen âge* (Montpellier, 2002), pp. 195–210; M. Boone et W. Lecupre-Desjardin, 'Espace vécu, espace idéalisé dans les villes des anciens Pays-Bas bourguignons', *Revue belge de philologie et d'histoire*, 89 (2011), pp. 111–128.
6   Small, *Late Medieval France*, pp. 200–202; G. D. Suttler, *The Social Construction of Communities* (Chicago, 1972), pp. 21–43, 189–232.
7   *Ordonnances*, III, pp. 297–8, 360–2
8   *Ordonnances*, V, pp. 66–9, 636–8; VI, pp. 538–41; VIII, pp. 420–2; IX, pp. 605–7, 658–61; XIII, pp. 483–4.
9   L. Crombie, *Archery and Crossbow Guilds in Medieval Flanders* (Woodbridge, 2016).
10 J. Shirley, *A Parisian Journal, 1405–1449* (London, 1968).
11 G. L. Thompson, *Paris and Its People under English Rule: The Anglo-Burgundian Regime, 1420–1436* (Oxford, 1991).
12 M. Keen, 'The End of The Hundred Years War: Lancastrian France and Lancastrian England', *England and Her Neighbours, 1066–1453: Essays in Honour of Pierre Chaplais*, ed. M. Jones and M. G. A. Vale (London: 1989), pp. 297–311; A. Curry, 'Soldiers Wives and the Hundred Years War', *Soldiers, Nobles and Gentlemen, Essays in Honour of Maurice Keen*, ed. P. Cross and C. Tyreman (Woodbridge, 2009), pp. 198–214; N. Murphy, 'War, Government and Commerce: The Towns of Lancastrian France under Henry V's Rule, 1417–22', *Henry V: New Interpretations*, ed. G. Dodd (Woodbridge, 2013), pp. 249–272.
13 A. de la Grange, 'Extraits analytiques des registres des consaulx de la ville de Tournai, 1431–1476', *Mémoires de la société royale d'histoire et d'archéologie de Tournai*, 23 (1893); E. Vandenbroeck, 'Extraits analytiques des anciens registres de la ville de Tournai, 1385–1422', *Mémoires de la Société historique et littéraire de Tournai* 7 (1861), pp. 1–302; idem, 'Extraits analytiques des anciens registres de la ville de Tournai (1422–30)', *Mémoires de la Société historique et littéraire de Tournai*, 8 (1863); G. Small, 'Centre and Periphery in Late Medieval France: Tournai, 1384-1477', *War, Government*, pp. 145-50.
14 Vandenbroekn, 'Extraits analytiques... Tournai (1422–30)', pp. 334–50.
15 For this situation and its later remedy see R. Moffett, 'Defense Schemes of Southampton in the Late Medieval Period, 1300–1500', *JMMH*, 11 (2013), pp. 215–27; idem, 'Military Equipment in the Town of Southampton during the Fourteenth and Fifteenth Centuries', *JMMH*, 9 (2011), pp. 167–98.
16 J. Watts, *The Making of Polities: Europe, 1300-1500* (Cambridge, 2009), p. 182; L. Crombie, 'A New Power in the Late Fourteenth-Century Low Countries; Philip the Bold's Planned Franco-Burgundian Invasion of England and Scottish Alliance, 1385-6', *History*, 101 (2016), pp. 3–19.

17 *The Chronica Maiora of Thomas Walsingham, 1376–1422*, ed. J. G. Clark, trans. D. Preest (Woodbridge, 2005), pp. 220–1.
18 *Knighton's Chronicle 1337–1396*, ed. G. H. Martin (Oxford, 1995), p. 349.
19 *Chronica Majora*, p. 241.
20 W. M. Ormrod, 'The Domestic Response to the Hundred Years War', *Arms, Armies and Fortifications in the Hundred Years War*, ed. A. Curry and M. Hughes (Woodbridge, 1994), pp. 83–101.
21 M. Strickland and R. Hardy, *The Great Warbow* (Stroud, 2005), p. 199.
22 C. Liddy, *War, Politics and Finances in Late Medieval English Towns, Bristol, York and the Crown, 1350–1400* (Woodbridge, 2005), pp. 43–57.
23 C. T. Allmand, *The Hundred Years War: England and France at War c.1300–c.1450* (Cambridge, 1988), pp. 120–35.
24 Liddy, *War, Politics and Finances*, especially pp. 20–43; P. M. Konieczny, 'London's War Effort during the Early Years of the Reign of Edward III', *HYW. Wider Focus*, pp. 243–61; L. Attreed, *The King's Towns: Identity and Survival in Late Medieval English Boroughs* (New York and Oxford, 2001).
25 R. Boutruche, 'The Devastation of Rural Areas During the Hundred Years War and the Agricultural Recovery of France', *The Recovery of France in the Fifteenth Century*, ed. P. Lewis (London, 1971), pp. 23–59.
26 C. J. Rogers, 'By Fire and Sword: *Bellum Hostile* and Civilians in the Hundred Years War', *Civilians in the Path of War*, ed. M. Grimsley and C. J. Rogers (Lincoln, NE, and London, 2002), pp. 41–8.
27 A. Curry, 'Les "gens vivans sur le pais" pendant l'occupation anglaise de la Normandie (1417–50)', *La guerre, la violence et les gens au moyen âge, v 1. Guerre et violence*, ed. P. Contamine and O. Guyotjeanin (Congrès national des sociétés historiques et scientifiques, 1996), pp. 209–21; C. Taylor, *Chivalry and the Ideals of Knighthood in France during the Hundred Years War* (Cambridge, 2013), pp. 210–11.
28 *Society at War*, pp. 131–62.
29 *Froissart* (Brereton), pp. 280–94.
30 J. Firnhaber-Baker, *Violence and the State in Languedoc, 1250–1400* (Cambridge, 2014), p. 116.
31 N. Wright, *Knights and Peasants: The Hundred Years War in the French Countryside* (Woodbridge, 1998), pp. 96–116.
32 P. Pégeot, 'L'armement des ruraux et des bourgeois a la fin du moyen âge. L'exemple de la region de Montbéliard', *Guerre et Société en France*, pp. 237–260.
33 S. K. Cohn, 'The "Modernity" of Medieval Popular Revolt', *History Compass*, 10 (2012), pp. 731–41; P. Freedman, 'Peasant Anger in the late Middle Ages', *Anger's Past: The Social Uses of an Emotion in the Middle Ages*, ed. B. H. Rosenwein (Ithaca, NY, 1998), pp. 171–88; J. Firnhaber-Baker, 'Formulating Opposition to Seigneurial War in the *Parlement de Paris*', *La formule au moyen âge*, ed. E. Louviot (Turnhout, 2013), pp. 209–18. In general see *The Routledge History Handbook of Medieval Revolt*, ed. J. Finharber-Baker and D. Schoenaers (London, 2016).

34 S. K. Cohn, *Popular Protest in Late Medieval Europe*, (Manchester, 2004), pp. 155–6.
35 Cohn, *Popular Protest*, pp. 143–200.
36 *The Chronicle of Jean de Venette*, ed. J. Birdsall (New York, 1953), pp. 75–7.
37 S. K. Cohn, *Popular Protest in Late Medieval English Towns* (Cambridge, 2012), pp. 1–5.
38 A. Musson, *Medieval Law in Context: The Growth of Legal Consciousness* (Manchester, 2001); R. W. Kaeuper, 'Law and Order in Fourteenth-Century England', *Speculum*, 54 (1979), pp. 734–84; E. Powell, 'Social Research and the Use of Medieval Criminal Records', *Michigan Law Review*, 79 (1980–1), pp. 967–78; J. G. Bellamy, 'The Coterel Gang: An Anatomy of Fourteenth-Century Criminals', *EHR*, 79 (1964), pp. 698–717.
39 P. J. P. Goldberg, *Women in England, c.1275–1525* (Manchester, 1995), p. 256.
40 B. Hanawalt, *Crime and Conflict in English Communities* (Cambridge MA, 1979), pp. 221–41.
41 A. Musson and W. M. Ormrod, *The Evolution of English Justice: Law, Politics and Society in the Fourteenth Century* (Basingstoke, 1998).
42 K. Philips, 'Introduction' to *A Cultural History of Women, Vol. 2: The Middle Ages*, ed. K. Philips (London and New York, 2013), pp. 1–14.
43 C. Taylor, *Joan of Arc, La Pucelle* (Manchester, 2006).
44 Wright, *Knights and Peasants*, p. 73.
45 C. Saunders, 'Women and Warfare in Medieval English Writing', *Writing War: Medieval Literary Responses to Warfare*, ed. C. Saunders, F. Le Saux and N. Thomas (Woodbridge, 2004), pp. 192–3.
46 A. Ramsay, 'On the Link Between Rape, Abduction and War in Christine de Pizan's *Cite des Dames*', *Contexts and Continuitie, Proceedings of the IVth International Colloquium on Christine de Pizan*, ed. A. J. Kennedy, R. Brown-Grant, J. C. Laidlaw and C. M. Müller (Glasgow, 2002), pp. 693–705; C. Cohn, 'Women and Wars: Towards a Conceptual Framework', in *Women and Wars*, ed. C. Cohn (Cambridge, 2013), pp. 1–12; A. Curry, 'The Theory and Practice of Female Immunity in the Medieval West', *Sexual Violence in Conflict Zones: From the Ancient World to the Era of Human Rights*, ed. E. Heineman (Philadelphia, 2011), pp. 173–88.
47 A. Curry, 'Sex and the Soldier in Lancastrian Normandy, 1415–1450', *Reading Medieval Studies*, 14 (1988), pp. 17–45.
48 M. McLaughlin, 'The Woman Warrior: Gender, Warfare and Society in Medieval Europe', *Women's Studies*, 17 (1990), pp. 193–209.
49 C. Brown, *The Second Scottish Wars of Independence* (Stroud, 2002), p. 60.
50 J. Heers, *Louis XI* (Paris: Perrin, 2003), p. 71; *Ordonnances*, XVII, pp. 581–5.
51 P. M. Kendall, *Louis XI* (London, 1971), pp. 303–5.
52 M. R. Evans, '"Unfit to Bear Arms": The Gendering of Arms and Armour in Accounts of Women on Crusades', *Gendering the Crusades*, ed. S. Edgington and S. Lambert (Cardiff, 2001), pp. 45–58.
53 D. Green, *The Hundred Years War: A People's History* (New Haven, CT, and London, 2014), pp. 195–6.

54 H. Nicholson, *Medieval Warfare* (Basingstoke, 2004), pp. 60–1.
55 Green, *People's History*, pp. 195–6; M. Villaret, *Histoire de France* (Saillant et Nyon, Desaint: Paris, 1770), pp. 261–3.
56 J. Firnhaber-Baker, 'Techniques of Seigneurial War in the Fourteenth Century', *JMH*, 36 (2010), pp. 90–103.
57 Firnhaber-Baker, *Violence and the State*, pp. 128–31.
58 J. E. Gilbert, 'A Medieval "Rosie the Riveter"? Women in France and Southern England during the Hundred Years War', *HYW. Wider Focus*, pp. 333–64.
59 I. Arthurson, 'Espionage and Intelligence from the Wars of the Roses to the Reformation', *Nottingham Medieval Studies*, 35 (1991), p. 147; Jehan Nicolay *Kalendrier des Guerres de Tournay (1477–1479)*, ed. F. Hennebert (Brussels, 1854), pp. 188–9, 197, 212, 277, 196.
60 London, College of Arms Arundel XLVIII folio 325r.
61 J. T. Rosenthal, 'Other Victims: Peeresses as War Widows, 1450-1500', *Upon my Husband's Death: Widows in the Literature and Histories of Medieval Europe*, ed. L. Mirrer (Ann Arbor, 1992), pp. 131–52.
62 B. Schnerb, 'Tournai et Azincourt; l'histoire d'un désastre', *Contexte, peinture et société dans la vallée de l'Escaut à l'époque de Robert Campin*, ed. L. Nys and D. Vanwijnsbergne (Valenciennes, 2007), pp. 51–62; R. E. Archer, 'War Widows', *The Battle of Agincourt*, ed. A. Curry and M. Mercer (London, 2015), pp. 216–25.
63 Green, *People's History*, pp. 179–94.
64 C. M. Bowie, *The Daughters of Henry II and Eleanor of Aquitaine* (Turnhout, 2014); M. Guade-Ferragu, *La reine au moyen âge: Le pouvoir au féminin XIVe–XVe siècle* (Paris, 2014); J. Bianchin, *The Queen's Hand: Power and Authority in the Reign of Berenguela of Castile* (Philadelphia, 2012); J. S. Bothwell, 'The More Things Change: Isabella and Mortimer, Edward III, and the Painful Delay of a Royal Majority (1327–1330)', *The Royal Minorities of Medieval and Early Modern England*, ed. C. Beem (New York, 2008), pp. 67–102.
65 C. T. Allmand, *Henry V* (London, 1997), pp. 404–25; G. L. Harris, *Shaping the Nation: England, 1360–1461* (Oxford, 2005).
66 Ormrod, 'The Domestic Response to the Hundred Years War', pp. 83–101; E. Danbury, 'English and French Artistic Propaganda during the Period of the Hundred Years War: Some Evidence from Royal Charters', *Power, Culture and Religion in France c. 1350–c.1550*, ed. C. Allmand (Woodbridge, 1989), pp. 75–97; Allmand, pp. 136–40.
67 *Medieval English Lyrics and Carols*, ed. T. G. Duncan (Woodbridge, 2013), pp. 296–7, 440–1.
68 Keen, 'End of the Hundred Years War', p. 297.
69 A. Curry, *Great Battles. Agincourt* (Oxford, 2015), pp. 67, 88; M. K. Jones, *Agincourt 1415: A Battle Guide* (Barnsley, 2005), pp. 6–12.
70 B. G. H. Ditcham, 'Mutton Guzzlers and Wine Bags: Foreign Soldiers and Native Reactions in Fifteenth-Century France', *Power, Culture and Religion in France*, pp. 1–13.

71 B. Guenée, 'Liturgie et politique. Les processions speciales à Paris sous Charles VI', *Saint-Denis et la Royauté, Etudes offertes a Bernard Guenée*, ed. F. Autrand, C. Gauvard and J.-M. Moeglin (Paris, 1999), pp. 23–49.
72 Allmand, pp. 136–50.
73 C. Taylor, 'War Propaganda and Diplomacy in Fifteenth-Century France and England', *War, Government*, pp. 70–91.
74 A. Brown and G. Small, *Court and Civic Society in the Burgundian Low Countries c.1420 – c.1520* (Manchester, 2007), pp. 222–3; L. Crombie, 'French and Flemish Urban Festive Networks: Archery and Crossbow Competitions Attended and Hosted by Tournai in the Fourteenth and Fifteenth Centuries', *French History*, 27 (2013), pp. 157–75.

6 Chivalry and the Hundred Years War

Andy King

The subject of 'Chivalry' is conspicuous only by its absence from the contents page of Kenneth Fowler's volume of essays *The Hundred Years War*. In 1971, when it was published, prevailing views of late medieval chivalry were still shaped largely by the work of the Dutch scholar Johan Huizinga, whose immensely influential *Herfsttij der Middeleeuwen* was first published in 1919, and translated into English as *The Waning of the Middle Ages* in 1924.[1] Written in the shadow of the First World War, it depicted chivalry as a decadent charade, a fantastical ritual which had been emptied of meaning, serving merely to distract from the brutality and shortness of life.[2] The longevity of this interpretation owed much to the gulf between twentieth-century perceptions of chivalry – viewed through the distorting lens of a Victorian romanticism purveyed by the likes of the Pre-Raphaelites and the French architect Eugène Viollet-le-Duc – and the brutal realities of the conduct of late medieval warfare.[3] It was not until the 1980s that this orthodoxy was challenged, by Maurice Keen's seminal work *Chivalry*, among others, which sought to understand chivalry on its own terms, and to examine what it meant to contemporaries, and how it influenced their conduct.[4]

The term 'chivalry' is first recorded in the twelfth century as a collective noun for a body of knights, a sense which it retained throughout the Middle Ages; but it soon gained the additional meaning of the conduct and behaviour associated with knights.[5] By the beginning of the fourteenth century, as the numbers of knights declined, those who were equipped and fought in the same fashion as knights – the men-at-arms – came to share their culture. 'Chivalry' derives from *chevalier*, the French term for a knight, which in turn derives from the late Latin *caballerius* ('horseman'): the connection between knights (*chevaliers*) and chivalry (*chevalerie*) is more literally obvious in French than in English. The association with horses remained integral to notions of chivalry long after knights and men-at-arms had become accustomed to fighting on foot; to the end of the period, chivalric romances almost invariably depicted warfare as a series of single combats between mounted knights.[6]

Medieval society was traditionally depicted as comprising three interdependent estates: the *oratores* (those who prayed); the *bellatores* (those who fought); and the *laboratores* (those who laboured). In his allegorical work on chivalry, *Le songe du vieil pèlerin*, Philippe de Mézières (a French contemporary of Chaucer, writing in 1389) referred to this tripartite division as something which 'everybody knows' and which was common to every realm, both Christian and pagan.[7] The nobility and the gentry were identified – and indeed, identified themselves – with the *bellatores*; bound up with this self-image was the concept of chivalry. Chivalry, then, was an aristocratic ethos, from which peasants and merchants were by definition excluded.

Nevertheless, though chivalry was, from the outset, clear in its social exclusivity, it developed as an uneasy amalgam of different, and potentially contradictory, values; chivalry often meant different things to different men. As it had come to be associated with concepts of nobility, so it became associated with *courtoisie*, or courtliness and good manners. Thus, the *Book of Chivalry* composed by Geoffroi de Charny, a councillor of Philip VI and John II, a few years before he was killed bearing the *oriflamme* (the royal French banner) at Poitiers in 1356, included, in its discussion of how a knight should conduct himself, the advice that he should eschew gambling and tennis in favour of 'jousting, conversation, dancing and singing in the company of ladies and damsels'.[8] In 1400, Jean le Meingre, the Marshal of France, known as Boucicaut, established a chivalric order, the *Emprise de l'Escu vert à la Dame Blanche* ('Enterprise of the Green Shield with the White Lady'). Its avowed main purpose, inspired by the literary ideals of courtly love, was to uphold the honour of women, being intended to provide opponents for knights who had sworn to perform specific deeds of arms.[9]

At the same time, however, the Church was making efforts to redirect chivalry along moral lines, promoting the ideal of chivalry as a moderating influence on the conduct of warfare and associating it with crusading, which thereby remained a potent force in chivalric culture. Following peace between France and England in 1389, John, count of Nevers (and later duke of Burgundy), sponsored a large French contingent for the crusade which ended in defeat at the battle of Nicopolis in 1396. Boucicaut balanced his career as Marshal of France with crusading in Prussia and in the Mediterranean whenever opportunity allowed; it was after his return from captivity following Nicopolis that he founded his chivalric order. It should be noted that much of Boucicaut's crusading activity was actually facilitated by his service to the French crown.[10] In his long and adventurous career, the Knight of Chaucer's

Canterbury Tales fought only on crusades against the heathen. Chaucer may have intended this as an implicit rebuke of the English knights of his day, and their enthusiasm for fighting within Christendom.[11] If so, such a rebuke would have been lost on most of them. For such men, the distinction between service on crusade and service in a just cause to an anointed king (who, after all, owed his position to God's providence) was one of degree rather than kind. The many enthusiastic English crusaders of the fourteenth century were equally enthusiastic in serving against the French, Scots and Spanish.[12]

It was in the conduct of war that chivalry had its greatest impact, as befitted the ethos of the *bellatores*. By the period of the Hundred Years War, there existed a body of customary law governing war which was recognised throughout Western Christendom and inseparable from the French chivalric culture in which it had developed. Legal theorists provided these customs with a retrospective intellectual justification resting on St Augustine's theory of just war. Particularly influential was the *Treatise on War* by John of Legnano, a professor of law at Bologna. This provided the basis for the *Tree of Battles* of c. 1387 by Honorat Bovet, a French Benedictine canon lawyer, which was in turn reworked in the early fifteenth century by Christine de Pizan at the French court in her *Book of Deeds of Arms and of Chivalry*. Christine's work was adapted into English by William Caxton as *The Book of Fayttes of Armes and of Chyualrye* in 1489.[13] Most knights and men-at-arms, however, learned the customs of war not from books but from their peers, and, as they did so, they imbibed the ethos of chivalry which governed these customs.

It is here that Huizinga's thesis of chivalry as an empty charade falls down, since the ethos of chivalry undoubtedly influenced the practical behaviour of men-at-arms at war. A prime example was the ransoming of prisoners. In the early medieval period, the fate of those defeated in combat was invariably to be slaughtered out of hand. With the development of chivalry, it became customary to take prisoners for ransom instead, though this extended only to the knights and men-at-arms; humble spearmen and archers could still expect to be slaughtered.[14] This class divide is highlighted by a revealing anecdote from the English chronicler Geoffrey le Baker (writing in the 1350s) in his account of the French raid on Southampton in 1338. The son of the king of Sicily, serving with the French, was clubbed to the ground by an English peasant. He shouted '*rancoun*' (i.e. 'ransom'), but the peasant replied, 'Yes, I know you're a *Francoun*' (i.e. 'Frenchman') and killed him, because, Baker writes, 'he did not understand the other's language, nor had he been taught to preserve noble prisoners for ransom'.[15]

Usually, though, the norms of chivalric practice dictated that noblemen could expect good treatment. Thus, it was common for prisoners captured in war to be released on parole so that they could raise the money to pay off their ransom.[16] In the absence of any overriding international legal framework to enforce such agreements, this depended to a great extent on the honour and chivalry of the captive to fulfil their side of the bargain – effectively a form of peer pressure: those who failed to pay their ransoms were denounced as dishonourable and unchivalric. Thus, Sir John de Lilleburn was denounced as acting 'contrarie to the order of Chivellrie the which all knightes & gent. oughte to have kepte inviolable' when he reneged on a ransom deal, leaving a fellow Northumbrian as a hostage.[17] The system generally worked because it was in everybody's interests that it should – for the captor, because it offered the chance of profit; for the captured, because paying a ransom was preferable to death. But it also ensured that the hard-headed business of prisoner ransoms remained inextricably tied up with notions of chivalry and honour, particularly in England where ransom disputes fell under the jurisdiction of the Court of Chivalry, the same court which adjudicated disputes over matters such as heraldic arms.[18] And so, when the English knight Sir Thomas Gray referred to chivalry explicitly as an ethical code in his *Scalacronica* (a chronicle he composed to while away the hours after he was captured in battle by the Scots in 1355), he did so in relation to a ransom dispute, where an Englishman was accused of breaching his parole 'contrary to the code of loyal chivalry'.[19] Jean Froissart, a clerk from Hainault and the foremost chronicler of late medieval chivalry, considered Poitiers a better-fought battle than Crécy because not only were more notable feats of arms achieved but also fewer nobles were killed, being taken prisoner instead, and (according to one variant of the text) because King John stayed on the battlefield to be captured, rather than fleeing.[20] Even freebooters and *routiers* serving in the mercenary companies were punctilious in observing the customs of war, since, so long as they could claim to be serving in the just cause of a sovereign prince, they could, if captured, expect to be ransomed as legitimate combatants rather than being hanged as common bandits.[21] Just as they followed the customs of war, so too they imbibed the culture of chivalry.

As a distinctively martial culture, chivalry placed great value on individual prowess in arms. The motivations behind such prowess were, to an extent, a secondary consideration; it was fighting well – and fighting successfully – that counted. Or as de Charny put it: 'He who does best is most worthy.'[22] Froissart wrote in the introduction to one of the recensions of his work: 'Just as firewood cannot burn without fire, the noble man cannot come to perfect honour nor glory in this world without prowess.'[23] Perhaps the classic expression of chivalry was the tournament and the joust. Until the end of the thirteenth century, tournaments, fought between large teams of men, had been regarded as good training for war. By the start of the Hundred Years War, however, tournaments had fallen from fashion, in favour of jousts between individuals;[24] and jousting was increasingly far removed from the actual practice of warfare. Nevertheless, it remained a highly fashionable and prestigious sport among the nobility and the gentry, and was generally regarded as a very honourable and chivalrous activity, while writers such as de Charny and Christine de Pizan recommended jousting as an exercise which developed the personal qualities necessary for war.[25]

As such, jousting found its place on campaign; it was not uncommon for men-at-arms to engage in jousts with their enemies during campaigns. According to the chronicler Henry Knighton, on Edward III's expedition of 1359–60, 'thirty newly-dubbed knights rode with their lances up to the gates of Paris asking for combat under the law of arms', while the *Scalacronica* records that on the same campaign, men of John of Gaunt's army engaged in formally arranged 'jousts of war' with the French garrison of Reims, in which one of the French was killed.[26] Such jousts could, on occasion, take on the trappings of chivalric romance, as when a Frenchman going under the romantic *nom de guerre* of 'le chevaler Blaunche' challenged the constable of an English castle to a 'batail personel'; the Englishman took up the challenge, dressing in vermilion for the occasion, and defeated and captured his opponent.[27] Such sporting challenges in the field seem, however, to have become less common from the late fourteenth century, though jousting remained hugely popular as an outlet for martial endeavour in times of peace. In 1390, the year after the sealing of an Anglo-French truce brought a halt to hostilities, the French knights Marshal Boucicaut, the Sire de Roye and the Sire de Sempny gained international renown by organising a tournament at Saint-Inglevert in the Marches of Calais; they held the field against all comers, including a large party of Englishmen who crossed the Channel to take them on.[28] Similarly, Duke René d'Anjou, titular king of Sicily, and one of the main French commanders of the French reconquest of Normandy in 1449–50, also found time to write a manual of jousting as well as organising a particularly splendid and celebrated tournament at Nancy in 1445.[29]

This taste for chivalric encounters was shared by the men of the *routier* companies. Perhaps the most famous chivalric contest of the Hundred Years War was the 'Combat of the Thirty', celebrated as a great feat of arms by Froissart.[30] It took the form of a pre-arranged tournament-style *mêlée*, fought on foot between two teams of thirty men-at-arms from the garrisons of the Breton castles of Josselin and Ploërmel, in the French and English allegiances respectively. The Anglo-Breton team was comprised largely of *routiers*, including Sir Robert Knolles and Sir Hugh Calveley, who both went on to careers as prominent captains in the service of the English crown; the Franco-Breton team, on the other hand, seems to have been composed largely of minor, though long-established, Breton nobles.[31]

Alongside prowess, prudence was ranked as a prime chivalric virtue – in the form of moral wisdom, but also of worldly wisdom, and due caution in waging war. After all, prowess was, arguably, only of value if it brought victory, and, as a martial ethos, chivalry placed a very high premium on success in war.[32] This provoked debate about the dividing lines between valour and rashness, and discretion and cowardice. The Norman chronicler Pierre Cochon blamed the catastrophic defeat at Agincourt on the overweening pride of the French men-at-arms:

> The French thought that they would carry the day given their great numbers, and in their arrogance had proclaimed that only those who were noble should go into battle. So all the men of lower ranks, who were enough to have beaten the English, were pushed to the rear.[33]

Conversely, when Bertrand du Guesclin had masterminded the French campaigns against the English after the resumption of war in 1369, he followed a cautious strategy of assiduously avoiding battle, even when the duke of Lancaster led a *chevauchée* across France in 1373. According to Froissart, this aroused widespread criticism among the French nobility and among townsmen, who publicly complained that because the might of French nobles was so renowned, their failure to fight the English brought them dishonour from the whole world.[34] Nevertheless, Charles V endorsed du Guesclin's strategy, and there was no battle. Later French writers such as Christine de Pizan lauded Charles as a great chivalric hero, even though he fought no battles, because this battle-avoiding strategy brought overall victory.[35]

This highlights another area of debate within the chivalric ethos over the extent to which ends could justify means. Some decried such caution, and the use of ruses and ambushes, as dishonourable or even cowardly. In response, a number of the chivalric biographies written in the late fourteenth and early fifteenth centuries appear to have intended, at least in part, to justify the Fabian tactics and trickery employed to great effect by such successful commanders as Bertrand du Guesclin or Robert the Bruce, and, indeed, to advocate the use of such tactics in the future.[36] Geoffroi de Charny, whose *Book of Chivalry* repeatedly advised that 'he who does best is most worthy', may have begun the work after being captured in 1349 while plotting to recapture Calais, in time of truce, by bribing Aimery de Pavia, a Lombard captain serving in the English garrison. Aimery revealed the plan to Edward III, who took the opportunity personally to lay a carefully planned and executed ambush which caught de Charny just after he had delivered the bribe money, and then gloatingly lectured him on his lack of chivalry.[37] The need to secure victory in battle could also override the convention that men-at-arms should be taken prisoner rather than killed. Thus, at Aljubarrota, in 1385, King John I of Portugal ordered the killing of French prisoners during the course of battle, a decision which, according to Froissart, he justified on the grounds of military necessity. And Henry V's reputation as an exemplar of chivalry remained entirely untarnished by his order to kill French prisoners at Agincourt. Even French writers accepted that this was justified by military necessity; far from criticising Henry for the massacre, they tended to blame the actions of French captains for provoking it.[38]

The use of ruses and trickery was regarded as entirely compatible with chivalry, and even commendable.[39] There were, however, limits to such trickery; breaches of faith or breaking an oath were completely beyond the pale, for personal honour was absolutely paramount in the tenets of chivalry.[40] As the English poet Thomas Hoccleve put it in the advice-poem he offered to the future Henry V, 'Amongst all things in a knight, *trouthe* is a thing he may not lack' ('trouthe' being the quality of good faith).[41] This was vital on a very practical level because core chivalric practices such as ransoming prisoners, agreeing terms for sieges or issuing safe-conducts, depended to a large extent on rival combatants being able to trust each other: the linking of personal honour with chivalric status served as a means of enforcing trust through peer pressure. Personal honour was also measured in terms of loyalty and faithful allegiance. Just how seriously this was taken is demonstrated by the treatment of the Frenchmen Jean d'Angennes who surrendered the town of Cherbourg to the English in 1418, and who was a given a safe-conduct to go to territory that remained in the French allegiance. The following year, he was captured when the English took Rouen, and put on trial before Henry V, who 'ordered his head to be cut off because he had taken money for the surrender of Cherbourg, which was still well supplied with provisions and artillery'.[42] To surrender a town while it was still defensible was considered to be treason. Henry's elevated conception of chivalry constrained him to punish d'Angennes as a traitor, even though Henry had himself benefitted from his treachery.

The tensions and contradictions within chivalry were particularly evident in the treatment of non-combatants (the *inermis*, or the unarmed).[43] Under the influence of the strictures of the Church, the non-combatants were supposed to be immune from war, and, at one level, members of the chivalric classes wholeheartedly endorsed this ideal. Thus, Sir Thomas Gray identified himself in the prologue of his *Scalacronica* as 'of that order [i.e. knighthood] which is enlightened by good customs, a support for the old, for maidens and for Holy Church'.[44] However, medieval warfare involved the deliberate destruction of enemy towns, villages and crops, both to destroy the economic base of the opponent's war effort and to undermine his political standing by demonstrating his failure to protect his subjects – a prime (perhaps *the* prime) duty of any medieval ruler. This method of warfare was summed up by the late twelfth-century English chronicler Jordan Fantosme: 'first lay waste the land, and then one's enemies.'[45] His maxim still held good in the Hundred Years War: up until the occupation of Normandy from 1417, the English made numerous *chevauchées*, large-scale mounted raids aimed at inflicting the maximum devastation through systematic plundering and ravaging. This deliberate targeting of non-combatants could be justified – if justification was required – on the grounds that, as subjects of the opposing prince, they were aiding his war effort through contributions such as taxation.[46]

There was, however, a long-standing opposing strand of criticism, mainly, though not exclusively, among clerical writers, which deplored such tactics, frequently harking back to a lost golden age of chivalry.[47] Bovet summed up this line of thought, commenting that:

> In these days all wars are directed against the poor labouring people and against their goods and chattels ... That way of warfare does not follow the ordinances of worthy chivalry or of the ancient custom of the noble warriors who upheld justice, the widow, the orphan and the poor ... Nowadays it is the opposite that they do everywhere, and the man who does not know how to set places on fire, to rob churches and usurp their rights and to imprison the priests, is not fit to carry on war.[48]

Even Froissart, that doyen of chivalric historians, deplored the sacking of Limoges by the Black Prince in 1370, writing: 'I do not know how [the English] could not have pity on the poor people who did not count enough to have done any treason; yet they paid for it, and paid more than the great lords who had done it.'[49] However, the prince was acting entirely within the customs of law, which allowed for any town taken by storm to be given over to plunder and rapine, as a condign and exemplary punishment for the defenders' refusal to submit.[50] Indeed, Henry V would claim biblical authority for such conduct, citing the book of Deuteronomy.[51]

For the majority of the chivalric classes, such plundering and ravaging were simply an inherent and natural part of warfare. Gray recounts how the Scots raided Northumberland in 1327, 'burning and devastating the country'. Tellingly, he does not condemn these tactics, even when inflicted by an enemy army upon his own home county; rather, he criticises the English defenders for failing to stop them, for 'none of them were willing to make a move, so much were they disheartened and unenterprising in war'.[52] As Henry V is alleged to have put it, when the citizens of Meaux complained that his conduct of his siege of their city overstepped the customary bounds, 'war without fire is worth nothing, no more than sausages without mustard'.[53]

Consequently, the acquisition of booty, far from being regarded as 'unchivalric', was seen as a mark of the proper and successful conduct of war; prisoners and plunder were a very tangible marker of martial prowess, and so, of honour.[54] According to the Hainaulter chronicler Jean le Bel, writing of the Gascon campaign of 1345:

> No greater or finer *chevauchée* was ever heard of, truly, than that conducted by the worthy earl of Derby ... And no man alive could count the vast wealth and incalculable riches that were won either from looting or by ransoming towns and captives.[55]

Similarly, looking back at the battle of Crécy and the capture of Calais in 1346–7, the English chronicler Thomas Walsingham gloried in the booty brought back from France: 'there was hardly any woman of name who did not possess something from the spoils of Caen, Calais and other overseas towns, such as clothes, furs, cushions, and utensils.'[56] Walsingham's account, written at the end of the century when the war was going badly for the English, may have been coloured by nostalgia for the glory days of Edward III's reign. Yet plentiful booty was still to be had in the latter part of the wars. Even after Henry V had embarked on the permanent occupation of Normandy, raiding into new territory still played an important role in the English invasion strategy; and so, writing to Henry in 1421, the earl of Salisbury described the results of a successful *chevauchée* in terms of the plunder gained: 'and we brought home the fairest and greatest prey of beasts, as all those said that saw them, that ever they saw.'[57] Similarly, Froissart describes Norman and Genoese sailors sharing out the huge plunder they acquired from their raid on Southampton in 1338 as a mark of their success.[58] What is noteworthy about these accounts is that they all record the taking of plunder with evident approval. The chivalric ethos was by no means incompatible with material motivations for military service; profit was not regarded as inherently dishonourable.

On the subject of 'men who do not want ... to bear arms for another if they do not reap great rewards before they are willing to depart', de Charny argued that 'these men-at-arms deserve praise for what they have achieved in the good combats in which they have participated, thus deserving the material rewards which they have had from this'.⁵⁹ Indeed, profit, lineage and honour are explicitly equated in the words of Sir Henry de Beaumont, in a speech reportedly made to encourage his vastly outnumbered men just before the battle of Dupplin Moor, in 1332:

> We should think of our great duty to prove that we are descended from good knights, and of the great honour and profit that God has destined for us, and the great shame which will befall us if we do not boldly prove ourselves in this great affair.⁶⁰

This account appears in the *Scalacronica*, written some twenty-five years after the event, so it may not be an accurate representation of Beaumont's words. Nevertheless, it undoubtedly represents a conception of chivalry current among men-at-arms, for the author of the *Scalacronica*, Sir Thomas Gray, enjoyed a long and prosperous military career serving the English crown, and may himself have been present at the battle.⁶¹ It should also be noted that (according to Gray) Beaumont claimed that the profits of war were ordained by God, a claim which would have appeared to be vindicated by the subsequent victory, which Gray (and other contemporary English chroniclers) attributed to 'a miracle of God'.⁶²

On a more fundamental level, neither French nor English armies could have been recruited or retained without pay. Both sides relied on captains who contracted to raise men, which offered them the prospect of making a profit. Accordingly, a career as a *routier* was regarded as entirely congruous with the tenets of chivalry. In 1484, when William Caxton printed his *Book of the Ordre of Chyualry*, he added a nostalgic epilogue calling on the knights of England to resume the chivalric calling. Looking back to the past, he held up the mercenaries Sir Robert Knolles and Sir John Hawkwood as exemplars of English chivalry, alongside such luminaries as Lancelot, Galahad and Tristram, and Richard *Coeur de Lion*, Edward I and Edward III, to be emulated by the slothful knights of his own day – and this despite the fact that Hawkwood made his reputation as a *condottiere* fighting for Italian princes rather than the English crown.⁶³

The influence of chivalry was not limited just to the battlefield; it was tightly woven into French and English society. In France, chivalry was increasingly integral to the very concept of nobility. Crucially, by the outbreak of the Hundred Years War, the French nobility, the *noblesse*, had collectively acquired certain rights, notably exemption from some forms of taxation. This in turn meant that the status of nobility acquired legal definition so that anyone claiming to be noble needed to prove their nobility in order to qualify for the privileges that went with it. In the absence of comprehensive registers or lists of noble families, entitlement to noble status was proved by conspicuous and public adherence to the norms of the noble lifestyle, of which chivalry was a primary element. Consequently, the *noblesse* gained a strong collective identity; military service and the right to bear arms were a vital part of that identity, particularly as exemption from taxation was justified by the idea that the nobility served under arms instead.[64] In England, too, gentility was portrayed as the virtue 'which falleth to men after as they be apt to have rule and dominion',[65] according to the clerical commentator and heraldic expert Nicholas Upton, writing in the 1440s. Command in war was a form of lordship, of 'rule and dominion' – indeed, a very honourable form of lordship. It was therefore natural that those who exercised such command could lay claim to gentility, no matter what their origin, particularly given the contemporary school of thought that nobility and gentility lay more in the exercise of virtue than merely in lineage.[66]

The linkage between military service, chivalry and social advancement was embodied by the practice of conferring knighthood, or even titles, at the beginning of campaigns or on the eve of battle. When the French royal host campaigned in the Low Countries in 1340, no fewer than 232 men-at-arms were knighted; 61 of them were knighted during the siege of Thun-l'Evêque, and another 38 before a skirmish against the Flemings near Saint-Omer.[67] Richard II created 'an incomparable multitude of knights' when he crossed the Scottish border at the head of the expedition of 1385;[68] and the Burgundian chronicler Jean Waurin, in his account of the English victory at Cravant, 1423, recorded that 'the day of this battle the earl of Salisbury made with his own hand four score new knights or more'.[69] And there are many further examples that could be quoted from throughout the course of the wars. It has been suggested that knighting on the battlefield was popular because it saved the expense of the costly ceremonies which usually accompanied dubbing to knighthood.[70] However, there was undoubtedly a high degree of honour attached to battlefield dubbings, which may have been more important than such pecuniary advantage. According to the Burgundian chronicler Enguerrand de Monstrelet, no less a figure than Charles, duke of Orléans, the nephew of King Charles VI, was dubbed a knight before a skirmish on the eve of the battle of Agincourt.[71]

Reputations formed by military service frequently translated into social advancement – or so it was widely perceived, during the fourteenth century at least. Writing in the late 1350s, the veteran warrior Sir Thomas Gray commented:

> These English had established themselves on their own account in many parts of the kingdom of France after this war. These were men who were

gathered, as unknown youths, from different regions of England, many beginning as archers, and then becoming knights, and some of them captains.[72]

Such opportunities also accrued in France, a prime example being Bertrand du Guesclin; the offspring of a cadet branch of a family of the middling Breton nobility, he gained promotion to the office of Constable of France, although his advancement owed much to John II's determination to reform his realm's conduct of war.[73] In English armies, there was a certain degree of social overlap between men-at-arms and archers, who were sometimes drawn from the cousins and younger sons of the gentry.[74] A man-at-arms was considered to be part of the chivalric class, and so could aspire to his own hereditary heraldic coat-of-arms, as a public signifier of his gentility – a privilege from which archers were generally excluded.[75] Thus, when archers were promoted to the ranks of the men-at-arms, this amounted to a social as well as a military promotion. The renowned English captain Robert Knolles, described by Walsingham as 'a poor and lowly valet, soon made a leader of knights',[76] appears to have started his career as an archer in 1346, serving in the retinue of his fellow Cheshireman, Hugh Calveley (who likewise became a renowned captain).[77] By 1351, Knolles was a knight, famed for his participation in the 'Combat of the Thirty'. By 1370, his reputation and status were such that he was put in charge of an expedition to France with some 4,000 men.

There were, however, limits to the degree of social mobility which a successful military career could afford, for chivalry remained a very class-based ethos. Knolles's comparative lack of social standing fatally undermined his command; he was unable to maintain his authority over his captains, and the army fell apart among acrimonious squabbles over strategy.[78] Tellingly, one of his captains, Sir John Minsterworth, complained to his fellows that 'it redounded to their great dishonour to be subjected to [Knolles]', calling him a 'veteran plunderer' (*vispilionem veterem*).[79] This was almost certainly a studied reference to Knolles's service in the mercenary companies, suggesting that such service was not held in universal regard. This was certainly so in France, which suffered from the attentions of these mercenary soldiers, who were barely, if at all, distinguishable from brigands. Indeed, writers such as Philippe de Mézières and Christine de Pizan pointedly contrasted the behaviour of 'true' knights, who defended the realm against the king's enemies, with that of *routiers* who acted like robbers and looters; these latter were characterised as low-born – a particularly pointed criticism in France, where chivalry was so closely linked with social standing and lineage. It remained possible for some French mercenaries to advance themselves, a prime example being du Guesclin, who made his fortune serving in the companies, where he became a brother-in-arms of the Englishman Sir Hugh Calveley. However, du Guesclin's origins were unimpeachably noble (if only of modest degree), which made his advancement acceptable to the French political establishment.[80] This association of chivalric status with birth in the eyes of contemporaries was made explicit in a memorandum sent by Sir Walter Bentley, Edward III's lieutenant in Brittany, in 1352. He complained that men in his service 'who fight for their own profit' were reluctant to muster to fight against invading French armies:

> because they are so rich and so laden with tribute that they have no wish to put themselves at risk, *for they are not knights, or esquires, but they are men of little value*, and they are never willing to remain in garrisons .. unless they take for wages 12*d.* a day, and 40 marks per year for their fees.[81]

As this suggests, central to the chivalric ethos was a strong imperative for the nobility and gentry to serve their king under arms. Indeed, the late medieval period saw a growing emphasis on service to the king; as Honorat Bovet put it, '[the soldier] does all that he does as the deputy of the king or of the lord in whose pay he is'.[82] In particular, under the influence of Classical concepts of the state, humanist thinking emphasised loyalty to the prince, and the precedence of his interests over personal goals. Edward III was particularly adroit at linking service in his wars with chivalric culture.[83] He was widely admired as perhaps the premier warrior in Christendom, and his success in recruiting the English gentry for his war effort en masse, and his linking of that war effort with the chivalric ethos, served to reinforce the link between chivalry and gentility. Indeed, it was in this very period that, in England, the rank of esquire, which had previously had a solely military connotation, emerged as a social rank.[84] In the Company of the Garter, founded in 1348, Edward III established an internationally renowned chivalric confraternity, celebrating and rewarding prowess in his service, and commemorating his victory at Crécy.[85] By contrast, John II's Company of the Star was founded not so much to harness chivalry as to reform it; according to his grant of 1352, establishing a clerical college to support the company, it was intended of its knights that:

> eager for honour and glory in the exercise of arms, [they] shall bear themselves with such concord and valiance that the flower of chivalry, which for a time ... had faded into the shadows, shall blossom in our realm, and shine resplendent in a perfect harmony to the honour and glory of the kingdom and of our faithful subjects.[86]

Both Edward and John saw companies of chivalry as a means of binding their nobility to the royal conduct of war. John had been appalled by the failure of French arms, particularly at Crécy, where his father, Philip VI, had fled the field; consequently, one of the regulations of his Company was that its knights should swear never to flee in battle. And so, according to Jean le Bel's account, when the knights of the Company of the Star were defeated at Mauron in 1352 by an Anglo-Breton force led by Sir Walter Bentley, they duly refused to withdraw: eighty-nine of them were killed, so that the Company '[came] to nothing and their house has been left empty'.[87] No such stipulation is be found in the Statutes of the Garter, but a similar concern for conduct on the battlefield undoubtedly drove its members. This was made clear in the aftermath of the defeat at Patay, in 1429, of an English force commanded by the fellow Garter knights John, Lord Talbot (the future earl of Shrewsbury) and Sir John Fastolf. Talbot, who been captured on the battlefield, accused Fastolf, who had managed to escape, of cowardice; Fastolf was suspended from the Order and only readmitted after spending considerable sums of money fighting a protracted series of court cases to try to clear his name.[88]

Fastolf was a hard-headed man who undoubtedly regarded serving under arms as a means of making his fortune and advancing his status. The status of nobility and gentility had become indissolubly intertwined with chivalry. Yet, after Henry V reignited the French war in the fifteenth century, the participation of the English gentry soon diminished greatly. This is made starkly clear by tracking the collective military experience of knights of the shire in parliament. The parliaments of Richard II were packed with active soldiers and veterans; by contrast, the parliaments of Henry VI contained far fewer representatives with such experience.[89] Paradoxically, as gentility had become more closely associated with chivalry, so it had begun to become less closely associated with war – for, in England at least, chivalry was losing its intrinsic association with military service.

At the same time, chivalric junketing became rather less common. Although Henry V was widely hailed as the flower of chivalry, his conception of it was notably austere, founded on hard martial endeavour, sanctioned by God.[90] There was no place here for the individual self-aggrandisement of the joust on the battlefield. Thus, Henry eschewed a tournament arranged to celebrate his marriage to Catherine of Valois, daughter of the king of France, ordering that:

> tomorrow morning we all of us be ready to go and besiege Sens where my lord the king's enemies are. There may we all tilt and joust and prove our daring and courage, for there is no finer act of courage in the world than to punish evildoers so that poor people can live.[91]

Furthermore, armies were composed of increasingly large proportions of non-chivalric soldiers such as archers and, increasingly, gunners. By the end of the Hundred Years War, English armies, in particular, had become less chivalric in their composition.[92] French armies tended to include a rather higher proportion of men-at-arms but this balance was altered after 1448, when Charles VII established a militia of *franc-archers*, to serve alongside standing companies of men-at-arms, all under control of the crown. The nobility remained more highly militarised than their English counterparts but Charles's reforms served to control their influence over the recruitment of armies, and instilled a higher level of professionalism in the French practice of arms.[93]

When Caxton published *The Book of the Ordre of Chyualry*, at a time when the English had long since lost all of their French lands except for Calais, he bemoaned the fact that, in England, chivalry was 'not used, honoured, nor exercised, as it has been in ancient time, at which time the noble acts of the knights of England that used chivalry were renowned through the universal world'.[94] For Caxton, this 'ancient time', a golden age of English chivalry, seems to have ended with 'that victorious and noble king Harry the fifth and the captains under him'. Thomas Montague, earl of Salisbury, killed in 1428 at the siege of Orléans by the shot of a French gun, is the last named of those chivalric heroes 'whose names shine gloriously by their virtuous noblesse and acts that they did in the honour of the order of chivalry'.[95] By this stage, it had becoming increasingly possible for those who aspired to gentility to advance their status through alternative forms of service, notably the law.[96] Writing in 1451, William Worcester, secretary of Sir John Fastolf, commented:

> But now of late days, the greater pity is, many one that be descended of noble blood and born to arms, [such] as knights' sons, esquires and others of gentle blood, set themselves to singular practice ... as to learn the practice of law or custom of land, or of civil matter, and so waste their time in such needless business.[97]

Conversely, it was already possible by the mid-fourteenth century for lawyers and merchants to acquire gentility, and even nobility, as the rapid social ascent of the Scrope and de la Pole families demonstrated.[98] The gentry continued enthusiastically to embrace the military trappings of chivalry as tokens of their gentility, taking up heraldic coats of arms, endowing church windows, and having themselves memorialised with martial effigies. Yet increasingly few of them troubled actually to serve under arms – even before the end of the wars with France in 1453 reduced their opportunities. For the French, faced with the English occupation of much of northern France, and the bitter rivalry between the crown and the dukes of Burgundy, the idea of nobility remained more closely tied with actual military service. But even here, the idea of a *noblesse de robe*, nobles who served in a civil capacity rather than under arms, was already starting to take root.[99] Chivalry remained a hugely influential force well into the sixteenth century; both Henry VIII of England and François I of France would fancy themselves the very embodiment of chivalric values. But, by the end of the Hundred Years War, chivalry was, in practice, becoming less and less a martial ethos.

NOTES

1. *The Waning of the Middle Ages: A Study of the Forms of Life, Thought and Art in France and the Netherlands in the XIVth and XVth Centuries* (London, 1924), with numerous reprints; a new translation was published in 1996 as *The Autumn of the Middle Ages* (Chicago, 1996). *Herfsttij* translates literally as 'autumn'.
2. M. H. Keen, 'Huizinga, Kilgour and the Decline of Chivalry', *Medievalia et humanistica*, new ser., 8 (1977), pp. 1–20.
3. R. W. Kaeuper, *Medieval Chivalry* (Cambridge, 2016), pp. 12–22.
4. M. H. Keen, *Chivalry* (New Haven, CT, and London, 1984); M. Vale, *War and Chivalry: Warfare and Aristocratic Culture in England, France and Burgundy at the End of the Middle Ages* (London, 1981).
5. See under 'chevalerie', 'chevaler', *Anglo-Norman Dictionary*, Online edition http://www.anglo-norman.net [accessed 1 November 2015].
6. R. W. Kaeuper, *Chivalry and Violence in Medieval Europe* (Oxford, 1999), pp. 174–5.
7. *Le songe du vieil pèlerin*, ed. G. W. Coopland, 2 vols (Cambridge, 1969), I, p. 526.
8. *The Book of Chivalry of Geoffroi de Charny*, ed. R. W. Kaeuper and E. Kennedy (Philadelphia, 1996), p. 113.
9. Keen, *Chivalry*, pp. 186, 193.
10. N. Housley, 'One Man and His Wars: The Depiction of Warfare by Marshal Boucicaut's Biographer', *JMH*, 29 (2003), pp. 27–40.
11. M. H. Keen, 'Chaucer and Chivalry Re-visited', *Armies, Chivalry and Warfare in Medieval Britain and France*, ed. M. Strickland (Stamford, 1998), pp. 1–12.
12. A. R. Bell, 'The Fourteenth-Century Soldier: More Chaucer's Knight or Medieval Career?', *Mercenaries and Paid Men: The Mercenary Identity in the Middle Ages*, ed. J. France (Leiden, 2008), pp. 301–15; idem, 'The Soldier, "hadde he riden, no man ferre"', *Soldier Experience*, pp. 208–19.
13. Late medieval writings on chivalry and war in French and English are surveyed respectively by C. Taylor, *Chivalry and the Ideals of Knighthood in France during the Hundred Years War* (Cambridge, 2013), pp. 19–53, and C. Nall, *Reading and War in Fifteenth-Century England: From Lydgate to Malory* (Woodbridge, 2012).
14. M. Strickland, *War and Chivalry: The Conduct and Perception of War in England and Normandy, 1066–1217* (Cambridge, 1996), pp. 183–203; J. Gillingham, '1066

and the Introduction of Chivalry into England', *Law and Government in Medieval England and Normandy*, ed. G. Garnett and J. Hudson (Cambridge, 1994), pp. 31–55 (reprinted in Gillingham, *The English in the Twelfth Century: Imperialism, National Identity and Political Values* (Woodbridge, 2000), pp. 209–310).

15 *Chronicon Galfridi le Baker de Swynebroke*, ed. E. M. Thompson (Oxford, 1889), p. 63 (author's emphasis).

16 For the ransoming and treatment of prisoners, see M. Keen, *The Laws of War in the Late Middle Ages* (London, 1965), pp. 156–85; R. Ambühl, *Prisoners of War in the Hundred Years War: Ransom Culture in the Late Middle Ages* (Cambridge, 2013); A. King, '"According to the Custom Used in French and Scottish Wars": Prisoners and Casualties on the Scottish Marches in the Fourteenth Century', *JMH*, 28 (2002), pp. 263–90.

17 *Pedigrees Recorded at the Herald's Visitations of the County of Northumberland*, ed. J. Foster (Newcastle, n.d.), p. 91; King, 'According to the Custom Used in French and Scottish Wars', p. 278.

18 M. H. Keen, 'The Jurisdiction and Origins of the Constable's Court', *War and Government in the Middle Ages: Essays in Honour of J. O. Prestwich*, ed. J. Gillingham and J. C. Holt (Woodbridge, 1984), pp. 159–69 (reprinted in Keen, *Nobles, Knights and Men at Arms in the Middle Ages* (London, 1996), pp. 135–48).

19 *Sir Thomas Gray: Scalacronica (1272–1363)*, ed. A. King (Surtees Society, 2005), p. 180; A. King, 'A Helm with a Crest of Gold: The Order of Chivalry in Thomas Gray's *Scalacronica*', *Fourteenth Century England I* (2000), pp. 34–5.

20 *Froissart* (Luce), V, pp. 42–3, 63–4, 270.

21 Keen, *Laws of War*, pp. 82–118.

22 Charny, *Book of Chivalry*, ed. Kaeuper and Kennedy. The comment is repeated as a refrain throughout the work.

23 *Froissart* (Luce), II, i, p. 2.

24 D. Crouch, *Tournament* (London, 2005), pp. 125–31; J. Barker, *The Tournament in England, 1100–1400* (Woodbridge, 1986), pp. 139–40.

25 Taylor, *Chivalry and the Ideals of Knighthood*, pp. 93–4.

26 *Knighton's Chronicle, 1337–1396*, ed. G. H. Martin (Oxford, 1995), p. 177; *Scalacronica*, p. 172.

27 *Scalacronica*, p. 176; King, 'A Helm with a Crest of Gold', pp. 25–6.

28 R. Barber and J. Barker, *Tournaments: Jousts, Chivalry and Pageants in the Middle Ages* (Woodbridge, 1989), pp. 42–3.

29 Taylor, *Chivalry and the Ideals of Knighthood*, pp. 58–9; Barber and Barker, *Tournaments*, pp. 114–16.

30 *Froissart* (Luce), IV, pp. 110–15. Froissart's account was based on Jean le Bel (The True Chronicles of Jean le Bel, 1290–1360, trans. N. Bryant (Woodbridge, 2011), pp. 212–214). For differing contemporary views, see S. Muhlberger, 'The Combat of the Thirty Against Thirty: An Example of Medieval Chivalry', *The Hundred Years War (Part II): Different Vistas*, ed. L. J. A. Villalon and D. J. Kagay (Leiden, 2008), pp. 285–94.

31 M. Jones, 'Breton Soldiers from the Battle of the Thirty (26 March 1351) to Nicopolis (25 September 1396)', *Soldier Experience*, pp. 157–74.

32 Taylor, *Chivalry and the Ideals of Knighthood*, pp. 157–74.
33 Curry, *Sources*, p. 113.
34 *Froissart* (Luce), VIII, pp. 160–3.
35 C. Given-Wilson, 'Chivalric Biography and Medieval Life-Writing', *Barbour's Bruce and its Cultural Contexts: Politics, Chivalry and Literature in Late Medieval Scotland*, ed. S. Boardman and S. Foran (Woodbridge, 2015), pp. 110–12.
36 Given-Wilson, 'Chivalric Biography and Medieval Life-Writing', pp. 108–13.
37 Charny, *Book of Chivalry*, pp. 10–14, 22.
38 A. King, '"Then a Great Misfortune Befell Them": The Laws of War on Surrender and the Killing of Prisoners on the Battlefield in the Hundred Years War', *JMH*, 43 (2017), pp. 106–17.
39 D. Whetham, *Just Wars and Moral Victories: Surprise, Deception and the Normative Framework of European War in the Later Middle Ages* (Leiden, 2009).
40 Taylor, *Chivalry and the Ideals of Knighthood*, pp. 74–86.
41 Thomas Hoccleve, *The Regiment of Princes*, ed. C. R. Blyth (Kalamazoo, MI, 1999), lines 2297–8 (spelling modernised).
42 *A Collection of the Chronicles and Ancient Histories of Great Britain, Now Called England, by John de Waurin*, trans. W. Hardy and E. L. C. P. Hardy, 3 vols (London, 1864–1891), II, p. 238; Keen, *Laws of War*, pp. 46–7.
43 N. Wright, *Knights and Peasants: The Hundred Years War in the French Countryside* (Woodbridge, 1998); C. T. Allmand, 'War and the Non-Combatant in the Middle Ages', *Medieval Warfare: A History*, ed. M. H. Keen (Oxford, 1999), pp. 253–72 (pp. 253–59); Taylor, *Chivalry and the Ideals of Knighthood*, pp. 208–30.
44 *Scalacronica*, p. 3.
45 *Jordan Fantosme's Chronicle*, ed. R. C. Johnston (Oxford, 1981), p. 34.
46 Allmand, 'War and the Non-Combatant', pp. 261–2.
47 Keen, *Chivalry*, pp. 233–4; J. Barnie, *War in Medieval Society: Social Values and the Hundred Years War, 1337–1399* (London, 1974), pp. 117–38.
48 *Tree of Battles of Honoré Bonet*, p. 189.
49 *Froissart* (Luce), VII, p. 250.
50 Keen, *Laws of War*, pp. 120–4; D. Green, *Edward the Black Prince* (Harlow, 2007), pp. 91–3.
51 *Gesta Henrici Quinti*, ed. F. Taylor and J. S. Roskell (Oxford, 1975), pp. 35, 49; and see Deuteronomy 20: 12–13.
52 *Scalacronica*, p. 97; A. King, 'Englishmen, Scots and Marchers: National and Local Identities in Thomas Gray's *Scalacronica*', *Northern History*, 36 (2000), p. 231.
53 Jean Juvénal des Ursins, 'Histoire de Charles VI, roy de France', *Nouvelle collection des mémoires pour servir à l'histoire de France*, ed. J.-F. Michaud and J.-J.-F. Poujoulat (Paris, 1836), II, p. 561.
54 Kaeuper, *Medieval Chivalry*, pp. 167–9.
55 *Jean le Bel*, pp. 159–60.
56 *Historia Anglicana*, ed. H. T. Riley, 2 vols (London, 1863–1864), I, p. 272.
57 *Fœdera*, x, 131 (spelling modernised).

58 *Froissart* (Luce), II, i, p. 158.
59 Charny, *Book of Chivalry*, p. 94.
60 *Scalacronica*, p. 108.
61 For Gray's career, see *Scalacronica*, pp. xxxiii–xliv; and A. King, 'Scaling the Ladder: The Rise and Rise of the Grays of Heaton, *c.*1296–*c.*1415', *North-East England in the Later Middle Ages*, ed. C. D. Liddy and R. H. Britnell (Woodbridge, 2005), pp. 57–74.
62 See note 59.
63 *The Book of the Ordre of Chyualry*, ed. A. T. P. Byles, Early English Text Society, 168 (1926), pp. 122–3. For Knolles, see note 77, and for Hawkwood, W. Caferro, *John Hawkwood: An English Mercenary in Fourteenth-Century Italy* (Baltimore, MD, 2006).
64 G. Prosser, 'The Later Medieval French Noblesse', *France in the Later Middle Ages, 1200–1500*, ed. D. Potter (Oxford, 2002), pp. 182–209; P. Contamine, 'The French Nobility and the War', *HYW*, pp. 139–142.
65 Cited by M. H. Keen, *Origins of the English Gentleman: Heraldry, Chivalry and Gentility in Medieval England, c.1300–c.1500* (Stroud, 2002), p. 110 (spelling modernised).
66 Keen, *Chivalry*, pp. 148–51; N. Saul, *For Honour and Fame: Chivalry in England 1066–1500* (London, 2011), pp. 172–7.
67 Contamine, 'French Nobility and the War', p. 146.
68 *Knighton's Chronicle*, p. 339.
69 *Waurin*, III, p. 47.
70 R. Barber, *The Knight and Chivalry* (2nd edn, Woodbridge, 1995), p. 35.
71 Curry, *Sources*, p. 156.
72 *Scalacronica*, p. 157. For a similar comment, see *Knighton's Chronicle*, p. 161.
73 R. Vernier, *The Flower of Chivalry: Bertrand du Guesclin and the Hundred Years War* (Woodbridge, 2003).
74 M. Strickland and R. Hardy, *The Great Warbow: From Hastings to the Mary Rose* (Stroud, 2005), pp. 202–6.
75 Keen, *Origins of the English Gentleman*, pp. 75–86.
76 *Historia Anglicana*, I, p. 286.
77 J. C. Bridge, 'Two Cheshire Soldiers of Fortune of the XIV Century: Sir Hugh Calveley and Sir Robert Knolles', *Journal of the Architectural, Archaeological, and Historic Society for the County and City of Chester and North Wales*, new ser., 14 (1908), pp. 112–231; M. Jones, 'Knolles, Sir Robert (*d.* 1407)', *ODNB*; K. Fowler, 'Calveley, Sir Hugh (*d.* 1394)', *ODNB*.
78 G. P. Baker, 'Sir Robert Knolles' Expedition to France in 1370: New Perspectives', *Military Communities in Late Medieval England: Essays in Honour of Andrew Ayton*, ed. C. Lambert, G. Baker and D. Simpkin (Woodbridge, 2018), pp. 147–79; *Divided Houses*, pp. 67–71, 84–93.
79 *Chronicon Angliæ, 1328–1388*, ed. E. M. Thompson (London, 1874), pp. 65–6.
80 Taylor, *Chivalry and the Ideals of Knighthood*, pp. 118–19, 223.

81 *Froissart* (Lettenhove), XVIII, pp. 340–1 (author's emphasis).
82 *Tree of Battles*, ed. Coopland, p. 135.
83 Saul, *For Honour and Fame*, pp. 93–114; Barnie, *War in Medieval Society*, pp. 83–5, 111–16.
84 N. Saul, *Knights and Esquires: The Gloucestershire Gentry in the Fourteenth Century* (Oxford, 1981); P. Coss, *The Origins of the English Gentry* (Cambridge, 2003); Keen, *Origins of the English Gentleman*.
85 R. Barber, *Edward III and the Triumph of England: The Battle of Crécy and the Company of the Garter* (London, 2013).
86 Translated by D'A. J. D. Boulton, *The Knights of the Crown: The Monarchical Orders of Knighthood in Later Medieval Europe, 1325–1520* (2nd edn, Woodbridge, 2000), p. 185.
87 *Jean le Bel*, p. 217; Boulton, *Knights of the Crown*, pp. 182–3.
88 H. Collins, 'Sir John Fastolf, John Lord Talbot and the Dispute over Patay: Ambition and Chivalry in the Fifteenth Century', *War and Society in Medieval and Early Modern Britain*, ed. D. Dunn (Liverpool, 2000), pp. 114–40.
89 A. King, '"What werre amounteth": The Military Experience of Knights of the Shire, 1369–1389', *History*, 95 (2010), pp. 418–36; S. J. Payling, 'War and Peace: Military and Administrative Service amongst the English Gentry in the Reign of Henry VI', *Soldiers, Nobles and Gentlemen: Essays in Honour of Maurice Keen*, ed. P. Coss and C. Tyerman (Woodbridge, 2009), pp. 240–58; A. Curry, 'Speakers at War in the Late 14th and 15th Centuries', *Parliamentary History*, 29 (2010), pp. 8–21.
90 C. Taylor, 'Henry V, Flower of Chivalry', *Henry V: New Interpretations*, ed. G. Dodd (Woodbridge, 2013), pp. 217–47.
91 *A Parisian Journal, 1405–1449*, trans. J. Shirley (Oxford, 1968), p. 151; Barber and Barker, *Tournaments*, p. 37.
92 *SLME*, pp. 56–59, 95–100, 139–44.
93 M. H. Keen, 'The Changing Scene: Guns, Gunpowder and Permanent Armies', *Medieval Warfare*, ed. Keen, pp. 273–91 (p. 283); Prosser, 'Later Medieval French *Noblesse*', pp. 197–9.
94 *Book of the Ordre of Chyualry*, p. 121 (spelling modernised).
95 *Book of the Ordre of Chyualry*, p. 123 (spelling modernised). For Montague's chivalric reputation, M. Warner, 'Chivalry in Action: Thomas Montagu and the War in France, 1417–1428', *Nottingham Medieval Studies*, 47 (1998), pp. 146–73.
96 Keen, *Origins of the English Gentleman*, pp. 87–142.
97 *The Boke of Noblesse*, ed. J. G. Nichols (London, 1860), pp. 77 (spelling modernised).
98 C. Given-Wilson, *The English Nobility in the Late Middle Ages* (London, 1987), pp. 48–50, 127–8.
99 Prosser, 'Later Medieval French *Noblesse*', pp. 194–203.

7 First-Hand Accounts and Reports of Warfare

Craig Taylor

Historians of modern warfare have becomingly increasingly interested in first-hand and eyewitness accounts of war that offer important information regarding the face of battle. For example, Joanna Bourke has explored the psychology and emotions of soldiers in warfare, drawing in significant part upon first-hand accounts of the protagonists themselves, recorded in 'ego documents' such as letters, diaries and memoirs.[1] Behind such research lie questions of great importance for contemporary military culture. Between 1943 and 1945, two American researchers serving in the Intelligence Section of the Psychological Warfare Division of the Supreme Headquarters Allied Expeditionary Force questioned 443 deserters from the German army. Drawing upon the direct testimony of these soldiers from the Wehrmacht, the two sociologists examined the importance of unit cohesion, arguing that such ties of comradeship were a decisive factor in providing good morale, unity and organisational framework. Their research paved the way for modern studies into the role of the bonds between soldiers in sustaining their will and commitment to each other, the unit, and the accomplishment of their mission in the face of combat and the stress of warfare.[2]

For the medieval historian, the opportunities to investigate the experience of soldiers in combat are frustratingly restricted because of the more limited availability of sources: comparatively few letters and memoirs written by soldiers survive from the Middle Ages. But it would be wrong to assume that there are no eyewitness accounts of medieval battles.[3] During the period of the Hundred Years War, for example, there was a remarkable flourishing of vernacular writing about warfare and military culture, including a range of different sources that either recorded the testimony of eyewitnesses or were themselves written by military veterans. These sources provide important evidence with which to reconstruct not just the narrative of campaigns and battles, but also to offer to address deeper questions regarding martial culture, and the emotional and psychological resonance of conflict.[4]

The most prominent witnesses to late medieval battles were often heralds who observed and recorded the names of casualties, echoing their role in tournaments and jousts. These men were therefore natural choices to write accounts of military campaigns and battles.[5] For example, the Chandos Herald was the author of a chivalric biography of the Black Prince, Edward of Woodstock, son of King Edward III. This account of Edward's life and deeds included a detailed description of the battle of Poitiers (19 September 1356), and of the Castilian campaign culminating in the battle of Nájera (3 April 1367) that the author had almost certainly witnessed while in service to Sir John Chandos.[6] At the battle of Agincourt (25 October 1415), a nineteen-year-old Frenchman named Jean Le Fèvre was positioned among the heralds on the English side, and nearly fifty years later he wrote an account of the battle, drawing upon his own memories together with written sources including the chronicle of Enguerrand de Monstrelet.[7]

Yet heralds were not the only eyewitnesses to battles during this period. Many clerics were eyewitnesses to the military events that they described.[8] In the *Vrayes chroniques,* Jean le including the chronicle of Jean e Bel recalled his youthful experience serving in the retinue of Jean de Hainaut, count of Beaumont, during Edward III's expedition to Scotland in 1327.[9] Similarly, an anonymous Parisian cleric compiled a journal of public events in the city of Paris from 1405 to 1449, including a vivid account of the failed Valois attack led by Joan of Arc upon the city of Paris on 8 September 1429.[10]

It was increasingly common for clerics to be effectively embedded in the military communities whose deeds they recorded and celebrated; clerics were eyewitnesses to the military events that they described.[11] Less than two years after Agincourt, an anonymous English priest composed a short Latin chronicle known as the *Gesta Henrici Quinti*.[12] This narrative offered an account of events from the coronation of Henry V on 9 April 1413 up to 20 November 1416, and in particular a very important report of the English victory at Agincourt. The *Gesta Henrici Quinti* presents one of the most trusted descriptions of this campaign, not just because it was written so soon after the battle of Agincourt, but also because the author was an eyewitness to these important events: 'I, who am now writing this and was then sitting on a horse among the baggage at the rear of the battle, and the other priests present, did humble our souls before God.'[13]

Just a few years later, John Page composed an eyewitness account of Henry V's siege of Rouen that had ended on 19 January 1419. Like the anonymous author of the *Gesta Henrici Quinti,* Page was most likely a royal chaplain accompanying the English army. He composed a verse chronicle of the siege of the Norman capital, inspired by literary models, but also providing graphic descriptions of the suffering of the French citizens.[14] A very different example is offered by the chivalric biography of Jean II Le Meingre, known as Boucicaut, the Marshal of France. The *Livre des fais du bon messire Jehan le Maingre* was completed in 1409 by an anonymous cleric, perhaps Nicolas de Gonesse, who claimed that the marshal's companions-in-arms had commissioned the biography. Whether this was true or just an attempt to protect Boucicaut from the charge that he had paid for his own biography, the author clearly had direct access to the marshal's military companions who had been eyewitnesses to a sequence of military campaigns between 1399 and 1407 for which the biography remains the most important primary source.[15]

Far more common, though, was the situation of the famous English chronicler Thomas Walsingham who was safely tucked away within the walls of the Benedictine abbey of St Albans when he wrote an account of the battle of Agincourt, littered with learned quotations from the Latin works of Lucan, Persius, Statius and Virgil.[16] But clerical chroniclers were able to base their accounts upon eyewitness reports provided by soldiers. Letters and dispatches from the front provided valuable information for civilian audiences.[17] The Augustinian author of the *Chronicle* of Lanercost Priory near Carlisle, like the writer of the *Anonimalle Chronicle* composed at Saint Mary's Abbey in York, drew upon such military newsletters regarding the fourteenth-century border wars with the Scots, as well as conflicts abroad.[18] More famously, Adam Murimuth and Robert of Avesbury included a number of official letters by key military commanders like Bartholomew lord Burghersh, Henry of Grosmont, Thomas Dagworth, Edward of Woodstock and even King Edward III, all relating to the campaigns from the first decades of the Hundred Years War.[19]

Chroniclers were also able to speak directly to military veterans. The author of the *Chronique du Religieux de Saint-Denys*, Michel Pintouin, derived his account of the battle of Nicopolis (25 September 1396) from one of the French survivors, a Burgundian nobleman named Gauthier des Roches.[20] But the most famous example of this practice is the great chronicler of the Hundred Years War, Jean Froissart. He was himself an eyewitness to many of the events that he recounted in his *Chroniques*, that he continued to compile, adapt and revise until the very end of the fourteenth century.[21] Yet Froissart was not usually present for any of the great battles or great military encounters that he described. He therefore had to rely heavily upon narratives written by other people, including the chronicle of Jean le Bel and the chivalric biography of the Black Prince, together with interviews with many of the soldiers who had participated in the events that he was describing. For example, he spoke with Bartholomew lord Burghersh, as well as many of the Frenchmen who had been captured at the battle of Poitiers or who served as hostages to ensure the fulfilment of the ransom of King John II and the terms of the treaty of Brétigny (1360), including his future patron Gui count of Blois. In October 1364, Froissart also spoke with a herald returning to England to report the Anglo-Breton victory at the battle of Auray on 29 September that year. Most famously, Froissart spoke with a number of individuals during his visit to the court of Gaston III Phébus, count of Foix, in late 1388 and early 1389, including the routiers Espan de Lion and Bascot de Mauléon. The latter presented a vivid picture of life as a routier fighting for money in the aftermath of the treaty of Brétigny: Mauléon claimed to have fought at both the battles of Cocherel (16 May 1364) and Auray (29 September 1364), as well as countless smaller frays such as his own capture of the town and castle of Thurie by entering the walls in disguise, dressed as a woman.[22]

In all of these cases, the voices and experiences of real soldiers were being filtered through narratives composed by chroniclers and biographers. Throughout the Middle Ages, writing remained almost entirely the province of outsiders, rather than of the soldiers who were directly involved in the martial culture. Indeed, one key reason why it is so easy to underestimate the medieval understanding of military strategy is the simple fact that the great commanders of the age rarely committed their thoughts and experiences to paper.[23] Even when they did, such documents were hardly likely to survive. A rare exception is a French plan for the invasion of England, originally drawn up in March 1339, that was seized by the English during the siege of Caen in 1346.[24] Another is a French battle plan for tackling the army led by Henry V, as the English raided through the Norman countryside from Harfleur just before Agincourt.[25] There is also a proposal written in 1435 by the English captain Sir John Fastolf, suggesting two punitive military expeditions sweeping from Calais or Le Crotoy across Artois, Picardy, Laonnois and Champagne.[26]

Nevertheless the late Middle Ages did witness a changing relationship between military men and the written word, marked by a dramatic increase in the ownership of books about warfare by soldiers.[27] The most famous example of this is the success of a Roman military manual entitled the *Epitoma rei militaris*, originally written between AD 383 and 450 by a Roman administrator named Flavius Vegetius Renatus. This was a medieval bestseller, surviving in nearly four hundred manuscripts, and was principally owned and read by members of the church. But this changed in the fourteenth and fifteenth centuries, when a series of translations made the work more accessible to military leaders.[28] Modern historians enthusiastically debate the extent to which this particular text influenced military activities in the late Middle Ages.[29]

But medieval military veterans also began to write manuals of advice of their own, informed by their direct experience of war. For example, in 1335, Jean de Vignay translated into French a brief treatise on the art of war originally written by Theodore Paleologus, marquis of Montferrat and second son of the emperor of Constantinople.[30] Around 1350, the prominent French knight Geoffroi de Charny wrote three texts on knighthood and the law of arms, almost certainly for the members of the Company of the Star that was founded by King John II in January 1352.[31] Shortly afterwards a Picard knight with extensive crusading experience named Philippe de Mézières began writing a series of books that offered extensive advice about warfare, crusading and knighthood within the context of wider themes.[32] Around 1419, the anonymous pamphlet *Debats et appointements* presented a highly practical set of suggestions for military reform, almost certainly written by a soldier, alongside a survey of the arguments surrounding the French royal succession.[33] Antoine de La Sale was the son of a mercenary captain and an experienced man-at-arms in his own right, having served under Louis II of Anjou during an expedition into Italy, as well as a crusade led by João I of Portugal against the Moors in 1415. In *La Salade* (1442–4), La Sale presented a discussion of military trickery inspired principally by the Roman writer from Valerius Maximus, but also advice on choosing military leaders and on preparations for battle and war, partially inspired by Vegetius. A few years later, La Sale composed a further didactic treatise, *La Sale* (1451), followed soon afterwards by his most famous work, the romance *Le petit Jehan de Saintré* (1456).[34]

The pinnacle of this tradition was *Le Jouvencel* written between 1461 and 1468. The author was Jean de Bueil, a very experienced military veteran who had fought at the siege of Orléans (1428–9) and the battle of Patay (18 June 1429) and had been appointed Admiral of France in 1450.[35] On the surface, *Le Jouvencel* seemed to present a military romance recounting the story of a fictional squire who slowly acquired the skills to be a successful military commander before moving on to accept wider political responsibility. But in a commentary on the text written shortly after Bueil's, his servant Guillaume Tringant revealed that the work was inspired by Bueil's own experiences: 'the majority of things that were written in the book of the *Jouvencel,* [Jean de Bueil] did and carried out.'[36] In other words, *Le Jouvencel* offered almost unprecedented eyewitness information regarding a series of military encounters including the defence of Orléans in 1428 and 1429, but more generally on the experience of warfare and the wider military culture during this formative period in the history of the French army. *Le Jouvencel* foreshadowed the post-medieval tradition of military memoires, sidestepping the usual celebration and glorification of the hero that was standard in chivalric biographies, in order to focus upon the didactic value of the experiences and advice offered by Bueil.

Other military veterans were more open in writing about their personal experiences of war. One important example is the *Scalacronica* written by the Northumbrian Sir Thomas Gray. This unusual text survives in just one incomplete manuscript and presented a universal chronicle recounting the histories of the Israelites, Trojans and Romans, before concluding with an account of more recent wars from 1066 to 1362, drawing in part upon the *Historia aurea* of John Tynemouth and the Anglo-Norman prose *Brut*.[37] For the Scottish campaigns of Edward I and Edward II, Gray relied upon the recollections of his own father, also called Thomas, who may have escaped during the battle at Roslin in February 1303, dramatically rescued Henry de Beaumont during the siege of Stirling Castle in 1304, and was captured at the battle of Bannockburn ten years later. For more recent events, Thomas Gray drew upon his own memories, having fought at the battles of Dupplin Moor in 1332 and Neville's Cross in 1346, and then been captured by the Scots outside of Norham Castle in late 1355 and held as a prisoner for just over a year in Edinburgh Castle, where he first began to compile the *Scalacronica*. His chronicle also presented a vivid and important account of the continental wars of Edward III, no doubt informed by a range of eyewitnesses and newsletters, as well as his own experiences in France from 1359 to 1360.

In France, a number of military veterans also composed chronicles and biographies recounting campaigns and battles during the Hundred Years War. Around 1436, Perceval de Cagny, master of the household of the dukes of Alençon, composed a chronicle covering the years 1239 to 1438 that included a great deal of original and valuable information about the campaigns of Joan of Arc, inspired and informed above all by his lord, Jean II, duke of Alençon.[38] Shortly after the death of Arthur de Richemont in 1458, one of his military entourage named Guillaume Gruel composed a biography of the Constable. Richemont had fought and been captured at Agincourt, and later took members of his retinue back to the battlefield in order to teach them about the tactics and deployments. So his knowledge and experience presumably informed Gruel's account of that battle, which explained that the battlefield had been too narrow, that the Lombard and Gascon cavalrymen had failed to attack the English flanks as had been agreed, and that the English archers had broken up the French formations.[39] Then, for the period from 1425 to 1458, Gruel was able to draw upon his own experiences, presenting an eyewitness account of a series of military expeditions.

Military veterans sometimes testified in court and so their witness statements can provide a different kind of record of their activities. For example, many English knights and squires testified before the Court of Chivalry in cases such as the famous dispute between Sir Robert Grosvenor and Sir Richard Scrope over the right to bear the heraldic arms *azure a bend or* in 1386. In that case, nearly four hundred witnesses gave evidence, with each describing their military careers to date, though often in limited detail.[40] Even more interesting and informative are the witness statements recorded at two inquiries organised at Rouen on behalf of Charles VII at the very end of the Hundred Years War. Between October and December 1449, Guillaume Juvénal des Ursins led an investigation into the complex skulduggery surrounding the English capture of Fougères in March 1448. Both civilians and soldiers testified regarding a covert operation led by François de Surienne to capture this Breton town for the English.[41] A few years later, Guillaume's brother Jean led an inquiry into the heresy trial of Joan of Arc that had been held at Rouen in 1431. Witnesses included a number of military veterans who had fought alongside *the Pucelle*. For example, Jean Count of Dunois, known as the Bastard of Orléans, had led the defence of the city of Orléans, while Jean Duke of Alençon had been the commander of the Valois army during the Loire campaign and then up to the siege of Paris in September 1429. The judges also heard from Jean de Nouillompont and Bertrand de Poulengy who had escorted Joan of Arc from Vaucouleurs to Chinon, as well as Joan's page and steward, Louis de Coutes and Jean d'Aulon.[42]

The testimony given by the military veterans at the Nullification trial of Joan of Arc in 1456 highlights the value of evidence provided by eyewitnesses, but also the great challenges presented by such sources. Dunois, Alençon and these other military men certainly offered a great deal of information about what actually happened during the course of the military encounters at Orléans, Patay and Paris, but their testimony must be handled with great care. Their testimony was controlled by the clerics who asked them questions and recorded their answers, shaping the evidence that they provided. They were being asked to recall events that had taken place some twenty-five years earlier, which raises questions about their ability to remember details with precision. There were certainly inconsistencies in their testimony. For example, almost every one of the military witness recounted a story of Joan of Arc being wounded in battle. Yet they disagreed not just about when she was hurt, but also about the nature of her injuries, so that it is impossible to know which of them was telling the truth. More frustratingly, Dunois confidently reported on 22 February 1456 that the Pucelle's military mission had been 'to have the siege of Orléans raised and to take the dauphin to Reims for his coronation'.⁴³ On the surface, this testimony provides invaluable evidence as to the strategy and military goals of Joan and her fellow captains, but it is contradicted by sources written during the Pucelle's lifetime. After she had been questioned at Poitiers in 1429 by theologians working for Charles VII, Joan had made no mention of a plan to crown Charles VII at Reims, and her first letter to the English on 22 March 1429 had certainly not referred to such a plan.⁴⁴ There is therefore a strong possibility that Dunois and other supporters of the French crown had deliberately reshaped the story in order to support their king at the time of the Nullification trial, a reminder of the powerful political pressures working in the background.⁴⁵

It is often true that eyewitness accounts in chronicles and other narrative sources provide our best evidence regarding military encounters that took place during the Hundred Years War. Thomas Gray's *Scalacronica* presents perhaps the best surviving report of Edward III's expedition of 1359, including important details of the division of the army into three units that reunited at Reims for the march upon Paris, the problems of securing supplies, and an attack upon the monasteries of Beauce.⁴⁶ Similarly, the anonymous author of the *Gesta Henrici Quinti* presented one of the best accounts of the battle of Agincourt. Yet care must still be taken in using such accounts, just like those of witnesses at the Nullification trial.⁴⁷ As Peter Ainsworth has noted, 'Even genuine eyewitnesses were strongly influenced in the composition of their works by stylistic, rhetorical and generic constraints or presuppositions'.⁴⁸ Moreover, the authors were rarely dispassionate witnesses to the events around them. The *Gesta Henrici Quinti*, for example, was not an objective record, but rather a piece of propaganda championing the cause of Henry V before an international audience. More practically, the anonymous author was neither located at the heart of the English lines during the battle nor experienced enough in military matters to offer an expert's eye on what was happening.⁴⁹

Beyond reconstructing the course of events, eyewitness reports potentially offer insight into wider and more subtle questions. For example, first-hand accounts may offer invaluable evidence with which to investigate contemporary soldiers' views of the moral framework for warfare, allowing us to peak behind the normal filters of medieval clerical commentary, and thereby test and challenge our modern romantic assumptions about chivalry. Witnesses at the Nullification trial reported on the way in which Joan of Arc behaved towards English soldiers who were captured in battle: Louis de Coutes praised the protection and mercy that she gave to English clerics captured in the assault upon the fortress of Saint-Loup, but made no comment whatsoever on her decision to leave the remaining English soldiers to be killed by the people of Orléans. Later in his testimony, he emphasised the piety of Joan by reporting that she had felt great pity at the deaths of so many English soldiers at the battle of Beaugency, and had personally comforted a prisoner who had been mortally wounded by a French soldier while held in captivity.[50] Whether factually accurate or not, such testimony that sought to distinguish Joan of Arc as a uniquely pious and compassionate individual would seem to suggest that such attitudes were not commonplace at the time.

Other sources also provide fascinating fragments of information. The *Scalacronica*, for example, demonstrated that for Thomas Gray 'the real business of war had little to do with the knightly heroics of chivalric romance'.[51] Particularly interesting in this regard is Gray's heartfelt warnings of the potential dangers of peace. Recounting the events in 1360 leading up to the signing of the treaty of Brétigny that had put an end to the first great phase of the Hundred Years War, Gray launched a powerful and emotional attack upon those who championed peace for the wrong reasons, such as idleness, lack of wealth, tiredness or old age. In his opinion, it was only valid to seek peace when this was truly pleasing to God and warned that anyone who ignored this important principle 'should never imagine that the throw of the dice will not go against him, even when he supposes he has the advantagee'.[52] These comments were undoubtedly shaped by his retrospective knowledge of the fragility of the great peace agreed at Brétigny, but also reveal a powerful sense of the value of war as a source of honour, profit and joy. They certainly give some flavour to the way that real military men reacted to the more pious pronouncements of the great medieval theologians and preachers. This might be compared, for example, with the unusual theological ideas of Geoffroi de Charny in the *Livre de chevalerie*, in which the great knight appeared at times to provide a blanket justification for almost any act of violence, but also championed the notion that the great risk and suffering endured by men-at-arms made them the equal if not the superior to clerics.[53]

Above all, first-hand accounts of war offer important crumbs of evidence regarding the ways in which medieval soldiers reacted emotionally to combat.[54] The soldiers who testified at the Nullification trial in 1456 spoke at length about the morale of both the Valois soldiers fighting alongside Joan of Arc and their English and Burgundian opponents. For example, on 28 May 1456, Jean d'Aulon recounted in some detail the attack upon the fortress of Les Tourelles on 7 May 1429, during the siege of Orléans. He graphically highlighted the importance of the Pucelle, and in particular her standard as the rallying point for the French troops. The fact that he also assigned himself a pivotal role in the story might call into question the historical accuracy of the tale. But this narrative would not have worked if there had not been some truth in the notion that such physical examples of leadership could help to motivate and drive soldiers forward in battle.[55]

Male bonding and peer pressure were naturally important factors in martial culture, too. Early in *Le Jouvencel*, the young hero of the tale announced that he had been inspired to bravery and to perform great deeds of arms by his companions, and returned to this theme later in the text when he famously declared:

> War is a joyful thing! ... When you see your friend's courage in a just cause, it brings tears to your eyes. The hardest heart softens, with affection and pity, when you see your friend risk his life in the service of Our Lord and Creator. You're prepared to live or die at his side, you'll never desert him. Such things bring an indescribable pleasure that no-one who hasn't experienced it can understand.[56]

Other statements made by witnesses at the Nullification trial reveal the importance of fear and terror on the battlefield during the Hundred Years War. Testifying on 22 February 1456, Dunois claimed that the greatest impact of Joan of Arc had been upon the Englishmen laying siege to Orléans, reporting that before her arrival

> around two hundred Englishmen would put to flight eight hundred or a thousand men of the royal army, but from that moment, four or five hundred men of the King fighting against the almost the whole of the English forces, put pressure on the Englishmen at the siege to the point that they did not dare to leave their shelters and fortresses.[57]

Again, it may be difficult to accept the historical veracity of this precise claim, and Dunois's related argument that English fear of Joan of Arc paved the way to the Valois victory at the siege of Orléans. Yet his testimony certainly acknowledged the importance of fear and morale on the battlefield, and can be read alongside the observations of other military veterans such as Geoffroi de Charny who repeatedly acknowledged the fear and horror occasioned by battle when calling upon his audience not to submit to the shame of cowardice.[58] Similarly, the author of the *Gesta Henrici Quinti* powerfully described how, at Agincourt, the previously 'sturdy' French knights became 'unmanly' and were seized with 'fear and trembling' as the battle turned against them.[59]

Such fragments of evidence are particularly important within the context of a wider historical debate about the willingness of pre-modern warrior cultures to acknowledge and debate fear and the negative emotions occasioned by war. In his study of military memoirs written after 1450, Yuval Noah Harari has highlighted the fact that pre-modern eyewitness accounts of war tended to focus upon actions rather than internal emotions. This observation has led Harari to conclude that these sources reveal a military culture that actively encouraged or even forced soldiers to focus upon their external behaviour, overriding their inner feelings and emotions. In his eyes, military memoirs were an active force, designed to protect readers from the true emotional cost of war, and to inspire young men to take up arms and conduct themselves well and honourably in war.[60] But it is important to think in more sophisticated ways about the relationship between memoirs and related first-hand accounts of war, and the 'truth' that they represent. It is essential to analyse the complex relationship in each case between those who were remembering warfare and the audiences to whom they were speaking. There is a very great difference, for example, between remembering for oneself and for those who had first-hand experience of combat, and representing the experience to others who had never seen battle. Added to that, there are different challenges for the historian in using documents that were composed close to the events in question versus memoirs that were written later and therefore were vulnerable not only to the pitfalls of memory, but also to the benefits of hindsight. Above all, if the descriptions of the emotions occasioned by war are muted, it is essential to recognise that this may tell us more about the representation of combat than the lived experience. Even in the twentieth century, writers of memoirs have struggled both with the cost of revealing their complex emotional reactions to war and with the simple challenge of representing the truth of combat.[61]

NOTES

1. J. Bourke, *An Intimate History of Killing: Face-to-Face Killing in Twentieth-Century Warfare* (London, 1999), and *Fear: A Cultural History* (London, 2005), pp. 197–221.
2. E. A. Shils and M. Janowitz, 'Cohesion and Disintegration in the Wehrmacht in World War II', *Public Opinion Quarterly*, 12 (1948), pp. 280–315. Their conclusions have since been tested and challenged by other scholars such as R. J. MacCoun, E. Kier and A. Belkin, 'Does Social Cohesion Determine Motivation in Combat? An Old Question with an Old Answer', *Armed Forces and Society*, 32 (2006), pp. 646–54, and L. Wong, T. A. Kolditz, R. A. Millen and T. M. Potter, *Why They Fight: Combat Motivation in the Iraq War* (Carlisle, PA, 2003), and L. Wong, 'Combat Motivation in Today's Soldiers', *Armed Forces and Society*, 32 (2006), pp. 659–63.

3   See, for example, M. Bull, *Eyewitness and Crusade Narrative: Perception and Narration in Accounts of the Second, Third and Fourth Crusades* (Woodbridge, 2018).
4   Scholars continue to debate whether the emotional reactions of soldiers to warfare are universal constants, or dependent upon specific historical culture and context. See, for example, J. Shay, *Achilles in Vietnam: Combat Trauma and the Undoing of Character* (New York, 1994).
5   M. H. Keen, 'Chivalry, Heralds and History', *The Writing of History in the Middle Ages. Essays Presented to R.W. Southern*, ed. R. H. C. Davis and J. M. Wallace-Hadrill (Oxford, 1981), pp. 393–414.
6   The Chandos Herald, *La Vie du Prince Noir [The Life of the Black Prince], by Chandos Herald: Edited from the manuscript in the University of London Library*, ed. D. B. Tyson (Tübingen, 1975), and also see *The Life and Campaigns of the Black Prince*, ed. R. Barber (2nd edition, Woodbridge, 1997).
7   Jean de Waurin [Wavrin], *Recueil des croniques et anchiennes istories de la Grant Bretaigne, a present nommé Engleterre par Jehan de Waurin, seigneur du Forestel*, ed. W. Hardy and E. L. C. P. Hardy, 5 vols (London, 1864–91), ii, pp. 185–222, and Jean Lefèvre de Saint-Rémy, *Chronique de Jean Le Fèvre, seigneur de Saint-Remy*, ed. F. Morand, 2 vols (Paris, 1876–1881), i, pp. 230–69. Also see Curry, *Sources*, pp. 135–71.
8   There are, of course, complex reasons why some medieval Latin and vernacular chroniclers chose to write themselves into their texts as eyewitnesses authenticating the narratives that they were presenting. See, for example, P. Ainsworth, 'Contemporary and "Eyewitness" History', *Historiography in the Middle Ages*, ed. D. Mauskopf Deliyannis (Leiden, 2003), pp. 249–76.
9   Jean le Bel, *Chronique de Jean le Bel*, ed. J. Viard and E. Déprez, 2 vols (Paris, 1904), I, pp. 35–77, and *The True Chronicles of Jean le Bel, 1290–1360*, trans. N. Bryant (Woodbridge, 2011), pp. 34–50, together with N. Chareyron, *Jean le Bel: Le Maître de Froissart, grand imagier de la guerre de Cent Ans* (Brussels, 1996), pp. 11–13.
10 *Journal d'un Bourgeois de Paris*, ed. A. Tuetey (Paris, 1881), pp. 244–6, together with *A Parisian Journal 1405–1449*, trans. J. Shirley (Oxford, 1968). Luke Giraudet is currently preparing a new scholarly edition of this important text.
11 There are, of course, complex reasons why some medieval Latin and vernacular chroniclers chose to write themselves into their texts as eyewitnesses authenticating the narratives that they were presenting. See, for example, Ainsworth, 'Contemporary and "Eyewitness" History', pp. 249–76.
12 *Gesta Henrici Quinti*, ed. J. S. Roskell and F. Taylor (Oxford, 1975), together with Curry, *Sources*, pp. 22–40.
13 *Gesta Henrici Quinti*, pp. 84–5. Curry has remarked that 'there can be no doubt of its central importance in every work on the subject' (*Sources*, p. 23).
14 *John Page's Siege of Rouen*, ed. J. Bellis (Heidelberg, 2015).
15 *Le livre des fais du bon messire Jehan le Maingre, dit Bouciquaut, Mareschal de France et gouverneur de Jennes*, ed. D. Lalande (Geneva, 1985), and *The Chivalric Biography*

of Boucicaut, Jean II Le Meingre, trans. C. Taylor and J. H. M. Taylor (Woodbridge, 2016), together with my monograph *A Virtuous Knight: Defending Marshal Boucicaut (Jean II Le Meingre, 1366–1421)* (Woodbridge, 2019), which examines the historical evidence provided by this book and also explores the questions of authorship, audience and purpose.

16 *The Saint Albans Chronicle: The Chronica Maiora of Thomas Walsingham, II, 1396–1422*, ed. J. Taylor, W. Childs and L. Watkiss (Oxford, 2011), pp. 672–82.

17 K. Fowler, 'News From the Front: Letters and Dispatches of the Fourteenth-Century', *Guerre et société en France*, pp. 63–92. Also note the eleven surviving letters attributed to Jeanne d'Arc, *De brieven van Jeanne d'Arc*, ed. J. M. van Winter and D. Th. Enklaar (Groningen-Jakarta, 1954), and *Joan of Arc, La Pucelle*, trans. C. Taylor (Manchester, 2006).

18 *Chronicon de Lanercost, MCCI–MCCCXLVI*, ed. J. Stevenson (Edinburgh, 1839), and *The Anonimalle Chronicle, 1333–1381*, ed. V. H. Galbraith (Manchester, 1927).

19 *Adae Murimuth continuatio chronicarum Robertus de Avesbury de gestis mirabilibus regis Edwardi tertii*, ed. E. M. Thompson (London, 1889).

20 *Chronique du Religieux de Saint-Denys contenant le règne de Charles VI, de 1380 à 1422*, ed. L. Bellaguet, 6 vols (Paris, 1839–1852), II, p. 520, and also see E. Gaucher, 'Deux regards sur une défaite: Nicopolis (d'après la *Chronique de Saint-Denis* et le *Livre des faits de Boucicaut*)', *Cahiers de recherches médiévales* 1 (1996), p. 95, and more broadly, B. Guenée, *L'opinion publique à la fin du moyen âge d'après la 'Chronique de Charles VI' du Religieux de Saint-Denis* (Paris, 2002).

21 M. Jones, 'Froissart, Jean (1337?–c.1404)', *ODNB*, and the Online Froissart digital edition at http://www.hrionline.ac.uk/onlinefroissart.

22 *Froissart à la cour de Béarn: L'écrivain, les arts et le pouvoir*, ed. V. Fasseur (Turnhout, 2009), and G. Pépin, 'Towards a Rehabilitation of Froissart's Credibility. The Non Fictitious Bascot de Mauléon', *Soldier Experience*, pp. 175–90.

23 C. Taylor, *Chivalry and the Ideals of Knighthood in France During the Hundred Years War* (Cambridge, 2013), pp. 231–75.

24 Robert Avesbury, *De gestis mirabilibus regis Edwardi tertii*, ed. E.M. Thompson (London, 1889), pp. 259–61. Also see E. Boutaric, 'Notices et extraits de documents inédits relatifs à l'histoire de France sous Philippe le Bel', *Notices et extraits des manuscrits de la Bibliothèque Nationale et autres bibliothèques*, 20 (1867), pp. 112–9; G. Templeman, 'Two French Attempts to Invade England During the Hundred Years War', *Studies in French Language, Literature and History Presented to R.L. Graeme Ritchie* (Cambridge, 1949), pp. 225–38; B. Schnerb, 'Un plan de guerre anglo-bourguignon en 1430', *Mémoires*, 5 (1986), pp. 106–11; idem, 'La préparation des opérations militaires au début du XVe siècle: L'exemple d'un document prévisionnel bourguignon', in *Guerre et société en France*, pp. 189–96.

25 C. J. Phillpotts, 'The French Battle Plan During the Agincourt Campaign', *EHR*, 99 (1984), pp. 59–66.

26 London, Lambeth Palace Library, MS 506, folios 38r–43v. There is an incomplete edition in *Letters and Papers Illustrative of the Wars of the English in France During*

the Reign of Henry VI, ed. J. Stevenson, 2 vols (London, 1861–4), II, ii, pp. 578–85. Also see M. G. A. Vale, 'Sir John Fastolf's "Report" of 1435. A New Interpretation Reconsidered', *Nottingham Medieval Studies*, 17 (1973), pp. 78–84.

27 C. Taylor, 'English Writings on Chivalry and Warfare During the Hundred Years War', *Soldiers, Nobles and Gentlemen: Essays in Honour of Maurice Keen*, ed. P. Coss and C. Tyerman (Woodbridge, 2009), pp. 64–84.

28 C. Allmand, *The De Re Militari of Vegetius: The Reception, Transmission and Legacy of a Roman Text in the Middle Ages* (Cambridge, 2011), and also see *Translations médiévales: Cinq siècles de traductions en français au moyen âge (XIe-XVe siècles). Étude et répertoire*, ed. C. Galderisi, 2 vols (Turnhout, 2011), II, pp. 256–60.

29 See, for example, the wide-ranging essays in the *Journal of Medieval Military History*, 2 (2004).

30 Jean de Vignay, *Les enseignements de Théodore Paléologue*, ed. C. Knowles (London, 1983).

31 Geoffroi de Charny, *The Book of Chivalry of Geoffroi de Charny: Text, Context and Translation*, ed. and trans. R. W. Kaeuper and E. Kennedy (Philadelphia, 1996), and M. A. Taylor, 'A Critical Edition of Geoffroy de Charny's *Livre Charny* and the *Demandes pour la joute, les tournois et la guerre*' (unpublished Ph.D. dissertation, University of North Carolina, 1977).

32 Philippe de Mézières, *Le songe du vieil pèlerin*, ed. G. W. Coopland, 2 vols (Cambridge, 1969), and *Une epistre lamentable et consolatoire adressée en 1397 à Philippe le Hardi, duc de Bourgogne, sur la défaite de Nicopolis (1396)*, ed. P. Contamine and J. Paviot (Paris, 2008), together with H. A. Hamid, 'Philippe de Mézières and the New Order of the Passion: II, The Sources', *Bulletin of the Faculty of the Arts of Alexandria University*, 18 (1964), pp. 1–105, and M. J. A. Brown, 'Philippe de Mézières' Order of the Passion: An Annotated Edition' (unpublished Ph.D. dissertation, University of Nebraska, 1971), pp. 93–213.

33 *L'honneur de la Couronne de France: Quatre libelles contre les Anglais (vers 1418 – vers 1429)*, ed. N. Pons (Paris, 1990), pp. 17–79.

34 Antoine de La Sale, *Oeuvres complètes d'Antoine de La Sale*, ed. F. Desonay, 2 vols (Liège-Paris, 1935–41), and *Jehan de Saintré*, ed. J. Misrahi and C. Knudsen (3rd edn, Geneva, 1978).

35 Jean de Bueil, *Le Jouvencel, suivi du commentaire de Guillaume Tringant*, ed. M. Szkilnik (Paris, 2018), together with the forthcoming translation by Jane Taylor and myself.

36 *Le Jouvencel*, 694.

37 Thomas Gray, *Scalacronica (1272–1363)*, ed. and trans. A. King (Woodbridge, 2005).

38 Perceval de Cagny, *Chroniques de Perceval de Cagny*, ed. H. Moranvillé (Paris, 1902).

39 Guillaume Gruel, *Chronique d'Arthur de Richemont, connétable de France, duc de Bretagne (1393–1458)*, ed. A. Le Vavasseur (Paris, 1890), pp. 17–8 and 126. Also see Curry, *Sources*, pp. 182–5.

40 *The Controversy Between Sir Richard Scrope and Sir Robert Grosvenor in the Court of Chivalry, AD 1385–1390*, ed. N. H. Nicolas, 2 vols (London, 1832), and A. Ayton,

'Knights, Esquires and Military Service: The Evidence of Armorial Cases Before the Court of Chivalry', *The Medieval Military Revolution: State, Society and Military Change in Medieval and Early Modern Europe*, ed. A. Ayton and J. L. Price (London, 1995), pp. 81–104.
41 Thomas Basin, *Histoire des règnes de Charles VII et de Louis XI par Thomas Basin*, ed. J. Quicherat 4 vols (Paris, 1855–9), IV, pp. 290–347, and M. H. Keen and M. J. Daniel, 'English Diplomacy and the Sack of Fougères in 1449', *History*, 59 (1974), pp. 375–91, and C. Taylor, 'Brittany and the French Crown: The Legacy of the English Attack upon Fougères (1449)', *The Medieval State: Essays Presented to James Campbell*, ed. J. Maddicott and D. Palliser (London, 2000), pp. 243–57.
42 *Procès en nullité de la condamnation de Jeanne d'Arc*, ed. P. Duparc, 5 vols (Paris 1977–89), together with *Joan of Arc, La Pucelle*.
43 *Procès en nullité de la condamnation de Jeanne d'Arc*, I, pp. 316–26, and *Joan of Arc, La Pucelle*, p. 278.
44 *Procès de condamnation et de réhabilitation de Jeanne d'Arc dite la Pucelle*, ed. J. E. J. Quicherat, 5 vols (Paris, 1841–9), III, pp. 391–2, and *Procès de condamnation de Jeanne d'Arc*, I, pp. 221–2.
45 C. T. Wood, 'Joan of Arc's Mission and the Lost Record of her Interrogation at Poitiers', *Fresh Verdicts on Joan of Arc*, ed. B. Wheeler and C. T. Wood (New York, 1996), pp. 19–30.
46 *Scalacronica*, pp. 170–88.
47 Ainsworth, 'Contemporary and "Eyewitness" History', p. 275.
48 J. S. Roskell and F. Taylor, 'The Authorship and Purpose of the *Gesta Henrici Quinti*', *Bulletin of the John Rylands Library*, 53 (1970–1), pp. 428–64 and 54 (1971–2), pp. 223–40.
49 For Curry's careful dissection of the consequence of these issues for the value of the text as a report on the battle, see *Sources*, pp. 24–6.
50 *Procès en nullité de la condamnation de Jeanne d'Arc*, I, pp. 361–7, and *Joan of Arc, La Pucelle*, pp. 296–7.
51 A. King, 'A Helm With a Crest of Gold. The Order of Chivalry in Thomas Gray's *Scalacronica*', *Fourteenth Century England*, 1 (2000), p. 25, and also see p. 35: 'For Gray, chivalry remained a thoroughly pragmatic (and entirely unromantic) arrangement.'
52 *Scalacronica*, pp. 190–4, and also see A. King, 'War and Peace: A Knight's Tale: The Ethics of War in Sir Thomas Gray's *Scalacronica*', *War, Government and Aristocracy in the British Isles, c.1150–1500. Essays in Honour of Michael Prestwich*, ed. C. Given-Wilson, A. Kettle and L. Scales (Woodbridge, 2008), pp. 148–62.
53 *The Book of Chivalry of Geoffroi de Charny*, pp. 96, 154–66 and 176.
54 A. Taylor, 'Chivalric Conversation and the Denial of Male Fear', *Conflicted Identities and Multiple Masculinities. Men in the Medieval West*, ed. J. Murray (New York, 1999), pp. 169–88, and C. Taylor, 'Military Courage in the Chivalric Imagination of Late Medieval France', *Cahiers de Recherches Médiévales et Humanistes* 23 (2012), pp. 129–47.

55 *Procès en nullité de la condamnation de Jeanne d'Arc*. I, 475–87, and *Joan of Arc, La Pucelle*, 344–5.
56 Bueil, *Le jouvencel*, pp. 291–2. The English quotation comes from the forthcoming translation by Jane Taylor and myself.
57 *Procès en nullité de la condamnation de Jeanne d'Arc*, I, pp. 316–26, and *Joan of Arc, La Pucelle*, p. 280.
58 *The Book of Chivalry of Geoffroi de Charny*, p. 194.
59 *Gesta Henrici Quinti*, p. 90.
60 N. Y. Harari, *Renaissance Military Memoirs: War, History, and Identity, 1450–1600* (Woodbridge, 2004); idem, 'Martial Illusions: War and Disillusionment in Twentieth-Century and Renaissance Military Memoirs', *Journal of Military History*, 69 (2005), pp. 43–72; idem, 'Military Memoirs: A Historical Overview of the Genre from the Middle Ages to the Late Modern Era', *War in History*, 14 (2007), pp. 289–309; and idem, *The Ultimate Experience: Battlefield Revelations and the Making of Modern War Culture, 1450–2000* (Basingstoke, 2008).
61 K. McLoughlin, 'War and Words', *The Cambridge Companion to War Writing*, ed. K. McLoughlin (Cambridge, 2009), pp. 15–24, and idem, *Authoring War: The Literary Representation of War from the Iliad to Iraq* (Cambridge, 2011).

8 Navies and Maritime Warfare

Andrew Ayton and Craig Lambert

In August 1371, an English naval force commanded by Humphrey Bohun, earl of Hereford and the two admirals, Guy, Lord Brian and John, Lord Neville, encountered a large Flemish fleet in the Bay of Bourgneuf. The Anonimalle Chronicle offers the fullest contemporary English narrative of the assembly of Hereford's fleet and the sea battle that it fought;[1] yet it neither identifies the 'enemy' nor locates the battle.[2] It provides no strategic background to the action and describes the fighting in only the most general of terms. We learn nothing of manoeuvres or tactics, only that it was a long drawn-out affair involving lances, swords and archery in which, owing to divine favour, the outnumbered English prevailed. What precision there is concerns the spoils of victory: that twenty-seven of the eighty Flemish ships were captured, of which twenty-five were taken back to London, the remaining two being burnt for want of mariners to crew them. But, for all its limitations, the Anonimalle account of the 'Bay of Flemings' is to be welcomed because encounters fought at sea captured the attention of mainstream chroniclers far less often than those fought on land, and their engagement with other aspects of maritime warfare was also, at best, selective. The brutality – or commendable bravado – of coastal raiders would often be commented upon;[3] a storm-wrecked fleet would come under the spotlight if contrasting fates of the villainous and the virtuous could be attributed to divine intervention;[4] as was his wont, Jean Froissart was often able to discern chivalry amidst the salt spray. Such morsels are certainly worth having: Diaz de Gamez's eyewitness account of the Castilian coastal raids on southern England in 1405 is a veritable feast,[5] but in general the naval historian will not find his staple fare, let alone his richest pickings, in the narrative sources.

Getting to grips with the maritime dimension of the Hundred Years War and with the naval resources deployed by its protagonists requires, on the one hand, controlled, imaginative deduction from a mass of non-explicit evidence, for strategy and operational aims are rarely explained in the sources. But, above all, it is necessary to engage closely with the administrative records: the documentation drawn up when naval operations were being planned, while they were taking place and after the event, when payments owed by the crown were accounted for. Such French archival material informed the pioneering work of Charles de la Roncière and, more recently, has been made accessible in a printed edition.[6] Few of the corresponding English records have as yet been published, but they survive in vast quantity, mainly at the National Archives.[7] The potential of these records is well illustrated by the richly (if not quite perfectly) documented English fleet at the Bay of Flemings. Payrolls and indentures reveal a force of forty-two vessels (21 ships, 21 barges), eight of them owned by the king, the remainder being requisitioned merchantmen, mostly from south-western ports.[8] In all, 1,724 mariners of all grades received wages, and the crews were stiffened by 243 armed men and 279 archers. Also serving on these vessels were the personal retinues of the earl of Hereford and the two admirals, a total of 420 men-at-arms and a further 460 archers in the king's pay.[9] The naming of masters and ships in the naval payrolls, and the preservation of full nominal rolls for the retinues of Hereford and Brian, means that the Bay of Flemings becomes a sea battle with a distinctive personality, involving identifiable vessels and men whose backgrounds, past experience and subsequent careers can be reconstructed. More surprisingly, perhaps, the administrative records also cast light on tactics and weaponry. The combined use of sailing ships and oared barges may well offer an insight into how tactical flexibility was achieved in the challenging environment of a marine 'battlefield'. Moreover, an inventory of the armour and weapons carried on this voyage by the king's ships reveals precisely what the men had to fight with, and how much of the equipment was lost or used up. Thus, while the Anonimalle Chronicle tells us simply that archers participated in the battle, the administrative records reveal how many archers there were, the names of 360 of them,[10] and how many sheaves of arrows were expended on the king's ships: 533.[11] As many as 180 sheaves were used up by the men on the *Rodecog*, which we can imagine at the centre of the action.

Although scarcely noticed in the modern secondary literature,[12] the sea battle at the Bay of Flemings in 1371 serves as an ideal entry point for investigating the maritime dimension of the Hundred Years War. In addition to illustrating rather well the relative merits of narrative accounts and administrative records as sources, it embodies in a single snapshot some of the key characteristics of the naval war: the prominence of ship-to-ship action – of sea fights – in a war whose land-based campaigns are often portrayed as exercises in battle avoidance; the large numbers of soldiers as well as seamen serving on the ships of a fighting fleet; the crown's heavy dependence, in raising such fleets, on privately owned merchant vessels; and the vulnerability, in the seascape of war, of the property and interests of neighbouring polities, whether or not they were allied with England or France. Additionally, and perhaps above all, what the Bay of Flemings exemplifies is the intensity of offensive naval (as contrasted with logistical) operations during the two decades prior to the truce of Leulingham (1389). It was during this phase of the conflict that the potential – but also the limitations – of seaborne operations for influencing the course and outcome of the war were most clearly demonstrated.[13] In presenting a new interpretation of the maritime dimension of the war, we shall assess the reasons for, and implications of, these and other distinctive features of the war at sea, and consider how, in terms of naval activity, the three broad phases of the war – 1337–60, 1369–89, 1415–53 – differed from each other and why.

Our investigation is driven by three key questions. To what extent and in what ways were strategy and naval operations of England and France, whether logistical or 'fighting' in nature, shaped by environmental constraints and geopolitical considerations, and how far by the maritime resources that were available for deployment? How effective were these operations in fulfilling the protagonists' strategic aims? What were the relative merits of the various types of naval resource that could be drawn upon?

THE WAR AT SEA: STRATEGY AND OPERATIONS

The Maritime Environment and Naval Warfare

It is something of a commonplace that the stretch of sea separating England from mainland Europe is at once a barrier and a highway. Shipping an army intended for a large-scale land campaign posed a formidable logistical challenge. Army size was constrained by the carrying capacity of the fleet of available transport vessels, and much depended on the vagaries of the weather. While assembling the hundreds of vessels required to transport the men, horses, equipment and supplies that an army of 5,000 men needed, commanders were ever conscious that contrary winds might cause delays or even cancellation, and that once at sea a fleet could be scattered by storms. Edward III's personal role in the war ended anticlimactically in October 1372 when a fleet carrying 6,000 men-at-arms and archers, having failed to make progress against headwinds, was forced to return to port.[14] Yet the relative rapidity and efficiency with which, in favourable conditions, a seaborne force powered by wind or oar could travel offered the possibility of mounting surprise amphibious operations against coastal and estuarine locations, while making it difficult for defenders to anticipate when and where such incursions would occur. It is this balance of advantage in favour of the attacker that explains the high success rate of the hit-and-run coastal raids that were so commonly employed by both sides. Given this potential for efficient movement had made the Channel into a major highway for shipborne merchandise, it was inevitable that predation of trading vessels, whatever their allegiance, would become a pervasive feature of the Anglo-French struggle. Although less easily executed than raids on fixed, land-based targets, the interception of merchantmen at sea could bring huge rewards, which meant that woven into this particularly brutal form of economic warfare, and finding convenient pretext in the wider war between polities, were the feuds of rival maritime communities and much private enterprise activity.

The environment of the Channel – an expanse of open water, animated by tides and volatile weather – combined with the necessarily episodic and usually non-coincident occurrence of the protagonists' naval operations, the limitations of maritime technology and the pervasiveness of private commercial predation resulted in the fluid and often unpredictable warfare that is both characteristic of the maritime sphere and very different from its land-based counterpart. 'The balance of initiative and fighting power shifted from one season to another';[15] there could be no real 'command of the sea' during the Hundred Years War. Temporary 'zones of control', whether static or moving, were the most that could be aspired to.[16] There were several different contexts to which this might apply. Ensuring the security of coastal waters against incursions from maritime raiders was difficult unless the latter's arrival at a particular locality could be anticipated. Waiting in a fixed location risked exposure to surprise attack, while embarking on a 'sweep' of the Channel resembled looking for a needle in a haystack. Maintaining localised control was crucial if blockades associated with sieges were to be maintained, but just how problematic that could be was seen during the siege of Calais (1346–7), which lasted nearly a year because the French were able to run in supplies.[17] French investment of Harfleur in 1416 failed because an English relief fleet reached the town after dispersing the blockading fleet.[18] The security of the routes plied by trading vessels, shipborne diplomatic missions and supply convoys depended on the presence of armed escort vessels, but this moving, localised 'control' was liable to be challenged. Even larger commercial convoys and army transport fleets, though moving like juggernauts, were vulnerable; their size made them all the more tempting as targets and easier to find. In the spring of 1380, aware that a Castilian galley fleet would be on the prowl in the western Channel, the English switched the embarkation of the duke of Buckingham's expedition, bound for Brittany, from the Devon ports to Sandwich.[19] The other way of ensuring localised security for an invasion armada was to deploy a separate war fleet tasked with fending off the interception threat – an option that paid off in July 1417 when, on the eve of Henry V's invasion of Normandy, the earl of Huntingdon's squadron, sent from Southampton, defeated the allied French-Castilian and Genoese fleet, probably near the mouth of the Seine estuary.[20]

The Maritime Battlefield

The environmental, organisational and technological constraints that shaped the character of maritime warfare naturally affected the incidence and wider impact of sea battles, but it would be misleading to present them as exceptional events of strictly limited significance. Indeed, in spite of these constraints and the particular hazards involved in shipboard combat, it was perhaps more at sea than on land that 'battle' was a defining feature of the Hundred Years War. Transports and convoys no doubt sailed in the hope of avoiding contact with the enemy; patrolling voyages might be as much (if not exclusively) concerned with information gathering as fighting. But many patrols were 'viages de guerre' involving ships packed with armed men and archers intent on neutralising enemy vessels on the high seas and taking lucrative prizes;[21] and when a full-scale war fleet put to sea its intention was to fight, or at least to deter by its presence. Two of the most striking examples occurred during the first phase of the war: on 24 June 1340 when Edward III successfully forced battle on the French fleet at Sluys,[22] and on 29 August 1350 when the same king confronted the Castilian armada off Winchelsea in an engagement dubbed 'Les Espagnols-sur-Mer'.[23] The latter shows that, given plenty of warning and good intelligence, interception in open water was possible, while the former illustrates a distinctive feature of the war at sea, namely that battles often occurred inshore. Fleets were most easily located and attacked before they left home, as at Sluys in 1340, or as they arrived at their destination, as happened in June 1372 at La Rochelle, where a Castilian squadron was waiting for the earl of Pembroke's under-strength flotilla.[24] As we have seen, a besieged port was also likely to witness inshore battles between blockading and relief fleets, that in the estuary of the Seine off Harfleur in August 1416 being a particularly large-scale, long, drawn-out and bloody affair.

For all the drama and strategic significance that attended the clash of war fleets, what really made the maritime sphere an arena of battle was that endemic feature of the war: the predation of merchant shipping. Armed commercial convoys were a natural response to the vulnerability of lone ships and they offered security of sorts, but they also presented so tempting a target that war fleets of commensurate size were organised to take them on. The resulting large-scale battles, like the Bay of Flemings, were a regularly occurring feature of that phase of the war. Four years later in the same location, thirty-six English merchantmen were seized or burnt, which the Anonimalle Chronicle considered 'the greatest loss of ships that England suffered at sea' at this time.[25] In 1387, the earl of Arundel's fifty-one-vessel war fleet, carrying nearly 2,500 soldiers and more than 2,600 seamen, took on a much larger Franco-Flemish fleet and captured about forty ships laden with 5,000 tonnes of wine,[26] probably one of the largest hauls since Sluys (1340) when the greater part of the French fleet was taken.[27] Measured by the intensity of the fighting and the numbers of combatants engaged, the sea fights of the 1370s and 1380s were major battles by medieval standards, their frequency all the more striking given that land battles had become less common during this phase. Moreover, if we scale down our expectations of what constitutes a 'sea battle' and take account of smaller actions, we find a seascape of war that was peppered by ship-to-ship combat, much of it centring on armed merchantmen.[28]

For the historian of warfare, sea battles large and small are of particular interest. In terms of frequency and the numbers of seamen and soldiers involved, they constitute an important subset of all medieval battles. While sharing much of the weaponry of land warfare, they had a distinctive character as a consequence of the maritime environment and the ship-centred focus of the action. The predominant aim was to capture an opponent's vessels, which were valued as prizes, though in the process of immobilising them or snuffing out resistance, they might be critically damaged. Given the limitations of available missile-weapon technology, sea battles were necessarily fought at close-quarters, by getting alongside, perhaps ramming, and then grappling and boarding.[29] This was bloody combat with hand-held weapons in which the armoured fighter had an advantage. It is small wonder that Edward III's experienced men-at-arms overwhelmed the Norman seamen at Sluys and that, later in the century, the mariners on the king's ships donned mail coats and bascinets when they went into action.[30] But, as on land, it was combat that was accompanied by a torrent of missiles.[31] Not for nothing were there more archers than armed men or men-at-arms in the English war fleet at the Bay of Flemings and elsewhere; as the equipment inventories make clear, arrows and throwing 'lances' (gads and darts), were expended in large quantities.[32] Once engaged, men could not easily flee from a sea battle, a prospect no doubt all the more terrifying when one side used fire as a weapon, as the Castilians did at La Rochelle.[33] The consequent 'prevail or perish' mentality meant that, by medieval standards, such engagements were often long, drawn-out affairs. The battle off Harfleur in 1416 reputedly lasted seven hours,[34] while the fighting at Sluys (1340) continued into the night. The engaged vessels' key characteristics as fighting platforms could make a crucial difference to the outcome. Oared craft (galleys; balingers and barges also had sail) offered greater flexibility of movement,[35] while sailing ships, especially carracks, had the advantage of height. Consequently, requisitioned cogs intended as escort vessels would have 'castles' added fore and aft to provide raised shooting platforms.[36] At Les Espagnols-sur-Mer in 1350, the Castilian ships towered over the English 'like castles above cottages',[37] though the latter ultimately prevailed. In late August 1416, the failure of five low-built balingers to take a single, large carrack in a running sea fight demonstrated that, as in a land battle, an elevated position could cancel out numerical superiority.[38] The tactical moral to be drawn from such asymmetrical sea battles was that the key to success might lie in a distinctively nautical form of 'combined arms': not Froissart's fanciful idea, influenced by land battles, that ships bristling with men-at-arms might be flanked by vessels stuffed with archers,[39] but the deployment of mixed fleets of low-built, manoeuvrable oared vessels and taller sailing ships – a combination offering real potential for tactical flexibility.[40]

Thus far, no mention has been made of gunpowder weapons. Shipboard deployment of guns is first suggested in a financial account of 1337–8: 'a certain iron instrument for firing quarrels and lead pellets, with powder' had been acquired for the *All Hallows Cog*, one of the English king's ships.[41] This remains something of a curiosity, since references to shipboard guns become frequent only in the later fourteenth century. The recent identification of 'masters of naval artillery' (or master gunners) in the earl of Cambridge's fleet bound for Portugal in 1381 is erroneous,[42] but records show that twenty-nine 'gonnes' were to have been used on Edward III's abortive naval expedition in 1372.[43] Turning to England's adversaries, the records reveal the delivery of gunpowder weapons to the ships of the *l'armée de la mer* at Harfleur in 1377 and 1383,[44] and chroniclers report that they were deployed in battle at La Rochelle (1372), St Malo (1379) and Dunkirk (1387).[45] By Henry V's reign, guns were frequently mounted on the king's ships, though in small numbers: with seven guns, the *Holigost* (760 tonnes) had the most.[46] At this stage, gunpowder weapons appear to have been used 'for the defence of the ship', as had been envisaged with the *All Hallow's Cog* in the 1330s, rather than for long-range, offensive gunnery.

If in terms of the scale and relative frequency of the larger sea fights and the everyday occurrence of ship-to-ship encounters the significance of shipboard combat can hardly be doubted, what of its wider impact? The key issue is not whether any kind of meaningful 'command of the sea' could be achieved by a single knock-out blow; even the destruction of the French fleet at Sluys in 1340 did not deliver such a result to the English. Sea battles mattered for other reasons. First, and most obviously, given the high capital value of ships and cargoes, the individual and community-level impact of gains and losses from major sea fights or piracy was quite as much a part of the essential fabric of warfare as the ravaging of town and country by land-based armies. Second, and most intriguingly, there could in so many ways be consequences for the balance of strategic advantage in the war. The losses suffered in the Bay of Flemings appear to be what prompted Count Louis of Flanders to ratify a trade agreement with England over which he had been prevaricating since 1370. By doing so, he made his neutrality in the Anglo-French war clear.[47] Although, in terms of the loss of ships, the destruction of the earl of Pembroke's flotilla at La Rochelle in 1372 was hardly a naval disaster, it had consequences, most obviously that there was less resistance to the subsequent French conquest of Poitou and Saintonge. It also had a 'highly stimulating effect' on the English effort at sea,[48] contributing thereby to the much increased emphasis on naval operations that is evident during this phase of the war.

Contrasting Strategies: The Protagonists' Responses to Maritime Imperatives

The very existence of the Channel as both environmental phenomenon and trading artery should ensure a centre-stage role for maritime logistics and economics in any study of the Hundred Years War. Yet just how much the fluctuating fortunes of the protagonists were bound up with their ability to overcome and exploit the attributes of the Channel has perhaps been insufficiently recognised. One of the most striking features of the war is that, while the English mounted repeated and deeply penetrative invasions of the French kingdom with armies that had been shipped across, their Valois adversaries failed to launch anything comparable throughout the entire war. Large-scale invasions of England were seriously planned in 1340, 1369 and 1385–7, the preparations at Sluys in 1386 being on a truly monumental scale. But all were aborted. The bulk of the French crown's naval operations involved, on the one hand, raids on English coastal communities or the predation of commercial shipping, the apparent aim being to degrade England's maritime resources and thus its capacity to conduct the war. On the other, there were inshore operations around the coast of France. Typical of the latter were attempts to interfere with invasion fleets, but also such coups de main as the amphibious operations that captured Bourg and Blaye, on the northern shore of the Gironde, in 1339.[49] For the English, 'fighting' naval operations such as these, whether offensive or defensive, were an accompaniment – not an alternative – to the core, logistical task of shipping armies to France. This fundamental contrast in scale and ambition between the maritime effort of the protagonists is reflected by the proportionately greater attention given to the naval dimension of the English war effort.

How are these contrasting responses to the maritime imperatives of the war to be explained? It could be argued that the English kings, with continental territories to defend, allies to support and the French crown to win by force of arms, had a much greater incentive to take on the maritime logistical challenge. The only alternative would have been to fight the war entirely by proxy. Yet a full-scale invasion of England would surely have been the most effective way for the king of France to put a stop to his rival's pretentions, to knock him out of the war, and bring peace to France.[50] Given that strategy is the art of the possible, a self-assessment of available maritime resources – how readily accessible they were and how effectively they could be managed – would surely have shaped what the protagonists considered to be realistic options and what they attempted operationally. From the outset, the English crown displayed a more consistent capacity for mobilising the realm's ships and shipboard manpower for the war effort; indeed this was essential if armies were regularly to be transported to France. By contrast, it is illustrative of the maritime constraints under which the French crown operated that one of the most ambitious plans to invade England was to have involved hiring an army of 12,000 mercenaries carried in a Danish fleet; and it is typical of the French war effort that the plan came to nothing.[51] But French kings were notably successful in gaining access to Castilian shipping and in particular to that realm's professional galley fleet.[52] These shallow-draught, oared vessels were ideally suited to the coastal and estuarine raiding and commercial predation that were central to French strategy, and they duly made a major contribution to France's maritime effort, particularly during the 1370s and 1380s in Biscay and the Channel, just as the Genoese galleys had in 1338–9. Competition to secure – or neutralise – the Castilian and Portuguese galley fleets was one aspect of Anglo-French diplomatic and military rivalry in Iberia during the 1360s, 1370s and 1380s: the consequent diversion of manpower and treasure into peninsular intrigues is nicely illustrative of both the wider implications of the war at sea and the indirect costs required to resource it.

English Strategy and Maritime Operations

The geopolitics of the Hundred Years War, which had profound effects on the protagonists' grand strategies and operational methods, was largely determined by the maritime environment of the Atlantic and Channel. At the heart of the war was a struggle to control the coastline of France from Biscay to Flanders, and especially its strategically located ports. For the French, this was a continuation of the quest for access to the open sea that had been informing its grand strategy since the early thirteenth century.[53] For the English king at the start of the war, maintaining direct access to continental fiefs and key economic partners went hand in hand with securing disembarkation points for armies shipped from England. A secure sea route to Aquitaine, important not least for wine shipments, would benefit greatly from friendly relations with the duke of Brittany, or at least his neutrality, while England's close economic relationship with Flanders, based on the supply of raw wool to the cloth industry there, depended on the security of sea lanes and disembarkation points. Breton and Low Countries ports at which English armies and supplies could be unloaded without hindrance also served as bases from which the sea could be patrolled and campaigns into the heart of France launched – a combination of naval and military potential that the capture of Calais in 1347 took to a new level.[54] Possession of strategically located French ports minimised occasions when it was necessary for an English army to attempt landfall on a hostile stretch of coastline, and provided the essential infrastructure underpinning Edward's ambitious multi-front strategies which drove the campaigns of 1345–7 and 1355–6.

During the gruelling two decades of war from 1369 to 1389 – a period generally remembered for the rapid territorial gains made by a resurgent Valois monarchy – control of strategically important ports from Bayonne in the south-west to Calais in the north-east, and beyond into Flanders, became a formally recognised centrepiece of English strategy. Through negotiation, Brest and Cherbourg were added to existing possessions in 1377 and 1378, and during the following decade unsuccessful attempts were made to take further ports.[55] As Richard, Lord Scrope argued in parliament in October 1378, these coastal strongholds were the barbicans of the kingdom beyond the sea that, it was hoped, would keep the war confined to France.[56] They would provide more bases for naval patrols and a range of starting points for penetrative land campaigns,[57] thereby posing a threat to French resources at sea while stretching them on land. Moreover, the barbicans were militarily and financially sustainable, making 'the best possible use of English resources'.[58] Crucial to that sustainability was naval support: there was now a far greater emphasis on the deployment of soldiers in naval expeditions, of which the earl of Hereford's voyage to the Bay of Bourgneuf in 1371 was an early, but typical example. Historians have long recognised the achievements of the leading French admiral during the 1370s and 1380s, Jean de Vienne, particularly his skilful employment of French and Castilian galleys in a series of coastal raiding campaigns.[59] But we should not overlook the sheer scale and cumulative effectiveness of the English naval effort during the same period; indeed, it is likely that Charles V's reforms of the Clos des Galées in 1374 were in part prompted by the increase in English naval activity.[60] Excluding the operations of small squadrons, eleven major 'fighting' fleets put to sea from 1369 to 1389: these were *viages de guerre* not army transport missions.[61] Given that each of the largest of these fleets (1372, 1377, 1378) carried as many soldiers as served in the major land campaigns, it is not surprising that, overall, from 1369 to 1380 almost as many men-at-arms and archers fought at sea as on land: 27,000 as compared with 30,000. And since more than 40,000 mariners were employed in fighting or transportation fleets, it can be seen that, in terms of manpower commitment to the French conflict, it was the war at sea that predominated. It was not significantly different during the 1380s. While land armies were sent to Iberia in 1381 and 1386, and Scotland in 1385, a series of naval expeditions sought to keep up the pressure on France, culminating in Arundel's *viage de guerre* during the summer of 1388, which involved 3,500 soldiers and 2,900 seamen. Given the scale of this expanded naval effort, that it consumed only 23 per cent of total war expenditure during the years 1369 to 1380[62] suggests that this was also a cost-effective way to wage war.[63] We might find fault with the planning or execution of individual expeditions,[64] which during times of financial stringency were as liable to be hit by sudden funding cuts as by adverse weather,[65] but overall we should surely conclude that the money was well spent. Whether tasked with intercepting enemy raiders or armed commercial convoys, with amphibious operations against coastal locations, or with relieving blockaded English-held ports, these naval operations complemented and reinforced the barbican strategy.[66] A steady focus on the war at sea helped England to weather the storm of raids and the threat of invasion – a threat that became very real when the French crown gained access to the Flemish merchant fleet following the duke of Burgundy's acquisition of the county of Flanders in 1384. That, by the late 1380s, the war had descended into what was for the English an acceptable stalemate was largely owing to sustained and generally well-targeted naval operations.

Control of the coastline of France remains the litmus test whereby the health of the English war effort under the Lancastrian kings is to be judged. Henry V's conquest of Normandy (1417–19) and his alliance with Burgundy, whose dukes controlled Flanders, brought both sides of the Channel under English influence. It was only this and the consequent neutralising of the enemy's naval resources – partly through the capture of Rouen and the destruction of the French royal naval base, the Clos des Galées – that allowed one of the protagonists in the war to aspire to genuine maritime security in the Channel, to the extent that even private commercial warfare was for a while brought under control. Whether in exploiting this grand strategic opportunity Henry deserves his reputation as a naval visionary is a moot point. He is justly celebrated for rebuilding the royal fleet of warships, which grew from eleven vessels in 1413 to thirty-six in 1419.[67] Such numbers had been achieved under Edward III; what was different about Henry's ships was, first, the size of the largest of them, including the king's four 'great ships', which were products of an arms race to match the towering Genoese carracks in French service; and, second, the improved sailing qualities possessed by those vessels fitted with the Mediterranean-style two-masted rig. This powerful fleet of warships spearheaded the naval operations that led to decisive victories in 1416 and 1417, but its heyday was brief. The rapidity of Henry's conquest meant that, upon completion, the largest and most costly of the great ships, the *Gracedieu*, which at 1,400 tonnes was of unprecedented size in northern waters, lacked an operational role.[68] After Henry's death in 1422, his fleet of warships – a personal asset rather than a state navy – was sold off or dismantled.[69]

Henry's grasp of the potential of sea power certainly contributed to the efficiency with which the conquest of Normandy was achieved,[70] though – as we have seen – such grasp can also be discerned in earlier reigns. While there can be no denying the purposefulness with which Henry's task forces were deployed to 'skim' the Channel, to counter interference with transport fleets,[71] the rapidity with which his adversary's naval resources were neutralised by territorial conquest and diplomatic alliance meant that he never had to grapple with the kind of persistent and slippery naval challenges that had so exercised the governments of Edward III and Richard II. The geopolitics of the war at sea could hardly have been more favourable – for the moment at least. Moreover, even his strongest advocates admit that 'Henry's fleet, powerful as it was, does not appear to have operated outside the Channel'.[72] No attempt was made to oppose Castilian naval operations in the Bay of Biscay, and comparatively little was done to counter Scottish maritime predation in the North Sea.[73] Within the Channel, once the royal fleet had been disposed of following Henry's death, everything depended on maintaining control of the French coastline. When the tide of the war began to turn, it is small wonder that Valois strategy targeted key ports like Harfleur and Dieppe, both of which were taken from the English in 1435,[74] and Le Crotoy, which was besieged unsuccessfully. The end of the Burgundian alliance in the same year was followed by the resumption of commercial predation in the Channel and the blockading of Calais, against which, with only two royal balingers in service, the government had by necessity to rely on licensed private enterprise.[75]

French Strategy and Maritime Operations

French efforts to take the war to the English yielded mixed results. As a means of inflicting economic damage that would affect tax revenues, of denting morale and tarnishing the reputation of the English crown, coastal raids and the interception of commercial traffic can be regarded as maritime counterparts to the *chevauchées* of land-based warfare. They were also intended to damage England's continental war effort and shipborne trade by undermining the maritime infrastructure of ports and shipping that sustained them. Much has been made of the impact of French amphibious landings, which resulted in the looting and burning of several important port towns (e.g. Southampton in 1338, Winchelsea in 1360, Poole in 1405), as well as more extensive damage to smaller coastal and estuarine communities. Less often commented upon, but no doubt common, was interference with fishing.[76] The direct effects – psychological as well as economic – of the notorious raids of 1377–80 would have been amplified by their concurrence with English reverses in France and domestic political instability. Moreover, with their attack on Gravesend in 1380, the Castilians brought the war almost to the very heart of English political life. That, at the height of the invasion scare in 1385, the crown was prepared to allow coastal villages in the Isle of Purbeck in Dorset to buy off the king's enemies who might suddenly appear from the sea speaks volumes for the government's impotence in the face of the threat of galley-borne raiders.[77]

Nevertheless, when viewed from the perspective of the war as a whole, the significance of French attacks on English coastal locations and, indeed, on commercial shipping on the high seas diminishes. First, in contrast with the English maintenance of footholds on the French seaboard, the Valois were unable to establish any permanent bases around the English coast. The Isle of Wight was overrun several times, but there was no attempt at permanent occupation. Scotland and Wales offered some potential as starting points for invasions of England, the former as a long-standing ally of France, the latter as an exploitable provincial fissure in the English realm. The Danish invasion plan of 1359 assumed a landing in Scotland; in 1385, the French succeeded in shipping there an army of 1,650 combatants under Jean de Vienne.[78] Subsequent Franco-Scottish operations in northern England exposed the extent to which these allies of convenience were separated by profound cultural and strategic differences and brought nothing new to a region that had long grown accustomed to the ravages of war.[79] The potential offered by Wales for back-door entry into England and also the unsustainability of such operations, were amply demonstrated by the events of 1405–6. Having landed at Milford Haven in August 1405, a French expeditionary force joined Owain Glyn Dŵr's troops, captured Carmarthen and, according to some accounts, advanced into England, engaging in a stand-off with Henry IV's army near Worcester.[80] However, hamstrung by the unreliability of sea communications, the French withdrew from south Wales in 1406.

Secondly, the damage inflicted by French and allied coastal raids should be kept in perspective. Not only does it pale into insignificance when compared with the ravaging that accompanied English land campaigns in France, but it is unlikely to have been greater than the corresponding havoc wrought on French coastal locations. The chroniclers' reporting of reprisal raids organised by vengeful coastal communities is surely showing us no more than the tip of an iceberg.[81] In addition to hit-and-run amphibious operations, destruction linked to land-based expeditions could be particularly sustained and thorough. For example, in July 1346, in a systematic assault on the maritime community of Normandy, the English fleet destroyed sixty-one 'warships' with castles fore and aft, twenty-three crayers and a similar number of 30-ton vessels – a huge blow, not matched by any comparable spell of raiding on the English coast.[82] Indeed, with respect to maritime infrastructure damage, it is far from clear that England suffered so disproportionately, either through coastal raids or through the harrying of commercial convoys, that its economic or naval capacity to wage war was significantly degraded. The third point stems from this. However much the French might aspire to disable England's maritime resources, such pressure could not be sustained for long enough or with sufficient concentration to determine the outcome of the war. The importance of the maritime sphere in the Hundred Years War is not that it was the arena where the conflict would be won and lost, but rather that it shaped the nature of the war as it was fought on land.

NAVAL RESOURCES: SHIPPING AND MANPOWER

When they needed to assemble fleets for maritime operations the protagonists had three broad options, rather similar in essence to those that they had when raising armies for land-based campaigns. First, they could draw upon the shipping and manpower of the maritime communities of their own realms, requisitioning or hiring ships and manpower that would normally be employed in commerce but which temporarily could be used as transports or fighting vessels. Second, they could maintain a royal fleet of ships, barges or galleys on a long-term basis: warships for strengthening the requisitioned fleets or for troubleshooting missions. In England, such a pool of vessels might be viewed as the maritime equivalent of the king's retinue of household knights; in France, perhaps as a proto-standing fleet, its 'barracks' being the shipyard, the Clos des Galées, founded by Philip IV on the tidal Seine at Rouen in 1295. Third, as a substitute for, or supplement to, indigenous maritime resources, they could acquire the services of foreign vessels, either by chartering them or through the provisions of military alliances. As a general rule, the English crown's maritime operations rested predominantly on requisitioned or hired indigenous shipping and manpower, while France's naval effort was more reliant on a centrally funded and maintained stock of vessels, combined with naval resources supplied by foreign powers. This, in a sense, is the maritime counterpart to England's heavy reliance on homegrown, short-service contract armies and France's greater experimentation with standing forces; as with their land armies, the protagonists' contrasting approaches to raising fleets were prompted by what would be required of them, as determined by war aims and strategy, and by what resources (ships, men and money) were most readily available.

Transport Fleets: The Scale and Impact of Ship Requisitioning

For much of the war, English effort rested squarely on the transportation of armies and supplies to France and elsewhere. The scale and fluctuating nature of these operations can be gauged from the number of ships involved. Nearly 400 were required for Edward III's first Channel crossing in July 1338, and thereafter, up to 1359–60, continental operations depended on a sequence of large transport fleets.[83] Although not all are well documented, clearly the largest, consisting of nearly 750 vessels, was that which conveyed Edward's army of about 14,000 combatants to Normandy in July 1346.[84] Complex, multi-front strategies like those attempted in 1345–6 and 1355–6 necessitated the deployment of several fleets at about the same time, each consisting of about 100 to 200 ships.[85] At least the capture of Calais in 1347 promised to ease the logistical burden, for it provided not only a secure entry point into France, but also one end of a short, cross-Channel shuttle route, which allowed shipping to be used more efficiently. During the period of intensive campaigning from 1369 to 1380, individual transport fleets continued to be of moderate size – in the region of 100–250 ships;[86] but they were regularly needed and when simultaneous deployments, including 'fighting' fleets, are aggregated we arrive at levels of demand similar to those normal during the pre-1360 period. Under the Lancastrian kings, after the huge invasion fleet of 1415,[87] which in size may have rivalled that of 1346, the war in France generally demanded fewer transports at any one time, but they were needed more often. The assembly of ninety-four ships that carried the duke of Somerset's army to Normandy in 1443 was large for this period,[88] but twice as many transport fleets sailed from 1423 to 1450 as compared with 1338 to 1360.

Although there was some reliance on foreign shipping, especially during the 1370s and 1380s, and following Henry V's resumption of the war, the only practical and economically sustainable way for the crown to assemble the larger of the transport fleets was to use its prerogative rights to requisition privately owned English and Welsh vessels and their crews, which would otherwise be employed in commerce. If prosecution of this trans-Channel war was made possible by the availability of a deep, well-stocked pool of suitable shipping and maritime manpower, there remained the problem of how to secure the services of ships from scattered coastal and estuarine communities large and small (there were more than 200 in total) and coordinate their arrival at one or more embarkation points at the same time as the army that needed to be transported.[89] It was important not to arrest too many ships from any single port, so as not to disrupt trade and therefore taxation; and important too that advances on wages be issued to ensure punctual appearance at the embarkation port. This bureaucratic and logistical challenge was made more manageable by dividing the long coastline of the kingdom into two admiralties (West and North) whose jurisdictions met at the Thames, and by associating departure ports with destinations: the south-western ports with Aquitaine, for example. Some of the ships had to be refitted to carry horses or to operate as fleet escorts, work that was managed at county level by the sheriffs.[90] It seems that the vessels arrived at embarkation ports with their usual commercial crews, but to man the king's ships and to supplement the manpower on escorts it was necessary to resort to impressment. All would be paid wages at set daily rates: 6d for the master, 3d for mariners. Overall, there were commonly more mariners crewing the ships of the transports than there were combatants carried.

Historians have tended to focus on the weaknesses of the system. Requisitioned commercial vessels, it is argued, would be slow to mobilise and were prone to desertion.[91] But, given that adverse weather and self-interest could affect any fleet however constituted, what is striking about this system is how often it operated efficiently. How else could Edward III have raised the bulk of the fleet of 750 ships needed to launch the Crécy campaign of 1346?[92]

Taking a different tack, perhaps the most weighty criticism of reliance on requisitioning has been that it was unsustainable. Constant interference with the trading activities of merchantmen, combined with the wider effects of warfare, including high seas commerce predation, had (it is argued) a devastating effect on the English merchant fleet, which by the time war resumed in 1369 was in serious decline[93] – a process to which the demographic and economic consequences of successive plague visitations can only have contributed.[94] Advocates of this view point to parliamentary petitions bemoaning losses, such as that concerning the thirty-six ships burnt or captured by the Castilians in the Bay of Bourgneuf in 1375.[95] Others have sought evidence of decline in the reduced numbers and tonnage of ships requisitioned for transport fleets or naval service. According to this interpretation, the number of merchant ships available for requisition shrank from about 250 in 1370 – a major drop from the 600 to 700 found in the naval records of the 1340s – to about 120 ten years later.[96] Moreover, for Buckingham's army in 1380, while 'only 123 English ships' were requisitioned, including some small vessels of 10 tonnes, 156 were chartered from ports in the Low Countries[97] – a notable instance of an increasing reliance on foreign shipping which continued into the fifteenth century.

The argument that English merchant shipping was in serious decline in the later fourteenth century, and that naval requisitioning was therefore no longer sustainable, is unconvincing. In particular, using the size of transport fleets as evidence of decline will not bear close scrutiny. First, it is important to recognise that vast fleets were no longer required during the last three decades of the fourteenth century because none of the armies deployed overseas was comparable in size with those of 1346 or 1359, and some could be shuttled in stages to Calais. Second, it is essential to examine the composition of the fleets that were assembled. Thus, the notion that the 1380 fleet offers a reliable guide to the size of the whole merchant marine simply dissolves when it is recognised that only thirty-two ports contributed ships, none from further west than Swanage in Dorset.[98] The south-western and Welsh ports – which had supplied nearly 40 per cent of naval shipping in 1373 – played no part in Buckingham's fleet. Third, shifting the spotlight from single transport fleets to the totality of naval operations, combined with maritime commercial activity, offers a more balanced, though still incomplete, picture of the merchant fleet. Taking 1373 as an example, we find that there were actually at least 330 ships, from eighty-two ports, employed in the various royal expeditions of that year,[99] and many more in overseas and coastal trade.[100] We may safely conclude from this that the Admirals' officers tasked with raising fleets were in no sense scraping the barrel during the 1370s.[101]

What can be suggested is that the switch from a predominant emphasis on logistical operations up to 1360 to the more active fighting role of the 1370s and 1380s may have increased the burden borne by the maritime communities of shipowners and mariners. *Viages de guerre* were often more time-consuming; given continuing logistical commitments, it is likely that just as many, if not more, ships and men as before were now required to maintain the war at sea. Seen in this light, the crown's increased reliance on foreign shipping for transport fleets in the 1370s and later looks like good sense.[102] Far from marking the 'lowest point to which the merchant fleet sank in the late middle ages',[103] the chartering of Low Countries transports in 1380 was intended to take the pressure off English maritime resources. While this was undoubtedly a time of increasing political influence for shipowners and merchants (as indicated by their petitioning in parliament), the fleet records suggest that governments under the Lancastrian kings took particular care to protect shrinking commercial taxation revenues by requisitioning fewer ships from the larger ports that were important exporters of wool. A small fishing port like Cromer, which had rarely been called upon in the past, was now contributing more ships to royal fleets than King's Lynn, which had regularly supplied large numbers during the fourteenth century.[104]

As we have seen, the French war effort rarely called for the raising of fleets as large as those frequently assembled by the English, but when major invasions of England were planned, the ship sourcing options were the same. Of the 202 ships, galleys and barges in the fleet destroyed at the battle of Sluys, 167 were drawn from two dozen Norman and Picard ports along the stretch of coast from Cherbourg to Calais.[105] The invasion fleet that gathered at Sluys in 1386 was of exceptional size. Independent sources attest that it consisted of about 1,200 vessels, the Florentine Buarnocorso Pitti, an eyewitness, adding that half were round ships.[106] Access to the merchant fleet of Flanders made it possible to raise a fleet of this size, though it seems that the chartering net had to be cast still more widely. It was to no avail. For all the elaborate planning, including a prefabricated fort designed to secure the beach landing site, the whole scheme was unwieldy, the vast fleet particularly vulnerable in the event of bad weather during the crossing.[107]

Fighting Fleets: The Organisation of Offensive and Defensive Naval Operations

The effectiveness of French naval resources is not to be judged from aborted invasion schemes, but rather from those activities that consumed most effort: inshore offensive and defensive operations around the coast of France and attritional raids on English coastal communities and commercial convoys. In this regard, we should not forget the role played by requisitioned shipping, nor indeed the courageous efforts of dozens of tiny Norman and Picard vessels that ran supplies into Calais during the English siege.[108] The operations requiring an aggressive edge were spearheaded, on the one hand, by a fleet of sailing ships and galleys maintained by the crown at the Clos des Galées at Rouen and, on the other, by foreign, professional squadrons drawn from two sources: Genoa and Castile. Although we should be careful not to exaggerate the significance of the Clos, especially prior to Charles V's reforms of 1374,[109] historians have generally considered this combination of royal and foreign naval resources to be ideal for the tasks required, with the allied French-Castillian fleet (thirty-five royal vessels and thirteen Iberian galleys) that put to sea in 1377 under de Vienne's command as the operational highpoint.[110] Against such an adversary the English would always struggle to mobilise an effective parry or riposte. For all the effort and money expended on naval expeditions, especially during the 1370s and 1380s, it is in the performance of these 'fighting' roles, whether defensive (patrolling, escort) or offensive (interception, coastal raids), that some historians have found England's 'non-professional' naval resources most deficient. 'For want of a professional fleet they were forever three months behind the enemy', notes Rodger dismissively.[111] However, this judgement takes insufficient account of what was actually achieved, given the constraints under which the English war effort operated. More fundamentally, it displays little understanding of practicalities – of what naval organisational options were realistically available to the English crown.

While lacking a navy in the modern sense, the crown did have specialised warships at its disposal. Their contribution to Henry V's war effort has been assessed already, but what of their role under Edward III, when the operational challenges were more varied and intractable? Like the French royal flotilla maintained at the Clos des Galées, Edward's ships, armed to the teeth and expertly mastered, were employed to stiffen larger fleets, whether as escorts for transport fleets or as the steely core of armadas tasked with offensive operations. He had similar numbers at his disposal: the expenses of thirty-one royal ships were met in 1345, twenty-one in 1357.[112] Twenty accompanied the king on his abortive naval expedition in 1372.[113] The 1370s, as we have seen, was a decade of intensive, flexible naval effort, and it is small wonder that the threat posed by the enemy's galley fleet prompted an appropriate organisational response. In 1373 and 1378, English towns were instructed to build, respectively, seventy barges and thirty-two balingers.[114] Many of them served, eleven newly built barges forming about a quarter of a war fleet operating in the Channel in 1374, for example.[115] Required to supply one barge, York actually built two, and one of them, the *Peter*, had a busy career in royal service, ended only in 1379 when it literally went down fighting.[116] As well as relieving pressure on the merchant fleet, deployment of these oared sailing vessels provided a fast, manoeuvrable response to the enemy's galleys. They contributed to that combination of sailing ships and oared craft that was a key feature of the war fleets raised during these years. Indeed, it was at this time of 'viages de guerre' that such a fighting fleet, manned by soldiers as well as seamen, first acquired a distinctive name in England: *armee* in Anglo-French indentures, which is translated as *armata* in the Latin pay records.[117]

The contribution to fighting fleets of the king's warships and of specially built barges and balingers was important, but, for the greater part of those fleets, the English crown had by necessity to rely on the services of the home merchant fleet and maritime community, just as it did for the logistical tasks of transporting armies and supplies. A sober assessment of this reliance reveals damaging consequences, but also advantages that have been insufficiently recognised. The issue of manpower illustrates this nicely. The hard-headed, pugnacious instincts of the mariner, as memorably portrayed in Chaucer's Shipman,[118] were admirably accommodated by the combatant role that the crown frequently required of him. It was usual for the escort vessels assigned to transport fleets and commercial convoys to have substantially supplemented crews (*duplex eskippamentum*), the extra men providing fighting muscle.[119] Moreover, as the fleet that fought at the Bay of Flemings in 1371 illustrates, the sailing ships and barges serving on *viages de guerre* would be stuffed with soldiers as well as seamen: 'marines' who, as impressment orders and muster records make clear, were recruited in the coastal zone from the same pool of manpower that supplied mariners.[120] So, although England lacked a professional navy at this time, we may be sure that the seamen serving on 'war voyages' knew how to handle weapons and that many of the shipboard soldiers had their sea legs. While this was of undoubted benefit to the king's war effort, heavy manpower demands during the 1370s and 1380s are likely to have had destabilising consequences within the coastal zone: we should not be surprised to find maritime communities, like Fobbing in Essex, at the centre of the Peasants' Revolt in May 1381.[121]

Another insufficiently recognised characteristic of the manpower of England's 'non-professional' fighting fleets is the role played by the nobility and gentry. The noblemen who served as admirals of the Northern or Western fleets were tasked primarily with administrative responsibilities, but that many of them also played a leadership role in naval expeditions – as well as owning ships of their own – is suggestive of a serious interest in the maritime sphere.[122] Sir Thomas Percy's exploits at sea in the 1370s are recorded by admiring chroniclers.[123] Oral testimony celebrating Robert, Lord Morley's vigorous naval command in the 1340s – from spearheading the attack at the battle of Sluys in a warship that proclaimed his heraldic identity to mounting raids on the coast of Normandy – is to be found in the records of the Court of Chivalry, where, among the witnesses, are members of the East Anglian lesser gentry who, like Morley, fought as often at sea as on land.[124] Their opponents did too. The French admiral, Jean de Vienne, who masterminded the assault on the south coast from 1377, ultimately died fighting the Turks at Nicopolis in 1396.[125] The Castilian, Pero Niño (from 1431, count of Buelna), scourge of the English Channel coast in 1405, followed a similar career path, mixing naval operations with campaigns in Iberia against a variety of adversaries.[126] The line of demarcation that traditionally separates the study of warfare on land and at sea reflects the prejudices of modern historians rather than the perceptions and experiences of medieval men, or indeed those of modern armed forces. The career of Edmund Rose, esquire, which involved spells of service at sea, including as captain of the Barge of London in 1373, interspersed with campaigns in France and garrison duty on Jersey, is not dissimilar to the life of a modern Royal Marines officer.[127]

If the shipborne manpower of England's fighting fleets was no less suited to their role than were the soldiers of armies campaigning in France, what of the ships and the mechanisms for getting them to sea when and where they were needed? Privately owned sailing vessels were perhaps not ideal for rapid, defensive mobilisation, but with the cards stacked in favour of the coastal raider, anticipation and forward planning were essential however the ships were sourced. There is admittedly more than a hint of desperation in some of the self-help initiatives, such as Scarborough's 1383 petition that they be allowed to raise men and money in the town to resource a barge and a balinger for defence against coastal raiders.[128] Such cases also serve to remind us that community-based naval forces brought a certain reliability to maritime defence that was rooted in a real incentive to succeed, combined with a profound knowledge of local waters. And there was *esprit de corps* too, as can be imagined among the 'doubled' crew of the *Blythe* of Newcastle in 1337–8, who were kitted out in matching red caps or hoods.[129] Activation of the Cinque Ports' long-standing obligation to provide naval service meant that along that sensitive stretch of coastline there were mechanisms in place to provide rapid reaction and patrolling.[130] Their raid on Boulogne in January 1340, which destroyed nineteen galleys and twenty-four other ships, was one of the most devastating of the entire war,[131] while the well-documented patrols of the 'narrow seas' by their armed squadrons during the 1370s and 1380s offered a robust response to 'the malice of the king's enemies', and a response that could be speedily deployed.[132] In 1372, for example, a task force of three ships and four barges, responding to an order dated 12 April, was at sea by the 25th of that month.[133]

As with the raising of a contract army, so with the assembly of a fleet of privately owned vessels: the crown thereby gained access to a vast pool of expertise and resources without the millstone of long-term commitments. Further, there was acceptance by government that private enterprise had a beneficial role to play in the king's war at sea. Allowing local mercantile elites to organise naval defence would be more likely to foster efficient deployments while minimising tensions with central government. There was recognition too, especially during the years of intensive naval demands, that financial incentives were needed to ensure willing participation. For shipowners and the crews of their vessels there had to be profit-making opportunities to balance the loss of commercially generated income and the risked damage to capital equipment as well as to life and limb. In 1380, shipowners supplying vessels for naval service were granted 3s 4d per quarter year for each ton of carrying capacity (i.e. £16 13s 4d per quarter for a 100-ton ship), an allowance ('tunnetight') for wear and tear that is reminiscent of *regard* paid to retinue commanders.[134] Before 1380, some spells of duty could be linked to commerce: having transported troops to Aquitaine, a master would hope to ship wine or salt back to England. Freightage payments might be offered to those willing to deploy their vessels on patrol or as escorts. During the late 1330s, the burgesses of Newcastle received £2 or £4 per week for each ship sent to protect supply convoys en route for Scotland.[135] The squadron of vessels escorting the wine fleet during the winter of 1372/3 was paid freightage at very favourable rates (from 16s to 22s per ton), thereby assuring for the owners the equivalent of a good commercial return from a potentially risky voyage soon after the defeat at La Rochelle.[136] Then there were the spoils to be won on the high seas. The owners of ships in paid royal service had a right to a quarter share of the value of prizes, with half going to the master and crew.[137] Sometimes the terms were still more favourable.[138] Given the number of prizes that were taken, either singly or in the large sea battles discussed earlier, we should not underestimate the appeal of potentially profitable naval service for owners, masters and ordinary mariners. Arundel's *viage de guerre* of 1387 proved so successful that shipowners scrambled to sign up for the fleet that sailed the following year, even waiving their right to ton-tight payments in the expectation of greater profits from prize money.[139]

It is in this light that we should interpret the 'self-help' naval operations, whether or not licensed, that became more common during the late fourteenth century and which are usually presented as evidence of the failure of centrally funded and organised naval defence, and, indeed, of weak kingship. The most notorious of the private initiatives occurred in 1378 when John Philpot, a London merchant, equipped a squadron to take on Scottish maritime raiders,[140] but men of other ports were quite as prepared to take matters into their own hands.[141] While patching the somewhat threadbare defence of the realm, such self-funded voyages were certainly intended to be profitable ventures; that is what gave them their vitality. From the crown's point of view, relying on licensed, self-financed ships was the least expensive sea-keeping option; the 'gallioters' might actually rise to the occasion rather well, as was the case during the months of crisis in 1436.[142] The drawback was that it became more likely that attacks on shipping would be indiscriminate, which exposed the crown to costly compensation claims and risked damaging relations with allies and neutrals.[143] Perhaps the worst instance occurred towards the end of the French war when, in May 1449 off the Isle of Wight, Robert Winnington captured a fleet of more than a hundred Hanseatic, Dutch and Flemish ships. As he noted in a letter: 'ye sawe never suche a syght of schyppys take into Englond.'[144] Retaliation against English interests in the Hanseatic sphere was swift and damaging.[145] Yet what the indiscriminate high seas predation by 'gallioters' represented was the worsening of an endemic problem of maritime life rather than the creation of a new one. That Winnington was apparently on indentured, royal service illustrates a long-standing phenomenon:[146] that ships doing the king's work would not pass over an opportunity for self-enrichment. This was a fact of maritime life that Henry IV was able to exploit when, in 1402, he called upon the services of the 'so-called pirates of the southern ports' to conduct an unofficial naval war against the shipping of France in response to that kingdom's attacks on English commercial vessels 'under cover of the conflict between England and Scotland'.[147] When, by contrast, Henry V used the reconstructed royal fleet to police the Channel and stamp out the scourge of 'piracy' he was, as we have seen, taking advantage of a more favourable geopolitical environment. When compared with the strategy and naval operations of Henry V, those of his less fortunate predecessors have attracted criticism. But the war managers of the 1370s and 1380s, with their backs to the wall in France and under severe financial and political constraints at home, had no choice but to make use of whatever naval resources were available, even if it meant some loss of control.

Permanent and Professional Fleets: An Unsustainable Option

Although the success of the earl of Arundel's *armee* in 1387 demonstrated what a 'non-professional' fleet could achieve, it is the perceived advantages to be gained from maintaining centrally organised, permanent naval resources and hiring true professionals in the art of naval warfare that have impressed historians. There has been a tendency to view the centrally managed fleets of the Hundred Years War, especially the resources of the Clos des Galées at Rouen and the naval establishment under Henry V, as proto-royal navies. As with the earliest permanent armies, so with standing fleets: their superiority can hardly be questioned because it was with such institutions that the future clearly lay, but projection of assumptions rooted in the early modern period onto an interpretation of late medieval war management risks distortion born of anachronism.

For the northern kingdoms at least, maintenance of a specialist, centrally funded war fleet for any length of time was scarcely possible, given the unreliability of funding streams, shifting operational needs and the discontinuities of political will. Henry V's management of his naval resources, while purposeful, was very much that of a late medieval king: he relied on established practices within his means. When, in August 1417, he issued retaining fees to the masters of his ships, he was attaching experienced and capable shipmen to his household, not founding 'a corps of regular sea officers'.[148] It was the same with naval infrastructure. A sheltered, fortified anchorage for the king's ships was established in the river Hamble, on Southampton Water, but there was nothing in England resembling the Arsenale of Venice.[149] His ships were built in various locations. Particularly important was the work done at Southampton under the supervision of William Soper, a merchant and (from 1420) clerk of king's ships; but – as we would expect with the English way of war – this was a privately owned facility rather than a true royal dockyard, for which it is necessary to wait until the reign of Henry VII.[150] Originating in the 1290s, the Clos des Galées had a long-term existence that seems to confirm its standing as a permanent royal shipyard. Yet it operated under the same constraints as affected English naval policy. The view of the Clos that has emerged since publication of the archival records is that, for much of its life, it was 'more a "winter shelter for warships and an arms workshop" than a state shipyard'.[151] The establishment of workmen was modest, and the vessels maintained there did not have permanent crews. While underpinning the sometimes important royal contribution to France's *armée de la mer*, centrally funded naval infrastructure in France, as in England, was dependent upon the strategic vision of particular war leaders, and the death of kings could have dramatic consequences. In England, the king's ships were sold off after the passing of Edward III (1377) and Henry V (1422). The death of Charles V of France in 1380 triggered a sharp decline in activity at the Clos des Galées. Even routine upkeep was neglected, the accounts for the years 1382–4 offering vivid glimpses of irreparable, out of service or half-built galleys and barges.[152] By contrast with England, there was no real recovery of vitality in the new century. The Clos contributed six old galleys to the fleet blockading Harfleur in 1416, and there can have been little of value there when it was destroyed in 1418.[153]

For both England and France, reliance for any length of time on standing naval forces to perform more than a supporting role was simply unsustainable. Until early modern state finance allowed for a permanent navy, and global commitments warranted it, a predominant reliance on the merchant fleet for fighting as well as logistics was the only realistic option. The other alternative – to hire foreign warships manned by their own professional crews – would have been subjected to careful cost/benefit analysis, for naval professionals came with a price tag that was generally beyond the means of the English crown.[154] Acquiring the services of a fleet through the terms of a military alliance was apparently cheaper, but there would always be strings attached. Thus, the Portuguese crown's financing of an imposing squadron of galleys for operations in the Channel during the mid-to-late 1380s was conditional on the dispatch of John of Gaunt's expedition in 1386,[155] and following the *chemin d'Espaigne* meant the redirection of scarce military resources from France into the Iberian theatre of war. Moreover, the contribution that foreign war fleets could make was likely to be time-limited and seasonal because, for galleys, the stormy waters of the Channel represented a hostile environment. In 1346, Carlo Grimaldi's thirty-two Genoese galleys, carrying 7,000 men, having arrived too late to interfere with the English crossing to Normandy went into winter quarters at Abbeville from November until May 1347, thus missing most of the siege of Calais.[156] There were reliability issues of other kinds, including those that we would expect to encounter with naval mercenaries; the Genoese mutiny in 1339[157] should serve as a reminder that such events were not confined to non-professional, requisitioned fleets.[158] The other risk accompanying dependence on foreign naval resources was that provision was subject to domestic priorities of the provider, against which treaty obligations were of secondary importance. Thus, once the threat of Gaunt's invasion had been removed by the treaty of Trancoso in 1387, and with it the need for French military assistance, John I of Castile lost interest in fulfilling his naval treaty obligations to France.[159]

CONCLUSIONS

It has been argued that 'the sea remained a secondary theatre in terms of decision', because 'it is unlikely ... that enough could be achieved at sea or in attacks from the sea by either England or France to bring the enemy to his knees or his senses'.[160] While this may be true if we adopt a narrow view of naval operations, in reality such operations were woven into the larger, multifaceted tapestry of the war, which included the more celebrated land-based campaigns and less showy diplomatic manoeuvres and economic fundamentals, which in various ways gave the war its recognisable form. The physical location of the protagonists in this war, and all the wider geopolitical issues associated with this, meant that grand strategies and operational specifics, the size and composition of armies and evolving political and cultural identities of the belligerent peoples were all conditioned by the constraints imposed and opportunities presented by the maritime environment. The Hundred Years War may have been won and lost on land, but from beginning to end its course was shaped by the sea.

In this regard, the two fundamental issues were the centrality of shipborne logistics for sustaining the English war effort and the vulnerability of maritime infrastructure and commerce to attack. Consequently, one way of explaining the protracted nature of the great Anglo-French conflict would be that the English crown was more successful, through thick and thin, in maintaining its capacity to ship armies and confine the war to continental Europe than were the Valois monarchy's efforts to degrade England's maritime infrastructure. These fundamentals of the war at sea, indeed of the whole war, are easiest to observe during the decades of undisputed English success under Edward III, from 1340 to 1360, and then under Henry V and John, duke of Bedford: years of victory built upon massive maritime logistical effort, which under the Lancastrians was assisted by territorial conquests that neutralised the French naval threat. But in many ways it is the years of intensive, attritional warfare from 1369 to 1389 that throw the maritime fundamentals of the Hundred Years War into sharpest relief. For despite having at its disposal a state-funded war fleet based at the Clos des Galées, the professional galley squadrons supplied by its Castilian allies and, from 1384, the well-stocked pool of Flemish commercial shipping, the French crown failed to break England's maritime capacity and therefore its war effort. What that crucial twenty-year period also demonstrates is that, in the world of uncertain revenue streams and 'personal' monarchy characteristic of many late medieval polities, an aspiration to maintain anything more than a small war fleet on a permanent, professional footing was unrealistic. This was evident to hard-headed statesmen at the time, as was the fact that 'standing' naval resources were not necessarily superior to those raised by prerogative right, contract or licence. The English crown's heavy dependence on the domestic merchant fleet for shipping and manpower to fuel *viages de guerre* as well as logistical operations was the only sustainable option, and it was also probably the best one, given the interlocking nature of strategic and commercial imperatives. But it was an option that placed an onerous burden of participation on England's coastal zone, which, during the two decades of intensive and time-consuming naval operations from 1369 to 1389, must have been the section of society most heavily involved in, and affected by, the king's war.

NOTES

1. *The Anonimalle Chronicle, 1333–1381*, ed. V. H. Galbraith (Manchester, 1927), pp. 68–9, 177. A shorter account in Thomas Walsingham (*Historia Anglicana, 1272–1422*, ed. H. T. Riley, 2 vols (London, 1863–4), I. pp. 313–14) assigns events to 1372 but the Flemings are identified and prizes confirmed at twenty-five.
2. *Froissart* (Lettenhove), VIII, pp. 92–5; *Istore et croniques de Flandres*, ed. K. de Lettenhove, 2 vols, (Brussels, 1879–80), II, pp. 161–2, where battle took place in 'un havene en Bretagne' called 'le Bay' and lasted three hours.
3. *Chronicon Anonymi Cantuariensis*, ed. and trans C. Scott-Stokes and C. Given-Wilson (Oxford, 2008), pp. 58–61; *Knighton's Chronicle, 1337–1396*, ed. G. H. Martin (Oxford, 1995), pp. 12–17.
4. The fate of Sir John Arundel's fleet, December 1379: *The St Albans Chronicle: The Chronica maiora of Thomas Walsingham, vol. 1, 1376–1394*, ed. J. Taylor, W. R. Childs and L. Watkiss (Oxford, 2003), pp. 324–43. Walsingham's coverage of maritime warfare reflects the intensity of naval activity during this period, but the attention given to Arundel's expedition is exceptional.
5. Rose, pp. 84–5; *Le Victorial. Chronique de don Pero Niño, comte de Buelna (1378–1453)*, ed. J.G. Dalché (Turnhout, 2001).
6. La Roncière; *Documents relatifs au Clos des Galées de Rouen*, ed. A. Merlin-Chazelas, 2 vols (Paris, 1977–8).
7. Transport fleet, 1338: *Wardrobe Book of William de Norwell, 12 July 1338 to 27 May 1340*, ed. M. Lyon et al. (Brussels, 1983), pp. 363–86. King's ships: S. Rose, *The Navy of the Lancastrian Kings. Accounts and Inventories of William Soper, Keeper of the King's Ships, 1422–1427*, Naval Records Society (London, 1982).
8. TNA, E 101/31/23; E 101/31/10 and 14; E 101/31/12, m. 1 and E 364/5, rot. 31d (a); E 101/30/13, m. 5 and E 101/30/15, m. 3. Three of the ships carried supplies for the fleet.

9   TNA E 101/31/11 (Brian); E 101/31/12 (Neville); E 101/31/15 and E 101/31/27 (Hereford). The earl was denied pay for an additional eighteen men-at-arms and twenty archers.
10 TNA E 101/31/11, mm. 1–5; E 101/31/15, m. 2.
11 TNA E 101/30/13, mm. 5-5d.
12 N. H. Nicolas, *History of the Royal Navy*, 2 vols (London, 1847), II, pp. 137–40 (from Froissart), La Roncière, II, p. 13, and M. Russon, *Les côtes guerrières: Mer, guerre et pouvoirs au Moyen Âge* (Rennes, 2004), p. 261, mention the battle but not Rodger, Sumption or Cushway.
13 For English, *War, Politics*; for French operations, La Roncière, II, pp. 1–100. Richmond, 'War at Sea', *HYW*, pp. 96–121.
14 Sherborne, 'The Battle of La Rochelle and the War at Sea, 1372-75', *War, Politics*, p. 48.
15 Sherborne, 'La Rochelle', p. 53.
16 Richmond, 'War at Sea', pp. 98–9.
17 Rose, pp. 60–1.
18 La Roncière, II, pp. 220–4; J. H. Wylie and W. T. Waugh, *The Reign of Henry the Fifth*, 3 vols (Cambridge, 1914–29), II, pp. 358–64; Allmand, *Henry V*, pp. 102–4, 107–8; Friel, pp. 118–26. The 1440 English blockade of Harfleur was more successful: C. Richmond, 'The Keeping of the Seas during the Hundred Years War, 1422–1440', *History* 49 (1964), pp. 296–7.
19 *St Albans Chronicle*, I, pp. 364–5; *Divided Houses*, p. 379.
20 La Roncière, II, pp. 226–8; Friel, pp. 126–31.
21 For a notable example in 1337–8, N. A. M. Rodger, *The Safeguard of the Sea: A Naval History of Great Britain, Volume 1: 660–1649* (London, 1997), pp. 107–8.
22 C. J. Rogers, *War Cruel and Sharp* (Woodbridge, 2000), pp. 190–8; Rose, pp. 64–5.
23 Richmond, 'War at Sea', pp. 100–1; Rose, pp. 65–6. *Chronicon Galfridi le Baker de Swynebroke*, ed. E. M. Thompson (Oxford, 1889), pp. 109–11.
24 Sherborne, 'La Rochelle', p. 43; *Divided Houses*, pp. 138–41.
25 *Anonimalle*, pp. 77, 99, 180, states seventy-two ships were taken. *Chronique des quatre premiers Valois (1327–1393)*, ed. S. Luce (Paris, 1862), p. 255, has eighty-four English ships defeated by a Castilian *armée* of eighty. The administrative records are more reliable: *PROME* V, pp. 351–2 (petition); TNA, C 47/30/8, no. 14, in Nicolas, *Royal Navy*, II, 510–14 (list of lost ships).
26 J. Sherborne, 'The English Navy: Shipping and Manpower, 1369-89', *War, Politics*, pp. 29–39 (p. 38); T. K. Moore, 'The Cost-Benefit Analysis of a Fourteenth-Century Naval Campaign: Margate/Cadzand, 1387', *Roles of the Sea in Medieval England*, ed. R. Gorski (Woodbridge, 2012), pp. 103–124. These rounded-up prize totals are based on extrapolation from the documented royal share. Chronicles give much higher figures for ships and wine captured: *The Westminster Chronicle, 1381–1394*, ed. L. C. Hector and B. F. Harvey (Oxford, 1982), pp. 183–4; *St Albans Chronicle*, I, pp. 810–11.
27 Nicolas, *Royal Navy*, II, pp. 501–2: Edward III's newsletter, which states that there were 190 'niefs, galeyes et grant barges' in the French fleet, whereas

(excluding three Genoese galleys) the naval payroll shows there to have been 199: *Clos des Galées*, II, pp. 33–49.
28 See *St Albans Chronicle*, I, pp. 214–15, 610–11, 708–11, 754–5.
29 Friel, pp. 92–8.
30 Sluys: A. Ayton, 'Edward III and the English Aristocracy at the Beginning of the Hundred Years War', *Armies, Chivalry and Warfare in Medieval Britain and France*, ed. M. Strickland (Stamford, 1998), pp. 179–81; Rogers, *War Cruel and Sharp*, p. 196. King's ships: TNA, E 101/30/13; E 101/30/15.
31 E.g. *St Albans Chronicle*, I, pp. 302–3.
32 TNA, E 101/30/13. On gads, thrown from a ship's topcastle, see Friel, p. 87.
33 Sherborne, 'La Rochelle', pp. 43–4. *Chronique des quatre premiers Valois*, pp. 233–4. See also *Le Victorial*, p. 263.
34 Wylie, *Henry V*, II, p. 361.
35 J. Sherborne, 'English Barges and Balingers of the Late Fourteenth Century', *War, Politics*, pp. 71–6.
36 Hewitt, p. 78.
37 *Chronicon Galfridi le Baker*, p. 110.
38 La Roncière, II, pp. 225.
39 As at Sluys: *Froissart* (Lettenhove), III, pp. 194, 200.
40 E.g. the sea battle fought in open water near Calais 1406: *Le Victorial*, p. 262.
41 TNA, E 101/20/27, m. 1d.
42 D. Biggs, 'A Voyage, or Rather an Expedition, to Portugal: Edmund of Langley's Journey to Iberia, June/July 1381', *JMMH*, 7 (2009), pp. 66–7, citing TNA, E 101/39/17, a misreading of the 'tuntyght' payments (m. 3), set at 3s 4d per quarter. The imagined 'masters of naval artillery' were in fact shipmasters. The ship's 'artillamentum' was its gear or equipment.
43 T. F. Tout, 'Firearms in England in the Fourteenth Century', *EHR*, 26 (1911), pp. 675, 694.
44 C. Bréard, ed., 'Le compte du clos des galées de Rouen au xiv siècle (1382–1384)', *Mélanges documents, deuxième serie* (Rouen, 1893), pp. 68–72; *Clos des Galées*, I. nos 1015, 1182.
45 K. DeVries, 'The Effectiveness of Fifteenth-Century Shipboard Artillery', *Mariner's Mirror* 84 (1998), pp. 389–99 (390).
46 Friel, pp. 89–90.
47 W.M. Ormrod, *Edward III* (New Haven & London, 2011), pp. 509–10.
48 Sherborne, 'La Rochelle', p. 49.
49 La Roncière, I, pp. 427–8; *Trial by Battle*, p. 258.
50 That this was Charles V's view in 1369, see J. Sherborne, 'John of Gaunt, Edward III's Retinue and the French Campaign of 1369', *War, Politics*, p. 81.
51 1359: the French were unable to raise the 600,000 florins demanded by Waldemar IV of Denmark (*Trial by Fire*, pp. 402–4).
52 Richmond, 'War at Sea', pp. 100–4; A. MacKay, *Spain in the Middle Ages* (Basingstoke and London, 1977), pp. 124–5.

53 Allmand, pp. 82–3.
54 Richmond, 'War at Sea', p. 100.
55 Harfleur, St Malo, Nantes, La Rochelle and Sluys. Ports on the Flemish coast were briefly held in 1383. J. Palmer, *England, France and Christendom, 1377–99* (London, 1972), p. 7; *Divided Houses*, pp. 304–6, 322–4.
56 *PROME VI*, pp. 78–9. *Divided Houses*, pp. 354–5.
57 The most important of the long-range chevauchées were in 1369, 1370, 1373, 1375 and 1380.
58 Palmer, *England, France and Christendom*, pp. 7–8. Cf. more sceptical assessments of the barbican strategy: Sherborne, 'The Cost of English Warfare with France in the Later Fourteenth Century', in *War, Politics*, p. 67; *Divided Houses*, pp. 310, 330.
59 H. Ph. A. Terrier de Loray, *Jean de Vienne, amiral de France, 1341–1396* (Paris, 1877), chapters 5–10; Richmond, 'War at Sea', pp. 105–6.
60 On the reforms, though not the part of English naval pressure, A. Merlin-Chazelas, 'La réforme du Clos des Galées de Rouen in 1374', *Revue historique des armées* 1 (1974), pp. 9–23.
61 For what follows: Sherborne, 'English Navy', pp. 35–9. All expeditions involved at least 1,000 soldiers and 1,000 mariners, and usually substantially more.
62 Sherborne, 'Cost of English Warfare', pp. 59–60, 66–67, 69.
63 See also conclusions of Moore, 'Cost-benefit analysis', on Arundel's 1387 naval expedition.
64 E.g Buckingham's fleet, 1377–8, which was at sea 'long after the French and Castilians had returned to winter berths': Sherborne, 'Cost', p. 66.
65 As in 1386: J. Sherborne, 'The Defence of the Realm and the Impeachment of Michael de la Pole in 1386', *War, Politics*, pp. 104–7.
66 The barbicans north of the Loire consumed 27% of war expenditure, 1369–80: Sherborne, 'Cost', p. 69.
67 Rose, pp. 18, 85–8; Rose, *Navy of Lancastrian Kings*, pp. 28–56; Friel, pp. 41–6, 164–88 (appendix 2). Ships captured from the enemy, of which Genoese carracks were particularly important, outnumbered new builds.
68 Friel, pp. 44, 75–6, 145–8, 152, 164–6; S. Rose, 'Henry V's *Gracedieu* and Mutiny at Sea: Some New Evidence', *Mariner's Mirror* 63 (1977), pp. 3–6.
69 Richmond, 'Keeping', pp. 285–90.
70 Allmand, pp. 220–32.
71 As in 1415: TNA, E 403/619, mm. 8, 13; *CPR, 1413–16*, p. 294.
72 Rodger, *Safeguard*, p. 144.
73 Friel, p. 102.
74 Harfleur was retaken by the English in 1440.
75 Richmond, 'Keeping', pp. 291–5.
76 In 1377 two French barges preyed on the Great Yarmouth herring fleet until driven away by five ships manned by the 'men of Norfolk'. *St Albans Chronicle*, I, pp. 168–9.

77 TNA, C 81/489, no. 3609; *CPR 1381–1385*, p. 554.
78 Terrier de Loray, *Jean de Vienne*, pp. 186–9, p.j.111.
79 *Divided Houses*, pp. 545–8.
80 R. R. Davies, *The Revolt of Owain Glyn Dwr* (Oxford, 1997), pp. 190–6.
81 In 1378 the men of Winchelsea and Rye raided St Pierre-en-Port and Veulettes in Normandy, recovering Rye's bells and church lead in the process. *St Albans Chronicle*, I, pp. 218–19.
82 Northburgh's newsletter in Robertus de Avesbury, *De gestis mirabilibus regis Edwardi Tertii*, ed. E.M. Thompson (London, 1889), pp. 359–60.
83 C.L. Lambert, *Shipping the Medieval Military: English Maritime Logistics in the Fourteenth Century* (Woodbridge, 2011), pp. 114–52.
84 Lambert, *Shipping*, pp. 136–40.
85 E.g. Hewitt, pp. 182–6 (Aquitaine, 1345); Lambert, *Shipping*, pp. 152–4 (Aquitaine, 1355).
86 Sherborne, 'English Navy', p. 35.
87 Records suggest a fleet of c. 700 vessels, a third from foreign ports: C. Lambert, 'Henry V and the Crossing to France: Reconstructing Naval Operations for the Agincourt Campaign, 1415', *JMH*, 43 (2017). The army of 1417 probably required a fleet of similar size, but the records are incomplete.
88 TNA E 403/750, mm. 12–16; E 101/53/39, mm. 4, 4d; E 101/54/4.
89 Lambert, *Shipping*, 1: 'Raising a fleet'.
90 Hewitt, pp. 78–9, 86–7.
91 Hewitt, pp. 83–4; Rodger, *Safeguard*, pp. 121–6; Lambert, *Shipping*, p. 129 (desertion 1342).
92 Of these ships, twenty-five were royal vessels and thirty-eight were hired from foreign ports. Lambert, *Shipping*, pp. 136–140.
93 Rodger, *Safeguard*, pp. 124–5; *Divided Houses*, pp. 132–5, 377–9; G. Cushway, *Edward III and the War at Sea: The English Navy, 1327–1377* (Woodbridge, 2011), pp. 187–9. This historiographical trend can be traced back to A. Saul, 'Great Yarmouth and the Hundred Years War in the Fourteenth Century', *BIHR* 52 (1979), pp. 105–15 and A. Saul, 'English Towns in the Late Middle Ages: The Case of Great Yarmouth', *JMH* 8 (1982), pp. 75–88. For a more positive view, M. Kowaleski, 'Warfare, Shipping and Crown Patronage: The Impact of the Hundred Years War on the Port Towns of England', *Money, Markets and Trade in Late Medieval Europe*, ed. L. Armstrong, I. Elbl and M. Elbl (Leiden, 2005), pp. 233–54.
94 'The Black Death … inevitably reduced the shipping resources of every kingdom, leaving fewer mariners to man ships and less demand for shipping': I. Friel, 'Oars, Sails and Guns: The English and War at Sea, c. 1200–c. 1500', *War at Sea in the Middle Ages and the Renaissance*, ed. J. B. Hattendorf and R. W. Unger (Woodbridge, 2003), p. 75.
95 *PROME V*, pp. 351–2; Nicolas, *Royal Navy*, II, pp. 510–14.
96 *Divided Houses*, pp. 132 & n. 26, 377 & n. 39. But note p. 153, where a contemporary report that a fleet of 376 ships had been assembled in 1372 is apparently accepted.

97 *Divided Houses*, p. 378.
98 TNA, E 101/39/2.
99 BL, Add MS 37494, fos 17r-20v, 23v-28r, 29v, 35v-37v, 40r, 41r-41v; TNA, E 101/31/29, mm. 4, 6, 7; E 101/32/28; E 101/32/35; E 101/33/2. *CCR 1369-74*, p. 516; *CPR 1370-74*, p. 350.
100 TNA, E 101/179/10; E 101/602/3; Devon Record Office, Exeter Customs Accounts, Mich. 1372–Mich. 1373 (46–47 Edward III), mm. 1–2. *CPR, 1370-74*, p. 307.
101 *Divided Houses*, p. 378.
102 Foreign ships were particularly important in 1373, 1379, 1380, 1415 and 1417.
103 *Divided Houses*, p. 378.
104 E.g. Cromer supplied about a dozen ships in 1417 and 1443, while King's Lynn contributed only three and two vessels to these fleets. *Rotuli Normanniae*, ed. T. D. Hardy (London, 1835), pp. 325–6, 329; E 101/53/39, mm. 4-4d.
105 There were thirty-two royal vessels and three Genoese galleys. La Roncière, I, pp. 438–43; *Clos des Galées*, II, pp. 33–49.
106 *Cronica di Buonaccorso Pitti*, ed. A. Bacchi della Lega (Bologna, 1905), p. 72; *St Albans Chronicle*, II. 804–05; Sherborne, 'Defence of the Realm', pp. 112-3
107 For the complex circumstances that prompted cancellation of the expedition, see Palmer, *England, France and Christendom*, pp. 73–85.
108 *Clos des Galées*, II, pp. 139–42.
109 *Clos des Galées*, II, pp. 157–9; Merlin-Chazelas, 'La réforme du Clos des Galées de Rouen in 1374'; Rose, pp. 13–16.
110 Richmond, 'War at Sea', pp. 105–6.
111 Rodger, *Safeguard*, pp. 105–8.
112 Rose, p. 17 & n. 53.
113 TNA, E 101/30/13, mm. 7, 8, 8d. For the king's ships during this period, see Sherborne, 'English Navy', p. 32.
114 Sherborne, 'English Navy', pp. 33–4; Sherborne, 'English Barges and Balingers'; Rose, p. 70.
115 Sherborne, 'La Rochelle', p. 51.
116 Liddy, *Bristol, York*, pp. 46–7, 54–5. *St Albans Chronicle*, I, pp. 294–5.
117 First noticed in 1371: E 101/31/11, no. 6 (indenture); E 364/5, mm. 30d-31d (enrolled account). For the 'petite armee' and 'grande armee' deployed at sea in 1386, see, Sherborne, 'Defence of the Realm', pp. 104–5. 'Armée de la mer' was a common term for the French war fleet.
118 *The Riverside Chaucer*, ed. L.D. Benson, 3rd edn (Oxford, 1988), pp. 29–30.
119 E.g. the crews of seven of the 1372 wine convoy escorts for which detailed records survive were more than twice their 'peacetime' size. E 101/32/3, 4, 6, 7, 9, 10, 11, 28. Figures in M. K. James, *Studies in the Medieval Wine Trade* (Oxford, 1971), p. 26 are unreliable.
120 E.g. 1371: *CPR 1370-74*, p. 88; *CCR 1369-74*, p. 229; TNA, E 101/31/11, m. 7 (Guy, Lord Brian's recruiting itinerary).

121 *Knighton's Chronicle*, pp. 208–9. A. Ayton and C. Lambert, 'Shipping the Troops and Fighting at Sea: Essex Ports and Mariners in England's Wars, 1337–1389', *The Fighting Essex Soldier*, ed. C. Thornton, J. Ward and N. Wiffen (Hatfield, 2017), pp. 129–33.
122 Rodger, *Safeguard*, pp. 130–6; D. Simpkin, 'Keeping the Seas: England's Admirals, 1369–1389', *Roles of the Sea*, ed. Gorski, pp. 79–101.
123 *St Albans Chronicle*, I, pp. 214–5, 270–71, 338–41.
124 TNA, C 47/6/1. A. Ayton, 'Knights, Esquires and Military Service: The Evidence of the Armorial Cases before the Court of Chivalry', *The Medieval Military Revolution*, ed. A. Ayton and J. L. Price (London and New York, 1995), pp. 89, 91.
125 Terrier de Loray, *Jean de Vienne*, pp. 273–4.
126 *Le Victorial*, pp. 14–20.
127 Captain of the Barge of London, with twenty armed men and twenty archers: TNA E 101/68/6, no. 134. Other naval service, 1371 and 1377: C 76/54, m. 11; C 76/61, mm. 20, 23. France, 1370: C 76/53, m. 27. Jersey, 1372, 1373, 1375–6: C 76/55, mm. 16, 46; C 76/56, m. 6; C 76/58, m. 9; C 76/59, m. 9. For the C 76 references www.medievalsoldier.org.
128 *PROME*, VI, p. 350.
129 TNA, E 101/20/34, m. 1.
130 In addition to a continuing role in army transport fleets: C. Lambert, 'The Contribution of the Cinque Ports to the Wars of Edward II and Edward III: New Methodologies and Estimates', *Roles of the Sea*, ed. Gorski, pp. 59–78.
131 Adae Murimuth, *Continuatio chronicarum*, ed. E. M. Thompson (London, 1889), pp. 103–04; La Roncière, I, p. 432.
132 Sherborne, 'English Navy', p. 33; Sherborne, 'La Rochelle', pp. 45, 50–1; *St Albans Chronicle*, I, pp. 610–11.
133 *CPR 1369–74*, pp. 369–70; TNA, E 101/31/32, mm. 1, 2, 3: in all, 210 armed men and 226 mariners served. For speed of deployment, see also C.J. Ford, 'Piracy or Policy: The Crisis in the Channel, 1400-1403', *TRHS*, 5th ser., 29 (1979), 63–78 (p. 72).
134 *PROME*, VI, pp. 179–80. Payments, generally at the lower rate of 2s, were made until 1388: Sherborne, 'English Navy', p. 31.
135 TNA, E 101/20/34.
136 TNA E 101/32/3, 4, 6, 7, 9, 10, 11, 28.
137 *Monumenta Juridica: The Black Book of the Admiralty*, ed. T. Twiss, 4 vols (London, 1871–6), I. 20–3. Some impression of the profits of 1373 is provided by the account of the crown's quarter share: BL, Add. MS 37494, folios 8v-9r. Cf. Friel, pp. 64–5.
138 Lambert, *Shipping*, p. 120.
139 Moore, 'Cost-Benefit Analysis', pp. 119–20 (division of prize money in 1387), 121 (ton-tight in 1388).
140 *St Albans Chronicle*, I, pp. 225–9.
141 E.g. 'the men of Portsmouth and Dartmouth': *St Albans Chronicle*, I, pp. 708–9, 754–5.

142 Richmond, 'Keeping', pp. 292–5. For 'gallioters' operating 'hors des gages du roy', see *Black Book of the Admiralty*, I, pp. 22–3.
143 Rodger, *Safeguard*, p. 116; Sherborne, 'La Rochelle', pp. 51–2.
144 Richmond, 'Keeping', pp. 295–6.
145 T. H. Lloyd, *England and the German Hanse, 1157–1611* (Cambridge, 1991), pp. 180–2.
146 *CPR 1446–52*, p. 270.
147 Ford, 'Piracy', pp. 71–2, 76. Cf. Rose, pp. 82–4.
148 *CPR 1416–22*, pp. 120–1. Cf. Rodger, *Safeguard*, p. 147; Friel, p. 53.
149 Note, for example, the inability of English shipwrights, familiar with clinker construction, to maintain the carvel-built hulls of captured carracks. Friel, p. 78.
150 Rose, pp. 18–19.
151 Rose, p. 14, quoting Merlin-Chazelas.
152 Bréard, 'Le compte du clos des galées', pp. 90–154. Note the poor condition of nearly half of Henry V's ships at his death: Richmond, 'Keeping', pp. 285–8.
153 *Clos des Galées*, I, pp. 72–3.
154 Richmond, 'War at Sea', pp. 102–3; Rodger, *Safeguard*, pp. 126–7.
155 P. E. Russell, *The English Intervention in Spain and Portugal in the Time of Edward III and Richard II* (Oxford, 1955), pp. 403, 414–17, 527–8.
156 La Roncière, I, pp. 474–7, 481–2; *Clos des Galées*, II, pp. 75–115. Cf. Russell, *English Intervention*, pp. 415–6.
157 *Trial by Battle*, pp. 265–6. Cf. Russell, *English Intervention*, p. 527.
158 E.g., Buckingham's naval expedition in 1378: *St Albans Chronicle*, I, pp. 212–3.
159 *Divided Houses*, pp. 618–22.
160 Richmond, 'War at Sea', p. 103.

9 Armies

Gary Paul Baker

ENGLISH AND FRENCH ARMIES AT THE BEGINNING OF THE WAR

The organisational structures and methods of recruitment employed by the English crown at the beginning of the Hundred Years War had changed little since the eleventh and twelfth centuries. Armies consisted of two martial arms operating largely independently – peasant infantry and 'heavy' cavalry – with occasional recourse to continental mercenaries and foreign allies. The cavalry, known collectively as men-at-arms, were the numerically smaller element, but were considered of greater martial value because they included men from the highest echelons of society. As the leaders of political society, which was intrinsically entwined with martial obligations and 'chivalric' mentality, war was the *raison d'être* of the nobility. The core of any royally led army was the contingent of mounted royal household troops: this remained a constant throughout the war.[1] The majority of the cavalry – knights and sub-knightly men-at-arms (the latter of heterogeneous socioeconomic origins) known by a variety of names including 'sergeants' or 'esquires' – were recruited as required via systems of 'feudal' obligation, whereby men owed their lord military service for forty days, usually in return for land, or in some cases for pay.[2]

The infantry (armed with weapons for hand-to-hand fighting and a few with bows) were recruited from among the peasantry through commissions of array in each county and organised into units of twenties, hundreds or thousands under *vintenars*, *centanars* and *milenars*. How men were selected for this service is unclear, but the system remained in place until at least the middle of the fourteenth century. At their peak in the 1290s, the shire levies constituted at least, and usually more, than three-quarters of an army's fighting strength, such as the 25,700 (out of an army of about 29,000 men) recruited for the Falkirk campaign (1298).[3] But with the notable exception of the campaign of 1346–7 (where there were about 8,000), by the early years of the Hundred Years War the large numbers of infantrymen raised by the shire levies had fallen dramatically. By the second half of the fourteenth century, they had virtually disappeared.[4] This was largely due to the changing composition of English armies later in the century, as we shall see, but also because these large infantry levies possessed little by way of martial value, especially for long overseas campaigns. They were derided by contemporaries as ill-disciplined, poorly armed, prone to desertion, lacking the will to fight and experience, and not sharing the martial *mentalité* of their social superiors.[5]

French armies were also essentially 'feudal' in nature; the king's vassals constituted the nucleus of his cavalry, recruited alongside a large body of infantry.[6] The extent of the summons for the cavalry varied but it always included the majority, if not all, of the king's immediate vassals (*vassaux*), and usually his *arrière vassaux* (vassals of his vassals) between the ages of eighteen and sixty, raised via the *semonce des nobles*. Like their English counterparts these men-at-arms were considered the elite of the French forces and were, by the end of the thirteenth century, paid for their service.[7] In times of necessity the king could issue a wider call to arms and summon the *arrière-ban*, requesting the service of all able-bodied men between the ages of eighteen and sixty. A similar provision existed in England, but whereas English kings resorted to a general call to arms only once during the Hundred Years War in 1385 (and that likely for financial reasons), in France the *arrière-ban* was called more regularly as Frenchmen were summoned to defend their kingdom; from 1338 to 1356, the summons was issued at least seven times.[8] Men were mustered and reviewed by local officials (*baillis* and *seneschals*) and placed into companies under the marshals and masters of crossbowmen (*maître des arbalétriers*) upon reaching their destination.

The French crown also utilised military contracts with individuals (similar to English contracts in the form of indentures, which will be discussed in more detail in the next section), known as *lettres de retenue* and *lettres de convenance*, which stipulated the conditions of service. These contracts had been used since at least the end of the thirteenth century to employ men who fell outside the bounds of the crown's feudal jurisdiction in regions like the Dauphiné. The French crown also drew on the assistance of neighbouring allied princes who either supported the French monarchy or fell within its political orbit. Mercenaries serving under their own captains were recruited to provide missile troops, in particular the prized Genoese crossbowmen. In the field, troops were organised into large units known as *batailles* consisting of thousands of men under the command of the king and prominent noblemen. Each battle was further divided into smaller units under watch chiefs (*chef de montre*). The count of Alençon's *bataille* in 1340, for example, consisted of 1,268 men-at-arms divided into 134 smaller units.[9]

Documents from 1339 to 1341 provide an indication of the sorts of numbers the French could field. From March to April 1339, 2,500 men-at-arms, as well as 11,000 foot soldiers in south-western France and 1,000 men in north-eastern France, were raised to counter potential English incursions in the south-west. This was in addition to *c.* 10,000 men-arms and 40,000 foot soldiers raised from June to September to confront Edward III in Flanders the same year. In September 1340, when fighting on two fronts simultaneously (the Low Countries and south-western France), it has been estimated that the Valois raised around 33,000 men-at-arms and 30,000 foot soldiers. With the two valets (*auxiliaires*) and one or two horses that accompanied each man-at-arms, this meant they had as many as 60,000 horses and 100,000 men (both combatant and non-combatants) in the field. Numbers in war are, of course, not everything, but they reveal the extent to which France's resources in both money and manpower could be translated into the military sphere, providing French monarchs with one of the largest potential forces in Western Europe but often lacking cohesion in the field.[10]

CHANGES IN ENGLISH MILITARY ORGANISATION DURING THE FOURTEENTH CENTURY

The middle decades of the fourteenth century saw a series of dramatic changes in the structural composition, strategic operations, and personnel, of English armies. The Italian poet Francesco Petrarch wrote in 1360 that the English, once militarily inferior to the even the, 'wretched Scots', were now a 'fiercely bellicose nation', having 'overturned the military glory of the French'.[11] By the resumption of war in 1369, there had emerged a new type of English army; a 'structurally-uniform' force replacing the 'feudal' or 'structurally-hybrid' armies of the past.[12] So profound were these changes that they were to influence military organisation, recruitment, strategy and tactics throughout Western Europe, and have often been described as a 'military revolution'. Whether such terminology is apposite is discussed at the end of the chapter. What is beyond doubt is that the changes English armies underwent saw them enjoy, if not unbroken, then at least, unprecedented levels of martial success in the opening phase of the war (1337–60).

'In broad brush-stroke terms, the feudal host, based upon the compulsory, unpaid provision of men-at-arms by tenants-in chief in fulfilment of their military obligations, was superseded by contract armies consisting of paid volunteers'.[13] Companies of heavy cavalry raised through obligation, and infantry levies raised via commissions of array, recruited separately and operating independently, were replaced by 'mixed' retinues of equal numbers of mounted men-at-arms and mounted archers. These mixed retinues were recruited and managed by captains – nobles and gentry – who entered into contracts with the crown. These were known as 'indentures' because they were written out twice, with a jagged cut made between the two copies resembling teeth (*dentes* in Latin) so that both halves could be brought together in the event of any dispute, the unique cuts proving the other party's copy was genuine. Indentures specified the number and type of troops the captain had agreed to recruit and the other terms of service under which he and his men were to serve, including rates of pay, service length and the division of spoils of war. These terms of service became largely standardised by the second half of the fourteenth century. Pay, for example, introduced en masse in the 1330s, became fixed at daily rates: dukes 13s. 4d.; earls 6s. 8d.; bannerets 4s.; knights 2s.; non-knightly men-at-arms 1s.; mounted archers 6d.; and the increasingly rare foot archers 3d.[14] The terms also evolved. From the 1340s, we see the first appearance of *regard*, a supplementary payment to captains at 100 marks (£66 13s. 4d.) for every thirty men-at-arms for every three months they were indented to serve. The purpose of this payment is unclear. It may have been pocketed by captains to cover their overheads or amounted to a supplementary payment of about 6d. a day for each man-at-arms, perhaps to help cover the ever-growing cost of plate armour, though it may be significant that it had begun to appear in indentures just as *restauro equorum* (compensation paid by the crown for horses lost by the men-at-arms on campaign) began to cease before finally disappearing in c. 1370.[15]

The provision of universal pay was a key factor in the emergence of contract armies. Paid military service had in some form or another existed for centuries, but, by the 1330s, it had become virtually the norm within English armies, since it was the only way to both entice men to serve abroad and presume they would do so for an extended period. In the early campaigns in France from 1338 to 1340, the crown offered double the customary rates of wages, presumably to encourage service overseas, but thereafter attitudes to fighting in France had shifted in favour of the endeavour.[16] Pay arguably improved the standard of recruits. As far as can be ascertained, those serving within mixed retinues did so voluntarily. Those from lower down the social scale in particular, along with potentially enriching themselves with booty, would have found that rates of pay offered for military service compared favourably to other avenues of employment, even if payment was not always prompt.[17] Despite its risks, military service was an attractive proposition and perhaps even competitively sought, with men hoping to serve the most prestigious captains whose potential patronage was a valuable social commodity.

The provision of pay helped end obligatory service as the crown could entice men to serve for the carrot, rather than being forced to fight by the stick.

War indentures were not new. Edward I had contracted with leading magnates to provide troops for a lump sum in the 1290s, and they had also been utilised to recruit garrison troops on the Anglo-Scottish border in the early fourteenth century.[18] It was not until 1337, however, that they were used to recruit an entire army – for the Scottish campaign of that year when Edward III was fighting in Flanders.[19] According to Ayton, the indenture system initially developed 'as a mechanism designed to fill the administrative vacuum which appeared when the king was not leading the army in person, and the clerical staff of the royal household were not on hand to supervise the distribution of wages and deal with related matters'.[20] When the king campaigned in person, such as in 1346–7 and 1359–60, indentures were not used. Only once during the fourteenth-century phase of the war, in 1341, does it appear that a royally led campaign was intending to use indentures, but this army never materialised.[21] However, as the war escalated during the 1340s and 1350s, and especially after 1369 with commitments on multiple fronts, the use of indentures became the standard method for raising armies, whether the king intended to be present or not. The hand of fate certainly played a part in the introduction of the system. After the reopening of war in 1369, Edward III was in reality too old to fight, despite plans to command in 1372. Edward's death in 1377, swiftly following that of the Black Prince in 1376, made the ten-year-old Richard II king, denying any prospect of a royally led campaign until Richard came of age. As a result, no army was led by an English king between 1360 and 1385. Richard's royal uncles utilised indentures to raise armies in the interim and the precedent became established practice. The indenture system, where pre-agreed numbers and types of troops were specified and where they fought together in battle within an integrated tactical system, had tangible benefits for the crown, captains and soldiers alike.

One of the most innovative features of mixed retinues was the inclusion of mounted archers, recruited by retinue captains alongside their men-at-arms rather than by commissions of array. This may originally have been intended as 'a move towards administrative simplicity, rather than being dictated by military logic', but it became clear that the integration of mounted archers and men-at-arms within a tactical system made for a far more effective military machine.[22] This recognition only occurred gradually. In Edward III's Scottish campaign of 1335, for example, mounted archers accounted for only $c.$ 25 per cent of the army, with around only a third of this number recruited within mixed retinues and the rest via commissions of array.[23] Indeed, commissions of array continued to be used to recruit foot archers in 1338, 1340,

1342 and 1346–7, and mounted archers in 1359. Edward III's abortive plans for a Low Countries expedition in 1341 did not feature mounted archers at all, the king instead preferring hobelars, a type of light horsemen armed not with bows but with spears and other melee weapons whose utility was rapidly diminishing at the time.[24] Nevertheless, after the resumption of war in 1369, arrayed archers only appear to have been utilised twice – in 1369 and 1373 – and then only in relatively small numbers, before disappearing entirely.[25] Mounted archers raised by captains in mixed retinues were already the norm. Initially recruited in equal numbers to men-at-arms, by the fifteenth century the archers began to predominate, as we shall see later in this chapter.

Another distinctive feature of mixed retinues was their size. As the fourteenth century progressed, the crown demanded that captains recruit on a more frequent basis ever greater numbers of men for extended periods of time. Early in the century, retinue sizes varied from between five to thirty men.[26] Edward III's army in 1359–60 included retinues which dwarfed these numbers, including the Black Prince with 1,487 men (including himself), the duke of Lancaster, with 1,006, and the earl of Warwick with 250.[27] This increasing retinue size was a trend evident even in retinues of gentry-level captains such as Sir John Minsterworth with 500 men in 1370.[28] Though Minsterworth's retinue was exceptionally large for a man of his status – most gentry-led retinues generally numbered between 20 to 100 men – his company highlights that some gentry-level captains were on occasion recruiting retinues comparable in size to those of the aristocracy fifty years earlier.

These changes in retinue sizes altered the structural composition of armies: on average there were fewer retinues, but they were numerically bigger in terms of personnel. This placed a greater strain on retinue captains whose personal recruitment networks – tenurial, personal, familial, household members and even formally indentured retainers – became increasingly inadequate.[29] To meet the challenge captains extended their 'recruitment reach' by entering into written agreements (sub-indentures) with 'sub-captains' so that the latter would provide some of the retinue's personnel.[30] As retinues became larger, these sub-captains often became the principal recruiting agents for the retinues.[31] Both captains and sub-captains recruited from their own personal networks and from among the growing pool of unattached 'professional' soldiers, in the realm. These 'professional' soldiers provided the predominant source of manpower within English retinues from the second half of the fourteenth century onwards.[32]

The influx of the 'professional' soldier had a direct impact upon retinue personnel and cohesion – the relationships between the captains and their men, and between the men themselves. Men who fought together on a regular basis brought tactical and disciplinary benefits. Research has shown that 'dynamic stability' of retinues – the number of men who served the same captain on multiple occasions – in English armies from 1337 to 1360 was relatively high. At least 65 per cent of those identified serving the earl of Warwick at Crécy, for example, had accompanied him to war before.[33] After 1369, however, the influx of 'professional' freelancers saw retinue-level stability fall dramatically. For example, of the 840 men who served with Sir William de Windsor in Ireland from 1371 to 1376, only 34 (4 per cent) were present in his retinue in France in 1380–1.[34] Yet, despite low levels of repeat service, it seems that the operational efficiency of English armies in the field remained high.

The structurally uniform English armies of the post-1369 period, barring the expedition of 1370, traversed the French countryside with near impunity just as their predecessors had done prior to 1360, with the fact they were fully mounted allowing them to devastate a much wider area. While they did not enjoy major battlefield successes from 1369 to 1389, as they had in the earlier phase, this was largely due to French avoidance of set-piece engagements on Charles V's orders. England's endeavours in these years should be measured not in battlefield victories but in their conduct of war. From 1369 to 1389, the war was fought far more intensively than it had been from 1337 to 1360; there were more expeditions, on both land and sea, and it was fought over a wider geographical area, with armies in the field for, on average, double the amount of time than in the earlier phase.[35] It should be pointed out that, despite the reorganisation, structurally uniform armies post-1369 were by no means free of disciplinary problems: desertion, fraudulently claiming letters of protection for service not performed, fighting, drunkenness and gambling were still a part of the soldierly life, and a headache to the authorities. The first complete set of surviving disciplinary ordinances of an English army, but probably building upon now-lost provisions for earlier armies, are those for Richard II's 1385 force in Scotland. Thereafter such ordinances survive with increasing frequency, all bolstering the authority of captains and army commanders.[36]

The emergence of structurally uniform armies also saw a decline in the use of charters of pardon for military service, issued to men serving unpaid for the expiation of past misdeeds. After a peak of several thousand issued for the Crécy-Calais expedition (1346–7), numbers began to fall. The 1370 expedition saw less than a hundred issued and though there was a brief revival in the early fifteenth century for service to counter the Glyn Dŵr rebellion, the practice disappeared completely thereafter.[37] The explanation was the realisation that pardons were an unreliable recruitment tool for providing the calibre of required combatant. Such men were no longer needed because of the growing militarisation, and arguably 'professionalism', of the men now constituting the English military community.[38]

Expeditions led by the king in person always attracted large turnouts, as did campaigns within the British Isles where there were fewer logistical difficulties of getting men to the front. Nevertheless, the general downward trend after 1369 through to the end of the Hundred Years War is self-evident, although we must also bear in mind the relative levels of frequency with which armies were raised, especially in the fifteenth century (Table 9.1).

Table 9.1 Average size of English land campaigns 1277–1453[39]

Years (and number of expeditions)	All Expeditions	Excluding Irish expeditions of less than 1,000 men	Expeditions to France Only
1277–1336 (16)	12,794	12,794 (16)	11,000 (1)
1337–1360 (11)	5,876	5,876 (11)	7,042 (6)
1361–1399 (34)	2,765	3,466 (26)	3,423 (15)
1400–1453 (56)	2,342	2,490 (52)	2,332 (47)

The decreasing size of armies was down to both financial and tactical reasons. The tactical reasons are discussed in the next section. Financially, the English crown struggled throughout the war to fund military spending.[40] Edward III's policy of hiring foreign allies in the Low Countries (c. £500,000 from 1338 to 1341) was unsustainable, virtually bankrupted the crown and led to a series of political crises.[41] Thereafter, though foreign soldiers were on occasion recruited during the fourteenth century, the English became largely self-reliant for its armies. Indeed, the rise of the mounted archer may well have been as much to do with finance as it was about tactical innovation. At 6d. per day it was cheaper to recruit archers than men-at-arms (although the decline of the latter in the fifteenth century may have been equally important).[42]

It is important to remember, however, that the emergence of the structurally uniform army was not an inevitability. Some facets of 'feudal' armies may well have disappeared in the fullness of time as the crown sought to raise forces more quickly and effectively, but the structurally uniform army which emerged by the late 1360s could have been markedly different had alternative circumstances prevailed at crucial points in its development. Some innovations were tried and then abandoned as either unworkable or a result of circumstance. Edward III, for example, attempted to extend the obligation of his subjects to perform military service based on wealth, as both his father and grandfather had done.[43] During the 1330s, he reissued the Statute of Winchester of 1285, itself derived from the Assize of Arms of 1181, requiring that all landholders serve the king when requested with arms appropriate to their station; but, in the following decade, in desperate need for troops in France, he went much further. He set out a schedule early in 1345 whereby men were to serve the king based upon the value of their lands: those with lands worth 100s (£5) were to serve as mounted archers; those with £10 a hobelar; those with £25 a man-at-arms and so forth up to £1,000.[44] In February and March 1346, further orders altered the assessment: landholders were now to provide troops based on their wealth, rather than serving in person, again with a proportional number of troops defined in a set schedule. Edward was thus able to raise an army of *c.* 14,000–15,000 in 1346, reducing his dependence on allies.[45] But the scheme provoked outrage and the crown was made to promise in parliament in September 1346 that it was not to be considered a precedent and formally abandoned it after a petition in the parliament of January 1352.[46] Similarly, had Edward's plans for the never-to-materialise campaign to the Low Countries in 1341 come to fruition – where captains were to be assigned wool to sell in lieu of wages, and retinues were to be comprised not of mounted men-at-arms and archers but men-at-arms with foot archers and armed men (*gentz armez*) – it would have been 'wholly untypical of the English armies of the Hundred Years War', perhaps even sending the development of English armies down a divergent path.[47]

TACTICAL IMPLICATIONS

The changes in English armies were also a reaction to changing tactical needs with two key changes made: the abandonment of heavy cavalry *destriers* in favour of smaller, nimbler mounts (a policy tailored for the needs of long-distance movement); and dismounting all troops to fight in set-piece engagements alongside the use of mass archery. The need for smaller, more agile mounts seems to have been recognised by Edward III and the wider military community as early as the 1327 campaign in Scotland. The Scots, on smaller, nimbler and thus more mobile horses, outmanoeuvred the English *destriers* with ease.[48] A generation earlier, at Bannockburn in 1314, the English horse had been defeated by Scottish infantry armed with spears and pole-arms in defensive hedgehog-like *schiltron* formations, part of a wider European phenomenon of infantry-based armies gaining the upper hand against cavalry.[49] These lessons – the importance of mobility on campaign and the value of infantry in fixed defensive positions – were utilised by the English in France. English armies used their mobile mounts to conduct lightning raids – *chevauchées* – plundering and burning the French countryside. The purpose of this activity was long seen by scholars as an attempt to weaken enemy resolve, forcing them to the negotiating table. It has been argued by Clifford Rogers, however, that the *chevauchée* was a stratagem intended to entice the French to pitched battle where the English could employ their new battlefield tactics, inflicting decisive defeats upon their opponent to end the war in England's favour.[50] The preferred modus operandi for English armies was to secure the tactical defensive, dismounting both men-at-arms and archers, and fighting in fixed positions; the latter employing heavy missile fire and the former being armed with lances and other pole-arms to protect the archers.[51]

The effect of massed archery was devastating and changed the nature of the war from the 1340s. Arrows broke up enemy formations, disrupted cavalry and caused attackers to crowd together. Then the men-at-arms and archers would engage hand-to-hand any attackers who had survived the withering fire. Use of archery on the battlefield was not, of course, new; it was the scale with which the English employed it which was truly revolutionary. Even when the French, attempting to copy English tactics, dismounted themselves and attempted to advance on foot, the fact that they had not developed a tradition of military archery meant that their unsupported men-at-arms were cut down by the incessant rate of fire of English bowmen, which was far higher than that of France's hired crossbowmen.[52]

Utilising these tactics, the English won a series of spectacular victories during the first phase of the Hundred Years War, and there would likely have been more after 1369 had the French not avoided battlefield encounters. Yet, barring mixed retinues, the English tactical and strategic innovations were nothing original in the annals of military history. But they were perceived as being new because of their novelty in contemporary eyes; it was this novelty which made them appear revolutionary and made English troops highly prized as mercenaries throughout Europe.[53] Moreover, in every region in which Englishmen fought, local military elites began adopting the 'English style' in tactical operations. The reforms of the Portuguese and Castilian armies in the late fourteenth century, for example, show how far both English and to an extent French military systems were seen as models to emulate.[54] It seems that 'English' tactics were not adopted wholesale, however, because of a combination of the obstinacy of military elites clinging to traditional practices and the prohibitive costs and difficulty of fostering a tradition of military archery in areas where it was largely non-existent. In England, a combination of Edward III's force of personality, the existing tradition of archery and the realisation by the elite of its battlefield effectiveness were the crucial factors.

THE FRENCH RESPONSE

The French did not fully appreciate the magnitude of the changes in English armies and tactics until they were utterly routed at Crécy, the first major land battle of the war. The defeat sent shockwaves throughout the French kingdom. In the wake of the defeat, towns throughout France gained greater autonomy in the organisation of local defence and repairing fortifications, yet little was done to reform the basic military system, largely because of the political upheaval the defeat caused.[55] The defeats at Poitiers a decade later, arguably worse because it saw the French king captured, and at Brignais (1362) against the military companies who ravaged France in the wake of the treaty of Brétigny, only served to emphasise the problem: French armies, and the military systems that brought them into being, were woefully inadequate to fight these more intensive conflicts.

Initial attempts at reform were made by John II in an ordinance of April 1351. To combat the lack of cohesion within the huge *batailles* raised prior to Crécy, he placed emphasis upon creating a more disciplined force, organised into companies, with men paid standard wage rates based upon social rank (much as in England), with minimum required standards for horses and equipment. Men-at-arms were to be formed into *grosses routes*, each comprising twenty-five to eighty men-at-arms, while the infantry was to be organised into units of twenty-five to thirty men under constables (*connétablies*). The primacy of loyalty to the king rather than regional magnates was reaffirmed along with a military hierarchy directly under the monarch comprising the Constable, Marshals, Master of Crossbowmen and so forth. Desertion, captains claiming wages for absent men and other unscrupulous practices were not to be tolerated, with wages withdrawn as a punishment for miscreants, aided by the introduction of more regular musters.[56] To encourage these practices, John issued further orders in July 1355 stipulating that 100 *livres tournois* a month was to be paid to each *chef de montre* (leader of the muster group) for every twenty-five men-at-arms provided from his household. The scheme seems to have borne fruit: a summons in Picardy in October–November 1355 reveals several bannerets mustered with companies of 25, 50, 60 and 100 men-at-arms. Records from Languedoc also show that the region provided for 5,000 men-at-arms, 1,000 mounted sergeants (*sergents à cheval*), 2,000 mounted crossbowmen (*arbalétriers à cheval*) and 2,000 *pavesiers à cheval*, for the year 1355/6, indicative of the general trend of an increase in mounted troops in French forces.[57] The French also began to try to replicate English tactics in the field. As early as 1351, French men-at-arms are recorded as dismounting to fight, and they certainly did so at Poitiers, perhaps influenced by Scottish knights in their ranks. The numbers of men being recruited also reduced significantly. The Black Death and financial problems experienced by the crown as the war dragged on certainly played a part, but most importantly was the realisation that it was the calibre, not number, of troops that was most important.

It was not until Charles V's much celebrated ordinance of 13 January 1374, however, that real change took place.[58] While continuing to use *letters de retenue*, mercenaries and feudal military obligation, the structure and discipline of French armies were henceforth to be heavily regulated, remedying abuses that had continued despite John II's ordinances. French captains were often not maintaining the numbers of men in their companies with whom they had initially mustered, fraudulently claiming absentees' pay and pocketing their wages. Charles's ordinance required that all soldiers, barring the households of the Constable and Master of Crossbowmen, were to be mustered and inspected regularly by the two Marshals of France or eight hand-picked lieutenants. Only those present at muster, adequately armed and mounted, were to receive wages. Absence was forbidden unless authorised by a captain for acceptable mitigating circumstances. The captains, paid 100 francs a month, were only to be appointed via the letters of authority from the king or his representatives. Soldiers were to purchase all goods at market price and do no intentional harm to the king's subjects, nor dally on their way to muster under pain of confiscation of their equipment. Captains were made responsible for any damages caused by their men, ensuring they had a vested interest in discipline.

To lessen the risk of fraud, payments to soldiers, rather than being made directly to captains, were to be made to smaller sub-divisions (*chambres*) within a company, who were responsible for paying a set number of men within the unit. Each company was to have no less than 100 men-at-arms divided into ten *chambres*, the main *chambre* consisting of the captain and his household. Pay was calculated monthly and paid more regularly: 60 francs a month for a banneret; 30 for a knight; 15 for a squire or rich (*étoffé*) archer; 12 for a mounted crossbowman; and 8 for a crossbowman on foot. For example, accounts detailing payments to Bertrand de Guesclin of 127,000 *livres tournois* for his retinue (1 March 1373–28 February 1374), numbering variously between 400 and 700 men, reveal payments in sixteen instalments at regular intervals.[59] Evidence for the structure and composition of the retinues of French captains is limited, but the duke of Anjou's company in Languedoc in 1374 may be representative: of 2,657 men-at-arms under his charge approximately half – 1,370 – were of southern origins, outside his sphere of influence; 1,007, or 41 per cent, were Bretons; 134 from Picardy; 345 were Normans; and the rest were from the Auvergne and its surrounding regions. In other words, French captains, especially those of more than regional prominence had, like their English counterparts, a wide geographic 'recruitment reach'. The development of small companies of archers and crossbowmen in the towns to provide a body of men who could be called upon in an emergency was also encouraged, emulating groups already present in the towns of Flanders.

Charles also continued the practice established in the later years of his father's reign of not summoning the *arrière-ban*, the last instance of which had been in 1356, although he did issue *semonces des nobles* in 1369, 1373, 1375, 1378 and, in all likelihood, in 1380, corresponding with the appearance of English armies. There were two reasons for the abandonment of the *arrière-ban*. First, as discussed in other chapters in this volume, new taxes like the *tailles* and *fouages*, better methods of collection and, more importantly, a steady income from these taxes – 800,000 to 1 million francs a year devoted to soldiers' pay – meant that funds that could have been raised from commutation of service were no longer desirable because of the uncertain amount and effort needed to collect them. Second, it reflected the government's desire – as in England – to move away from a reliance on large numbers of untrained, ill-disciplined infantrymen.

The army that Charles V created was thus, in theory, a more disciplined body of largely mounted fighting men, comprising in the main lower-ranking French nobles with a smattering of mercenary crossbowmen. This was on a regional basis with men paid and recruited by the local nobility, providing a semi-permanent army, potentially 6,000-strong, in addition to the troops of the permanent royal garrisons in northern France and twenty men-at-arms and twenty-four mounted crossbowmen who formed the royal *garde du corps* – an embryonic French royal household guard – who from 1369 to 1379 were permanently employed by the king.[60] With this rejuvenated army, the French did experience a brief period of success against the English in the early years after the war recommenced in 1369, reconquering many of the lands in south-western France ceded to the English in 1360. But the traditional argument – that the French enjoyed untrammelled superiority in the second half of the fourteenth century – can be challenged.[61] On a purely martial level, the interpretation fails to recognise that the English conduct of war from 1369 to 1389 had changed. English strategy in these years was the acquisition of

French coastal fortresses like Brest and Cherbourg to act as 'barbicans of the realm', accompanied by an increased naval effort. Although initially the French held the upper hand, the English continued to be able to land troops in French territory with impunity. Moreover, as we have seen, Charles V publicly ordered his captains not to engage the English in pitched battle no matter the provocation, as clear an indication as any of French respect, even fear, of English arms.

The success of Charles's reforms should therefore not be overstated. It does not appear that he intended them to create a standing army.[62] Indeed, the reforms did not survive his death in 1380. Charles himself was a key architect in the failure, for on his deathbed he cancelled the *fouage*, the tax which had been the foundation of French fiscal and military rejuvenation.[63] Consequently, the strict standards of recruitment and discipline lapsed due to lack of funding. Moreover, the continuing reliance on mercenary crossbowmen, indicative of a failure to develop a tradition of military archery with the longbow, was arguably France's greatest martial failure in the period as it prevented the adoption of the successful English tactical system. Attempts were made to stimulate archery practice among the French populace after the truce with England in the 1380s, but the fear of popular insurrection by militarising the lower orders caused Charles VI to limit the number of archers that could be recruited in each region.[64] What can be said about the long-term efficacy of Charles V's reforms is that, when the political climate was calmer in the 1440s, Charles VII used them as the basis for martial recovery.

ENGLISH ARMIES OF THE FIFTEENTH CENTURY

From 1415, the English changed their strategic modus operandi by concentrating on conquest and occupation of territory.[65] It is not clear why this change occurred, but perhaps it was the realisation that the only realistic method of winning the war was through conquest and having the French people recognise English kings as the legitimate rulers of France. Initially, the English were the aggressors, aided by the French civil war between Armagnacs and Burgundians. However, after the fateful siege of Orléans (1428-9) and the subsequent defeat at Patay (1429), the death of John, duke Bedford (1435), and Henry VI's lack of interest in pursuing the war upon reaching maturity, the conflict took on a distinctively defensive character for the English as they tried to hold what they had won.

The indenture system continued to be utilised to recruit armies in England, even when the king was present in person. There were, however, subtle changes, perhaps linked to the fact that, from 1422, the king was a minor. With the earl of Salisbury's campaign of 1428, for instance, we see the introduction of the 'great' indenture.[66] Rather than indenting with numerous captains individually, the crown contracted with one nobleman, who in turn entered into sub-indentures with other captains, a development presumably intended to streamline the administrative process. Another observable change is the rise in the proportion of archers in English armies with one man-at-arms to every three mounted archers becoming the norm from 1406, although the proportion of archers increased in the years of crisis of the 1440s to as high as 90 per cent.[67] While this development was likely because archers were both cheaper and easier to recruit than men-at-arms, as well as highly flexible for all kinds of war, it was also likely a response to the continuing fall in the number of dubbed knights serving in the war. This was a sign of a wider disengagement from the war among the gentry: a war of occupation suited men from lower down the social scale – archers – with fewer domestic ties in England.[68]

It was no longer enough, however, to raise expeditionary armies in England. Henry V began a strategy of granting out conquered lands so that some of the burden of defence would be placed upon their recipients, both easing the financial burden on the crown's financial responsibilities and ensuring that, in theory, those in receipt of lands were invested in their protection.[69] In addition, Henry sought to emphasise the legitimacy of his rule by appealing to the Normans by attempting to revive the traditional feudal obligations of landholders in Normandy, an echo of the structurally hybrid forces of the past. Henry issued the *semonce des nobles* on at least four occasions during his lifetime. From 1422 to 1444, it was issued at least fifty times, though its political significance was greater than the numerical contribution made by the *semonce* to English forces. However, many of the English who had been granted lands were non-resident and had to be reminded of their duties on several occasions. The frequency of issue of the *semonce* decreased after 1436, indicating the failure of the settlement policy as a means of providing soldiers and the increasingly delicate relationship with the Norman nobility. Attempts to summon the *arrière-ban* in 1435–6 were disastrous, leading to revolt and the loss of a large swathe of Upper Normandy, highlighting the problem of attempting to utilise such forms of recruitment on an already overstretched population.[70]

Occupying garrisons had been the cornerstone of the fourteenth-century 'barbicans strategy' and of Edward III's capture of Calais, but the fifteenth-century conquests saw an unprecedented number of places held and many more men needed to garrison them. At least forty-five garrisons were held in

Normandy and the *pays de conquête* (the Seine valley between Normandy and Paris) from 1422 to 1448, amounting to between c. 2,000 and 7,000 soldiers, depending on the French threat and strategic needs.[71] Most garrison soldiers were English or Welsh, some of whom had crossed initially with expeditionary armies. Some were settlers who came to France as a result of the English conquests. Henry V's policy of conciliation towards the French (so he would be seen as a legitimate ruler rather than a foreign conqueror) encouraged local recruitment, a position much enhanced by the treaty of Troyes of May 1420 which gave access to all means of French military provision and financial resources, including local taxation to pay for defence. There were therefore Norman and French soldiers in the garrisons and a smattering of men from other European countries, although after the successes of Joan of Arc the English had concerns about the loyalty of local men and sought to limit their service.[72] Almost all garrisons followed the ratio of one man-at-arms for every three archers, although the sedentary nature of these defensive installations led to the service of foot alongside mounted soldiers.

Garrisons were not simply for defence and policing the population; they also provided detachments for service in the field. Field armies recruited within France had the ability to react quickly to emergencies and potential opportunities which the process of raising an army and shipping it from England could never hope to match. The drawback of utilising garrison personnel too intensively to provide troops for field armies was that it weakened the defensive networks the English had put in place. Reforms of the duke of Bedford in October 1434 tried to solve this by assigning field companies to certain garrisons.[73] Other stratagems included the recruitment of veterans living in Normandy but not in royal pay (the 'gens vivans sur le pais'), who might also be used to reinforce vulnerable places for short periods or to fill gaps in field armies.[74] By the 1440s, the English were on the defensive, having lost Paris in 1436 as well as Burgundian support in the previous year. Even the Normans, initially loyal to the English, were increasingly reluctant to pay heavy taxation to pay for garrisons, which made the English increasingly reliant on troops recruited in England at a time when English tax payers were equally reluctant to support the war effort.

It was the general failure of the English to fully integrate their continental possessions into a successful means of raising and maintaining troops which was one of the long-term reasons for the eventual French victory. Of the major protagonists in the fifteenth-century phase of the war, only England failed to establish anything akin to a permanent standing army, largely due to a lack of permanent and heavy taxation. As Sir John Fortescue observed in the 1470s, a crucial difference between the English and French monarchies was that French kings could arbitrarily demand taxation of their subjects; English kings had to ask parliament to acquiesce to the raising of funds.[75] The availability and ease of raising money, was not, however, the only explanation for the ultimate French victory in 1449–53. The reasons for this dramatic reversal in English fortunes have long been debated,[76] but arguably most important were the reforms that took place in French military organisation.

FRENCH MILITARY REFORMS IN THE FIFTEENTH CENTURY

The campaigns of Henry V saw the near complete collapse of the French military system. Attempts at reform had proven transient. The unwieldy 'feudal' methods of recruitment persisted. However, the rapprochement between Charles VII and Philip, duke of Burgundy in 1435, ending the Armagnac-Burgundian civil war and diplomatically isolating England, created a unity of purpose among the French – removing the English from France. Changes in the French military sphere can also be viewed as the monarchy overcoming the long-standing near political autonomy of many of the territorial French princes, made more pressing still after the *Praguerie* revolt of French noblemen in 1440. The need 'not only to end the war with the English, but to deprive the potentially rebellious magnate of the means of revolt' was an absolute necessity.[77] It is important, however, not to think of the French military reforms in the mid-fifteenth century as a new army created from scratch. The innovations of Charles VII should be seen as a development, albeit a large one, of practices that had slowly emerged since Crécy.

The immediate problem for the French in the 1430s and 1440s was that the Armagnac-Burgundian rapprochement of 1435 left large numbers of soldiers – *écorcheurs* – without employment and, like the *routier* companies of the previous century, many took to brigandage. Solving this problem was a crucial test of Charles VII's authority and that of the French crown over the territorial magnates, because many of these *écorcheurs* claimed allegiance to their local lords. To counter the problem, Charles issued the first of his celebrated *ordonnances* in May–June 1445, taking advantage of the break in hostilities with the English after the truce of Tours (1444).[78] The king stated that he intended to retain a large number of the unemployed *écorcheurs* within several mounted *compagnies d'ordonnance* under royally commissioned captains. Fifteen cavalry companies were envisaged, each with its own captain, and 100 men-at-arms (*lances fourni*), with each man-at-arms supported by five other men: one lightly armoured horseman (*coutiliers*); two mounted archers (*archers à cheval*); and two servants (thus 600 men per company). The men chosen were to be of the best calibre available based upon both their equipment and their loyalty to the crown, severing the link between the men and the regional magnate power bases and cemented by Charles's stipulation that the king alone had the right to wage war.[79] Most important was that the companies were to be retained permanently, paid for by local resources from new taxes. To ease this burden, Charles divided up his troops within garrisons in different French provinces (*élections*) in numbers small enough that they would, in theory, be unthreatening to local inhabitants, who were to maintain the troops and pay their wages either in money or in kind.[80] Charles's master stroke was allowing local officials to organise the distribution and billeting of these men and only later appointing his personal representatives in supervisory roles. His administration thus presented itself as showing respect for local rights and privileges, helping to win over those who held the reins of power in the localities, without whose cooperation the scheme would surely have failed.

The system was not perfect. A second *ordonnance* of January 1446 attempted to enforce the changes Charles had intended the previous year by requiring monthly musters, scrutinised tri-monthly by French marshals to prevent soldiers selling their horses or equipment, or simply taking the king's pay and disappearing. There was also a degree of resentment among the populace upon whom soldiers were billeted, in the absence of formal barracks. Nevertheless, the system, no matter how difficult to administer, with regular troops paid permanently and available quickly in times of need, was a vast improvement on what had gone before. Charles's reforms thus created a body of 9,000 fully mounted men of whom 6,000 were combatants – the first permanent standing army in Western Europe since the fall of the Western Roman Empire.

To supplement his cavalry, Charles also created a body of 8,000 *franc-archers* in April 1448, to address the need for highly trained infantry after the abandonment of the *arrière-ban*, and a desire to have a body of missile troops comparable to the English archers. The men were selected based upon their skill with arms and were chosen, supplied and equipped locally by each parish.[81] They were to exercise and practice regularly, have their names and addresses recorded in a register and swear an oath that they would serve only the crown. As an incentive, they were exempted from paying the *taille* (thereby joining those liable to the *semonce* – the nobles and others 'following the wars' – who were traditionally exempt) and other local obligations. The *franc-archers* were certainly instrumental in helping drive the English out of France, notably at the siege of Caen (1450) and the battle of Castillon (1453). Charles also sought, through his orders of 22 May 1448, to reorganise the obligation of nobles to give service, primarily as a defensive force. Service was henceforward to be fully paid at rates comparable to those of the *compagnies d'ordonnance*: 15 *livres tournois* monthly for each man-at-arms with three horses and 7 *livres* 10 *sous* (shillings) for each archer. Although Charles never summoned these men for service in the final years of the war, many served of their own volition.[82] Furthermore, the Bretons turned out to be valuable allies for Charles VII in 1449–50: Breton dukes issued their own military ordinances in the mid-to-late fifteenth century intended to modernise their forces and military institutions on a French model.[83]

The development undertaken by the French government in the 1440s that arguably had the greatest repercussions for the future of warfare was the organisation and supervision of France's gunpowder artillery by the brothers Jean and Gaspard Bureau.[84] Looking back on the achievements of French arms after the expulsion of the English, the herald Gilles le Bouvier wrote that the king:

> had such a large number of great bombards ... canon [and other firearms], that no one can remember a Christian king ever having such great artillery, nor of one so well furnished with powder, shields, and all other necessaries for approaching and taking castles and towns.[85]

Firearms in warfare were nothing new, emerging in rudimentary fashion in Europe as early as the 1320s, firing existing missiles like stones and utilised alongside traditional siege equipment like trebuchets.[86] Small artillery pieces had appeared on some western European battlefields in the mid-to-late fourteenth century; but, because even the smaller pieces were heavy, difficult to manoeuvre and aim with precision, with a slow rate of fire and the possibility of rupture, and because traditional missile weapons were far more effective in killing and harassing the enemy from afar, gunpowder artillery remained largely unsuitable for battlefield deployment, even when an army remained in a fixed position on the defensive. They were utilised primarily as siege weapons because, despite the logistical difficulties of their use for the besieger, they could undoubtedly reduce the length of a siege. Even then, however, difficulties of transport and repair, as well as the limited availability of saltpetre used to make gunpowder, meant that, in the fourteenth century, the effect of firearms was primarily psychological. It was often the threat of the guns which could hasten a garrison's surrender, such as at St Sauveur-le-Vicomte in 1375.[87]

The real advent of gunpowder artillery in Western Europe came from the 1380s with expanding production and increased availability on the European market of saltpetre. When Henry V invaded France he brought an extensive siege train with him (though his gunners were largely foreign), and, as the century progressed, the general trend is clear: an increase in the size and number of huge artillery pieces, and the utilisation of smaller guns, like *ribauldequins*, as anti-personnel weapons against defenders on city walls. The French guns at St Sauveur in 1375 had fired stones weighing 100 pounds; those in Henry's army at the siege of Harfleur fired stones about 400 pounds.[88] Historians remain divided on whether guns gained the upper hand over fortifications or whether walls were still strong enough to resist.[89] Nevertheless, English guns had been essential in the conquest of Normandy. The key to controlling territory was the occupation and maintenance of fortifications and the English provided the French with a stark lesson in the effectiveness that artillery could play in warfare.

The reorganisation of the French siege train by the Bureau brothers was not the result of new types of artillery technology; significant developments in the art of gunnery including corned powder, cast-iron shot and specialised gun carriages only occurred in 1453 at the earliest.[90] Nor was there any real improvement in battlefield artillery. French successes at Formigny (1450) and Castillon (1453), while rightly being attributed to artillery, were in fact the result of siege guns pressed into field service. Nor were the brothers' reforms related to any improvement in personal firearms. While handguns and shoulder arms did find their way into garrisons, the days of large numbers of *arquebusiers* and other small arms on the battlefield were for later centuries.[91] The key to the brothers' success was 'the replacement of older and somewhat haphazard methods of procuring ordnance' with 'an organised system of personnel, arsenals, and magazines all geared toward providing a large, reliable supply of siege guns and supporting firearms wherever and whenever the king might demand them'.[92] They were simply able to build, purchase, acquire, transport, supply and maintain large numbers of existing pieces, fully exploiting their potential, rather than exploiting new technological changes.

Burgundian influences on French martial developments and vice versa should also not be discounted. The Burgundian dukes transformed the duchy from an apanage of the French crown in the fourteenth century, dependent on the latter for troops, into the third major power in the fifteenth-century phase of the war, and an ally first of the English and then, critically for the outcome of the conflict, the French.[93] They recruited troops from all their territories, including the wealthy Low Countries, as well as drawing on mercenaries. In the late fourteenth century, these were largely Italian crossbowmen but, in the fifteenth century, English archers were particularly prized. From the 1430s, the numbers and proportions of archers in Burgundian armies increased exponentially to about three-quarters, a figure reminiscent of English forces.[94] But most important of all was the reorganisation of the Burgundian artillery by John the Fearless, well before this happened in France. He created a *maître d'artillerie* to manage his guns for all the Burgundian territories, bringing pieces not within fortifications to a central arsenal at Dijon, and kept detailed records of his artillery and an inventory of the ducal cannons.[95] One such piece in 1409, for example, weighed three-and-a-half tons and fired missiles of 700–900 pounds.[96] It would not be until the third quarter of the fifteenth century, however, that a true arms race between the French and the Burgundians took place over the size and technological developments of their artillery. In this competition, the English were very much a part-player, although the need to defend their remaining toehold in France at Calais prompted them to build up a suitable arsenal there.[97]

The role of foreign mercenary troops in French armies should also not be overlooked. Both England and France employed mercenaries throughout the war – via a formal alliance, because they provided expertise not readily available within their native populations, or simply because they were mercenaries looking to serve for profit and plunder. The Franco-Castilian alliance of 1368, for example, provided the French with much-needed naval support, while the English crown employed mostly foreign gunners, at least initially, because of a lack of Englishmen with this expertise.[98] During the fourteenth century, foreign soldiers never constituted more than a significant minority of the overall forces employed, but, during the fifteenth century, though they were utilised by the English, it was the French crown for whom mercenaries played a significant role, riddled as it was by a major military defeat in 1415, an English invasion and occupation, and civil war. In the 'dark days of the 1420s' after the treaty of Troyes, the dauphin Charles (the future Charles VII)

> organised his armed forces on the basis of the much-truncated kingdom still left to him ... [and] foreign troops were considerably more than the essentially auxiliary forces they had been in the past; they were to become, for the next decade and more, a major, and at times preponderant element in French royal armies.[99]

These men came from all over Europe, like the Castilian *routier* Rodrigo de Villandrando, who fought in French service from 1410 to the 1440s, and also large numbers of soldiers from the British Isles; like the 4,000 Scots slain by English forces fighting for the French at Verneuil (1424).[100] This utilisation of foreign troops continued even after the creation of the *compagnies d'ordonnance*.

Unlike Charles V's reforms, those of Charles VII remained a permanent fixture of French military organisation. The transition from the 'feudal' to the permanent army was far from smooth, but the reforms succeeded because they were 'traditional in conception, realistic in ambition, and simple in application' and ultimately because the French populace, by their acquiescence to increased taxation (coerced or otherwise), were willing to fund the changes if it meant ridding the countryside of both large numbers of master-less soldiers and the English.[101] Without the lubricant of money, Charles VII's reforms would doubtlessly have failed.

CONCLUSION: THE HUNDRED YEARS WAR AND THE MILITARY REVOLUTION

Do the changes which took place within, first, English and then, later, French armies during the Hundred Years War deserve to be categorised as a military revolution? The idea of a military revolution, first proposed in the 1960s for developments in early modern Swedish armies, was quickly adopted by scholars of other periods.[102] Medievalists have been keen to highlight that many of the supposed changes seen by early modernists as revolutionary – including the supplanting of heavy cavalry with infantry; the introduction of universal pay; and rising cost of armies – had, in fact, precedents in the Middle Ages.[103]

The whole notion of military revolution has not been without its critics. How, for example, can a 'transformation which took place over such an extended period – perhaps from the early fourteenth to the end of the eighteenth century – be usefully be called a revolution at all'?[104] The notion of revolution also falls into the trap of 'technological determinism', seeing history as an unending arms race with technological developments in the military sphere giving one particular group or armament supremacy for a period of time until new developments overtake it.[105] This view is not without merit, but it does not adequately cater for factors such as regional differences, terrain, the military-political objectives of belligerents and the fact that there were often transitional periods (sometimes decades) between the introduction of new technologies and their widespread adoption – gunpowder artillery being a classic example.[106] Nor is technological determinism easily reconcilable with the remarkable success that English armies enjoyed in the early-to-mid fourteenth century in dismounting to fight. This was based upon tactical effectiveness not technological change.

The 'military revolution problem' has been skilfully tackled by Clifford Rogers. He argued that there were in fact several military revolutions in Europe from 1300 to 1800, occurring in all areas of war – infantry, artillery, cavalry, navy and fortification – with each dramatically altering warfare for a brief period. For Rogers, the answer was 'punctuated equilibrium evolution ... short bursts of rapid change interspersed with long periods of near stasis, rather than constant, slow alteration'.[107] Within the Hundred Years War, he saw two periods of rapid change: the rise of the archer infantry, which brought the English so much initial success; and the increased use and power of gunpowder artillery in the fifteenth century, which facilitated, first, the English and, finally, the French triumph.

Furthermore, recent research is revealing just how important interpersonal relationships (the *esprit de corps*) between the men were to the operation of armies during the Hundred Years War. For medieval armies, 'personnel was paramount' to their cohesion and operational efficiency in the field, arguably more so than the barracks-based, professional armies of later periods where the individual recruit was 'subordinated to the collective and enduring identities of, on one level, the regiment and, on another, the armed forces of the state'.[108] Into organisational and technological changes, therefore, always need to be placed the men themselves. The most significant conclusion to emerge from this military-community-focussed research is the widening and diversification of the socioeconomic origins of serving personnel because of the intensity of the Anglo-French conflict. It was in this period that the socio-professional (serving as a by-product of their status) began to be joined by the military careerist, serving for financial return; in that combination lies the foundation of modern armies.[109] The application of the term 'military revolution', therefore, is aptly applied to developments that occurred during the Hundred Years War.

NOTES

1   A. Ayton, 'English Armies in the Fourteenth Century', *Arms, Armies and Fortifications in the Hundred Years War*, ed. A. Curry and M. Hughes (Woodbridge, 1994), p. 25.
2   'Feudal', though a problematic term, remains 'the most appropriate way of describing the military service rendered by tenants-in-chief in return for lands': D. Simpkin, *The English Aristocracy at War* (Woodbridge, 2008), p. 152 n. 2. On sub-knightly combatants, ibid, pp. 91–102.
3   M. Prestwich, 'Edward I's Armies', *JMH*, 37 (2011), pp. 237–9.
4   A. Ayton, 'The English Army and the Normandy Campaign of 1346', *England and Normandy in the Middle Ages*, ed. D. Bates and A. Curry (London, 1994), p. 268.
5   M. Prestwich, *Armies and Warfare in the Middle Ages: The English Experience* (London, 1996), pp. 124–9.

6   Contamine, *GES*, pp. 26–55; X. Hélary, *L'armée du roi de France. La guerre de Saint Louis à Philippe le Bel* (Paris, 2012), pp. 39–64, 111–72.
7   B. Schnerb, 'De l'armée féodale a l'armée permanente', *Le Miracle Capétien*, ed. S. Rials (Paris, 1987), pp. 123–32.
8   Allmand, pp. 92–3.
9   A. Blanchard et al, *Histoire militaire de la France. 1: Des origines à 1715* (Paris, 1992), pp. 135–40.
10 B. Schnerb, 'Vassals, Allies and Mercenaries: The French Army Before and After 1346', *The Battle of Crécy, 1346*, ed. A. Ayton and P. Preston (Woodbridge, 2005), p. 268.
11 *Knights and Warhorses*, p. 9.
12 A. Ayton, 'Armies and Military Communities in Fourteenth-Century England', *Soldiers, Nobles and Gentlemen: Essays in Honour of Maurice Keen*, ed. P. Coss and C. Tyreman (Woodbridge, 2009), pp. 215–19.
13 Ayton, 'English Armies', p. 22.
14 A. Prince, 'The Payment of Army Wages in Edward III's Reign', *Speculum*, 19 (1944), pp. 137–60.
15 Ayton, 'English Armies', pp. 24–5.
16 Ayton, 'English Armies', p. 28.
17 C. Dyer and S. A. C. Penn, 'Wages and Earnings in Late Medieval England: Evidence from the Enforcement of the Labour Laws', *EcHR*, 43 (1990), reprinted in C. Dyer, *Everyday Life in Medieval England* (2nd edn, London, 2000), p. 167.
18 Prestwich, *English Experience*, p. 91; *Knights and Warhorses*, pp. 11–12.
19 N. B. Lewis, 'Recruitment and Organisation of a Contract Army. May to November 1337', *BIHR*. (1964), pp. 1–19.
20 Ayton, 'English Armies', p. 25.
21 M. Prestwich, 'English Armies in the Early Stages of the Hundred Years War: A Scheme of 1341', *BIHR*, 56 (1983), pp. 102–13.
22 Prestwich, *English Experience*, p. 125.
23 R. Nicholson, *Edward III and the Scots* (Oxford, 1965), pp. 199–200.
24 Prestwich, 'Scheme of 1341', p. 109; R. W. Jones, '*Cum Equis Discoopertis*: The "Irish" Hobelar in English Armies of the Fourteenth Century', *Military Communities in Late Medieval England: Essays in Honour of Andrew Ayton*, ed. G. P. Baker, C. Lambert and D. Simpkin (Woodbridge, 2018), pp. 15–30.
25 J. Sherborne, 'Indentured Retinues and English Expeditions to France', *EHR*, 79 (1964), pp. 718–46, reprinted in *War, Politics*, pp. 24–5.
26 Simpkin, *Aristocracy*, pp. 59–62.
27 TNA E101/393/11, folios 79r–79v.
28 G. P. Baker, 'Sir Robert Knolles' Expedition to France in 1370: New Perspectives', *Military Communities*, p. 159. For examples of retinue sizes: Sherborne, 'Indentured Retinues', p. 4, 11, 13, 15.
29 N. B. Lewis, 'The Organisation of Indentured Retinues in Fourteenth-Century England', *TRHS*, 4th series, 27 (1945), pp. 29–39.

30   Ayton, 'Armies and Military Communities', pp. 217–24.
31   Sherborne, 'Indentured Retinues', pp. 25–7.
32   A vast literature exists on military communities and whether medieval soldiers can be considered as 'professional'. For introductory reading, SLME, pp. 19–22, 260–70; A. Ayton 'The Military Careerist in Fourteenth Century England', *JMH*, 43 (2017), pp. 4–23; D. B. Trim, 'Introduction', *The Chivalric Ethos and the Development of Military Professionalism*, ed. D. B. Trim (Leiden, 2003), pp. 1–41.
33   A. Ayton, 'Military Service and the Dynamics of Recruitment in Fourteenth Century England', *Soldier Experience*, p. 16.
34   G. P. Baker, 'The English Way of War, 1360–1399', unpublished PhD thesis (University of Hull, 2012), p. 143.
35   J. J. N. Palmer, *England, France and Christendom 1377–99* (London, 1972), p. 2.
36   M. Keen, 'Richard II's Ordinances of War 1385', *Rulers and Ruled in Late Medieval England. Essays presented to Gerald Harriss*, ed. R. E. Archer, and S. Walker (Michigan, 1995), pp. 33–48; A. Curry, 'Disciplinary Ordinances for English and Franco-Scottish Armies in 1385: an International Code?', *JMH*, 37 (2011), pp. 269–94; A. Curry, 'The Military Ordinances of Henry V: Texts and Contexts' *War, Government and Aristocracy in the British Isles c.1150–1500: Essays in Honour of Michael Prestwich* (Woodbridge, 2008), pp. 214–49.
37   Baker, 'Way of War', pp. 32–5.
38   On militarisation, and later demilitarisation, of the gentry: P. Coss, 'Andrew Ayton, 'The Military Community and the Evolution of the Gentry in Fourteenth-Century England', *Military Communities in Late Medieval England*, pp. 31–50; SLME, pp. 75, 81, 238.
39   Figures: Baker, 'Way of War', pp. 59–60; SLME, pp. 271–4. Naval expeditions excluded.
40   G. L. Harriss, 'War and the Emergence of the English Parliament, 1297–1360', *JMH*, 2 (1976), pp. 35–56; J. Sherborne, 'The Cost of English Warfare with France in the Later Fourteenth Century', *BIHR*, 50 (1977), pp. 135–50, reprinted in *War, Politics*, pp. 55–70.
41   W. M. Ormrod, *The Reign of Edward III* (London, 1990), p. 11.
42   SLME, pp. 75–81.
43   M. Powicke, *Military Obligation in Medieval England* (Oxford, 1962), pp. 142–47, 182–212.
44   *CPR 1343–45*, pp. 414–16, 427–8.
45   Ayton, *Battle of Crécy*, p. 15.
46   Prestwich, *English Experience*, p. 80.
47   Prestwich, 'Scheme of 1341', p. 111.
48   C. J. Rogers, *War Cruel and Sharp: English Strategy under Edward III, 1327–1360* (Woodbridge, 2000), pp. 10–26.
49   C. J. Rogers, 'The Military Revolutions of the Hundred Years War', *Journal of Military History*, 57 (1993), pp. 247–57.

50 C. J. Rogers, 'Edward III and the Dialectics of Strategy, 1327-60', *TRHS* 6th series, 4 (1994), reprinted in Rogers, *The Wars of Edward III*, pp. 265–84.
51 For a useful summary of English tactics, B. S. Hall, *Weapons and Warfare in Renaissance Europe* (London, 1997), pp. 28–38.
52 D. Whetham, 'The English Longbow: A Revolution in Technology?', *The Hundred Years War II: Different Vistas*, ed. L. J. A. Villalon and D. J. Kagay (Leiden, 2008), pp. 213–32. Cf. in the same volume, pp. 233–60, R. Mitchell, 'The Longbow-Crossbow Shootout at Crécy: Has the "Rate of Fire Commonplace" been Overrated?'.
53 W. P. Caferro, '"The Fox and the Lion": The White Company and the Hundred Years War in Italy', *HYW Wider Focus*, pp. 189–99.
54 P. E. Russell, *English Intervention in Spain and Portugal in the Time of Edward III and Richard II* (Oxford, 1955), pp. 128–9, 202, 333–4.
55 F. Autrand, 'The Battle of Crécy: A Hard Blow for the Monarchy of France', *Battle of Crécy*, pp. 273–86.
56 *Ordonnances* IV, pp. 67–70, partially translated in *Society at War*, pp. 45–8.
57 Blanchard, *Histoire militaire*, pp. 138–40.
58 For what follows, see Contamine, *GES*, pp. 135–83; *Ordonnances* V, pp. 658–61.
59 Blanchard, *Histoire militaire*, p. 149.
60 P. Contamine, 'Batailles, bannières, compagnies', *Cahiers Vernonnais* 4 (1964), pp. 29–30.
61 Baker, 'Way of War', pp. 1–14, 238–44; Palmer, *England, France and Christendom*, p. 6.
62 P. Contamine, *War in the Middle Ages*, translated by M. Jones (London, 1984), p. 168.
63 *Divided Houses*, pp. 395–6, 399–400.
64 Contamine, *War in the Middle Ages*, p. 217.
65 For what follows, A. Curry, 'English Armies in the Fifteenth Century', *Arms, Armies and Fortifications*, pp. 39–68, and 'The Organisation of Field Armies in Lancastrian Normandy', *Armies, Chivalry and Warfare in Britain and France*, ed. M. Strickland (Stamford, 1998), pp. 207–31, as well as case studies of the armies of 1415 and 1416 in her *Agincourt. A New History* (Stroud, 2005), 'After Agincourt, What Next? Henry V and the Campaign of 1416', *The Fifteenth Century*, VII (2007), pp. 23–51.
66 TNA E101/71/2 no. 825.
67 *SLME*, pp. 272–4.
68 A. Curry, 'Guns and Goddams. Was there a Military Revolution in Lancastrian Normandy 1415-50?', *JMMH*, 8 (2010), pp. 174–81.
69 A. Curry, 'Towns at War: Relations between the Towns of Normandy and their English Rulers, 1417–50', *Towns and Townspeople in the Fifteenth Century*, ed. J. A. F. Thomson (Gloucester, 1988), pp. 148–72.
70 A. Curry, 'Le service féodal en Normandie pendant l'occupation Anglaise (1417–1450)', *La France Anglaise: Actes du 111e Congrès National de Sociétés Savantes, Poitiers, 1986* (Paris, 1988), pp. 233–57.

71 Curry, 'English Armies', pp. 48–60.
72 A. Curry, 'The Nationality of Men-at-Arms Serving in English Armies in Normandy and the *Pays de Conquête*, 1415–1450: A Preliminary Study', *Reading Medieval Studies* 18 (1992), pp. 135–63; A. Curry, 'Foreign Soldiers in English pay: Identity and Unity in the Armies of the English Crown, 1415–1450', *Routiers et mercenaires pendant la guerre de Cent Ans*, ed. G. Pépin, F. Boutoulle and F. Lainé (Bordeaux, 2016), pp. 303–16.
73 A. Curry, 'John, duke of Bedford's Arrangements for the Defence of Normandy in October 1434: College of Arms MS Arundel 48, folios 274r-276v', *Annales de Normandie*, 62 (2012), pp. 235–51.
74 Curry, 'English Armies', p. 62; A. Curry, 'Les gens vivans sur le pays pendant l'occupation de Normandie, 1417–1450', *La guerre, la violence et les gens au moyen age. 1. Guerre et violence* (Paris, 1996), pp. 209–21.
75 E. W. Ives, 'Fortescue, Sir John (c.1397–1479)', *Oxford Dictionary of National Biography*, online edition (2004).
76 M. H. Keen, 'The End of the Hundred Years War: Lancastrian France and Lancastrian England', *England and Her Neighbours, 1066–1453: Essays in Honour of Pierre Chaplais*, ed. M. Jones and M. Vale (London, 1989), pp. 297–311.
77 M. G. A. Vale, *Charles VII* (London, 1974), p. 77.
78 Contamine, *GES*, pp. 277–319.
79 Blanchard, *Histoire militaire*, pp. 201–2.
80 P. D. Solon, 'Valois Military Administration on the Norman Frontier, 1445–1461: A Study in Medieval Reform', *Speculum*, 51 (1976), pp. 93–105.
81 For examples of their equipment: Contamine, *GES*, pp. 657–8.
82 Blanchard, *Histoire militaire*, pp. 204–5.
83 M. Jones, 'L'armée Bretonne, 1449–1491: structures et carrières', *La France de la fin du XVe siècle: renouveau et apogée*, ed. B. Chevalier and P. Contamine (Paris, 1985), pp. 147–65.
84 For development of gunpowder weapons in this period Hall, *Weapons*, pp. 41–133.
85 *Narratives of the Expulsion of the English from Normandy 1449–1450*, ed. J. Stevenson (London, 1863), pp. 372–3.
86 Contamine, *War*, p. 139.
87 Hall, *Weapons*, pp. 56–7.
88 D. Spencer, '"The Scourge of the Stones": English Gunpowder Artillery at the Siege of Harfleur', *JMH*, 43 (2017), pp. 59–73; A. King, 'Gunners, Aides and Archers: The Personnel of English Ordnance Companies in Normandy in the Fifteenth Century', *JMMH*, 9 (2011), pp. 65–75; Rogers, 'Military Revolutions', p. 260.
89 Allmand, pp. 80–2; cf. K. DeVries, 'The Walls Come Tumbling Down': The Campaigns of Philip the Good and the Myth of Fortification Vulnerability to Early Gunpowder Weapons', *HYW. Wider Focus*, pp. 429–46.
90 Hall, *Weapons*, p. 119.
91 Curry, 'Guns and Goddams', p. 188.
92 Hall, *Weapons*, p. 115.

93 See: B. Schnerb, 'Aspects de l'organisation militaire dans les principautés Bourguignonnes (v.1315–v.1420)', unpublished PhD thesis, 3 vols (Paris Sorbonne, 1988); idem, 'Le recrutement social et géographique des armées des ducs de Bourgogne (1340–1477)', *Guerre, Pouvoir, Principauté* 18 (2002), pp. 53–67; R. Vaughan, *John the Fearless* (Woodbridge, 2002), pp. 138–52.
94 Schnerb, 'Le Recrutement social', pp. 55–60.
95 K. DeVries and R. Douglas Smith, *The Artillery of the Dukes of Burgundy 1363–1477* (Woodbridge, 2005), pp. 319–39.
96 Rogers, 'Military Revolutions', p. 260.
97 D. Grummitt, *The Calais Garrison: War and Military Service in England, 1436–1558* (Woodbridge, 2008), pp. 133–9.
98 King, 'Gunners, Aides, and Archers', pp. 65–75; *Soldier*, pp. 191–202; Schnerb, 'Vassals, Allies, and Mercenaries', p. 271.
99 B. D. H. Ditcham, 'The Employment of Foreign Mercenary Troops in the French Royal Armies, 1415–1470', unpublished PhD thesis (University of Edinburgh, 1978), p. 11.
100 Contamine, *GES*, p. 254, ft.100; B. Chevalier, 'Les Ecossais dans le armées de Charles VII jusqu'à la bataille de Verneuil', *Jeanne d'Arc, une époque, un rayonnement* (Paris, 1982), pp. 85–94; Ditcham, 'Employment', p. 3.
101 Solon, 'Valois Military Reforms', p. 91.
102 M. Roberts, *The Military Revolution, 1560–1660* (Belfast, 1956).
103 For an introduction, see the editors' introduction to *The Medieval Military Revolution: State, Society and Military Change in Medieval and Early Modern Europe*, ed. A. Ayton and J. L. Price (London, 1995), pp. 1–22.
104 *Medieval Military Revolution*, p. 17.
105 Originally formulated by L. White Jr, *Medieval Technology and Social Change* (Oxford, 1962).
106 For criticism of technological determinism, see K. DeVries, *Medieval Military Technology* (Ontario, 1992), pp. 99–111.
107 Rogers, 'Military Revolutions', p. 277.
108 Ayton, 'Armies and Military Communities', pp. 215.
109 See, for example, Ayton, 'Military Careerist', pp. 4–23.

Index

Adam of Usk, 126
Agincourt, battle of (1415)
    contemporary accounts, 154–55, 158, 160, 162
    English victory, 7, 45–46, 125, 154
    French conduct and demeanour, 138, 162
    Henry V's conduct and demeanour, 13
    killing of French prisoners, 124, 139
    place in English consciousness, 126
    political goodwill generated by victory, 7
    Walsingham's account, 155
Agincourt Carol, 125–26
Agnes of Dunbar, 123
aides, 48, 61–62, 67–68, 87
Aimery de Pavia, 138
Alcock, John, bishop of Rochester, 24–25
Alençon, Jean I, duke of, 46
Alençon, Jean II, duke of, 49, 158–59
Anjou, 39, 48
Anjou, Louis I, duke of, 45–46
Anjou, Louis II, duke of, 46
Anjou, René, duke of, 48, 122, 137
Anonimalle Chronicle, 155, 169–70, 174
Armagnac, Bernard VIII, count of, 45–46
Armagnac-Burgundian rapprochement, 219
armies, 203–25
    English and French armies at the beginning of the war, 203–5
    the Hundred Years' War and the military revolution, 224–25
    see also English army; French army
arquebusiers, 222
Arras
    Congress of (1435), 94
    treaty of (1435), 23, 49

artillery, 139, 222–23
Artois, 46
Arundel, Richard Fitzalan, earl of, 19, 174, 179, 190, 192
Arundel, Thomas, bishop of Ely, archbishop of Canterbury, 15
Augustine, Saint, 135
Aulon, Jean d', 159, 161
Auray, battle of (1364), 44, 156
Auvergne, 39
Avesbury, Robert of, 155
Avignon Peace Conference (1344), 94

Bannockburn, battle of (1314), 158
barbican strategy, of maritime warfare, 178–79, 216–17
Basin, Thomas, 117
Battle Abbey, 93
battle avoidance, French policy (disengagement), 9, 11, 17, 67, 85, 91, 111, 115, 117, 138, 170, 173, 209, 212
Baugé, battle of (1421), 47
'Bay of Flemings' *see* Bourgneuf, battle of
Bayonne, 178
Beaugency, action at (1429), 161
Beaumont, Henry de, 158
Beaumont, Jean de Hainaut, count of, 154
Bedford, John, duke of, 47, 99, 114, 194, 216, 218
Bel, Jean le, 10, 141, 146, 154–55
Benedict XII, Pope, 94
Bentley, Sir Walter, 145–46
Berry, 41
Black Death, 59, 118, 214
    see also plague

Black Prince *see* Edward, Prince of Wales
Blaye, 177
Blois, Gui, count of, 156
Bolton, Nicholas de, 120
Boniface VIII, Pope, 87
Book of Chivalry (Charny), 134, 138
Book of Deeds of Arms and of Chivalry (Pizan), 135
Book of the Ordre of Chyualry (Caxton), 142, 147
books about warfare, increase in ownership by soldiers, 156
booty, 100–101, 103, 121, 141, 206
Boroughmuir, battle of (1335), 122
Boucicaut, Jean le Maingre, Marshal of France, 134, 137, 155
Boulogne, 189
Bourbon, 41
Bourg, 177
Bourgneuf
　battle of (1371) ('Bay of Flemings'), 169–71, 174, 176, 179, 188
　Bay of, 185
Bouvet, Honoré de (Bovet, Honorat), 135, 140, 145
Bouvier, Gilles le, Berry Herald, 221
Bouvines, battle of (1214), 112
Bower, Walter, 122
Brest, 178, 216
Brétigny, treaty of (1360), 44, 156, 161, 213
Brignais, battle of (1362), 213
Bristol, 116
Brittany, 145
　civil war, 41
　succession crisis, 43–44
Brittany, Jean IV, duke of, 41–42
brokerage, 35
Bruges Conference (1375–7), 94
Brut chronicle, 158
Buckingham, Thomas, earl of (later duke of Gloucester), 173, 185
Bueil, Jean de, 157–58

Bulgnéville, battle of (1431), 122
Bureau, Jean and Gaspard, 221–22
Burghersh, Bartholomew, lord, 155
Burgundy, 38, 41–42
　Armagnac-Burgundian rapprochement, 219
　Henry V's alliance with, 179
Burgundy, Charles the Bold, duke of, 42
Burgundy, John the Fearless, duke of, 45, 47, 134, 223
Burgundy, Odo IV, duke of, 43
Burgundy, Philip the Bold, duke of, 45–46, 179
Burgundy, Philip the Good, duke of, 23, 42, 47, 49, 219

Caen, 7
　capture (1346), 11, 99, 101, 111
　discovery of French plan for invasion of England, 156
　siege of (1450), 220
Cagny, Perceval de, 158
Calais, 7, 17
　capture (1347), 112, 141, 178, 183, 217
　garrison, 18, 71, 74–75
　Philip the Good's unsuccessful attack, 23
　place of in English strategy, 178, 223
　siege of (1346–7), 75, 99, 172, 187, 193
Calveley, Sir Hugh, 100, 145
Cambrai, 103
Cambridge, Edmund, earl of, see York, Edward duke of
Canterbury Tales (Chaucer), 134
Castillon, battle of (1453), 220, 222
Caxton, William, 135, 142, 147
Champagne, 47
Chandos, Sir John, 154
　herald's biography of the Black Prince, 154
Chapel of St George, Windsor, 100

Charles, dauphin, son of Charles VI (*see also* Charles VII), 47, 62, 69, 94, 104–5, 113, 223
Charles of Navarre, 35, 40, 43–44, 51, 118
Charles of Spain, 40, 44
Charles V, King of France, 34, 36
  Fabian tactics, 35
  and the recovery of the crown's authority, 44–45
  reforms of the Clos des Galées (1374), 179
Charles VI, King of France
  impact of incapacity on French finances, 62
  onset of mental illness (1392), 45
  political administration, 34
  processions in Paris, 126
Charles VII, King of France, 94, 97
  conservation of royal resources, 35
  crowning, 47
  fiscal system, 37, 48, 62, 65
  military reforms, 103, 147, 219–21, 223–24
  striking of medals to celebrate victory, 126
Charny, Geoffroi de, 35, 137, 139, 141
  writings, 138, 157, 161
Chaucer, Geoffrey, 188
chemin d'Espaigne, 193
Cherbourg, 139, 178, 216
chevauchées, 17, 111, 117, 119, 138, 140–41, 181, 209, 212
chivalry, 133–48
  and the acquisition of booty, 141–42
  and the Church, 134
  'Combat of the Thirty', 137, 144
  the concept, 133–34
  and the conduct of war, 135
  Court of Chivalry testimony, 159
  decline of, 147
  etymology and first recording, 133
  exemplars of English chivalry, 142
  and Fabian tactics, 3, 138–39
  Henry V's conception, 146
  Huizinga's depiction, 133
  influence in French and English society, 142–48
  Order of the Star (*see also* Company of the Star), 44
  and personal honour, 139
  and prowess in arms, 136, 138
  prudence as prime virtue, 138
  and the ransoming of prisoners, 135–36
  tournaments as classic expression of (*see also* jousts), 136–38
  and the treatment of non-combatants, 139–41
  values, 134
Chronicle (Lanercost Priory), 155
chroniclers, 136, 155–58
  see also under individual names
Chronique du Religieux de Saint-Denys (Pintouin), 97, 155
Chroniques (Froissart), 155
the Church, 85–105
  chivalry and, 134
  coastal raids and the mobilisation of, 91–93
  damage to property, 85
  and dissemination of the case for war, 12–13
  English and French ecclesiastical contributions, 86
  French and English appeals to divine authority, 86
  granting of financial relief by, 103
  and Joan of Arc, 104–5
  militarisation of Church architecture, 90, 117–18
  military participation of clergy, 90–93
  peace making role, 93–94
  propaganda role, 86, 93, 97–100
  relationship with the French crown, 87
  spiritual function of patronage, 100–104
  taxation of, 13
  and the theoretical underpinnings of justified violence, 95

churches, French fortification of, 117–18
Cinque Ports, 189
city walls, impact on Edward III's campaign, 50
civic militias, 112
Clement V, Pope, 93
Clement VI, Pope, 69, 74, 94
Clisson, Olivier de, 35, 42, 45
Clos des Galées, Rouen
  destruction (1418), 180, 193
  founding and location, 183
  function, 187
  operation, 192
  reforms (1374), 179
coastal raids
  eyewitness account, 169
  impact on England, 182
  as maritime counterparts to *chevauchées*, 181
  and the mobilisation of the Church, 91–93
  success rate, 141, 172
Cocherel, battle of (1364), 156
Coeur, Jacques, 73
coinage, debasement of, 69–71
'Combat of the Thirty', 137, 144
commercial predation, 177, 182
  in the Channel, 172, 174, 181, 191
compagnies d'ordonnance, 58, 219, 221, 223
Company of the Star, 145, 157
confraternities, 112–13
Council of Constance (1414–18), 94
courtoisie, 134
Coutes, Louis de, 159
Cravant, 143
  battle of (1423), 47
Crécy, battle of (1346), 4, 40, 99, 141, 146, 184, 213
criminals, recruitment to the English army, 119–20
Cromer, 186
crusades, and international knightly camaraderie, 101

Dagworth, Thomas, 155
d'Angennes, Jean, 139
David II, King of Scotland, 26
debasement of coinage, 69–71
Debats et appointements (anon.), 157
de Beaumont, Henry, Earl of Buchan, 142
defence of England, lack of, 18–20
de la Pole family, 147
  see also Suffolk
depopulation, of the French countryside, 117
Despenser, Henry, bishop of Norwich, 93
Díaz de Gámez, Gutierre, 169
Dieppe, 180
domestic context in France and England, 111–27
  the countryside, 116–18
  disorder and protest, 118–20
  influence of the war on French and English society, 124–27
  towns, 111–16
  women, 120–24
domestic politics, link between foreign warfare and, 25–26
dual monarchy wording (double monarchy in text), 10, 13, 47
Dunkirk, 175
Dupplin Moor, battle of (1332), 142, 158

écorcheurs, 102, 219
Edward, Prince of Wales (The Black Prince), 15, 44, 89, 93, 104, 112, 140, 154–55, 207–8
Edward I, King of England, 25, 158
  recruitment of criminals, 120
Edward III, King of England, 2, 94, 155
  appeals to God and justice, 95
  battle at Sluys (1340), 173
  character, 13, 25
  claim to the French throne, 4, 10, 24
  comparison with King Arthur, 3–4
  death, 207
  expedition of 1359, 160

extension of military service
obligations, 211
finances, 8–9, 11, 58, 61, 64, 71–73, 75, 78, 89, 116
and the French campaign, 6–8
and King Arthur, 13
lands in France, 43
and the limitations of royal authority, 9
linking of war service with chivalric culture, 145
multi-front strategies, 178
and Parliament, 18
political dealings at home, 8–9
public relations, 125
ships at the disposal of, 187
withdraws from politics, 17
Edward IV, King of England, 50
proposed invasion of France, 24
Emprise de l'Escu vert à la Dame Blanche, 134
England
breakdown of law and order in, 119
grants of extraordinary taxation, 64–65
implications of the war for the population, 111
military expectations of the adult male population, 115–16
ordinary revenues, 63–64
raids on (*see also* coastal raids), 114
urban fortifications, building of, 115
English army
cavalry and infantry recruitment, 203–4
charters of pardon, 209
discipline, 204, 209
in the fifteenth century, 216–19
indenture system, 206–7, 216–17
massed archery, 211–13
mounted archers, 207, 210
occupying garrisons, 217–18
pardons issued for military service, 119–20
pay, 206
preferred modus operandi, 212

professionalization, 208–10
reorganization, 205–11; French response 213–16; tactical implications 211–13
in the fifteenth century, 216–19
retinue size, 208
soldiers' relations with the female population of Normandy, 121
sustainability issues, 210
English identity, influence of the war, 36, 124–26, 127
English language
in churches, 98
Henry V's use of, 14
English politics, 1–26
contextual considerations, 2–6
military decline and, 14–23
military success and, 6–14
Epitoma rei militaris (Vegetius), 156
Estates-General, 38, 65, 88
Eu, count of, 40, 43
Eu, Bertrand Carit, archdeacon of, 103
Eugenius IV, Pope, 94

Fabian tactics, 35, 138
Fantosme, Jordan, 140
Fastolf, Sir John, 96, 146–47, 156
financing the war, 57–79
comparison of English and French finances, 61–63
comparison of English and French fiscal policies, 65–71
comparison of extraordinary expenditure and extraordinary revenues, 71–72
contemporary financial system, 72–78
and debasement of coinage, 69–71
the demand for money, 58–63
English military expenditure, 58
English soldiers' wages, 74
English taxation, 64–65
French military expenditure, 58
French taxation, 65

financing the war (*continued*)
   and the royal jewels, 75
   sources of royal revenues in England and France, 63–72
   use of credit, 72–8
firearms, 221–22
first-hand accounts, 153–63
   advice manuals written by military veterans, 157
   chroniclers, 155–58
   courtroom testimony of military veterans, 159–61
   documents produced by French religious houses, 102
   emotional reactions to combat, 161–63
   French chroniclers, 155–56
   letters by key military commanders, 155
   ownership of books about warfare by soldiers, 156
   personal experiences of war, 158
Flanders, 18, 46, 113, 123, 178–79, 186, 205, 207, 215
   rebellions, 119
Flanders, Jeanne of, 123
Flanders, Louis II, count of, 176
fleur de lis, English appropriation, 10, 13, 100
Fobbing, Essex, 188
Foix, Gaston III Phébus, count of, 156
Formigny, battle of (1450), 222
fouage, 61, 68, 215–16
Fougères, 159
France
   claim of English kings, 4, 10–11
   English immigration, 114
   fortification of churches, 117–18
   mobilisation of the population, 112–13
   ordinary revenues, 64
   political life of rural localities, 39
   proves military superiority, 10
   sources of indirect taxation, 67
   town walls, 111–12

Franco-Castilian alliance, 223
freebooters, 112, 117, 136
   see also mercenaries
French army
   arrière-ban, 204
   Burgundian influences, 222–23
   cavalry and infantry recruitment, 204–5
   Charles V's ordinance (1374), 214
   creation of the standing army, 49
   and English barbican strategy, 216
   fifteenth century reforms, 219–24
   garde du corps, 215
   gunpowder artillery, 221–23
   influence of English tactics, 214
   pay, 213–14
   reform attempts in the fourteenth century, 213
   response to English military reorganization, 213–16
   retinue size, 215
   role of foreign mercenary troops, 47, 223
   taxation and, 215
French identity, influence of the war, 36, 124, 126–27
French politics, 33–52
   eastern and western noble networks, 42–50
   power of French princes, 40–42
   role of the towns, 50–52
   trends in the study of, 34–40
Froissart, Jean, 9–10, 93, 101, 111, 117–18, 136–41, 155–56, 169, 175

gabelle, 61, 68
Gascony, 42
Gaunt, John of, duke of Lancaster, 16–19, 137, 193
gentry, militarisation under Edward III, 9–10
Gerson, Jean, 36

Gesta Henrici Quinti (anon.), 154, 160, 162
Gloucester, Humphrey, duke of, 21
Glyn Dŵr, Owain, 182
God
   on the side of the English, 7, 10, 12, 92, 96, 98, 125–26, 135, 142, 146
   on the side of the French, 98, 104–5
Gonesse, Nicolas de, 155
Gower, John, 19
Grandes Chroniques de France, 97
Gravesend, 181
Gray, Sir Thomas, 139–40, 142–43, 158, 161
Great Companies, 117, 119
Great Schism (1378–1418), 86, 93–94
Gregory XI, Pope, 94
Gresham, James, 125
Grimaldi, Carlo, 193
Grosmont, Henry of, duke of Lancaster, 100, 155
Grosvenor, Sir Robert, 159
Gruel, Guillaume, 158
Guernsey, 114
Guesclin, Bertrand du, 138, 144–45
Guesclin, Julienne du, 123
Guienne, conflicts (1294–7, 1324–5), 10
Guines peace talks (1352–4), 94
gunpowder artillery in Western Europe, advent of, 221–23

Harcourt, Godefroy of, 43
Harewell, John, Chancellor of Aquitaine, 104
Harfleur, 17, 172, 173, 175, 180, 193, 222
Hawkwood, Sir John, 142
Henry I, King of England, 25
   income, 63
Henry II, King of England, 25
Henry III, King of England, 25
Henry V, King of England, 2, 94
   character, 13–14, 25
   claim of biblical authority, 140
   conquest of Normandy (1417–19), 179–80
   coronation, 154
   death, 180
   as exemplar of chivalry, 139
   formal entry to Paris (1420), 113
   granting of conquered lands, 217
   Hoccleve's advice, 139
   inter-dynastic marriage, 7
   letters to the citizens of London, 14
   management of naval resources, 192
   order to kill French prisoners, 139
   overhaul of England's financial system, 8
   parliamentary subsidies awarded to, 7
   rebuilds the royal fleet of warships, 180
   victory at Agincourt, 7
Henry VI, King of England
   early years, 20–21
   and English finances, 62
   finances, 22, 71–72, 74
   lack of interest in pursuing the war, 216
   political situation, 25
   union with Margaret of Anjou, 21
Hereford, Humphrey Bohun, earl of, 169, 170, 179
Historia aurea (Tynemouth), 158
Hoccleve, Thomas, 139
Holland, Sir Thomas, 101
Hundred Years' War
   a better date for the close, 50
   contemporary conceptions, 4
   and the development of French identity, 23, 36
   and the emergence of popular politics, 26
   English kings involved in, 1–2
   as family squabble, 7
   flourishing scholarship, 2
   political impact, 24–25
   and taxation, 17
Huntingdon, John Holland, earl of, 173

imposition foraine, 67
Innocent VI, Pope, 94, 102
invasion of England, French plans, 11, 20, 43, 156, 176–77, 181, 186
Isabella of France (wife of Richard II), 15
Isabella of Lorraine, 122
Isle of Wight, 181
    capture of fleet of ships (1449), 191

Jacquerie, 118–19
Joan of Arc, 47, 104, 218
    attack on Paris (1429), 154
    burning in Rouen, 48, 105
    Nullification trial, 159–62
    writings on, 121, 158
John I, King of Castile, 193
John I, King of Portugal, 139
John II, King of France, 26, 35, 40, 91, 134, 145
    capture, 37, 44, 88, 93, 118
    chivalric order, 145
    military reform, 213–14
    personal failings, 43–44
    ransom and French finances, 61, 65
jousts/jousting, 134, 136–37, 146, 154
just war, St Augustine's theory, 135

killing of prisoners, at Aljubarrota (1385) and Agincourt (1415), 124, 139
King's Lynn, 186
Knighton, Henry, 137
Knolles, Sir Robert, 100, 137, 142, 144

Laisné, Jeanne (Hachette), 122
Lanercost Priory, *Chronicle*, 155
Langland, William, 98
La Rochelle, 175
    destruction of the English fleet (1372), 18, 72, 173, 176
La Sale, Antoine de, 157
law and order, reasons for breakdown, 119
le Bel, Jean *see under* Bel

Le Crotoy, 181
Le Fèvre, Jean, 154
Legnano, John of, 135
Le jouvencel (Bueil), 157, 162
Le petit Jehan de Saintré (La Sale), 157
'Les Espagnols-sur-Mer' (1350) (Winchelsea), 173, 175
Le Songe du Vieil Pèlerin (Mézières), 134
Les Tourelles, attack on the fortress (1429), 161
letters of remission, 118–19, 121
Leulingham, truce of (1389), 171
Limoges, 140
Limousin, 39
Lion, Sir Espan de, 156
Livre de chevalerie (Charny), 161
Livre des fais du bon messire Jehan le Maingre (anon.), 155
loans, provided by English towns, 116
Lollardy, 8, 98
London, 116
Louis X, King of France, 43
Louis XI, King of France, 37, 49

Malestroit, truce of (1343), 94
Mare, Peter de la, Speaker of the Commons, 18–19
maritime warfare, 169–95
    barbican strategy, 178–79, 216–17
    characteristics of engaged vessels, 175
    contemporary records, 169–71
    contrasting responses to maritime imperatives, 176–77
    documentation of the English fleet, 170
    English strategy and operations, 178–81
    environmental and geopolitical considerations, 171, 173
    fire, use of as a weapon, 175
    and French access to Castilian shipping, 177
    and French access to the Flemish merchant fleet, 179

French strategy and operations, 181–82
gunpowder weapons, 175
and Henry V's conquest of Normandy (1417–19), 179–80
hit-and-run coastal raids (*see also* coastal raids), 172
offensive and defensive naval operations, 186–91
permanent and professional fleets, sustainability, 192–93
reliance on foreign shipping, 184, 186
requisitioning of ships (scale and impact), 183–86
role of and benefits for private enterprise, 190
self-help naval operations, 191
shipping and manpower, 183
and taxation, 186
see also coastal raids; ships
Marmousets, 34–35, 45
marriage
and Anglo-French diplomacy, 4–7
intermarriage between English men and Norman women, 114, 123
Martin V, Pope, 94, 102
Mauléon, Bascot de, 117, 156
Mauron, battle of (1352), 44, 146
Meaux, siege of (1421–22), 141
mercenaries, 48, 117, 136, 142, 144, 157, 177, 204, 212, 214–16, 222–23
merchant shipping, predation *see* commercial predation
Mercier, Jean Le, 35
Merton, Eleanor de, 120
Mézières, Philippe de, 101, 134, 144, 157
Michelet, Jules, 39
Milemete Treatise, 3
Milford Haven, 182
militarisation, of French urban society, 112–13
military revolution, the Hundred Years' War and, 224–25

military service
and exemption from taxation, 143
and social mobility, 143–44
military veterans
advice manuals written by, 157
courtroom testimony of, 159–61
militias, civic, 112
Minsterworth, Sir John, 144, 208
Monstrelet, Enguerrand de, 143, 154
Montferrat, Theodore Paleologus, marquis of, 157
Montfort, Jean de, 123
Montreuil, Jean de, 36
Morley, Robert, Lord, 189
Murimuth, Adam, 155

Nancy, tournament (1445), 137
national identity, influence of the war for French and English societies, 23, 36, 124–27
navies, and maritime warfare (*see also* maritime warfare), 169–95
Neville, Sir John, 169
Neville's Cross, battle of (1346), 26, 158
Newcastle, 189
Nicopolis, battle of (1396), 101, 134, 155, 189
Niño, Pero, count of Buelna, 189
noble networks
eastern, 42–43, 46–47, 50
in late medieval France, 39–47, 50–51
western, 42–43, 46, 48–50
non-combatants, 102–3, 121, 139, 205
chivalry and the treatment of, 139–41
deliberate targeting of, 140
impact of the war on, 111
role of in equipping and feeding the English army, 116
supposed immunity from war, 139
Normandy, 38
acceptance of English rule, 114
assault on (1346), 182

Northampton, William de Bohun, earl of, 75
Nouillompont, Jean de, 159

Oeuvres complètes d'Antoine de La Sale (La Sale), 157
Order of the Garter (1348), 13, 100, 145
Order of the Star, 44
  see also Company of the Star
oriflamme, 134
Orléans, siege of (1428–29), 50, 104–5, 147, 157, 159, 161–62, 216
Orléans, Charles, duke of, 46, 143
Orléans, Jean, Bastard of, Count of Dunois, 159
Orléans, Louis, duke of, 45, 113

Page, John, 154
pardons, issued for military service, 119–20
Paris, 113, 218
  acceptance of English rule, 114
  disorder in, 119
  Henry V's formal entry to (1420), 113
parliament
  attendees, 7
  military service and, 146
  rolls, 2
Paston, John, 125
Patay, battle of (1429), 146, 157, 216
peasants, 85, 117–18, 134–35
  defence initiatives, 117–18
  rights of, 118
  suffering, 119
Peasants' Revolt (1381), 17, 19–20, 65, 119, 188
Pembroke, earl of, 173, 176
Petrarch, 116–17, 205
Philip IV, King of France, 38, 73
  founds Clos des Galées, 183
Philip VI, King of France, 34, 40, 49, 64–65, 73, 87, 94, 101, 134, 146
  finances, 61, 74

  plans invasion of England, 11, 43
  and political society, 42
Philpot, John, 191
Pin, Guiot de, 121
Pintouin, Michel, 155
piracy, 191
Pitti, Buarnocorso, 186
Pizan, Christine de, 36, 104, 122, 135, 137–38, 144
plague, 64, 102, 120, 124, 185
  see also Black Death
plunder/plundering, 102–3, 140–41, 212, 223
Poitiers, battle of (1356), 26, 35, 37–38, 88, 91, 93, 117–18, 134, 154–55, 213
Poitou, 176
Pole, William de la, earl of Suffolk *see* Suffolk
poll taxes, 17, 65, 68, 119
Poole, 181
popular protest, 111, 118–19
Portsmouth, 114
Poulengy, Bertrand de, 159
Praguerie, 49, 219
prisoners, 124, 135–6, 139
propaganda, 2, 98–100, 111, 125–26, 160
Provence, 38
public opinion, 9–10, 12–13, 23, 26, 51, 86, 96, 105
  French political history scholarship and, 36
  Henry V's handling, 14
  influence of the Church, 96, 98–99

raiding, role of in English invasion strategy, 141, 212
ransoms, 61, 102, 105, 117, 135–36, 139, 156
Raoul I, count of Eu and Guînes, 40
Raoul II, count of Eu and Guînes, 40, 43
rape, 113, 120–21
regard, 206

ribauldequins, 222
Richard I, King of England, 25
Richard II, King of England, 2, 207
　attitude to war, 15–16
　campaigns in Ireland and Scotland, 15
　loss of power, 20
　political situation, 25
　pursuit of peace, 20
Richemont, Arthur de, 48, 158
Roches, Gauthier des, 155
Roncière, Charles de la, 170
Rose, Edmund, 189
Rouen, 180, 187
　siege of (1418–19), 154
routiers, 65, 102, 113, 121, 136–37, 142, 144, 223
　first-hand accounts, 156
　see also mercenaries

Saint-Denis, abbey of, 97, 100
Sainte-Chapelle, Paris, 100
Saint-Mary's Church, Warwick, 100
Saintonge, 176
Salisbury, Thomas Montague, earl of, 141, 147, 217
saltpetre, 221
Scalacronica (Gray), 136–37, 139, 142, 158, 160–61
Scarborough, 189
Scotichronicon (Bower), 122
Scots
　French army's use of mercenaries, 47
　slain by English forces at Verneuil (1424), 223
Scrope, Sir Richard, 159, 178
Scrope family, 147
Secreta Secretorum, 3
seigniorage, 60, 64, 69–71
semonce des nobles, 204, 215, 217, 220
Sens, siege of (1429), 146
Sens, Guillaume de Melun, archbishop of, 91

Shipman's Tale (Chaucer), 188
ships
　All Hallow's Cog, 175
　Blythe, 189
　disposal of warships after Henry V's death, 180
　Gracedieu, 180
　Holigost, 175
　Peter, 188
　Rodecog, 170
The Siege of Rouen (poem, 1418–19), 112
Sluys
　battle of (1340), 7, 43, 50, 173–76, 186, 189
　invasion fleet, 115, 176, 186
social mobility, military service and, 143–44
Somerset, John Beaufort, duke of, 184
Song Against the King's Taxes (anon.), 8
Soper, William, 192
Southampton, 141, 181
　fortified anchorage for the king's ships, 192
　French attack (1338), 114–15
　militarisation, 115
South coast of England, vulnerability to attack (*see also* coastal raids), 18, 20, 115
Speakers, election, 18
St Augustine Abbey, Canterbury, 93
Stirling Castle, siege of (1304), 158
St Malo, 175
Stratford, John, 8
St Sauveur-le-Vicomte, 221, 222
Suffolk, William de la Pole, earl of, 21–23, 73
Swanage, 185

tailles, 61–62, 65, 68–69, 87, 215, 220
Talbot, John, Lord, later earl of Shrewsbury, 146

tallies, 75–78
taxation
   challenges for English and French kings, 58–59
   clerical, 68–69
   comparison of French and English systems of, 219
   of English ecclesiastical property, 89
   and English failure to integrate continental possessions, 218
   English wool and cloth exports and income from indirect taxation, 66
   French contributions for defence of Normandy, 114
   of French ecclesiastical property, 87
   French resentment, 119
   French system, 37–38, 51, 61
   funding of war through, 6–7
   Hundred Years' War and, 17
   internal differences within France, 67
   maritime warfare and, 186
   military service and exemption from, 143
   poll taxes, 17, 65, 68, 119
   raised by the English government over the whole War, 59
   royal tax revenues as a percentage of GDP, 59, 60, 61
   for war, 13, 17–18, 22, 62
Thierry, Augustin, 39, 51
Toulouse, 112
Tournai, 50, 114, 124
   shooting competition, 126–27
Tours, truce of (1444), 219
trading vessels, predation of *see* commercial predation
Trancoso, treaty of (1387), 193
Treatise on War (Legnano), 135
trebuchets, 221
Tree of Battles (Bouvet), 135

Trémoille, Georges de la, 48
Tringant, Guillaume, 157
Troyes, treaty of (1420), 22, 47, 62, 94, 117, 223
Tynemouth, John, 158

Upton, Nicholas, 143
Ursins, Guillaume Juvénal des, 159
Ursins, Jean Juvénal des, 159

Vegetius Renatus, Flavius, 156–57
Venette, Jean de, 119
Verneuil, battle of (1424), 47, 223
Vienne, Jean de, 179, 181, 189
Vignay, Jean de, 157
Villandrando, Rodrigo de, 48, 223
Vrayes chroniques (Bel), 154

Waldegrave, Richard, 19
Wales, 182
Walsingham, Thomas, 7, 20, 115, 141, 144, 155
war
   experience of most English people, 10
   generation of support for, 6–14
warfare
   fourteenth century attitudes, 3
   impact on state development, 24
   relationship with politics, 1
Waurin, Jean, 143
Wilton Diptych, 15
Winchelsea, 115, 181
   'Les Espagnols-sur-Mer' (1350), 173
Windsor, Sir William de, 209
Windsor Castle, rebuilt, 13
   Chapel of St George 100
Winnington, Robert, 191
women
   domestic context in France and England, 120–24
   impact of the war on, 111
   improved economic position, 124
   medieval writers' views, 121

    participation in disorder, 120
    participation in warfare, 122–23
    treatment of, 103, 121
    use of as spies, 123
Woodstock, Edward of (*see* Edward, Prince of Wales)
wool subsidy, 7, 22
wool trade, 65, 67, 73, 75, 89, 186

Worcester, Thomas Percy, earl of, 189
Worcester, William, 147
Wyclif, John, 93, 98
Wykeham, William, bishop of Winchester, 12–13

York, 116
York, Edward duke of, 175

www.ingramcontent.com/pod-product-compliance
Lightning Source LLC
Chambersburg PA
CBHW071819300426
44116CB00009B/1369